PROGRAMMING LOGICS

AN INTRODUCTION TO VERIFICATION AND SEMANTICS

Raymond D. Gumb
University of Lowell

WILEY
John Wiley & Sons
New York Chichester Brisbane Toronto Singapore

Library of Congress Cataloging in Publication Data:

Gumb, Raymond D.
Programming logics: An Introduction to Verification and Semantics
by Raymond D. Gumb.
p. cm.

Includes indexes.
ISBN 0-471-60539-5
1. Computer programs—Verification. 2. Programming languages
(Electronic computers)—Semantics. I. Title.
QA76.76.V47G86 1989
005.1′4—dc19

Printed in the United States of America

10 9 8 7 6 5 4 3 2 1

To
Albert and Rebecca, in memoriam,
and
Christopher and Robert

Preface

This text is intended for a first course in program verification systems, and consistent and complementary definitions of the semantics of programming languages. In order of emphasis, it treats axiomatic, operational, translational, and denotational semantics. Although program proving is covered extensively, this text also shows that the different semantics are appropriately related. Finally, because of its focus on Hoare-style Axiomatizations and semantics of **while** programs, this text serves as an introduction to programming (or Hoare) logics.

I began writing this text after being drafted to teach advanced undergraduate and graduate-level courses in program verification and the semantics of programming languages, a subject for which there were no adequate introductory texts. Excellent advanced texts existed, but they were too difficult for the graduate students who had not taken the undergraduate course. Because most computer science students enjoy programming, I feel that an introductory text should emphasize program proving and suggest relevant programming projects. At the same time, students need to realize that verification systems and semantics are not self-evident formalisms to the *cognoscenti* that should be applied uncritically. Consequently, this text highlights the importance of consistent and complementary definitions of programming language semantics by, for example, stressing the role of soundness proofs in vindicating verification systems. Furthermore, relevant aspects of first-order logic and Peano arithmetic are accented here for two reasons: first, they are needed in program proving, and second, they facilitate the explication of key semantic concepts (e.g., the weakest precondition).[1] A novel feature of this text is its use of "free" logic and arithmetic to handle run-time errors in the final two chapters.

Advanced undergraduates and beginning graduate students in computer science at three universities have used drafts of this text. Professional programmers should also find it suitable for independent study (without formal classroom instruction). The text presumes that the student has some background in concepts of programming languages and in discrete structures (in particular, sets, relations, functions, mathematical induction, first-order logic, formal proofs, and the Peano axioms for the natural numbers). However, Chapter 0 reviews the basic mathematical tools used in the text and, in general, the text covers preliminary material in enough detail so that it should be comprehensible to a diligent reader with little background in some of these areas. Students who have mastered the material in this text should be prepared for a second course using one of the more advanced texts listed in *Suggestions for Further Reading.*

When feasible, the text follows standard notational conventions as represented in de Bakker's excellent advanced text. And, to make semantic analysis tractable in this introductory text, we impose a number of restrictions on the syntax of our programming languages. Our approach is to introduce a minilanguage in each chapter to simplify treatment of new concepts. Although we deal primarily with extensions of the class of **while** programs, represented by dialects of Pascal (Chapters 1 and 4 through 6), we also treat flowchart programs, represented by dialects of BASIC (Chapters 2 and 3). Despite the fact that BASIC's **goto** command complicates semantic description, so do the restricted transfer of control statements advocated by proponents of program intelligibility. In program verification today, the methods of Floyd remain a viable alternative to Hoare Axiomatizations, and flowchart programs provide a convenient framework for developing the power and simplicity of Floyd's methods. Furthermore, the commands of flowchart programs are more similar to the instruction sets of conventional machines than the statements of **while** programs, and flowchart programs are the "meanings" of **while** programs under the translational semantics presented in Chapter 4.

Figure P.1 presents a checklist of chapter contents. To avoid developing the intricacies of many-sorted logic, only integer-type variables are used.

[1] Applications of the Consequence Rule in programming (Hoare) logic are justified, in part, by proofs in arithmetic. In Chapter 5, the symbiosis of arithmetic and programming logic is most perfect: Proving programmer-defined functions correct in programming logic justifies the introduction of function-call axioms into arithmetic.

The sections numbered 0 in Chapters 5 and 6 introduce two critical mathematical concepts—free arithmetic and concepts of denotational semantics that are essential for understanding subsequent sections.

In Chapter 0, it is important for students to work through enough natural deduction proofs and proofs in arithmetic to develop an intuition of when, in the Hoare Axiomatization, the Consequence Rule can be applied and, in the Floyd Method, when a verification condition holds. Furthermore, by working through some formal proofs in arithmetic, students will come to appreciate the fact that a natural deduction system is truth-preserving, as contrasted with the Hoare Axiomatization of Chapter 1, which is only validity-preserving. Chapter 0 can be reviewed in about a week by mathematically mature students. In Chapter 1, it is essential for students to work through at least three or four program-proving exercises for them to understand the Hoare Axiomatization. Because program proofs in the formalism of Chapter 1 can be rather long, I generally postpone the proofs of more intricate programs until Chapter 2. And, as students will learn, program-proving can be fun! In Chapters 3 and 4, more interesting algorithms such as sort programs can be proven, but I generally emphasize finding loop invariants and semantic issues because thorough program proofs are long and complex. Students should work through one or two of the program-proving exercises in enough detail to appreciate the aspects of the minilanguage giving rise to these complexities (e.g., assignments to subscripted variables), as these aspects are obstacles to practical program proving. Either program proving or semantic issues can be emphasized in Chapters 5 and 6. Many students will be motivated by the programming exercises. I usually do not assign more than one programming exercise in a semester because meaningful programming exercises tend to be long.

I recommend working through the chapters in the order they are presented. If there is not enough time in a one-semester course to cover all seven chapters and you wish to spend some time on subprograms and rudimentary denotational semantics (Chapters 5 and 6), you can cover lightly—or even skip altogether—Chapters 3 and 4. If you wish to skim over the more mathematical material, it can be found in Sections 0.2, 0.3, 0.5, and 0.6, Section 1.4, Section 2.4, Sections 3.4 and 3.6, Section 4.3, Sections 5.0 and 5.4, and Sections 6.0, 6.5, and 6.6.

I wish to thank Russ Abbott, Paul Kenison, Hugues Leblanc, Donald Martin, Edward Smith, Ivan Sudburough, George Weaver, Anita Gleason, Paul Lee, Faith Lin, Phil Mahler, Paul Mayer, Ridge McGhee, Kevin Meier, and Weidong Wang for their comments on earlier versions of this text. Faith Lin created the subject index and assisted in proofreading.

Tyngsboro, Massachusetts
June 1988

Figure P.1 Checklist of Topics by Chapter

CHAPTER 0

First-order logic, natural deduction, axiomatization and the intended semantics of the first-order theory of the integers (Peano arithmetic extended to the negative integers), properties of relations (e.g., orderings), and Nötherian induction.

CHAPTER 1

While programs in a Pascal dialect, operational semantics (Cook – de Bakker style), the concepts of partial and total correctness, Hoare Partial Correctness Axiomatization, and soundness.

CHAPTER 2

Flowchart programs in a BASIC dialect, operational semantics, the Floyd Method (inductive assertions for proving partial correctness and well-founded sets for proving termination), and soundness.

CHAPTER 3

Extension of the BASIC dialect in Chapter 2 to cover arrays and sequential input/output.

CHAPTER 4

Extension of the Pascal dialect in Chapter 1 to cover arrays, stacks, and input/output, Hoare Total Correctness Axiomatization, correctness of a translation of the new dialect of Pascal into the BASIC dialect of Chapter 3, comparison of the Hoare and Floyd Methods, and difficulties expressing specifications in first-order languages.

CHAPTER 5

Free logic for handling run-time errors, extension of the Pascal dialect in Chapter 1 to cover nonrecursive functions and procedures, environments, static scoping, call-by-value and call-by-reference, Hoare Total Correctness Axiomatization, and soundness.

CHAPTER 6

Rudimentary concepts of denotational semantics, modification of the Pascal dialect in Chapter 1 yielding a class of tail recursive procedures, Hoare Total Correctness Axiomatization, correctness of a translation of tail recursive programs into **while** programs, equivalence of the denotational and operational semantics, weakest preconditions, and relative completeness.

Contents

List of Figures

Introduction

Some time ago, while working as a programming consultant, I was asked to implement an algorithm for scheduling plant shutdown times. The specification for the "algorithm" had been written by an accountant in an informal, but seemingly thorough, manner. I developed a program and, after considerable program testing, turned it over to the plant's computer center for production runs. A few months later, I received a frantic call. My program had begun assigning plant workers negative vacation times, which, needless to say, the workers did not appreciate! After studying the unfortunate runs for some time, I discovered that the problem lay in the specification. It became apparent that no program could be written for the specification. That is, the specification was unsatisfiable. When I pointed out the problem to the accountant, he simply replied that "the world is filled with inconsistencies." At first, I was impressed by his response, but not for long, as higher-level management soon made it clear that they did not want any of the world's inconsistencies running around in their scheduling programs.

Computer users in government and industry constantly are demanding more reliable computer systems. Part of this demand is for fault-tolerant systems that will continue to perform *correctly* when components fail or faults occur. But what does it mean to speak of a system, consisting of hardware and programs (software and firmware), "performing correctly"? In this text, we study this question in the case of programs. We analyze what it means for a program to be correct, and present verification techniques for proving programs correct. For as my accountant friend and I discovered at the expense of the plant workers, testing a program does not always establish its correctness; crucial test cases may be overlooked or there may be too many cases to test. Program correctness must be understood in the context of a mathematical theory.

No user wants an incorrect program, but some users cannot afford even a single "bug" in their programs, as program failures could result in the loss of life and expensive resources. To that end, for example, the Department of Defense Security Center has developed standards for evaluating the security features of commercially available computer systems. For a computer system to receive the highest security rating, the tools of formal logic must be used in establishing the correctness of the system. The reliability of the "Star Wars" system, for example, hinges in part on the possibility of proving that programs meet their specifications. Another government agency has funded development of a provably fault-tolerant computer system to control future commercial aircraft that will be inherently unstable to improve fuel efficiency. Similar efforts in program verification are contemplated in England and other countries. Like it or not, ready or not, program verification is with us. Soon we will see demands for provably correct computer systems for controlling nuclear power plants, life support equipment in hospitals, electronic funds transfer systems, and other critical applications.

Program correctness is a semantic concept. In keeping with the tradition of mathematical semantics developed by Alfred Lindenbaum, Alfred Tarski, Leon Henkin, Saul Kripke, Dana Scott, Christopher Strachey, and others, we understand semantics to give meaning to linguistic expressions by assigning them denotations. Typical denotations are an object (an integer), a set of objects (the even integers), and a set of ordered pairs of objects (the greater than relation $>$ on the integers), and so forth. In the study of logics, one typically distinguishes between syntax, semantics, and a deductive system. In the case of a programming language, one typically specifies the context-free aspects of the syntax in terms of a BNF grammar. The semantics assigns denotations to the syntactic objects specified by the grammar. For example, the semantics assigns to an integer expression (a syntactic or linguistic object) an integer (a mathematical, nonlinguistic object), and it assigns to an assertion (a syntactic object) a truth-value (true or false) as a denotation. The deductive system (verification system) provides a means of arranging assertions into proofs. In other words, the deductive system lets us prove (verify) that our programs do what they were intended to do (as formalized in specifications, which we discuss in the following paragraphs).

In programming language semantics, many writers distinguish between "axiomatic" semantics (discovered by Anthony Hoare), "translational" semantics, "operational" semantics (developed, as we shall study it, by Stephen Cook and Jaco de Bakker), and "denotational" semantics (discovered by Dana Scott and Christopher Strachey). Roughly, these semantics may be characterized as follows. The axiomatic semantics is a program verification system consisting of axioms and rules of inference. The translational semantics is provided by a programming language translator that specifies a mapping of a source program to a target program (the meaning of the source program). The operational semantics is given by a description of the sequence of machine states passed through during program execution. The denotational semantics is more abstract, as it denotes the meaning of a program in the form of a mapping from machine state to machine state.

These different semantics are said to be "complementary" because they can serve different purposes, and they are said to be "consistent" because they can define one and the same programming language. Complementary semantics are needed because many writers believe that the fundamental semantics is denotational semantics for the language designer, operational semantics for the language implementor developing an interpreter, translational semantics for the implementor developing a compiler, and axiomatic semantics for the language user writing reliable programs. The different semantics must be mutually consistent (or equivalent in some sense) if the implementors are to realize properly the language design and the users are to write software correctly. To illustrate the point on consistency in the extreme, consider the absurdity of selecting a Pascal compiler to translate LISP (as opposed to Pascal) source code.

The terminology used in the last paragraph underscores the importance of different semantic definitions being consistent and complementary, but it also has some problems. The terms "axiomatic semantics" and "translational semantics" are somewhat out of keeping with existing mathematical practice, because axiomatic semantics does not (directly) assign denotations to programs, and translational semantics does not assign the usual sort of mathematical entities (set theoretic objects). The "operational"–"denotational" terminology is somewhat misleading as the operational semantics as well as the denotational semantics can deliver denotations for syntactic expressions. In fact, whenever both the operational and denotational semantics assign a denotation to the same syntactic object, they must deliver the same denotation (or denotations that are equivalent in some suitable sense). If the two semantics do not deliver the same denotation, something is seriously wrong with one or both of them. The difference between the two semantics is in how the denotations are "delivered." In particular, the meaning of a program is a function mapping the set of states (memory configurations) into itself. The operational semantics is described in terms of a machine executing program statements, leaving a trace or sequence of machine states. Roughly, it specifies the meaning of a program point-wise: given an initial state, the meaning of a program is the state (if it exists) in which the program terminates. The denotational semantics abstracts from machine implementations, describing the semantics in terms of various mathematical constructions (e.g., the least fixed points of appropriate functions). If we restrict our attention to nonrecursive programs, the only structured programming construct for which the operational and denotational semantics differ substantially is the **while** statement. We shall examine that difference in Chapter 6.

Program correctness, as we shall study it, is a relativized concept because it is defined in terms of a specification and we will presume that any given specification is correct. A specification consists of a pair of assertions—the precondition (or input assertion) and the postcondition (or output assertion). The precondition describes the permissible values of variables when program execution begins, and the postcondition prescribes the values variables must have when the program terminates. A program is totally correct with respect to a specification consisting of a precondition p and a postcondition q provided that, if p is true when execution begins, then the program *will* terminate and q will be true on termination. The program is partially correct provided that, if p is true when execution begins and *if* the program terminates, then q will be true on termination. Total correctness is the more natural concept in most contexts. However, partial correctness is usually easier to work with, and many important works on program correctness have dealt with it exclusively. We shall define these two concepts of program correctness more rigorously in the chapters that follow.

A deductive or verification system is said to be sound if no incorrect program can be "proven" correct. Beginning in Chapter 1, we will prove the soundness of most of our verification systems immediately after presenting them. We do this to make sure that each verification system contains no "bugs" as well as to fortify your intuitions with the sense of what makes each verification system tick. A deductive system is also said to be complete if every correct program can be proven correct. As we shall see, our verification systems are not complete in this sense, but most of them are complete in a weaker, relative sense. A verification system is called "relatively complete" if the programming part of the verification system does its work fully. The incompleteness of arithmetic (which Kurt Gödel proved in 1931) is entirely responsible for the incompleteness of relatively complete verification systems. The relationships between syntax, operational and denotational semantics, and verification system are depicted in Figure I.1.

A verification system must be proven correct with respect to a semantics —operational or denotational—for it to be trustworthy. An unsound verification system is at best useless and at worst dangerous, for in it one can prove falsehoods. Suppose, for instance, that you were given a verification system in which you could write down (prove) any assertion you choose. You could prove many properties about programs or whatever. You could prove, say, that your very first program gave a constructive proof of Fermat's Last Theorem, that your program established that $x=x+1$, or that (assuming an appropriate encoding of assertions into the language of arithmetic) the moon was made of green cheese. You could prove many things, but that certainly

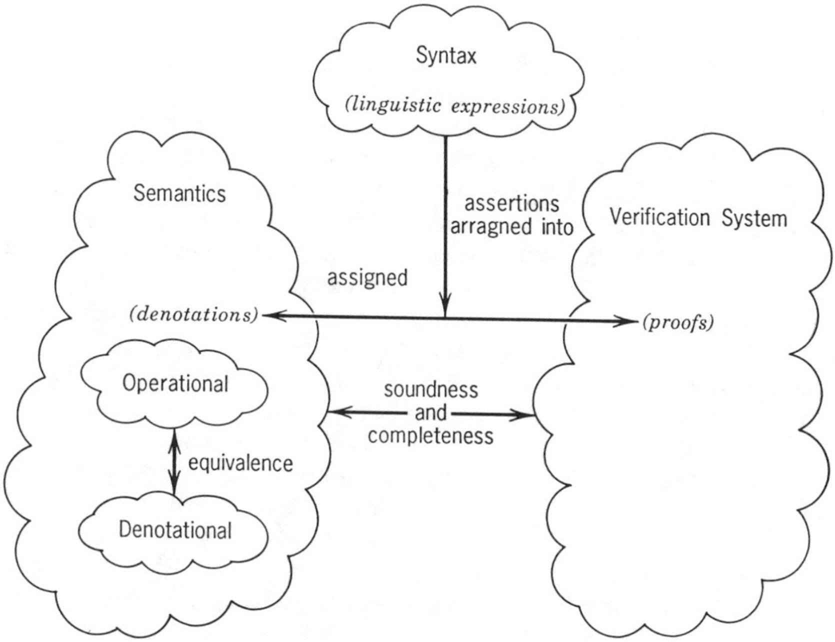

FIGURE I.1. Relationships between syntax, semantics, and verification systems.

would not mean that they were true. You would have been swept away by the *runaway inference ticket* that licenses one to prove anything.

You may say that this is all very silly, that you would never use an unsound verification system. In the unfortunate history of program verification technology, however, many systems for specifying and verifying programs have been developed without a mathematical semantics. And although these systems have been used to "prove" programs correct, many of these systems themselves have not been correct. As a result, incorrect programs have been "proven" correct. And, as a case in point, technical papers on the Assignment Axiom for arrays were, for years, filled with errors. (We shall explore some of the intricacies of the Axiom of Assignment for arrays in Chapter 3.)

Unsound verification practices can surface anywhere. For instance, in the late 1970s, an office of the Department of Defense funded the development of the programming language EUCLID, which was intended to facilitate the development of programs that could be easily verified. The designers of EUCLID did develop proof rules, but they neglected to provide a semantics. In the end, they were forced to admit that they could not vouch for the correctness of their verification system. Indeed, they could not show correctness without first providing a semantics, for correctness is a semantic concept. In another instance, as recently as 1983, the Department of Defense Security Center's evaluation criteria for secure computer systems included only one sentence about semantics, and nothing about the correctness of specification and verification systems.

In my opinion, program verification and semantics are most worthy of study as mathematical aspects of computer science. Further, I am convinced that study of these subjects has practical import. At the least, some basic understanding of them is required to understand the advanced literature on programming languages as well as the ongoing debate on the practicality of verification. More importantly, their study enhances one's ability to reason informally about programs and write correct programs. Furthermore, their study may suggest criteria for evaluating and designing programming languages if, as I believe, only programming languages with reasonable formal verification systems and semantics can be used to develop reliable software.

I do not believe, however, that large-scale program verification, as demanded by some of the systems mentioned previously, is practical in the near future. As will be seen in the following chapters, verification of even moderately realistic programs is complicated. Due to results in undecidability and complexity theory, we know that mechanical theorem-proving techniques are of limited assistance, and that we must depend on human-oriented proof techniques such as the natural deduction system presented in Chapter 0. There are also technical problems in expressing certain specifications, both of a formal and an informal nature. The formal problems are touched upon in Chapter 3. The informal problems relate to the difficulty of spelling out a user's needs in a formal specification, as might be gleaned from the scheduling algorithm fiasco mentioned at the beginning of this introduction. A formal specification may not capture the user's informally stated objectives, and, even if it does, the user's articulated objectives may be misguided, immoral, or just plain wrong.

On the other hand, I am not convinced that program verification will never become a practical activity. Some events that would make program proving more practical are basic discoveries in the mathematical theory of definitions, acceptance of semantic standards for programming language designs, development of software tools to assist humans in program proofs, and initiation of training programs for "proof engineers." I make no prediction on the practicality of program verification in the twenty-first century.

CHAPTER 0

Mathematical Preliminaries

In this chapter, we present the basic mathematical tools used throughout our text. As mentioned in the Preface, we expect this material to be somewhat familiar to most readers, except for the material in Sections 0.3 and 0.4 on the theory of integers (insofar as it differs from Peano arithmetic) and that in Section 0.6 on the Coincidence Lemma. However, to become acquainted with our notational conventions, the reader should glance through all the sections, including those that deal with familiar concepts.

Normally, we will use the language of first-order logic with equality and operation symbols to express mathematical relationships. On those few occasions in which it is necessary to express higher-order concepts, we will do it informally. We describe the language of arithmetic (the first-order theory of integers) in Section 0.1 and a typical natural deduction system in Section 0.2. In Section 0.3, we present an axiomatization of arithmetic. In later chapters, our deductive system (the axiomatization of Section 0.3 together with the natural deduction system of Section 0.2) can be used in establishing facts about the integers essential for proving program correctness.

In Section 0.4, we provide a semantics for our language in terms of *states*. A state extends what is called in logic "the intended interpretation" of our language to encompass integer variables (the variables to which programs can assign values). In subsequent chapters, we extend states to obtain an operational semantics for our programming languages. In Section 0.5, we provide an introduction to the theory of relations to help the reader understand basic semantic concepts and the principle of induction that is introduced in Section 0.6 and used throughout this text. In Section 0.6, we prove the Coincidence Lemma, a basic model theoretic result that states, roughly, that syntactic and semantic substitutions are equivalent. The Coincidence Lemma is essential to understanding the semantics of the assignment statement presented in Chapters 1 and 2. At the end of Section 0.6, we outline a proof of the soundness of our deductive system for arithmetic.

0.1. SYNTAX

In this section, we describe the language of arithmetic. We expect that most of the concepts, terminology, and notational conventions will be familiar to most readers. Readers who are merely glancing through this section should note that we distinguish between the integer variables of our programs and the quantified variables of our assertions.

First, we list the *primitive vocabulary of integer expressions* (along with their intended meanings in parentheses), and then we define the class of integer expressions. The vocabulary consists of a countably infinite number of integer variables (alphabetically ordered), the numeral '0', and the unary and binary operation symbols:

Integer variables:	'x', 'y', 'z', . . .	
Numeral:	'0'	
Unary operation symbol:	'succ'	(successor)
Binary operation symbols:	'+'	(addition)
	'*'	(multiplication)
	'**'	(exponentiation)

Later, in Section 1, we will introduce the *defined symbols* consisting of the numerals . . . '−2', '−1', '1', '2', . . . , the unary operation symbols 'pred' (predecessor), '−' (negative), and 'abs' (absolute value), and the binary operation symbols '−' (subtraction), '/' (division), and 'mod' (remainder). We shall briefly discuss legitimate methods by which new defined symbols can be introduced into the language of arithmetic.

The *integer expressions* (usually called "terms" in logic) of the language of arithmetic are defined inductively as follows:

(1) A numeral m is an integer expression.
(2) An integer variable x is an integer expression.
(3) If e is an integer expression and o_u is an unary operation symbol, then $o_u(e)$ is an integer expression.
(4) If e and e' are integer expressions and o_b is a binary operation symbol, then $(e\ o_b\ e')$ is an integer expression.
(5) Nothing else is an integer expression.

An integer expression is *simple* if it is either a numeral (clause (1)) or an integer variable (clause (2)); otherwise, it is *complex*. For example, '0' and 'x' are simple integer expressions, whereas 'succ(x)', '($x*y$)', and '(succ(x)$-$($x*y$))' are complex integer expressions.

It is convenient to introduce some notational conventions and related terminology. Let x be an integer variable and e be an integer expression. We write $\mathfrak{ivar}[e]$ for the set of integer variables occurring in e. We say that e is *free* of x (*x-free,* for short) and that x is *foreign* to e if x does not occur in e. For example, $\mathfrak{ivar}[(x*2)+x]=\{x\}$, and the integer variables y and z are foreign to the integer expression $(x*2)+x$. We use the backward slash \ to indicate the syntactic operation of *substitution* (as distinguished from the forward slash / used for the integer division operator) and the square brackets [and] to delimit substitutions. We understand $e[y\backslash x]$ to be the integer expression obtained from the integer expression e by substituting the integer variable y for all occurrences of the integer variable x in e. For example, using the triple bar $\equiv$ to indicate *syntactic identity,* we have the following:

$$x[y\backslash x] \equiv y$$

$$z[y\backslash x] \equiv z \qquad \text{(when } x \text{ and } z \text{ are distinct integer variables)}$$

$$(x/y)[y\backslash x] \equiv y/y$$

We will use the same notation to indicate substitution in other linguistic contexts. For example, substituting the integer expression $(y-z)$ for the integer variable x in the integer expression $((x*2)+x)$, we have the following:

$$((x*2)+x)[(y-z)\backslash x] \equiv ((y-z)*2)+(y-z)$$

Similarly, we understand $e[e'\backslash\backslash e'']$ to be any of the integer expressions that can be obtained from e by substituting the integer expression e' for zero or more occurrences of the integer expression e'' in e. For example, $(x+x)[y\backslash\backslash x]$ can be any of $x+x$, $y+x$, $x+y$, or $y+y$.

We will now define the class of assertions (the sentences describing the integers and the integer variables of our programs). The *primitive vocabulary of assertions* consists of a countably infinite number of quantified variables, the binary predicate symbols, and the assertion connectives (frequently called "logical operators"), together with the vocabulary of integer expressions. They are as follows:

Quantified variables:	'X', 'Y', 'Z', . . .	
Binary predicate symbols:	'$=$'	(equal)
	'$\geqslant$'	(greater-than-or-equal)
Unary assertion connectives:	'$\sim$'	(negation)
	'$\forall$'	(the universal quantifier)
	'$\exists$'	(the existential quantifier)
Binary assertion connectives:	'&'	(conjunction)
	'$\vee$'	(disjunction)
	'$\rightarrow$'	(conditional)
	'$\leftrightarrow$'	(biconditional)

In Section 0.2, we will introduce, as defined symbols, the binary predicate symbols '$\neq$' (not-equal), '$\leqslant$' (less-than-or-equal), '$>$' (greater-than), and '$<$' (less-than).

To distinguish the integer variables (to which programs can assign values) and the quantified variables (to which the quantifiers $\forall$ and $\exists$ can be prefixed), we are using the small letters 'x', 'y', 'z', . . . for integer variables and the capital letters 'X', 'Y', 'Z', . . . for quantified variables. Discrete structures and logic texts differ considerably in their terminology and treatment of variables, so it is important to understand how our treatment is related to other treatments. We use two runs of variables (the quantified variables and the integer variables), a style derived from Leblanc and Wisdom's *Deductive Logic.* Our quantified variables are called "term variables" by Leblanc and Wisdom; other texts often refer to them as "individual variables." Our integer variables are called "terms" by Leblanc and Wisdom, whereas others may call them "arbitrary names" or "individual parameters." In a text that uses only one run of variables, an occurrence of one of our quantified variables corresponds to "a bound occurrence" of a variable, and an occurrence of one of our integer variables corresponds to "a free occurrence."

The *assertions* are defined inductively as follows:

(1) If e and e' are integer expressions and r is a binary predicate symbol, then $(e\ r\ e')$ is an assertion.

(2) If p is an assertion, then $\sim p$ is an assertion.

(3) If p and q are assertions and c_b is a binary assertion connective, then $(p\ c_b\ q)$ is an assertion.

(4) If X is a quantified variable and $p[0\backslash X]$ is an assertion, then $\forall Xp$ and $\exists Xp$ are assertions.

(5) Nothing else is an assertion.

An assertion is *simple* if it is of the form specified by clause 1; it is *complex* otherwise. The notation $\mathfrak{ivar}[p]$ and the terms *foreign* and *x-free* are extended to an assertion p in the natural manner.

To illustrate our grammar, we show the following assertions (with the clauses justifying them in parentheses):

$(x=0)$	(clause (1))
$(\sim(x\geqslant 0))$	(clauses (1) and (2))
$((x=0)\rightarrow(\sim\sim(x\geqslant 0)))$	(clauses (1)–(3))
$\forall X((X=0)\rightarrow(\sim\sim(X\geqslant 0)))$	(clauses (1)–(4))
$\forall X\exists Y(X=Y)$	(clauses (1) and (4))

The first assertion is simple, and the rest are complex. The string

$$\forall X\exists X(X=X)$$

is not an assertion because

$$\exists 0(0=0)$$

is not an assertion.[1]

We adopt the standard conventions for eliminating parentheses. First, we take the precedence of the assertion connectives, in order of decreasing binding power, as follows: first the unary connectives ('∼', '∀', and '∃'), second '&', third '∨', fourth '→', and fifth '↔'. So, instead of writing

$$\forall X(((x\leqslant X)\&(X\leqslant y))\rightarrow((x=y)\vee(x<y)))$$

we can write (using our precedence convention and dropping inessential parentheses around simple assertions):

$$\forall X(x\leqslant X\ \&\ X\leqslant y\rightarrow x=y\vee x<y)$$

Similarly, we take the precedence of the primitive and defined operation symbols, as follows: first the unary symbols ('succ', 'pred', '−', and 'abs'), second '**', third '*', '/', and 'mod', and fourth '+' and the binary '−'.

Second, we take the binary connectives and operations to associate to the left, except for '**', which associates to the right. For example, instead of writing

$$(x+((5*y)**(w**z)))$$

[1] As illustrated by this last example, the language of assertions is not context-free due to clause (4). If we did allow $\forall X\exists X(X=X)$ to be an assertion, we could derive the nonassertion $\exists 0(0=0)$ by Rule ∀∃ in the natural deduction system, which is presented in the next section.

we can write simply

$$x+(5*y)**w**z$$

Substitution associates to the left and has greater binding power than any operation symbol or assertion connective. If parentheses have been eliminated according to our conventions, some of the parentheses may need to be reinserted when making substitutions. For example, we have

$$x[y\backslash x][z\backslash x] \equiv y$$

$$x-x[y-1\backslash x] \equiv x-(y-1)$$

$$(x-x)[y-1\backslash x] \equiv y-1-(y-1)$$

Third, we write '$\forall X_1, X_2, \ldots, X_n$' as an abbreviation for '$\forall X_1 \forall X_2 \ldots \forall X_n$'. We use a similar abbreviation with the existential quantifier $\exists$. When an assertion is of the form '$\forall X_1, X_2, \ldots, X_n p$', we sometimes follow the practice of eliminating the prefix of universal quantifiers '$\forall X_1, X_2, \ldots, X_n$'. For example, we understand

$$\forall X, Y(X*Y=Y*X)$$

and

$$X*Y=Y*X$$

to be short for

$$\forall X \forall Y(X*Y=Y*X)$$

Let true $\equiv$ 0=0 and false $\equiv$ ~true. It is convenient to adopt the following convention regarding arbitrarily long (finite) conjunctions of the form $p_1 \& \ldots \& p_n (n \geq 0)$. We understand

$$p_1 \& \ldots \& p_n \equiv \text{true if } n=0$$

Otherwise,

$$p_1 \& \ldots \& p_n \equiv (p_1 \& \ldots \& p_{n-1}) \& p_n$$

Similarly, in the case of disjunctions of the form $p_1 \vee \ldots \vee p_n (n \geq 0)$, we understand

$$p_1 \vee \ldots \vee p_n \equiv \text{false if } n=0$$

Otherwise,

$$p_1 \vee \ldots \vee p_n \equiv (p_1 \vee \ldots \vee p_{n-1}) \vee p_n$$

When no ambiguity can result, we will use other commonly used abbreviations.

Our grammar of integer expressions and assertions is sometimes called a "logician's grammar." This is due to the style in which it is presented. In Chapter 1, we will offer the grammar of integer expressions in the style of John McCarthy's abstract syntax, an abbreviated form of BNF that abstracts the semantically relevant features of the grammar from purely syntactic considerations dealing with parsing[2].

0.2. NATURAL DEDUCTION

A *natural deduction* system mirrors the structure of mathematical discourses in which rigorous reasoning is expressed. The name is derived from the fact that its rules enable one to derive (prove) an assertion from a set of assumptions (premises) in a way that closely resembles mathematical practice. In this section, we describe the rules of our natural deduction system and illustrate their use. The next section contains more examples, which follow a discussion of an axiomatization of arithmetic. Our natural deduction system is taken largely from the Fitch-style system in Leblanc and Wisdom's *Deductive Logic* (supplemented with standard rules for equality). Readers familiar with other natural deduction systems for classical first-order logic may skim this section and need note only Figure 0.1, where our natural deduction rules are schematized and named.[3]

The *m assumptions* (assumed assertions) $p_1, \ldots, p_m$ in a *derivation* are written above a horizontal line. Assertions derived by the rules of inference are written below the line in the order in which they are derived and are numbered consecutively. For example, in the Reiteration Rule (**R**) schema-

[2] The reader should bear in mind that the grammar of assertions is not context-free, as might be suggested by the use of abstract syntax in subsequent chapters. This slight complexity in the grammar of assertions is more than compensated for by the simplicity it contributes to the deductive system and the semantics. In most of the logic literature, the grammar of assertions is context-sensitive, though this is frequently not stated explicitly.

[3] For those readers with a limited background in logic and who would like additional experience in using a natural deduction system, we suggest supplemental reading in Leblanc and Wisdom or any one of the many other excellent introductory texts covering natural deduction.

tized in Figure 0.1

$$\begin{array}{r|lll} 1 & p_1 & & \\ 2 & p_2 & & \\ \cdot & \cdot & & \\ m & \underline{p_m} & & \\ \cdot & \cdot & & \\ n & p_i & (\mathbf{R},i) & (1\leqslant i\leqslant m) \end{array}$$

the assertion $p_i\,(1\leqslant i\leqslant m)$ on line n is derived because it is one of the assumptions $p_1, \ldots, p_m$. We say that line n is *derived* from line i by the Reiteration Rule, which the *annotation* $(\mathbf{R},i)$ on line n indicates.

Figure 0.1 displays an introduction rule and an elimination rule for each of the assertion connectives. Our natural deduction system permits finitely many nested derivations, which are used in the Conditional Introduction Rule ($\rightarrow$**I**), the Negation Introduction Rule ($\sim$**I**), the Disjunction Elimination Rule ($\vee$**E**), the Biconditional Introduction Rule ($\leftrightarrow$**I**), and the Existential Quantifier Elimination Rule ($\exists$**E**). For example, in Rule ($\rightarrow$**I**)

$$\begin{array}{r|ll} 1 & p_1 & \\ 2 & p_2 & \\ \cdot & \cdot & \\ m & \underline{p_m} & \\ \cdot & \cdot & \\ a & \begin{array}{|l} \underline{\;q\;} \end{array} & \\ \cdot & \begin{array}{|l} \;\cdot \end{array} & \\ b & \begin{array}{|l} \;r \end{array} & \\ b+1 & q\rightarrow r & (\rightarrow\mathbf{I},a-b) \end{array}$$

a nested derivation begins on line a and ends on line b. Rule $\rightarrow$**I** allows us to derive $q\rightarrow r$ (line $b+1$) if we can derive r (line b) from the assumption q (line a) in a nested derivation. The annotation $(\rightarrow\mathbf{I},a-b)$ on line $b+1$ indicates that line $b+1$ was derived by Rule $\rightarrow$**I** from the nested derivation on lines $a-b$ (lines a through b).

We now turn to a formal description of nested derivations. (On a first reading, the reader might skim this paragraph, returning for a more careful reading after having studied the example derivations at the end of this section.) Let d_1 and d_2 be the derivations:

$$d_1 \qquad\qquad\qquad\qquad d_2$$

$$\begin{array}{r|l} 1 & p_1 \\ 2 & p_2 \\ \cdot & \cdot \\ m & \underline{p_m} \\ \cdot & \cdot \\ n & p_n \end{array} \qquad\qquad \begin{array}{r|l} 1 & q_1 \\ 2 & q_2 \\ \cdot & \cdot \\ a & \underline{q_a} \\ \cdot & \cdot \\ b & q_b \end{array}$$

THE REITERATION RULE (R)

R

1	p_1		
2	p_2		
·	·		
m	p_m		
·	·		
n	p_i	(**R**,i)	$(1 \leq i \leq m)$

THE CONDITIONAL INTRODUCTION RULE (→I) AND THE CONDITIONAL ELIMINATION RULE (→E)

→I

1	p_1		
2	p_2		
·	·		
m	p_m		
·	·		
a		q	
·		·	
b		r	
$b+1$	$q \to r$		(→**I**,$a-b$)

→E

1	p_1	
2	p_2	
·	·	
m	p_m	
·	·	
a	$q \to r$	
·	·	
b	q	
·	·	
n	r	(→**E**,a,b)

THE NEGATION INTRODUCTION RULE (~I) AND THE NEGATION ELIMINATION RULE (~E)

~I

1	p_1		
2	p_2		
·	·		
m	p_m		
·	·		
a		q	
·		·	
b		r	
·		·	
c		$\sim r$	
$c+1$	$\sim q$		(~**I**,$a-c$)

~E

1	p_1	
2	p_2	
·	·	
m	p_m	
·	·	
a	$\sim\sim q$	
·	·	
n	q	(~**E**,a)

FIGURE 0.1. The natural deduction rules.

THE CONJUNCTION INTRODUCTION RULE (&I) AND THE CONJUNCTION ELIMINATION RULE (&E)

&I

1	p_1	
2	p_2	
.	.	
m	p_m	
.	.	
a	q_1	
.	.	
b	q_2	
.	.	
n	$q_1 \& q_2$	(**&I**,a,b)

&E

1	p_1	
2	p_2	
.	.	
m	p_m	
.	.	
a	$q_1 \& q_2$	
.	.	
n	q_i	(**&E**,a) (i=1 or 2)

THE DISJUNCTION INTRODUCTION RULE (∨I) AND THE DISJUNCTION ELIMINATION RULE (∨E)

∨I

1	p_1	
2	p_2	
.	.	
m	p_m	
.	.	
a	q_i	(i=1 or 2)
.	.	
n	$q_1 \vee q_2$	(∨**I**,a)

∨E

1	p_1	
2	p_2	
.	.	
m	p_m	
.	.	
a	$q_1 \vee q_2$	
.	.	
b	q_1	
.	.	
c	r	
d	q_2	
.	.	
e	r	
$e+1$	r	(∨**E**,a,b–c,d–e)

FIGURE 0.1. *(Continued)*

THE BICONDITIONAL INTRODUCTION RULE (↔I) AND THE BICONDITIONAL ELIMINATION RULE (↔E)

↔I

1	p_1	
2	p_2	
·	·	
m	p_m	
·	·	
a	q	
·	·	
b	r	
c	r	
·	·	
d	q	
$d+1$	$q \leftrightarrow r$	(↔**I**,$a-b$,$c-d$)

↔E

1	p_1	
2	p_2	
·	·	
m	p_m	
·	·	
a	$q \leftrightarrow r$	(or $r \leftrightarrow q$)
·	·	
b	q	
·	·	
n	r	(↔**E**,a,b)

THE UNIVERSAL QUANTIFIER INTRODUCTION RULE (∀I) AND THE UNIVERSAL QUANTIFIER ELIMINATION RULE (∀E)

∀I

1	p_1	
2	p_2	
·	·	
m	p_m	
·	·	
a	$q[x \backslash X]$	
·	·	
n	$\forall Xq$	(∀**I**,a)

∀E

1	p_1	
2	p_2	
·	·	
m	p_m	
·	·	
a	$\forall Xq$	
·	·	
n	$q[e \backslash X]$	(∀**E**,a)

X may be any quantified variable, e any integer expression, and x any integer variable subject to the following restriction:

Restriction: In the Rule **∀I**, x must be foreign to $\forall Xq$ and each p_i $(1 \leq i \leq m)$.

FIGURE 0.1. *(Continued)*

THE EXISTENTIAL QUANTIFIER INTRODUCTION RULE ($\exists$I) AND THE EXISTENTIAL QUANTIFIER ELIMINATION RULE ($\exists$E)

$\exists$I

$$
\begin{array}{r|ll}
1 & p_1 & \\
2 & p_2 & \\
\cdot & \cdot & \\
m & \underline{p_m} & \\
\cdot & \cdot & \\
a & q[e\backslash X] & \\
\cdot & \cdot & \\
n & \exists Xq & (\exists\mathbf{I}, a)
\end{array}
$$

$\exists$E

$$
\begin{array}{r|lll}
1 & p_1 & & \\
2 & p_2 & & \\
\cdot & \cdot & & \\
m & \underline{p_m} & & \\
\cdot & \cdot & & \\
a & \exists Xq & & \\
\cdot & \cdot & & \\
b & \quad| \; \underline{q[x\backslash X]} & & \\
\cdot & \quad| \; \cdot & & \\
c & \quad| \; r & & \\
c+1 & r & & (\exists\mathbf{E}, a, b-c)
\end{array}
$$

X may be any quantified variable, e any integer expression, and x any integer variable subject to the following restriction:

Restriction: In the Rule **$\exists$I**, x must be foreign to $\exists Xq$, r, and each p_i $(1 \leq i \leq m)$.

THE EQUALITY INTRODUCTION RULE (=I), THE EQUALITY REPLACEMENT RULE (=R), AND THE EQUALITY SYMMETRY RULE (=.sym)

=I

$$
\begin{array}{r|ll}
1 & p_1 & \\
2 & p_2 & \\
\cdot & \cdot & \\
m & \underline{p_m} & \\
\cdot & \cdot & \\
n & e=e & (=\mathbf{I})
\end{array}
$$

=R

$$
\begin{array}{r|ll}
1 & p_1 & \\
2 & p_2 & \\
\cdot & \cdot & \\
m & \underline{p_m} & \\
\cdot & \cdot & \\
a & e_1=e_2 & \\
\cdot & \cdot & \\
b & q & \\
\cdot & \cdot & \\
n & q[e_2\backslash\backslash e_1] & (=\mathbf{R}, a, b)
\end{array}
$$

FIGURE 0.1. *(Continued)*

=.sym

1	p_1	
2	p_2	
.	.	
m	p_m	
.	.	
a	$e_1 = e_2$	
.	.	
n	$e_2 = e_1$	(**=.sym**, a)

e, e_1, and e_2 may be any integer expressions.

FIGURE 0.1. *(Continued)*

From derivations d_1 and d_2, we can form a new derivation d_3 by writing down the derivation d_1 followed by the derivation d_2 (after renumbering the lines from $n+1$ to $n+b$) and one or more additional lines (ending with line c):

d_3

1	p_1	
2	p_2	
.	.	
m	p_m	
.	.	
n	p_n	
$n+1$		q_1
$n+2$		q_2
.		.
$n+a$		q_a
.		.
$n+b$		q_b
.	.	
c	r	

The derivation on lines $n+1$ to $n+b$ (the derivation d_2 with renumbered lines) is said to be an *immediate subordinate derivation* of the derivation d_3. A derivation d_j is called a *subordinate derivation* of a derivation d_i if d_j is an immediate subordinate derivation of d_i or if d_j is an immediate subordinate derivation of a third derivation d_k and d_k is a subordinate derivation of d_i. A derivation d_j is in the *scope* of an assumption for a derivation d_i if d_j is d_i or if d_j is a subordinate derivation of d_i. Each line in a derivation d is in the scope of an assumption if d is. So that we do not have to repeat assumptions in a subordinate derivation, we understand that the set of assumptions for a derivation d is the set consisting of each assumption p such that d is in the scope of p. With this understanding, *we relax the Reiteration Rule* **(R)** *by allowing the reiteration of an assumption, provided the derived line is in the scope of that assumption.*

In the Conditional Elimination Rule (**→E**)

1	p_1	
2	p_2	
.	.	
m	p_m	
.	.	
a	$q \rightarrow r$	
.	.	
b	q	
.	.	
n	r	(**→E**,a,b)

we understand that line b may occur before line a in the derivation. That is, it does not matter whether p or $p \rightarrow q$ occurs first, just as long as they both occur in the *same* derivation before line n. A similar understanding is implicit in the schematics of other rules, shown in Figure 0.1.

In the Universal Quantifier Introduction Rule (**∀I**)

1	p_1	
2	p_2	
.	.	
m	p_m	
.	.	
a	$q[x \backslash X]$	
.	.	
n	$\forall Xq$	(**∀I**,a)

we understand that X may be any quantified variable and x any integer variable, subject to the restriction that x must be foreign to $\forall Xq$ and each p_i ($1 \leq i \leq m$). The restriction blocks illicit derivations such as (1) $\forall X(X=x)$ from $x=x$ and (2) $\forall X(X=0)$ from the assumption $x=0$. A similar restriction applies to the Existential Quantifier Elimination Rule (**∃E**). As an exercise, the reader is asked to exhibit illicit derivations that could be obtained if the restriction on the integer variable x was dropped in Rule **∃E**.

We say that an assertion p is *derivable* from a set of assertions A—written $A \vdash p$—if there is a derivation of p from a finite subset of A. If p is derivable from the finite set of assertions $A=\{p_1, \ldots, p_n\}$, we usually omit the set brackets and write $p_1, \ldots, p_n \vdash p$. When $A=\{\}$ (i.e., A is the empty set), we write $\vdash p$, short for $\{\} \vdash p$, and call p a *theorem of first-order logic.*

The following examples illustrate the use of each of the natural deduction rules.

EXAMPLE 1

We illustrate the use of the Rules **R**, **→I**, and **→E** by showing that

$$y>z, x>y\rightarrow(y>z\rightarrow x>z) \vdash x>y\rightarrow x>z$$

The subordinate derivation of $x>z$ (line 8) from the assumption $x>y$ (line 3) allows us to apply Rule **→I** and obtain $x>y\rightarrow x>z$ (line 9).

1	$y>z$	
2	$x>y\rightarrow(y>z\rightarrow x>z)$	
3	$\mid\ x>y$	
4	$\mid\ x>y$	(**R**,3)
5	$\mid\ x>y\rightarrow(y>z\rightarrow x>z)$	(**R**,2)
6	$\mid\ y>z\rightarrow x>z$	(**→E**,4,5)
7	$\mid\ y>z$	(**R**,1)
8	$\mid\ x>z$	(**→E**,6,7)
9	$x>y\rightarrow x>z$	(**→I**,3–8)

EXAMPLE 2

We illustrate the use of the Rules Conjunction Introduction **(&I)**, Disjunction Introduction **(∨I)**, and Disjunction Elimination **(∨E)** (in addition to the Rules **R**, **→I**, and **→E** illustrated in Example 1) by showing that

$$p\&q\rightarrow r,\ s\rightarrow p,\ s\rightarrow q,\ t\vee u\rightarrow s,\ w\rightarrow t,\ x\rightarrow u \vdash w\vee x\rightarrow r$$

A subordinate derivation runs from line 7 to line 28 and sets up an application of Rule **→I** (line 29), and nested within that subordinate derivation are its two immediate subordinate derivations (lines 9 to 13 and 14 to 18) that set up an application of Rule **∨E** (line 19).

1	$p\&q\rightarrow r$	
2	$s\rightarrow p$	
3	$s\rightarrow q$	
4	$t\vee u\rightarrow s$	
5	$w\rightarrow t$	
6	$x\rightarrow u$	
7	$\mid\ w\vee x$	
8	$\mid\ w\vee x$	(**R**,7)
9	$\mid\ \mid\ w$	
10	$\mid\ \mid\ w$	(**R**,9)
11	$\mid\ \mid\ w\rightarrow t$	(**R**,5)
12	$\mid\ \mid\ t$	(**→E**,10,11)
13	$\mid\ \mid\ t\vee u$	(**∨I**,12)

14	x	
15	x	(**R**,14)
16	$x \rightarrow u$	(**R**,6)
17	u	($\rightarrow$**E**,15,16)
18	$t \vee u$	($\vee$**I**,17)
19	$t \vee u$	($\vee$**E**,8,9–13,14–18)
20	$t \vee u \rightarrow s$	(**R**,4)
21	s	($\rightarrow$**E**,19,20)
22	$s \rightarrow p$	(**R**,2)
23	p	($\rightarrow$**E**,21,22)
24	$s \rightarrow q$	(**R**,3)
25	q	($\rightarrow$**E**,21,24)
26	$p \& q$	(**&I**,23,25)
27	$p \& q \rightarrow r$	(**R**,1)
28	r	($\rightarrow$**E**,26,27)
29	$w \vee x \rightarrow r$	($\rightarrow$**I**,7–28)

EXAMPLE 3

We illustrate the use of the Rules **∀I**, **∀E**, **∃I**, and **∃E** in a demonstration of the following:

$$\forall Y \exists X(X \leqslant Y \vee X > Y) \vdash \forall Y(\exists X(X \leqslant Y) \vee \exists X(X > Y))$$

1	$\forall Y \exists X(X \leqslant Y \vee X > Y)$	
2	$\forall Y \exists X(X \leqslant Y \vee X > Y)$	(**R**,1)
3	$\exists X(X \leqslant y \vee X > y)$	(**∀E**,2)
4	$x \leqslant y \vee x > y$	
5	$x \leqslant y \vee x > y$	(**R**,4)
6	$x \leqslant y$	
7	$x \leqslant y$	(**R**,6)
8	$\exists X(X \leqslant y)$	(**∃I**,7)
9	$\exists X(X \leqslant y) \vee \exists X(X > y)$	($\vee$**I**,8)
10	$x > y$	
11	$x > y$	(**R**,10)
12	$\exists X(X > y)$	(**∃I**,11)
13	$\exists X(X \leqslant y) \vee \exists X(X > y)$	($\vee$**I**,12)
14	$\exists X(X \leqslant y) \vee \exists X(X > y)$	($\vee$**E**,5,6–9,10–13)
15	$\exists X(X \leqslant y) \vee \exists X(X > y)$	(**∃E**,3,4–14)
16	$\forall Y(\exists X(X \leqslant y) \vee \exists X(X > y))$	(**∀I**,15)

EXAMPLE 4

We illustrate the use of the Rules Equality Introduction (**=I**), Equality Replacement (**=R**), and Biconditional Elimination (**↔E**) in a demonstration of the following:

$$y+z=z+z \leftrightarrow y+z=2*z, y=z \vdash y+z=2*z$$

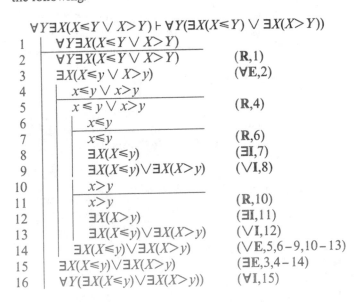

The Rule **=R** allows us to substitute z for only one occurrence of y in line 3 to obtain line 5.

1	$y+z=z+z \leftrightarrow y+z=2*z$	
2	$y=z$	
3	$y+z=y+z$	(**=I**)
4	$y=z$	(**R**,2)
5	$y+z=z+z$	(**=R**,3,4)
6	$y+z=z+z \leftrightarrow y+z=2*z$	(**R**,1)
7	$y+z=2*z$	(**↔E**,5,6)

EXAMPLE 5

We illustrate the use of the Rules Biconditional Introduction **(↔I)** and Equality Symmetry **(=.sym)** in a demonstration of the following:

$$\vdash x=y \leftrightarrow y=x$$

Notice that the final line in the derivation (line 7) is not in the scope of any assumption. The assumptions on lines 1 and 4 are said to have been *discharged.*

1	$x=y$	
2	$x=y$	(**R**,1)
3	$y=x$	(**=.sym**,2)
4	$y=x$	
5	$y=x$	(**R**,4)
6	$x=y$	(**=.sym**,5)
7	$x=y \leftrightarrow y=x$	(**↔I**,1–3,4–6)

EXAMPLE 6

This derivation can be incorporated into a proof showing that Rule **=.sym** is dispensible in the sense that, for any integer expressions e and e', we can demonstrate $e=e' \vdash e'=e$ without using Rule **=.sym.** Several other of our rules are also dispensible, but eliminating **=.sym** or any of the other rules would lead to long and unnatural proofs.

1	$e=e'$	
2	$e=e'$	(**R**,1)
3	$e=e$	(**=I**)
4	$e'=e$	(**=R**,2,3)

EXAMPLE 7

Our final sample derivation, which illustrates the use of the Rules **~I**, **~E**, and **&E**, demonstrates the disastrous consequences of inconsistency. That is, from a contradiction, one can derive anything whatsoever (in this case, that all integers are equal):

1	$z=0\&\sim z=0$	
2	$\quad \sim x=y$	
3	$\quad z=0\&\sim z=0$	(**R**,1)
4	$\quad z=0$	(**&E**,3)
5	$\quad \sim z=0$	(**&E**,3)
6	$\sim\sim x=y$	(**~I**,2–5)
7	$x=y$	(**~E**,6)
8	$\forall Y(x=Y)$	(**∀I**,7)
9	$\forall X \forall Y(X=Y)$	(**∀I**,8)

In the next section, when no ambiguity can result, we will periodically collapse two or more lines into one line. For example, lines 8 and 9 are both derived by Rule **∀I**, so we might replace these two lines with

8 | $\forall X \forall Y(X=Y)$ (**∀I**,7)

0.3. THE THEORY OF INTEGERS: AXIOMATIZATION

In this section, we present an axiomatization of *arithmetic (the theory of integers),* building on the natural deduction system presented in the preceding section. Our axioms are intended to characterize the integers and are adapted from the *Peano Axioms* for the *natural numbers* (the nonnegative integers 0, 1, 2, . . .) to suit the negative integers as well as the natural numbers.[4] The reader should fully understand the concept of a proof in arithmetic to contrast it with the concept of a proof in the Hoare axiomatization (Chapter 1). As we will see in Chapter 1, the two concepts of proof are quite different, and failure to appreciate the differences can lead to disastrous consequences. Even those readers familiar with the Peano Axioms should note how we name our axioms as well as our conventions regarding proofs. We will begin with our list of axioms, and then proceed to define the concept of a proof, discuss briefly the role of definitions, and finally exhibit a few sample proofs.

An assertion p in which no integer variable occurs is said to be *integer variable free.* Let $p(x)$ be any assertion in which (1) the integer variable x occurs, (2) no integer variable other than x occurs, and (3) the quantified variables X and Y do not occur. We understand $p(e)$ to be the assertion

[4] Although the Peano Axioms are covered in many excellent introductory texts (see, for example, Kleene (1967)), we do not know of any direct axiomatization for the integers similar to the one presented in this section. See Feferman for a standard treatment of the integers in mathematics.

$p(x)[e\backslash x]$. For example, $p(0) \equiv p(x)[0\backslash x]$ and, similarly, $p(X) \equiv p(x)[X\backslash x]$. In the axiomatization of arithmetic presented in Figure 0.2, the first axiom is the axiom of (complete) induction for the integers.[5] In the antecedent of the induction axiom, the second conjunct serves for induction over the *positive integers* (the natural numbers greater than 0), and the third conjunct serves for induction over the negative integers.

From this section forward, our use of the symbol $\vdash$ will differ somewhat from its use in the preceding section. Let A be a set of assertions, and let Ax be the set of axioms of arithmetic. A *proof* (in arithmetic) of an assertion p from A is a derivation of p from any finite subset of $A \cup \text{Ax}$. An assertion p is *provable* from A,—written as $A \vdash p$,—if there is a proof of p from A. When $\{\} \vdash p$, we call p a *theorem (of arithmetic)* and write $\vdash p$. We say that A is *consistent* if there is an assertion p such that not $A \vdash p$, and A is *inconsistent* if A is not consistent.

The axioms shown above the dashed line in Figure 0.2 are expressed in terms of the *primitive symbols* of arithmetic, which are $\geq$, 'succ', '+', '*', '**', and '0'.[6] The axioms shown below the dashed line in Figure 0.2 are used to introduce the symbols $\neq$, '$\leq$', and so forth by definition. Each of the axioms **(D.pred)**, **(D.n)**, and **(D.mod)**, which introduce the unary operation symbols 'pred' and '—' and the binary operation symbol 'mod', is said to be an "equational definition" because the symbol being defined is the only operation symbol on the left side of the equation and the only operation symbols occurring on the right side are *more primitive* (i.e., are primitive or have been previously defined). For example, in **(D.mod)**, 'mod', the binary operation symbol being defined, occurs on the left side, while on the right side, '*' is the only primitive operation symbol. The only other operation symbols are the previously defined binary '—' and '/'. One can think of the integer expression (e mod e') as abbreviating the integer expression $(e-(e/e')*e')$ so that, by using Rule **=R**, any simple assertion p can be converted into the equivalent assertion $p[(e-(e/e')*e')\backslash(e \bmod e')]$. This eliminates all occurrences of 'mod' in favor of the more primitive '*', '—', and '/'. Considering, for the moment, each numeral m to be a 0-ary operation symbol, the axioms of the form **(D.m)** equationally define the numerals other than 0.

More formally, we say that an equation of the form

$$o_n(X_1, \ldots, X_n) = e(X_1, \ldots, X_n)$$

introducing the new n-ary operation symbol o_n is an *equational definition*

[5] The induction axiom is often called an *axiom schema* because $p(0)$ can be any integer variable free assertion having one or more occurrences of the numeral 0, and X and Y can be any distinct quantified variables. The schema stands for a countably infinite set of axioms.

[6] The variables, the assertion connectives, and the predicate symbol '=' are *logical symbols* common to all mathematical theories. Consequently, they are not counted as primitive symbols peculiar to arithmetic. Their role in proofs is governed by the rules of our natural deduction system, not by the axioms of arithmetic.

(Ind)	$p(0) \,\&\, \forall X(X \geqslant 0 \rightarrow (p(X) \rightarrow p(\mathrm{succ}(X))))$
	$\&\, \forall X(0 \geqslant \mathrm{succ}(X) \rightarrow (p(\mathrm{succ}(X)) \rightarrow p(X))) \rightarrow \forall Y p(Y)$
(⩾.tr)	$X \geqslant Y \,\&\, Y \geqslant Z \rightarrow X \geqslant Z$
(⩾.as)	$X \geqslant Y \,\&\, Y \geqslant X \rightarrow X = Y$
(⩾.di)	$X \geqslant Y \vee Y \geqslant X$
(succ.⩾)	$\mathrm{succ}(X) \geqslant X$
(succ.=)	$\mathrm{succ}(X) = \mathrm{succ}(Y) \rightarrow X = Y$
(succ.≠)	$X \geqslant 0 \rightarrow \sim(\mathrm{succ}(X) = 0)$
(+.0)	$X + 0 = X$
(+.succ)	$X + \mathrm{succ}(Y) = \mathrm{succ}(X + Y)$
(*.0)	$X * 0 = 0$
(*.succ)	$X * \mathrm{succ}(Y) = X * Y + X$
(.0)**	$X ** 0 = \mathrm{succ}(0)$
(.+)**	$Y \geqslant 0 \rightarrow X ** \mathrm{succ}(Y) = (X ** Y) * X$
(.−)**	$0 \geqslant \mathrm{succ}(Y) \rightarrow X ** Y = 0$
(D.≠)	$Y \neq Y \leftrightarrow \sim(X = Y)$
(D.⩽)	$X \leqslant Y \leftrightarrow Y \geqslant X$
(D.>)	$X > Y \leftrightarrow \sim(X \leqslant Y)$
(D.<)	$X < Y \leftrightarrow Y > X$
(D.−)	$X - Y = Z \leftrightarrow Z + Y = X$
(D.pred)	$\mathrm{pred}(X) = X - \mathrm{succ}(0)$
(D.n)	$-X = 0 - X$
(D.abs)	$\mathrm{abs}(X) = Y \leftrightarrow (X \geqslant 0 \rightarrow Y = X) \,\&\, (X < 0 \rightarrow Y = -X)$
(D./)	$X/Y = Z \leftrightarrow ((Y = 0 \rightarrow Z = 0) \,\&\, (Y \neq 0 \rightarrow (\mathrm{abs}(Y * Z) \leqslant$
	$\mathrm{abs}(X) < \mathrm{abs}(Y) * \mathrm{succ}(\mathrm{abs}(Z)) \,\&\, (Z \geqslant 0 \leftrightarrow Y * X \geqslant 0)))$
(D.mod)	$X \bmod Y = X - (X/Y) * Y$
(D.−1)	$-1 = \mathrm{pred}(0)$
(D.1)	$1 = \mathrm{succ}(0)$
(D.−2)	$-2 = \mathrm{pred}(-1)$
(D.2)	$2 = \mathrm{succ}(1)$
:	:

FIGURE 0.2. The axioms of arithmetic.

and that o_n is a *defined symbol* if the following conditions are satisfied:

(1) The X_i ($1 \leqslant i \leqslant n$) are distinct quantified variables,

(2) The X_i are the only quantified or integer variables occurring in $e(X_1, \ldots, X_n)$, and

(3) The only nonlogical symbols occurring in $e(X_1, \ldots, X_n)$ are either primitive symbols or previously defined symbols.

Each of the axioms **(D.≠)**, **(D.⩽)**, **(D.>)**, and **(D.<)**, which define the predicate symbols other than '=', is called an "explicit definition." This is true because the symbol being defined is the only predicate or operation symbol occurring on the left side of the biconditional and only more primitive symbols occur on the right side. Much as Rule **=R** can be used to eliminate occurrences of symbols introduced by equational definitions, Rule **↔E** can be used to eliminate predicate symbols introduced by explicit definitions. Similarly, each of the axioms **(D.−)**, **(D.abs)**, and **(D./)** defining the remaining nonprimitive operation symbols is called an "explicit definition" because the operation symbol being defined and '=' are the only operation and predicate symbols occurring on the left side of the biconditional. Clearly, any equational definition can be mechanically translated into an equivalent explicit definition. In the case of a unary operation symbol o_u, for example, if the equational definition is of the form

$$o_u(X) = e(X)$$

then

$$o_u(X)=Y \leftrightarrow Y=e(X)$$

is an equivalent explicit definition. However, it is known that exponentiation ('**'), for example, has an explicit definition but can have no equational definition.[7]

For those operations that cannot (or cannot conveniently) be equationally defined, an explicit definition of the corresponding operation symbol must be shown to be "proper" in the sense that it must be possible to prove (in the theory prior to introducing the explicit definition) theorems expressing appropriate existence and uniqueness conditions. That is, the result of performing any operation must be a unique integer. More formally, we say that a biconditional of the form

$$o_n(X_1, \ldots, X_n)=Y \leftrightarrow p(X_1, \ldots, X_n, Y)$$

introducing the new n-ary operation symbol o_n, is an *explicit definition* and that o_n is a *defined symbol* if the following conditions are satisfied:

(1) The X_i $(1 \leq i \leq n)$ and Y are distinct quantified variables.
(2) The biconditional is of the form

$$\forall X_1 \ldots \forall X_n \forall Y(o_n(X_1, \ldots, X_n)=Y \leftrightarrow p(X_1, \ldots, X_n, Y))$$

when the quantifiers in the prefix of the biconditional are written out fully and explicitly.
(3) No integer variable occurs in $p(X_1, \ldots, X_n)$.

[7] See de Bouvere for a proof that exponentiation is not equationally definable.

(4) The only nonlogical symbols occurring in $p(X_1, \ldots, X_n)$ are either primitive symbols or previously defined symbols.

(5) The assertions

$\forall X_1 \ldots \forall X_n \exists Y p(X_1, \ldots, X_n, Y)$ *(the existence condition)* and $\forall X_1 \ldots \forall X_n \forall Y \forall Y'(p(X_1, \ldots, X_n, Y) \& p(X_1, \ldots, X_n, Y') \rightarrow Y=Y')$ *(the uniqueness condition)* are provable from the axioms and preceding definitions.

The conditions on explicit and equational definitions insure that defined symbols are *eliminable* in favor of the primitive symbols and that definitions are *noncreative* in the sense that, after the definition is introduced, no previously unprovable assertion containing only logical and primitive symbols becomes provable.[8]

For example, to establish condition (5) in the case of **(D.−)**, we must establish that, for any X and Y, $Z=X-Y$ exists and is unique. That is, the existence condition is

$$\exists Z(Z+Y=X)$$

and the uniqueness condition is

$$Z+Y=X \;\&\; Z'+Y=X \rightarrow Z=Z'$$

The proofs are straightforward, and we leave them as exercises.

The conditions on explicit and operational definitions enable us to regard definitions as "abbreviations" although, strictly speaking, definitions are axioms. That is, definitions provide convenience, while at the same time do not alter the basic mathematical content of the original theory. Regarding eliminability, for example, we can replace the assertion

$$x \neq 0 \rightarrow x*y>0$$

(which is not a theorem) containing the defined symbols $\neq$ and $>$ with the equivalent assertion

$$\sim(x=0) \rightarrow \sim(0 \geqslant x*y)$$

containing only primitive symbols because, using **(D.≠)**, **(D.>)**, and **(D.≤)**,

[8] The importance of explicit definitions can be underlined using a slightly different terminology. A *theory* is a set of assertions. A theory $T+$ is said to be an *extension* of a theory T if every theorem of T is a theorem of $T+$. An extension $T+$ of T is *conservative* if no unprovable assertion of T is a theorem of $T+$. The conditions on explicit (and equational) definitions insure that, when a theory $T+$ is obtained from a theory T by adding explicit definitions, the theory $T+$ (called an *extension by explicit definitions*) is a conservation extension of T.

we can show

$$\vdash (x \neq 0 \rightarrow x * y > 0) \leftrightarrow \sim(x=0) \rightarrow \sim(0 \geqslant x * y)$$

The following example illustrates how the stricture against creative definitions could be violated if condition (5) was dropped. If condition (5) was not imposed on explicit definitions in the case of operation symbols, an explicit definition could introduce inconsistency into arithmetic. Consider the pseudodefinition

(D.?) $\quad ?X = Y \leftrightarrow X \neq Y$

purporting to introduce the unary operation symbol '?'. Because $0 \neq 1$ and $0 \neq 2$ are provable, we can prove $?0 = 1$ and $?0 = 2$, and hence, by Rule =**R**, that $1=2$. And, because $\sim 1=2$ is also provable, we have a contradiction. If allowed, the definition of the operation symbol '?' would be creative indeed.

The conditions imposed on *explicit definitions* in the case of *n*-ary predicate symbols are much the same as those imposed on explicit definitions of *n*-ary operation symbols, except that there is no need for a condition analogous to (5).

A few other features of the axiomatization should be noted. First, we have formulated **(D./)** and **(D.mod)** so that the division and remainder operations are totally defined while preserving the law

$$X = (X/Y) * Y + (X \bmod Y)$$ [9]

Second, we have made the exponentiation symbol '**' primitive because, not only is no equational definition possible, but no simple, intuitive definition is known.

In subsequent sections and chapters, we will introduce other new operation and predicate symbols. We will provide an explicit definition (or equational definition in the case of an operation symbol) whenever feasible. Some of the axioms used to introduce new symbols will not be in the form of explicit definitions. Many of these symbols are, in principal, explicitly definable, but we do not know simple explicit definitions. In the case of the Ackermann function ('ack'), for example, we will introduce axioms that are not in the form of an explicit definition. Nevertheless, when we do introduce the operation symbol 'ack' in Section 0.6, we will provide an informal justification that existence and uniqueness conditions are satisfied.[10]

[9] Until we reach Chapter 5, we shall understand all of our operations to be totally defined.

[10] We will introduce some symbols in subsequent chapters, such as the unary operation symbols *'in'* and *'out'* (which are associated with sequential files) of Chapter 3, without any accompanying axioms. Symbols such as *'in'* and *'out'* should be thought of, in the context of the present chapter, as "function parameters," contributing nothing to the mathematical content of the theory of integers. Although such symbols are not eliminable, they are noncreative. Their

We will now present some sample proofs. In our proofs, *we will not explicitly list our axioms as assumptions, and we will annotate a line by writing the axiom's name to indicate that the line was derived by an application of the Reiteration Rule* **(R)** *to that axiom. Similarly, we will permit the use of Rule* **R** *to introduce previously established theorems.*

THEOREM 1: pred(succ(X))=X

Proof

1	pred(X)=X−succ(0)	**(D.pred)**
2	pred(succ(x))=succ(x)−succ(0)	**(∀E,**1)
3	succ(x)−succ(0)=pred(succ(x))	(**=.sym**,2)
4	$X-Y=Z \leftrightarrow Z+Y=X$	**(D.−)**
5	succ(x)−succ(0)=pred(succ(x)) ↔ pred(succ(x))+succ(0)=succ(x)	**(∀E,**4)
6	pred(succ(x))+succ(0)=succ(x)	(**↔E**,3,5)
7	X+succ(Y) = succ($X+Y$)	**(+.succ)**
8	pred(succ(x))+succ(0) = succ(pred(succ(x))+0)	**(∀E,**7)
9	$X+0=X$	**(+.0)**
10	pred(succ(x))+0 = pred(succ(x))	**(∀E,**9)
11	pred(succ(x))+succ(0) = succ(pred(succ(x)))	(**=R**,8,10)
12	succ(pred(succ(x))) = succ(x)	(**=R**,6,11)
13	succ(X)=succ(Y) → $X=Y$	**(succ.=)**
14	succ(pred(succ(x)))=succ(x) → pred(succ(x))=x	**(∀E,**13)
15	pred(succ(x))=x	(**→E**,12,14)
16	pred(succ(X))=X	**(∀I,**15)

□

---

introduction will make provable no previously unprovable assertion in which the primitive symbols of arithmetic are the only nonlogical symbols. The theory of integers in Chapter 3 is a conservative extension of the theory of integers presented in this chapter, and so the introduction of the symbols *'in'* and *'out'* cannot introduce inconsistency. These later claims can be justified by the Robinson Joint Consistency Theorem or, equivalently, the Craig Interpolation Lemma. See Boolos and Jeffrey, Kleene (1967), or Shoenfield for details concerning the Craig Lemma and the Robinson Theorem.

For more detailed discussions of definitions and the criterion requiring that defined symbols be eliminable, see (arranged in order of increasing difficulty) Suppes, Shoenfield, and de Bouvere. We will discuss the practical difficulty of supplying explicit definitions further in Section 3.6.

THEOREM 2: $\mathrm{succ}(\mathrm{pred}(X))=X$

Proof

1	$X+\mathrm{succ}(Y)=\mathrm{succ}(X+Y)$	**(+.succ)**
2	$\mathrm{pred}(x)+\mathrm{succ}(0)=\mathrm{succ}(\mathrm{pred}(x)+0)$	(**∀E**,1)
3	$X+0=X$	**(+.0)**
4	$\mathrm{pred}(x)+0=\mathrm{pred}(x)$	(**∀E**,3)
5	$\mathrm{pred}(x)+\mathrm{succ}(0)=\mathrm{succ}(\mathrm{pred}(x))$	(**=R**,2,4)
6	$\mathrm{pred}(X)=X-\mathrm{succ}(0)$	**(D.pred)**
7	$\mathrm{pred}(x)=x-\mathrm{succ}(0)$	(**∀E**,6)
8	$x-\mathrm{succ}(0)=\mathrm{pred}(x)$	(**=.sym**,7)
9	$X-Y=Z\leftrightarrow Z+Y=X$	**(D.−)**
10	$x-\mathrm{succ}(0)=\mathrm{pred}(x)\leftrightarrow \mathrm{pred}(x)+\mathrm{succ}(0)=x$	(**∀E**,9)
11	$\mathrm{pred}(x)+\mathrm{succ}(0)=x$	(**↔E**,8,10)
12	$\mathrm{succ}(\mathrm{pred}(x))=x$	(**=R**,5,11)
13	$\mathrm{succ}(\mathrm{pred}(X))=X$	(**∀I**,12)

□

THEOREM 3: $0+Y=Y$

Proof: The proof runs by induction on Y. Line 2 constitutes the basis, lines 3 to 11 constitute the induction step on the positive integers, and lines 12 to 23 are the induction step on the negative integers. Line 24 conjoins the basis and induction steps and constitutes the antecedent of line 25, the Induction Axiom. The theorem $0+Y=Y$ (line 26) is then derived from lines 24 and 25.

1	$X+0=X$	**(+.0)**
2	$0+0=0$	(**∀E**,1)
3	$x\geqslant 0$	
4	$0+x=x$	
5	$X+\mathrm{succ}(Y)=\mathrm{succ}(X+Y)$	**(+.succ)**
6	$0+\mathrm{succ}(x)=\mathrm{succ}(0+x)$	(**∀E**,5)
7	$0+x=x$	(**R**,4)
8	$0+\mathrm{succ}(x)=\mathrm{succ}(x)$	(**=R**,6,7)
9	$0+x=x\rightarrow 0+\mathrm{succ}(x)=\mathrm{succ}(x)$	(**→I**,4−8)
10	$x\geqslant 0\rightarrow(0+x=x\rightarrow 0+\mathrm{succ}(x)=\mathrm{succ}(x))$	(**→I**,3−9)
11	$X\geqslant 0\rightarrow(0+X=X\rightarrow 0+\mathrm{succ}(X)=\mathrm{succ}(X))$	(**∀I**,10)
12	$0\geqslant \mathrm{succ}(x)$	
13	$0+\mathrm{succ}(x)=\mathrm{succ}(x)$	
14	$X+\mathrm{succ}(Y)=\mathrm{succ}(X+Y)$	(+.succ)
15	$0+\mathrm{succ}(x)=\mathrm{succ}(0+x)$	(**∀E**,14)
16	$0+\mathrm{succ}(x)=\mathrm{succ}(x)$	(**R**,16)
17	$\mathrm{succ}(0+x)=\mathrm{succ}(x)$	(**=R**,15,16)

18	$\;\;\parallel\parallel$ $\text{succ}(X)=\text{succ}(Y)\to X=Y$	**(succ.=)**
19	$\;\;\parallel\parallel$ $\text{succ}(0+x)=\text{succ}(x)\to 0+x=x$	$(\forall\text{E},18)$
20	$\;\;\parallel\parallel$ $0+x=x$	$(\to\text{E},17,19)$
21	$\;\;\parallel$ $0+\text{succ}(x)=\text{succ}(x)\to 0+x=x$	$(\to\text{I},13-20)$
22	$\;\;\parallel$ $0\geqslant\text{succ}(x)\to(0+\text{succ}(x)=\text{succ}(x)\to 0+x=x)$	$(\to\text{I},12-21)$
23	$\;\;\parallel$ $0\geqslant\text{succ}(X)\to(0+\text{succ}(X)=\text{succ}(X)\to 0+X=X)$	$(\forall\text{I},22)$
24	$0+0=0\;\&\;\forall X(X\geqslant 0\to(0+X=X\to$ $0+\text{succ}(X)=\text{succ}(X)))\;\&\;\forall X(0\geqslant\text{succ}(X)\to$ $(0+\text{succ}(X)=\text{succ}(X)\to 0+X=X)$	$(\&\text{I},2,11,23)$
25	$0+0=0\;\&\;\forall X(X\geqslant 0\to(0+X=X\to$ $0+\text{succ}(X)=\text{succ}(X)))\;\&\;\forall X(0\geqslant\text{succ}(X)\to$ $(0+\text{succ}(X)=\text{succ}(X)\to 0+X=X)\to$ $\forall Y(0+Y=Y)$	**(Ind)**
26	$0+Y=Y$	$(\to\text{E},24,25)$

$\square$

THEOREM 4: $\text{succ}(X)+Y=\text{succ}(X+Y)$

Proof: The proof runs by induction on Y. We outline the proof and leave the details to be filled in by the reader. Note that line 6 constitutes the basis of the inductive proof, and that lines 7 to $j+3$ constitute the induction step on the positive integers. The induction step on the negative integers begins at line $j+4$.

1	$X+0=X$	**(+.0)**
2	$\text{succ}(x)+0=\text{succ}(x)$	$(\forall\text{E},1)$
3	$x+0=x$	$(\forall\text{E},1)$
4	$x=x+0$	$(=\text{.sym},3)$
5	$\text{succ}(x)+0=\text{succ}(x+0)$	$(=\text{R},2,4)$
6	$\text{succ}(X)+0=\text{succ}(X+0)$	$(\forall\text{I},5)$
7	$\;\;\parallel$ $z\geqslant 0$	
8	$\;\;\parallel\parallel$ $\underline{\text{succ}(X)+z=\text{succ}(X+z)}$	

$\cdot\;\;.\;\;.\;\;.\;\;.$

j	$\;\;\parallel\parallel$ $\text{succ}(X)+\text{succ}(z)=\text{succ}(X+\text{succ}(z))$	
$j+1$	$\;\;\parallel$ $\text{succ}(X)+z=\text{succ}(X+z)\to$ $\text{succ}(X)+\text{succ}(z)=\text{succ}(X+\text{succ}(z))$	$(\to\text{I},8-j)$
$j+2$	$z\geqslant 0\to\forall X(\text{succ}(X)+z=\text{succ}(X+z)\to$ $\text{succ}(X)+\text{succ}(z)=\text{succ}(X+\text{succ}(z)))$	$(\to\text{I},7-(j+1))$
$j+3$	$Z\geqslant 0\to\forall X(\text{succ}(X)+Z=\text{succ}(X+Z)\to$ $\text{succ}(X)+\text{succ}(Z)=\text{succ}(X+\text{succ}(Z)))$	$(\forall\text{I},j+2)$
$j+4$	$\;\;\parallel$ $\underline{0\geqslant\text{succ}(z)}$	

$\cdot\;\;.\;\;.$

$\square$

THEOREM 5: $X+Y=Y+X$[11]

Proof: The proof runs by induction on X and uses Theorems 3 and 4. We give the basis and the induction step on the positive integers, leaving the rest as an exercise. Line 7 constitutes the basis of the induction. The induction step on the positive integers runs from line 8 to line 21. The induction step on the negative integers begins on line 22.

1	$0+Y=Y$	**(Theorem 3)**
2	$X+0=X$	**(+.0)**
3	$0+y=y$	**(∀E,**1)
4	$y+0=y$	**(∀E,**2)
5	$y=y+0$	**(=.sym,**4)
6	$0+y=y+0$	**(=R,**3,5)
7	$0+Y=Y+0$	**(∀I,**6)
8	$z\geqslant 0$	
9	$z+Y=Y+z$	
10	$z+y=y+z$	**(∀E,**9)
11	$X+\mathrm{succ}(Y)=\mathrm{succ}(X+Y)$	**(+.succ)**
12	$\mathrm{succ}(X)+Y=\mathrm{succ}(X+Y)$	**(Theorem 4)**
13	$y+\mathrm{succ}(z)=\mathrm{succ}(y+z)$	**(∀E,**11)
14	$\mathrm{succ}(y+z)=y+\mathrm{succ}(z)$	**(=.sym,**13)
15	$\mathrm{succ}(z)+y=\mathrm{succ}(z+y)$	**(∀E,**12)
16	$\mathrm{succ}(z)+y=\mathrm{succ}(y+z)$	**(=R,**10,15)
17	$\mathrm{succ}(z)+y=y+\mathrm{succ}(z)$	**(=R,**14,16)
18	$\mathrm{succ}(z)+Y=Y+\mathrm{succ}(z)$	**(∀I,**17)
19	$z+Y=Y+z\rightarrow \mathrm{succ}(z)+Y=Y+\mathrm{succ}(z)$	**(→I,**9–18)
20	$z\geqslant 0\rightarrow \forall Y(z+Y=Y+z\rightarrow \mathrm{succ}(z)+Y=Y+\mathrm{succ}(z))$	**(→I,**8–19)
21	$Z\geqslant 0\rightarrow \forall Y(Z+Y=Y+Z\rightarrow \mathrm{succ}(Z)+Y=Y+\mathrm{succ}(Z))$	**(∀I,**20)
22	$0\geqslant \mathrm{succ}(z)$	
23	$\mathrm{succ}(z)+Y=Y+\mathrm{succ}(z)$	

. . . . □

Many other important theorems of arithmetic are listed in the exercises. We note that the principle of strong mathematical induction (course of values induction),

$$p(0)\ \&\ \forall X(X>0\rightarrow(\forall Y(0\leqslant Y\& Y<X\rightarrow p(Y))\rightarrow p(X)))$$
$$\&\ \forall X(X<0\rightarrow(\forall Y(X<Y\& Y\leqslant 0\rightarrow p(Y))\rightarrow p(X)))\rightarrow p(Z)$$

[11] It is known that, in Robinson Arithmetic (Peano Arithmetic without the Induction Axiom), Theorem 5 is unprovable, and the same negative result holds for the theory of integers. See Boolos and Jeffrey for a sketch of a proof.

is a theorem (schema) that permits sometimes, shorter proofs of other theorems.

A proof in the sense that we have just defined and illustrated is sometimes called a *formal proof* because it is defined purely in terms of forms (symbols) and is *effective* because each line can be checked mechanically for legitimacy. An informal proof might be thought of as a prose-rendering of a formal proof, minus some symbolism and details. An informal proof is *rigorous* if it can be converted (by a competent person) into a formal proof. Mathematicians and computer scientists frequently use informal, rigorous proofs, and we will sometimes follow this practice in this text. Informal proofs are often preferred over formal proofs because the latter tend to be long and tedious, and a person attempting to follow a long, formal proof can easily become lost in the details. However, in informal proofs, essential details may be overlooked. Many errors have arisen in the technical literature for this exact reason. An important area of current research is directed towards developing software tools to partially mechanize the generation of formal proofs, and to extract and display salient structural features of proofs to make them more comprehensible to the reader.

0.4. THE THEORY OF INTEGERS: SEMANTICS

In this section, we present the semantics of the theory of integers in terms of states. On one level, a state is simply a memory configuration. That is, an integer variable may be thought of as a memory location having some integer as its contents. An *unextended state* is a total function (a "contents" function) assigning an integer to each integer variable. The integer m assigned an integer variable x by a state $\mathfrak{s}$ is called the *value* or *denotation of* x in $\mathfrak{s}$, and so we write $\mathfrak{s}[x]=m$. On another level, an *(extended) state* extends an unextended state to encompass the intended (standard) interpretation of arithmetic.[12] Although there are no proofs in this section, the reader should study it carefully to become conversant in the notational conventions governing our semantic descriptions.

In describing our semantics, we write $\mathfrak{t}$ for the truth-value true and $\mathfrak{f}$ for the truth-value false. We have two *domains:* the set of integers $\mathfrak{Z}$ and the set of truth-values $\mathfrak{Tv}=\{\mathfrak{t},\mathfrak{f}\}$.[13] The semantic equations in Figure 0.3 define an (extended) state inductively by assigning an integer to each integer expres-

[12] In the intended or standard interpretation, for any integer variable x, $\mathfrak{s}[x]$ is some integer m. As a consequence of Gödel's results, there can be nonstandard interpretations (models) of first-order arithmetic in which $\mathfrak{s}[x]>m$ for every integer m. We will be concerned only with the standard interpretation. For a discussion of nonstandard interpretations in model theory, see Boolos and Jeffrey.

[13] In logic, it is customary to refer to $\mathfrak{Z}$ as *the* domain of discourse. Our reasons for departing from the traditional terminology will become apparent in Chapter 6 when we describe the denotational semantics of a class of programs with tail recursive procedures.

(1) $\mathfrak{S}[m] = m$
(the integer m)

(2) $\mathfrak{S}[\mathrm{succ}(e)] = \mathrm{succ}(\mathfrak{S}[e])$
(the successor of the integer denoted by e)

(3) $\mathfrak{S}[e+e'] = \mathfrak{S}[e]+\mathfrak{S}[e']$
(the sum of the integers denoted by e and e')

(4) $\mathfrak{S}[e*e'] = \mathfrak{S}[e]*\mathfrak{S}[e']$
(the product of the integers denoted by e and e')

(5) $\mathfrak{S}[e**e'] = \mathfrak{S}[e]**\mathfrak{S}[e']$
(the integer denoted by e raised to the power of the integer denoted by e')

(6) $\mathfrak{S}[e=e'] = \mathfrak{S}[e]=\mathfrak{S}[e']$
(the truth-value $\mathfrak{t}$ if e and e' denote the same integer, and the truth-value $\mathfrak{f}$ otherwise)

(7) $\mathfrak{S}[e\geqslant e'] = \mathfrak{S}[e]\geqslant\mathfrak{S}[e']$
(the truth-value $\mathfrak{t}$ if the integer denoted by e is greater-than-or-equal to the integer denoted by e', and the truth-value $\mathfrak{f}$ otherwise)

(8) $\mathfrak{S}[\sim p] = \sim\mathfrak{S}[p]$
(the truth-value $\mathfrak{t}$ if the truth-value denoted by p is $\mathfrak{f}$, and the truth-value $\mathfrak{f}$ otherwise)

(9) $\mathfrak{S}[p\&p'] = \mathfrak{S}[p]\ \&\ \mathfrak{S}[p']$
(the truth-value $\mathfrak{t}$ if the truth-value denoted by p is $\mathfrak{t}$ and the truth-value denoted by p' is $\mathfrak{t}$, and the truth-value $\mathfrak{f}$ otherwise)

(10) $\mathfrak{S}[p\vee p'] = \mathfrak{S}[p] \vee \mathfrak{S}[p']$
(the truth-value $\mathfrak{t}$ if the truth-value denoted by p is $\mathfrak{t}$ or the truth-value denoted by p' is $\mathfrak{t}$, and the truth-value $\mathfrak{f}$ otherwise)

(11) $\mathfrak{S}[p\rightarrow p'] = \mathfrak{S}[p] \rightarrow \mathfrak{S}[p']$
(the truth-value $\mathfrak{t}$ if the truth-value denoted by p is $\mathfrak{f}$ or the truth-value denoted by p' is $\mathfrak{t}$, and the truth-value $\mathfrak{f}$ otherwise)

(12) $\mathfrak{S}[p\leftrightarrow p'] = \mathfrak{S}[p] \leftrightarrow \mathfrak{S}[p']$
(the truth-value $\mathfrak{t}$ if p and p' denote the same truth-value, and the truth-value $\mathfrak{f}$ otherwise)

(13) $\mathfrak{S}[\forall Xp] =$ For each numeral m, $\mathfrak{S}[p[m\backslash X]]$
(the truth-value $\mathfrak{t}$ if $p[m\backslash X]$ denotes $\mathfrak{t}$ for each numeral m, and $\mathfrak{f}$ otherwise)

(14) $\mathfrak{S}[\exists Xp] =$ For some numeral m, $\mathfrak{S}[p[m\backslash X]]$
(the truth-value $\mathfrak{t}$ if $p[m\backslash X]$ denotes $\mathfrak{t}$ for some numeral m, and $\mathfrak{f}$ otherwise)

FIGURE 0.3. The semantics of integer expressions and assertions.

sion and a truth-value to each assertion. On the left side of each equation, we have the linguistic entity being assigned a denotation by the state $\mathcal{S}$, and on the right side, we have the denotation assigned. The '=' sign (in the middle of the equation) should be read as "denotes." Underneath each equation, in parentheses, is a reading for the denotation. For example, the first equation might be read: "In state $\mathcal{S}$, the numeral m denotes the integer m." To keep our semantic description from becoming too lengthy, we have not provided semantic equations for the nonprimitive symbols of arithmetic (except for the numerals other than 0). A semantic equation for each nonprimitive symbol can be constructed readily using its equational or explicit definition and the semantic equations (1) through (14).

Following a common practice in mathematics, we understand the integer 0 to be the denotation of $\mathcal{S}[e/0]$ (the denotation of the integer expression '$e/0$') and the integer $\mathcal{S}[e]$ to be the denotation of $\mathcal{S}[e \bmod 0]$. For the present semantics to work, $\mathcal{S}$ must be extended in a manner so that it never becomes undefined for some syntactic element in its domain.[14]

As an example, we show that, for any state $\mathcal{S}$, $\mathcal{S}[\forall X(X+1=1+X)]$ evaluates to t. We have

$\mathcal{S}[\forall X(X+1=1+X)]$ = for each numeral m, $\mathcal{S}[m+1=1+m]$	Clause (13)
= for each numeral m, $\mathcal{S}[m+1]=\mathcal{S}[1+m]$	Clause (6)
= for each numeral m, $\mathcal{S}[m]+\mathcal{S}[1] = \mathcal{S}[1]+\mathcal{S}[m]$	Clause (3)
= for each integer m, $m+1 = 1+m$	Clause (1)
= t	by the laws of arithmetic

Our semantic equations for universal and existential quantifications (equations (13) and (14)) are given in the style known as the "substitution" interpretation of the quantifiers. Frequently, these two equations are stated in a somewhat different (model theoretic) style. Before displaying the alternatives to the semantic equations (13) and (14), some additional notational conventions must be introduced. Let m be a numeral, e and e' be integer expressions, p and p' be assertions, X be a quantified variable, x be an integer variable, and $\mathcal{S}$ be a state. We say that a state $\mathcal{S}'$ is an *x-variant* of $\mathcal{S}$ provided that, for every integer variable y distinct from x (i.e., not $y \equiv x$), $\mathcal{S}'[y]=\mathcal{S}[y]$. Notice that any state is an x-variant of itself. The state $\mathcal{S}\{m\backslash x\} = \mathcal{S}-\{\langle x,\mathcal{S}[x]\rangle\}\cup\{\langle x,m\rangle\}$ is the x-variant of $\mathcal{S}$ such that $\mathcal{S}\{m\backslash x\}[x]=m$. For example, if $\mathcal{S}'=\mathcal{S}\{0\backslash x\}$, then $\mathcal{S}'[x]=0$ and, for every integer variable y distinct from x, $\mathcal{S}'[y]=\mathcal{S}[y]$. That is, if $\mathcal{S}=\{\langle x,1\rangle,\langle y,1\rangle, \ldots\}$, then $\mathcal{S}' = \{\langle x,0\rangle,\langle y,1\rangle, \ldots\}$. More generally, for distinct integer variables $x_1, \ldots, x_n$, a state $\mathcal{S}'$ is an x_1- . . . -x_n-variant of $\mathcal{S}$ ($n \geq 1$) provided that,

[14] This is because we are following the customary practice in computer science of using standard first-order logic in our semantics. In a semantics for first-order logic, all integer expressions must be regarded as denoting some member of the underlying domain. In Chapter 5, we will replace standard first-order logic with "free" first-order logic, and we will then no longer need to make the rather artificial assumption that $\mathcal{S}[e/0]$ is an integer.

for every integer variable y distinct from each of the x_i $(1 \leq i \leq n)$, $\mathfrak{s}'[y] = \mathfrak{s}[y]$. The state $\mathfrak{s}\{m_1, \ldots, m_n \backslash x_1, \ldots, x_n\}$ is the x_1- . . . -x_n-variant of $\mathfrak{s}$ such that $\mathfrak{s}\{m_1, \ldots, m_n \backslash x_1, \ldots, x_n\}[x_i] = m_i$ for every i from 1 to n.

The (model theoretic) alternatives to (13) and (14) are as follows:

(13′) $\mathfrak{s}[\forall Xp] =$ For each integer m, $\mathfrak{s}\{m \backslash x\}[p[x \backslash X]]$, where x is the alphabetically first integer variable foreign to $\forall Xp$. (The truth-value t if $p[x \backslash X]$ denotes t on every x-variant of $\mathfrak{s}$, and f otherwise.)

(14′) $\mathfrak{s}[\exists Xp] =$ For some integer m, $\mathfrak{s}\{m \backslash x\}[p[x \backslash X]]$, where x is the alphabetically first integer variable foreign to $\exists Xp$. (The truth-value t if $p[x \backslash X]$ denotes t on some x-variant of $\mathfrak{s}$, and f otherwise.)

The semantic equations (13) and (13′) ((14) and (14′)) are equivalent (at least in the present context) in the sense that, for any assertion p and any state $\mathfrak{s}$, $\mathfrak{s}[p]$ has the same truth-value whether evaluated by the equations (1) to (14) or by the equations (1) to (12), (13′), and (14′). We prefer the pair of semantic equations (13) and (14) over the pair (13′) and (14′) because of the naturalness and simplicity of the former.

Now we turn to important semantic definitions. A set of assertions A is *satisfiable* if there is some state $\mathfrak{s}$ such that $\mathfrak{s}[p]=$t for every assertion $p \in A$. A set of assertions A is *unsatisfiable* if it is not satisfiable. A set of assertions A *entails* an assertion p provided that, for every state $\mathfrak{s}$, if $\mathfrak{s}[q]=$t for every $q \in A$, then $\mathfrak{s}[p]=$t. As an immediate consequence of the definitions, we have the following:

PROPOSITION ON ENTAILMENT: A entails p iff $A \cup \{\sim p\}$ is unsatisfiable.

Proof: A entails p iff (if and only if) for any state $\mathfrak{s}$, if $\mathfrak{s}[q]=$t for every $q \in A$, then $\mathfrak{s}[p]=$t iff for any state $\mathfrak{s}$, if $\mathfrak{s}[q]=$t for every $q \in A$, then $\mathfrak{s}[\sim p]=$f iff there is no state $\mathfrak{s}$ such that $\mathfrak{s}[q]=$t for every $q \in A \cup \{\sim p\}$ iff $A \cup \{\sim p\}$ is unsatisfiable. □

If A entails p, we also say that p is a *consequence* of A and write $A \models p$. When A is a finite set of assertions $\{p_1, \ldots, p_n\}$, we omit the set brackets and write $p_1, \ldots, p_n \models p$. An assertion p is *valid*, written $\models p$, provided $\{\} \models p$. It follows from these definitions that p is valid iff $\mathfrak{s}[p]=$t for every state $\mathfrak{s}$.

The correctness of a deductive system is determined by the intended semantics. A deductive system is said to be *strongly sound* provided that, for every assertion p and every set of assertions A, $A \models p$ if $A \vdash p$. A deductive system is *weakly sound* provided that, for every assertion p, $\models p$ if $\vdash p$. Similarly, a deductive system is *strongly complete* provided that, for every assertion p and every set of assertions A, $A \vdash p$ if $A \models p$. Finally, it is *weakly complete* provided that, for every assertion p, $\vdash p$ if $\models p$. Soundness and completeness theorems (whether of the strong or weak variety) are referred to as *bridge results.*

There are two classic results bridging the deductive system presented in the last section and our semantics. The first, due to Gödel, states that there is an assertion p such that $\models p$ but not $\vdash p$. For this reason, (our deductive system for) arithmetic is *incomplete* (even in the weak sense). The second result, due largely to Gentzen, states that $A \models P$ if $A \vdash P$. For this reason, arithmetic is strongly sound. (An overview of the proof of the Soundness of Arithmetic Theorem will be given in Section 0.6.) As we mentioned in the Preface, a deductive system must be sound for it to be of any value. Completeness is also desirable but not obtainable. In the original proof of incompleteness, Gödel exhibited a valid but unprovable sentence that read, roughly, "I am not a theorem." The Gödel sentence is of little mathematical interest aside from its role in demonstrating incompleteness. However, in recent years, valid but unprovable sentences have been discovered that do have an intrinsic mathematical content.[15]

The significance of Gödel's result may be better appreciated in terms of what is sometimes called "semantic completeness" (the terminology varies considerably in the literature). The theory of integers is *semantically complete* in the sense that, for every integer variable free assertion p, we have either $\models p$ or $\models \sim p$.[16] Suppose we find, in attempting to prove a program correct, that our proof hinges on our being able to prove an integer variable free assertion p, but that we are unable to do so. If we could prove $\sim p$, we would know that our program (or our proof) would need considerable alteration, but we cannot show that either. Now, either p is valid or $\sim p$ is, but, by Gödel's result, there is no mechanical test to give us the correct answer. It may be the case that we are not clever enough in our attempted proofs, or there may be no proof of p and no proof of $\sim p$ either. Fortunately, such

[15] The following simple example shows that arithmetic is not strongly complete. Consider the set of assertions

$$A = \{x > m: m \text{ is a numeral}\}.$$

First, note that A is unsatisfiable, because, if it were satisfiable, then some state $\mathfrak{s}$ would assign x "the largest integer." However, there is no largest integer, and so there can be no state $\mathfrak{s}$ such that $\mathfrak{s}[p] = \mathrm{t}$ for every $p \in A$. Hence, $A \models \sim x = x$. Second, note that $A \cup \{\sim\sim x = x\}$ is consistent by the strong soundness of arithmetic because proofs are finite in length (and so can use only a finite set of assumptions) and every finite subset of A is satisfiable. Hence, not $A \vdash \sim x = x$. Because $A \models \sim x = x$ but not $A \vdash \sim x = x$, arithmetic is not strongly complete.

[16] Second-order arithmetic has predicate variables and permits quantifying over sets, as in $\forall p(q(p))$ ("for every set of integers p, $q(p)$") and $\exists p(q(p))$ ("there is some set of integers p such that $q(p)$"). In model theoretic terminology, the second-order integer variable free theory of integers obtained by prefixing $\forall p$ to the axiom schema of induction, therefore converting it into an axiom, is *categorical* in the sense that, up to isomorphism, it has only one model. The semantic completeness of second-order arithmetic follows from its being categorical. For more details, see Boolos and Jeffrey.

situations seem to be rare, but where they will occur is somewhat unpredictable. After three centuries, for example, we still do not know whether Fermat's last theorem is valid or whether its negation is! (Recall that Fermat's last theorem states that there are no positive integers m, m', and m'', and no integer n greater than 2 such that $m{**}n + m'{**}n = m''{**}n$.)

0.5. PROPERTIES OF RELATIONS

A *(binary) relational system* is an ordered pair $\mathfrak{A} = \langle A,R \rangle$, where A is a nonempty set and R is a (binary) relation on A. A relational system is said to have a property P when a set of assertions expressing property P hold in the relational system. For example, $R(X,X)$ expresses the property of reflexivity. If $\mathfrak{A}=\langle A,R \rangle$, where $A=\{a,b\}$ and $R=\{\langle a,a \rangle,\langle a,b \rangle,\langle b,b \rangle\}$, then $\mathfrak{A}$ is a reflexive relational system and R is said to be a reflexive relation (on A). The following list supplies some of the important properties of relations and the sets of assertions that express them:

Property	**Expressed By**
Reflexivity	$R(X,X)$
Symmetry	$R(X,Y) \rightarrow R(Y,X)$
Transitivity	$R(X,Y) \& R(Y,Z) \rightarrow R(X,Z)$
Irreflexivity	$\sim R(X,X)$
Antisymmetry	$R(X,Y) \& R(Y,X) \rightarrow X=Y$
Asymmetry	$R(X,Y) \rightarrow \sim R(Y,X)$
Dichotomy	$R(X,Y) \vee R(Y,X)$
Trichotomy	exactly one of the following holds: $X=Y$, $R(X,Y)$, or $R(Y,X)$. That is, $(\sim R(X,Y) \& \sim R(Y,X) \leftrightarrow X=Y) \;\&$ $(\sim R(X,Y) \vee \sim R(Y,X))$
Equivalence	Reflexivity, Symmetry, and Transitivity
Partial Order	Reflexivity, Antisymmetry, and Transitivity
Strict Partial Order	Asymmetry and Transitivity

When R is a strict partial ordering, we write $x \prec y$ as a stronger graphic representation of $R(x,y)$. We then define the relations $\preccurlyeq$, $\succ$, and $\succcurlyeq$ in terms of $\prec$ (and identity):

$$X \preccurlyeq Y \leftrightarrow X \prec Y \vee X=Y$$

$$X \succ Y \leftrightarrow Y \prec X$$

$$X \succcurlyeq Y \leftrightarrow Y \preccurlyeq X$$

So we have, continuing our list of properties of relations and the sentences that express them:

Weak Total Order	Partial Order and Dichotomy
Total Order	Strict Partial Order and Trichotomy
Finite Descending Chains	There is no infinite sequence $\langle x_0,x_1,x_2, \ldots \rangle$ such that $x_0 \succ x_1 \succ x_2 \ldots$
Least Element	Every nonempty subset of A has a least element, that is, $\forall A' \subset A(A' \neq \{\} \rightarrow \exists X \in A', \forall Y \in A'(X \preccurlyeq Y))$
Well-Founded Order	Strict Partial Order and Finite Descending Chains
Well-Order[17]	Total Order and Least Element

We give some examples of well-orderings and well-founded orderings. The relation $<$ on the integers is a total order and, restricted to the natural numbers, it is a well-ordering. The integers are not well-ordered by $<$ because they have no first element. The rational numbers greater than 0 are not well-ordered by the usual less-than relation for the same reason—consider the infinite sequence $\langle 1,½,¼, \ldots \rangle$. Another example of a well-ordering is the *lexicographic ordering* $\prec$ on the set of ordered n-tuples ($n \geqslant 1$) of natural numbers defined by $\langle m_0,m_1, \ldots m_n\rangle \prec \langle m'_0,m'_1, \ldots ,m'_n\rangle$ if there is some k such that $0 \leqslant k \leqslant n$ and $m_k < m'_k$, and, for every i such that $0 \leqslant i < k$, $m_i = m'_i$. For example, in the case of ordered pairs of natural numbers, we have $\langle 0,0\rangle \prec \langle 0,1\rangle \prec \langle 1,0\rangle$.

Let $\prec_i$ be a well-ordering of the set A_i ($1 \leqslant i \leqslant n$), and let $x_i, y_i \in A_i$. An example of a well-founded ordering that is usually not a well-ordering is the ordering $\prec\!\cdot$, where the *direct product ordering* $\preccurlyeq\!\cdot$ is defined on the Cartesian product $A_1 \times \ldots \times A_n = \{\langle x_1, \ldots ,x_n\rangle : x_i \in A_i \ \& \ 1 \leqslant i \leqslant n\}$ as follows: $\langle x_1, \ldots ,x_n\rangle \preccurlyeq\!\cdot \langle y_1, \ldots ,y_n\rangle$ iff $x_1 \preccurlyeq_1 y_1 \& \ldots \& x_n \preccurlyeq_n y_n$. We say that the orderings $\preccurlyeq_i$ *induce* the ordering $\preccurlyeq\!\cdot$. For example, in the case of ordered pairs of natural numbers, we have $\langle 0,0\rangle \preccurlyeq\!\cdot \langle 0,1\rangle$ and $\langle 0,0\rangle \preccurlyeq\!\cdot \langle 1,0\rangle$ but neither $\langle 0,1\rangle \preccurlyeq\!\cdot \langle 1,0\rangle$ nor $\langle 1,0\rangle \preccurlyeq\!\cdot \langle 0,1\rangle$. Another example of a well-founded ordering that is not a well-ordering is the *complexity ordering* $\prec$ on the set of integer expressions defined by $e \prec e'$ if e is a constituent of e'. That is, understanding o_u to be a unary operation symbol and o_b to be a binary operation symbol, we have $e \prec e'$ if (1) $e' \equiv o_u(e)$, or (2) $e' \equiv e o_b e''$, or (3) $e' \equiv e'' o_b e$, or (4) there is some e'' such that $e \prec e''$ and $e'' \prec e'$. A complexity ordering is defined on the set of assertions in an entirely similar manner. (That is, understanding $\subset$ to be a binary assertion connective and Q to be either $\forall$ or $\exists$, we take $p \prec p'$ if (1) $p' \equiv {\sim} p$, or (2) $p' \equiv QXp[X \backslash e]$, or (3) $p' \equiv p \subset p''$, or (4) $p' \equiv p'' \subset p$, or (5) there is some p'' such that $p \prec p''$ and

[17] The last four properties are not expressible in first-order logic. They are higher-order properties of relations. For more on higher-order properties of relations, see Shapiro and Gurevitch.

$p'' \prec p'$.) We say that e is *simpler* than e' if $e \prec e'$. The complexity ordering is not a well-ordering because, for example, the set of integer expressions $\{2,x,2+x\}$ has no first element; both 2 and x are simple and, therefore, neither one is simpler than the other. Well-founded orderings are most important as they are the underlying structures for *Nötherian Induction,* our fundamental principle of induction that we introduce in the next section.

There are many interrelationships between the properties we have just listed. To illustrate how we will present informal but rigorous proofs when working outside of the theory of integers, we state and prove a few of these interrelationships.

EXAMPLE 8: Every asymmetric relation is irreflexive.

Proof: Suppose R is an asymmetric relation. Suppose further that there is some element a such that $R(a,a)$. Because R is asymmetric, we have $R(a,a) \rightarrow \sim R(a,a)$. Hence, $\sim R(a,a)$. This contradicts the assumption that $R(a,a)$. Hence, $\sim R(a,a)$. As a was arbitrarily chosen, we have $\forall X \sim R(X,X)$. Hence, R is irreflexive. □

EXAMPLE 9: The binary relation ' is an x-variant of ' holding between pairs of states is an equivalence relation.

Proof: It is easily shown that the relation is reflexive, symmetric, and transitive. □

EXAMPLE 10: $\prec$ is a well-ordering iff $\prec$ is a well-founded ordering satisfying the trichotomy law.

Proof: *(if)* Suppose $\prec$ is a well-ordering. It suffices to show that $\prec$ has only finitely descending chains. Suppose the contrary: that is, there is an infinite sequence $\langle x_0,x_1, \ldots \rangle$ such that $x_0 \succ x_1 \succ \ldots$. The set of elements in the sequence is a nonempty subset having no least element, contradicting the supposition that $\prec$ is a well-ordering. Hence, if $\prec$ is a well-ordering, then $\prec$ is a well-founded ordering.

(only if) Suppose $\prec$ is a well-founded ordering satisfying the trichotomy law. It suffices to show that every nonvoid subset has a least element. Suppose the contrary: there is a nonempty subset A' having no least element. Because the trichotomy law holds, A' is totally ordered and certain of the elements x_i of A' can be selected and arranged in an infinite sequence $\langle x_0,x_1, \ldots \rangle$ such that $x_0 \succ x_1 \succ \ldots$, as follows. Pick any member of A' and let that be x_0. Because A' is totally-ordered and has no least element, there is some member y of A' such that $x_0 \succ y$. This is true because, if there were no such y, then x_0 would be the least element, contradicting the assumption that A' has no least element. Choose as x_1 any element y such that $x_0 \succ y$. Reasoning in an entirely similar manner, for each $i \geqslant 0$, we select as

our x_{i+1} an element of A' such that $x_i > x_{i+1}$. So we have constructed an infinite sequence $\langle x_0, x_1, \ldots \rangle$ such that $x_0 > x_1 \ldots$. So $<$ is not well-founded, contradicting the assumption stated previously. Hence, if $<$ is a well-founded ordering satisfying the trichotomy law, then $<$ is a well-ordering. □

0.6. NÖTHERIAN INDUCTION

The principle of mathematical induction on the integers is expressed by the first axiom **(Ind)** in our axiomatization of arithmetic in Section 0.3. Restricting attention to the domain of natural numbers, the principle of mathematical induction can be represented schematically as follows:

Basis:	$p(0)$
Induction Step:	$p(X-1) \rightarrow p(X) \quad (X \geqslant 1)$
Conclusion:	$\forall Y p(Y)$

The assertion $p(X-1)$, the antecedent of the assertion in the induction step, is called the *induction hypothesis* (the *IH* for short).

Sometimes it is convenient to give informal proofs using the principle of mathematical induction, as illustrated by the following example:

EXAMPLE 11: The 4-ary function h4 is "inductively defined" as follows:

$$\begin{aligned} \mathrm{h4}(a,x,y,s) &= s \text{ if } a>y+1 \\ &= \mathrm{h4}(2,x,y,1) \text{ if } a=1\leqslant y+1 \\ &= \mathrm{h4}(a+1,x,y,s*x) \text{ if } a\neq 1 \text{ and } a\leqslant y+1 \end{aligned}$$

Although the operation symbol 'h4' should be introduced into arithmetic with the explicit definition,

$$\textbf{(D.h4)} \qquad \begin{aligned} &\mathrm{h4}(A,X,Y,S) = Z \leftrightarrow \\ &\qquad (A>Y+1 \rightarrow Z=S)\ \& \\ &\qquad (A\leqslant Y+1 \rightarrow \\ &\qquad\qquad (Y\geqslant 0\ \&\ A\leqslant 1 \rightarrow Z=X**Y)\ \& \\ &\qquad\qquad ((Y\geqslant 0\ \&\ A>1) \lor Y<0 \rightarrow \\ &\qquad\qquad\quad Z=S*(X**(Y+2-A)))) \end{aligned}$$

we shall assume (to illuminate an example in Chapter 6) that the simple explicit definition **(D.h4)** has not been discovered and that we are forced to use the "inductive definition." It can be shown that h4 as introduced in the "inductive definition" is uniquely defined for all a, x, y, and s, and is, in fact, equal to the explicitly defined h4. We shall demonstrate a more restricted proposition. Let

$$g3(x,y,s) = h4(1,x,y,s)$$

We show here that

$$\begin{aligned} g3(x,y,s) &= s \text{ if } y<0 \\ &= x{**}y \text{ if } y\geqslant 0 \end{aligned}$$

That is, the 3-ary operation symbol 'g3' should be introduced into arithmetic with the following explicit definition:

(D.g3) $g3(X,Y,S) = Z \leftrightarrow (Y<0 \rightarrow Z=S) \ \&\ (Y\geqslant 0 \rightarrow Z=X{**}Y)$

If $y<0$, then, by the definition of g3, we have

$$\begin{aligned} g3(x,y,s) &= h4(1,x,y,s) \\ &= s \quad \text{by the ("inductive") definition of h4 because } 1>y+1 \end{aligned}$$

Next, we show that, for $y\geqslant 0$, $g3(x,y,s) = x{**}y$. Below, we prove

(*) $h4(1,x,y,s) = h4(d+2,x,y,x{**}d)$ $(y\geqslant 0)$ for each d such that $0\leqslant d\leqslant y$.

We have

$$\begin{aligned} g3(x,y,s) &= h4(1,x,y,s) \\ &= h4(y+2,x,y,x{**}y) \quad \text{by (*) taking } d \text{ to be } y \\ &= x{**}y \quad \text{by the definition of h4 because } y+2>y+1 \end{aligned}$$

The proof of (*) proceeds by mathematical induction on d such that $0\leqslant d\leqslant y$.

BASIS: $d=0$
Because $1\leqslant y+1$, by the definition of h4 we have

$$\begin{aligned} h4(1,x,y,s) &= h4(2,x,y,1) \\ &= h4(0+2,x,y,x{**}0) \end{aligned}$$

INDUCTION STEP: $d\geqslant 1$
By the IH, we have

$$\begin{aligned} h4(1,x,y,s) &= h4((d-1)+2,x,y,x{**}(d-1)) \\ &= h4(d+1,x,y,x{**}(d-1)) \end{aligned}$$

$= \text{h4}(d+2,x,y,(x**(d-1))*x)$ by the definition of h4 because $2 \leqslant d+1 \leqslant y+1$
$= \text{h4}(d+2,x,y,x**d)$

The principle of strong mathematical induction on the natural numbers, which is provable in arithmetic, can be expressed formally as

$$p(0) \;\&\; \forall X(\forall Z(0 \leqslant Z < X \rightarrow p(Z)) \rightarrow p(X)) \rightarrow \forall Y(Y \geqslant 0 \rightarrow p(Y))$$

If we restrict attention to the domain of natural numbers and use *relativized quantifiers,* so that $\forall Z<X.p(Z)$ abbreviates $\forall Z(Z<X \rightarrow p(Z))$, the principle of strong mathematical induction can be represented schematically, as follows:

Basis:	$p(0)$	
Induction Step:	$\forall Z<X.p(Z) \rightarrow p(X)$	$(X \geqslant 1)$
Conclusion:	$\forall Y p(Y)$	

The assertion $\forall Z<X.p(Z)$, the antecedent of the assertion in the induction step, is the *induction hypothesis.*

EXAMPLE 12: We present an informal but rigorous proof of the fundamental theorem of arithmetic, which states that every integer $n \geqslant 2$ is equal to a product of one or more prime numbers. Note that we consider n to be a product of prime numbers if n is a prime number. The predicate symbol 'prime' can be introduced into our axiomatization of the integers with the explicit definition

(D.prime) $\quad \text{prime}(X) \leftrightarrow X \geqslant 2 \;\&\; \forall Y(Y \geqslant 2 \;\&\; X \bmod Y = 0 \rightarrow X = Y)$

Fact: For all $n \geqslant 0$, $n+2$ is equal to a product of prime numbers.

Proof: By mathematical induction on n.

BASIS: $n=0$.
We have $0+2=2$, and 2, a prime number, is a product of prime numbers.

INDUCTION STEP: $n \geqslant 1$.
If $n+2$ is a prime number, then $n+2$ is also a product of prime numbers. Suppose $n+2$ is not prime. By the definition of a prime number, there is an integer $m+2 \geqslant 2$ such that $(n+2) \bmod (m+2)=0$. By the laws of arithmetic, it follows that $m+2<n+2$ and that there is also an integer $m'+2 \geqslant 2$ such that $(m+2)*(m'+2)=n+2$ and $m'+2<n+2$. Now, by the IH (induction hypothesis), for each integer k such that $0 \leqslant k<n$, $k+2$ is equal to a product of primes. So, by the IH, $m+2$ is equal to a product of primes and so is $m'+2$. Hence, $n+2=(m+2)*(m'+2)$ is equal to a product of primes. □

In principle, a formal proof of the fundamental theorem of arithmetic could be carried out using the axiomatization of arithmetic in Section 0.3. However, we presume that such a formal proof would be long and tedious. Consequently, even in arithmetic we are often content to present our proofs in the informal style just illustrated.

Notice that the set of natural numbers ordered by the usual $<$ relation is a well-founded ordering. The principle of mathematical induction is, in fact, a special case of *Nötherian Induction.*[18] In Nötherian induction, we have a well-founded set A under an ordering $\prec$. We understand a member x of A to be a *minimal element* if $\forall X \in A. \sim X \prec x$ and to be *nonminimal* otherwise. If the well-founded ordering is a well-ordering, there will be exactly one minimal element, *the least element* of A. For simplicity, we take it that the quantifiers range over the domain A. Then, the principle of Nötherian Induction is $\forall X(\forall Z \prec X.p(Z) \rightarrow p(X)) \rightarrow \forall Y p(Y)$. Frequently, it is convenient to have a basis in which $p(X)$ is proved for every minimal element X, and then to proceed with the induction step. Schematizing Nötherian Induction in a form similar to the one we used to express the principle of strong mathematical induction, we have

Basis:	$p(X)$ for each minimal element X	
Induction Step:	$\forall Z \prec X.p(Z) \rightarrow p(X)$	(X nonminimal)
Conclusion:	$\forall Y p(Y)$	

EXAMPLE 13: Ackermann's function ack is "inductively defined" on ordered pairs of natural numbers as follows:

$$\text{ack}(0,n) = n+1$$

$$\text{ack}(m+1,0) = \text{ack}(m,1)$$

$$\text{ack}(m+1,n+1) = \text{ack}(m,\text{ack}(m+1,n))$$

We will first illustrate Nötherian Induction by proving that ack(m,n) is uniquely defined on the set of ordered pairs of natural numbers. We understand the set of pairs of natural numbers to be ordered by $\prec$ as in the lexicographical ordering, except that we take each pair of the form $\langle 0,n \rangle$ to be a minimal element. Because of the ordering, this form of Nötherian induction is sometimes called generalized induction or, more specifically, lexicographic induction.

Fact: For every pair of natural numbers $\langle m,n \rangle$, ack(m,n) is uniquely defined.

[18] The principle of Nötherian Induction was discovered by the great German mathematician Emmy Nöther. The principle is known to many as *The Strongest Induction Principle Known to Man.*

Proof: By Nötherian Induction on $\langle m,n \rangle$.

BASIS: $\langle m,n \rangle = \langle 0,n \rangle$
By the "inductive definition" of ack, we have ack$(0,n)=n+1$. Hence, ack$(0,n)$ is uniquely defined because it is equal to the unique natural number $n+1$.

INDUCTION STEP: $\langle m,n \rangle \succ \langle 0,n \rangle$
Note that the IH states that ack(m',n') is uniquely defined for every pair of natural numbers $\langle m',n' \rangle$ such that $\langle m',n' \rangle \prec \langle m,n \rangle$.

Case 1: $m \geq 1$ & $n=0$
We have ack$(m,0)$ = ack$(m-1,1)$, which is uniquely defined by the IH because $\langle m-1,1 \rangle \prec \langle m,0 \rangle$. (Note that $m-1 \geq 0$ because $\langle m,n \rangle \succ \langle 0,n \rangle$ and $n=0$, and so $\langle m-1,1 \rangle$ is sure to be an ordered pair of natural numbers.)

Case 2: $m \geq 1$ & $n \geq 1$
We have ack(m,n) = ack$(m-1$,ack$(m,n-1))$. By the IH, ack$(m,n-1)$ is uniquely defined because $\langle m,n-1 \rangle \prec \langle m,n \rangle$ and so, for some natural number n', ack$(m,n-1)=n'$. Applying the IH a second time, we have that ack(m,n) is uniquely defined because $\langle m-1,n' \rangle \prec \langle m,n \rangle$ and ack(m,n)=ack$(m-1,n')$. □

Now we could introduce the operation symbol ack into the theory of integers with the following axioms:

$$
\begin{aligned}
&X<0 \vee Y<0 \rightarrow \text{ack}(X,Y)=0 \\
&Y \geq 0 \rightarrow \text{ack}(0,Y)=Y+1 \\
&X \geq 1 \rightarrow \text{ack}(X,0)=\text{ack}(X-1,1) \\
&X \geq 1 \;\&\; Y \geq 1 \rightarrow \text{ack}(X,Y)=\text{ack}(X-1,\text{ack}(X,Y-1))
\end{aligned}
$$

As mentioned in Section 0.3, no simple explicit definition of ack is known. Note that, for any unary operation symbol o_u introduced into the theory of integers, we can prove $\forall X \exists Y(o_u(X)=Y)$ and $\forall X \forall Y \forall Y'(o_u(X)=Y \& o_u(X)=Y' \rightarrow Y=Y')$. Similar results are provable for any n-ary operation symbol. Hence, we cannot legitimately prove the existence and uniqueness conditions for ack *after* the operation symbol ack has been introduced into arithmetic. As a result, we must be content with the informal proof just given that the existence and uniqueness conditions for ack are satisfied.[19]

[19] The proof is easily extended to the case when ack is applied to a pair of integers $\langle m,n \rangle$ and either m or n is a negative integer. In recursive function theory, Ackermann's function is an example of a recursive function that is not primitive recursive. It follows that ack can be computed by a **while** program (Chapter 1) but not by a **for** program. See footnote 5 in Chapter 1 and Greibach for further details.

Nötherian Induction is also used in the proof of the Coincidence Lemma, which will be used repeatedly in the following chapters. Intuitively, part (a) of the Coincidence Lemma expresses the fact that, in a state $\mathfrak{s}$, the value assigned an integer variable x foreign to an integer expression e are irrelevant to the value assigned to e. Part (b) expresses a similar relevance result for an assertion p. Parts (c) and (d) express the fact that "semantic substitutions" (the left sides of the equations) and syntactic substitutions (the right sides) coincide (i.e., are equivalent in a suitable sense).

COINCIDENCE LEMMA: Let $\mathfrak{s}'=\mathfrak{s}\{\mathfrak{s}[e']\backslash x\}$. Then
(a) If x is foreign to e, then $\mathfrak{s}'[e]=\mathfrak{s}[e]$
(b) If x is foreign to p, then $\mathfrak{s}'[p]=\mathfrak{s}[p]$
(c) $\mathfrak{s}'[e] = \mathfrak{s}[e[e'\backslash x]]$
(d) $\mathfrak{s}'[p] = \mathfrak{s}[p[e'\backslash x]]$

Proof: *(a)* By Nötherian Induction on the complexity of the integer expression e. Suppose $x \notin \mathfrak{ivar}[e]$.

BASIS: e is simple.
Because e is simple, e is either a numeral m or an integer variable y. If $e \equiv m$, then $\mathfrak{s}'[m]=m=\mathfrak{s}[m]$ by the definition of a state. If $e \equiv y$, then y is distinct from x because $x \notin \mathfrak{ivar}[y]$, and so $\mathfrak{s}'[y]=\mathfrak{s}[y]$ by the definition of $\mathfrak{s}'$.

INDUCTION STEP: e is complex.
The proof is by cases depending on the form of e. Let o_u be a unary operation symbol and o_b be a binary operation symbol.

Case: $e \equiv o_u(e')$
By the IH, we have that $\mathfrak{s}'[e']=\mathfrak{s}[e']$ because e' is simpler than e. Hence,

$$\begin{aligned}\mathfrak{s}'[o_u(e')] &= o_u(\mathfrak{s}'[e'])\\ &= o_u(\mathfrak{s}[e']) \quad \text{by the IH}\\ &= \mathfrak{s}[o_u(e')]\end{aligned}$$

Case: $e \equiv e' o_b e''$
Because e' and e'' are simpler than e, we have by the IH that $\mathfrak{s}'[e']=\mathfrak{s}[e']$ and $\mathfrak{s}'[e'']=\mathfrak{s}[e'']$. Hence,

$$\begin{aligned}\mathfrak{s}'[e' o_b e''] &= \mathfrak{s}'[e'] o_b \mathfrak{s}'[e'']\\ &= \mathfrak{s}[e'] o_b \mathfrak{s}[e''] \quad \text{by the IH}\\ &= \mathfrak{s}[e' o_b e'']\end{aligned}$$

(b) The proof is left as an exercise.

(c) The proof is by Nötherian Induction on the complexity of e. We consider

the case in the basis when e is an integer variable y. If y is distinct from x, we have $\mathfrak{s}'[y]=\mathfrak{s}[y[e'\backslash x]]$ by part (a). On the other hand, suppose $y\equiv x$. We have $\mathfrak{s}'[x]=\mathfrak{s}[e']$ by the definition of $\mathfrak{s}'$. Due to the fact that $e'\equiv x[e'\backslash x]$, we have $\mathfrak{s}'[x]=\mathfrak{s}[x[e'\backslash x]]$. The other case in the basis (when $e\equiv m$) and the induction step are left as an exercise.

(d) The proof is by Nötherian Induction on the complexity of p. We consider the case in the induction step when $p\equiv\forall Xq$. We have

$$\begin{aligned}
\mathfrak{s}'[\forall Xq] &= \text{For every numeral } m,\ \mathfrak{s}'[q[m\backslash X]] \\
&= \text{For every numeral } m,\ \mathfrak{s}[q[m\backslash X][e'\backslash x]] \\
&\qquad \text{by the IH} \\
&= \text{For every numeral } m,\ \mathfrak{s}[q[e'\backslash x][m\backslash X]] \\
&= \mathfrak{s}[\forall Xq[e'\backslash x]] \\
&= \mathfrak{s}[(\forall Xq)[e'\backslash x]]
\end{aligned}$$

The basis and the other cases in the induction step are left as an exercise. □

A sketch of the strong soundness of our deductive system for arithmetic developed in Sections 0.2 and 0.3 provides our final example of Nötherian Induction. We will not give a detailed proof of the Soundness of Arithmetic Theorem for two reasons; first, it would lead us too far away from our main concern, the "programming part" of program verification systems, and second, similar proofs can be found in introductory logic texts. Strictly speaking, though, the soundness of the Hoare axiomatization of **while** programs (Chapter 1) hinges on the Soundness of Arithmetic Theorem. We will discuss this in more detail in the next chapter.

SOUNDNESS OF ARITHMETIC THEOREM: Let p be an assertion and A be a set of assertions. If $A\vdash p$, then $A\models p$.

Proof Sketch: We break the proof into two parts. First, each of the rules of our natural deduction system is truth-preserving in the following sense: For any state $\mathfrak{s}$, if an assertion p_n is derived by a rule and each assumption p_i such that line n is in the scope of line i is true, then p_n will also be true. For example, in the case of Rule **&E**, we derive p from $p\&p'$. It is easily shown that, for any state $\mathfrak{s}$, if $\mathfrak{s}(p\&p')=\mathrm{t}$, then $\mathfrak{s}(p)=\mathrm{t}$. (Phrased in terms of higher-order logic, we have $\forall\mathfrak{s}(\mathfrak{s}[p\&p']\rightarrow\mathfrak{s}[p])$.) The soundness of the natural deduction system follows by Nötherian induction on the set of pairs of positive integers $\langle d+1,l\rangle$ under the lexicographic ordering, where d is the depth of a derivation (the number of derivations to which the derivation is subordinate) and l is the length of the derivation.[20] Finally, the axioms of arithmetic are shown

[20] Further details regarding the soundness of our natural deduction system can be retrieved from Leblanc and Wisdom. Their proof runs by a nested (double) mathematical induction, with

easily to be valid with respect to our semantics. Therefore, because the axioms of arithmetic are valid and our natural deduction system is truth-preserving, every theorem is also sure to be valid. More generally, if $A \vdash p$, then $A \models p$. □

EXERCISES

Natural Deduction

1. Using the natural deduction system of Section 0.2, show the following:
   (a) $\vdash p \vee \sim p$
   (b) $\vdash (p \rightarrow \sim p) \rightarrow \sim p$
   (c) $\vdash (p \rightarrow q) \rightarrow (\sim q \rightarrow \sim p)$
   (d) $\vdash \sim p \rightarrow (p \rightarrow q)$
   (e) $\vdash \sim\sim p \leftrightarrow p$
   (f) $\vdash \sim(\sim p \& \sim q) \leftrightarrow p \vee q$
   (g) $\vdash \sim(\sim p \vee \sim q) \leftrightarrow p \& q$
   (h) $\vdash \sim(p \rightarrow q) \leftrightarrow p \& \sim q$
   (i) $\vdash (p \rightarrow q) \& (q \rightarrow p) \leftrightarrow (p \leftrightarrow q)$
   (j) $\vdash \sim(p \leftrightarrow q) \leftrightarrow (p \& \sim q \vee \sim p \& q)$
   (k) $\vdash (p \vee q) \& \sim p \rightarrow q$
   (l) $\vdash (p \vee (q \leftrightarrow r)) \leftrightarrow ((p \vee q) \leftrightarrow (p \vee r))$
2. Using the natural deduction system of Section 0.2, show the following:
   (a) $p \vee q, q \rightarrow r \vdash \sim p \rightarrow r$
   (b) $p \rightarrow q, \sim(q \vee r) \vdash \sim(p \vee r)$
   (c) $p \vee q, (p \rightarrow r) \& (\sim r \rightarrow \sim q) \vdash r$
   (d) $p \rightarrow q, q \rightarrow r \vdash p \rightarrow r$
   (e) $p \leftrightarrow q, (q \leftrightarrow r) \vdash (r \leftrightarrow q)$
   (f) $q \leftrightarrow p, (q \rightarrow r), \sim r \vdash \sim p$
   (g) $(p \rightarrow q) \rightarrow (p \rightarrow r) \vdash p \rightarrow (q \rightarrow r)$
   (h) $p \& (q \vee r) \vdash p \& q \vee p \& r$
   (i) $p \& q \vee p \& r \vdash p \& (q \vee r)$
   (j) $p \vee (q \& r) \vdash (p \vee q) \& (p \vee r)$
   (k) $(p \vee q) \& (p \vee r) \vdash p \vee (q \& r)$
   (l) $(p \vee q), p \rightarrow r, q \rightarrow r' \vdash r \vee r'$

---

the induction on l nested within the induction on d. All of the Nötherian Inductions in this text could be run by nested mathematical inductions. Although the Nötherian Induction principle is more powerful than nested mathematical inductions, we use it because of its naturalness and simplicity.

3. Using the natural deduction system of Section 0.2, show the following:
   (a) $\vdash \sim \exists X(p \& \sim p)$
   (b) $\vdash \exists X(p \vee \sim p)$
   (c) $\vdash \forall X(p \rightarrow q) \rightarrow (\forall Xp \rightarrow \forall Xq)$
   (d) $\vdash \forall X(p \& q) \leftrightarrow \forall Xp \& \forall Xq$
   (e) $\vdash \exists Xp \vee \forall X(p \rightarrow q)$
   (f) $\vdash \exists X(p \& q) \& \forall X(q \rightarrow r) \rightarrow \exists X(p \& r)$
   (g) $\vdash \forall X(p(X) \vee q(0)) \leftrightarrow \forall Xp(X) \vee q(0)$
   (h) $\exists X(p \vee q) \vdash \exists Xp \vee \exists Xq$
   (i) $\sim \exists X \sim p \vdash \forall Xp$
   (j) $\sim \forall X \sim p \vdash \exists Xp$
   (k) $\exists X \forall Y p(X,Y) \vdash \forall Y \exists X p(X,Y)$
   (l) $\forall X \forall Y(p(X) \& q(Y) \rightarrow r(X,Y)), \exists X \exists Y(p(X) \& \sim p(Y) \& \sim r(X,Y))$
   $\vdash \exists X(\sim p(X) \& \sim q(X))$
   (m) $p(0) \rightarrow \forall Xq(X), \exists Xq(X) \rightarrow p(0) \vdash \forall X(p(0) \leftrightarrow q(X))$

Arithmetic

4. Using our axiomatization of arithmetic (Section 0.3), show the following:
   (a) $\vdash \sim X<X$
   (b) $\vdash X \neq 0 \rightarrow X>0 \vee X<0$
   (c) $\vdash X \neq Y \rightarrow X>Y \vee X<Y$
   (d) $\vdash \text{succ}(X)>X$
   (e) $\vdash \text{pred}(X)<X$
   (f) $\vdash \sim(X<Y<X+\text{succ}(X))$
   (g) $\vdash (X+Y)+Z=X+(Y+Z)$
   (h) $\vdash X*1=X$
   (i) $\vdash 0*X=0$
   (j) $\vdash X*Y=Y*X$
   (k) $\vdash x \neq 0 \rightarrow 0**x=0$
   (l) $\vdash \exists Y((X \geqslant 0 \rightarrow Y=X) \& (X<0 \rightarrow Y=-X))$
   (m) $\vdash (X \geqslant 0 \rightarrow Y=X) \& (X<0 \rightarrow Y=-X) \& (X \geqslant 0 \rightarrow Y'=X) \&$
   $(X<0 \rightarrow Y'=-X) \rightarrow Y=Y'$
   (n) $\vdash \text{abs}(\text{abs}(X))=\text{abs}(X)$
   (o) $\vdash 1 \neq 2$
   (p) $\vdash X-X=0$
   (q) $\vdash -0=0$

5. Using our axiomatization of arithmetic, show the following:
   (a) $\vdash X*(Y+Z)=X*Y+X*Z$
   (b) $\vdash X+(-X)=0$
   (c) $\vdash X-Y=X+(-Y)$
   (d) $\vdash X \geqslant Y \ \& \ X' \geqslant Y' \rightarrow X+X' \geqslant Y+Y'$
   (e) $\vdash X \geqslant Y \ \& \ X' \leqslant Y' \rightarrow X-X' \geqslant Y-Y'$
   (f) $\vdash X \geqslant 0 \ \& \ Y \geqslant Y' \rightarrow X*Y \geqslant X*Y'$
   (g) $\vdash X>0 \ \& \ X*Y \geqslant X*Y' \rightarrow Y \geqslant Y'$
   (h) $\vdash \text{abs}(X*Y)=\text{abs}(X)*\text{abs}(Y)$
   (i) $\vdash \text{abs}(X**2)=X**2$
   (j) $\vdash X \bmod 0 = X$
   (k) $\vdash X=(X/Y)*Y+(X \bmod Y)$
   (l) $\vdash X \geqslant 0 \& Y>0 \rightarrow \exists Q \exists R(0 \leqslant R<Y \ \& \ X=Y*Q+R)$
   (m) $\vdash \text{abs}(x+y) \leqslant \text{abs}(x)+\text{abs}(y)$
   (n) $\vdash x/1=x$
6. Demonstrate that *The Principle of Strong Mathematical Induction* is a theorem of arithmetic. That is, show that

$$\begin{aligned}&\vdash p(0) \ \& \ \forall X(X>0 \rightarrow (\forall Y(0 \leqslant Y \& Y<X \rightarrow p(Y)) \rightarrow p(X)))\\ &\quad \& \ \forall X(X<0 \rightarrow (\forall Y(X<Y \& Y \leqslant 0 \rightarrow p(Y)) \rightarrow p(X))) \rightarrow \forall Z p(Z)\end{aligned}$$

HINT: The proof runs by induction on X. The proof begins as follows:

1	$p(0) \ \& \ \forall X(X>0 \rightarrow (\forall Y(0 \leqslant Y \& Y<X \rightarrow p(Y)) \rightarrow p(X)))$ $\& \ \forall X(X<0 \rightarrow (\forall Y(X<Y \& Y \leqslant 0 \rightarrow p(Y)) \rightarrow p(X)))$	
2	$p(0) \ \& \ldots$	**(R,1)**
3	$p(0)$	**(&E,2)**
4	$z \geqslant 0$	
	.	
	.	
	.	

Line 2 constitutes the basis, and the induction step on the positive integers begins at line 3.

7. Eliminate the defined symbols (in favor of primitive symbols) from the following assertions. That is, state an assertion in the primitive vocabulary, which holds iff the given assertion holds. *Example:* Eliminating the defined symbols from $x \neq 1$, we obtain $\sim x=\text{succ}(0)$.
   (a) $x \neq y \leftrightarrow x \neq z$
   (b) $x>y \ \& \ y>z \rightarrow x>w$
   (c) $x-y=-2$

(d) pred(succ(x))=y
(e) $-0=x$
(f) abs($x+y$)$\leqslant$abs(w)+abs(z)
(g) $x/y=3$
(h) x mod $0 = y$
(i) abs(x/y) $<$ (x mod z)

8. Provide explicit or equational definitions of the following predicates and operations:
   (a) The unary predicate is_odd (i.e., is_odd (X) is to hold iff X is odd).
   (b) The unary predicate is_even.
   (c) The binary predicate divides (divides (X, Y) iff X divides Y without remainder).
   (d) The binary predicate is_a_multiple_of.
   (e) The unary predicate is_a_power_of_2.
   (f) The binary predicate is_a_power_of.
   (g) The binary operation is_the_greatest_common_divisor_of.
   (h) The binary operation is_the_least_common_multiple_of.
   (i) The binary operation is_the_minimum_of.
   (j) The binary operation is_the_maximum_of.
   (k) The binary operation is_the_rounded_average_of.
   (l) The unary operation sum_of_the_integers_from_0_to.
   (m) The binary operation sum_of_the_integers_from_–_to.
   (n) The unary operation (schema) is_the_smallest_integer_$\geqslant$0_such_that_p.

Semantics

9. In the style of Section 0.4, state the semantic equations for the following:
   (a) $\neq$, $\leqslant$, $>$, and $<$
   (b) $-$ (subtraction), pred, $-$ (negative), and abs
   (c) / and mod

10. Using the semantic equations in Section 0.4, show that
   (a) $\mathcal{S}[1+1] = 2$
   (b) $\mathcal{S}[x+0] = \mathcal{S}[x]$
   (c) $\mathcal{S}[x*\text{succ}(y)] = \mathcal{S}[x] + \mathcal{S}[x]*\mathcal{S}[y]$
   (d) $\mathcal{S}[x*(y+z)] = \mathcal{S}[x*y+x*z]$
   (e) $\mathcal{S}[x\geqslant y \vee y\geqslant x] = \text{t}$
   (f) $\mathcal{S}$[(**succ.=**)] = t (i.e., $\mathcal{S}[\text{succ}(X)=\text{succ}(Y)\rightarrow X=Y] = \text{t}$)
   (g) $\mathcal{S}$[(**Ind**)] = t

11. Prove or give a counterexample disproving the following:

(a) $e[y\backslash x][e'\backslash y] \equiv e[e'\backslash x]$

(b) $e[y\backslash x][e'\backslash y] \equiv e[e'\backslash x]$ if y is foreign to e

(c) $e[y\backslash x][e'\backslash z] \equiv e[e'\backslash z][y\backslash x]$ if x is distinct from z, y is distinct from z, and y is foreign to both e and e'

12. Prove the following:

(a) $\mathcal{S}\{\mathcal{S}[x]\backslash x\} = \mathcal{S}$

(b) $\mathcal{S}\{m\backslash x\}\{m'\backslash x\} = \mathcal{S}\{m'\backslash x\}$

(c) If x and y are distinct integer variables, then $\mathcal{S}\{m\backslash x\}\{m'\backslash y\} = \mathcal{S}\{m'\backslash y\}\{m\backslash x\}$

13. Let $\mathcal{S}$ be a state in which the truth-value of assertions is evaluated according to the semantic equations (1)–(14) (Section 0.4), and let $\mathcal{S}'$ be like $\mathcal{S}$ except that the truth-value of assertions is evaluated according to the semantic equations (1)–(12), (13′), and (14′). Using Nötherian induction, prove that, for any assertion p, $\mathcal{S}[p]=\mathcal{S}'[p]$.

14. Prove that the complexity ordering on the integer expressions is a well-founded ordering.

15. Prove the principle of Nötherian Induction.

Programming Projects

16. In your favorite programming language, write a proof-checker for the natural deduction system described in Section 0.2. The input file contains an alleged proof consisting of lines in much the same format illustrated in the text. (Use –>, <–>, (X), and (EX) instead of $\rightarrow$, $\leftrightarrow$, $\forall X$, and $\exists X$.) Your output should indicate whether the alleged proof is, in fact, a proof and, if it is not, it should output the first line number in error and an indication of the type of error.

17. In your favorite programming language, write a "recognizer" for the axioms of arithmetic listed in Section 0.3. The input file contains assertions in much the same format illustrated in the text. (Use –>, <–>, (X), and (EX) instead of $\rightarrow$, $\leftrightarrow$, $\forall X$, and $\exists X$.) Your output should indicate which of the assertions are axioms. Output a diagnostic if an input line is not an assertion.

CHAPTER 1

The Partial Correctness of **while** Programs

In this chapter, we present the **while** programs, the basic building blocks of structured programs. Their name derives from the fact that the only control structures building on the assignment statement are the composition, conditional, and **while** statements.[1]

In Section 1.1, we present the syntax of **while** programs in the framework of a Pascal-like dialect that has only simple integer variables. In Section 1.2, the more rigorous definitions of partial and total correctness, promised in the Introduction, are stated in the context of the operational semantics. We develop the related concepts of truth and validity for a program taken together with its specification (an asserted program).

In Section 1.3, we present Hoare's method (the Hoare Axiomatization) for proving the partial correctness of **while** programs. We will postpone the

[1] The fundamental theorem of structured programming, usually attributed to Böhm and Jacopini, states that a **while** program can be written to compute any computable function. See Ledgard and Marcotty for an intuitive exposition.

development of a method for proving the total correctness of **while** programs until Chapter 4, as Hoare's partial correctness formalism is simpler and more intuitive than the total correctness formalism. Furthermore, because the Hoare method for proving even partial correctness becomes unwieldy when applied to programs consisting of more than a dozen lines or so, we treat only short programs in our sample proofs in this chapter. Consequently, we will consider primarily **for** programs (more accurately, **while** programs having a particular syntactic form), conforming to our policy of keeping our sample proofs simple. Limiting attention to the **for** programs also carries an advantage in that Hoare's method of proving partial correctness suffices for proving total correctness.

In Section 1.4, we prove the (weak) soundness of the Hoare Axiomatization (with respect to the semantics of Section 1.2), noting that the Soundness of Arithmetic Theorem (Chapter 0) plays a key role in the proof. Finally, in Section 1.5, we illustrate the use of the Hoare Axiomatization by proving the correctness of a few simple programs.

1.1. SYNTAX

The syntax of integer expressions and assertions is as given in Chapter 0. However, in this section we develop abstract syntax as well as some additional notational conventions. The set of *numerals* is **Num** with typical members $m, m', \ldots$, and the set of integer variables is **Ivar** with typical members $x, y, z, \ldots$. The set of *integer expressions* is **Iexp** with typical members $e, e', \ldots$. Now let us turn to the grammar of integer expressions in the style of abstract syntax

Iexp: $e, e', \ldots$ (typical members)
$e ::= m \mid x \mid \mathrm{succ}(e) \mid \ldots \mid e+e' \mid \ldots$

The first ellipsis ('. . .') indicates where the other unary operation symbols ('pred', etc.) are introduced, and the second ellipsis indicates location of the other binary operation symbols. A rough reading of the abstract syntax of **Iexp** is: "An integer expression is either a numeral or an integer variable or the successor of an integer expression or. . . ." The reader should compare the abstract syntax of **Iexp** with the logician's grammar on page 8. When we consider the parenthesis-omitting conventions in Chapter 0 and the complementary parenthesis-insertion conventions adopted in abstract syntax to disambiguate integer expressions, the two grammars are equivalent (with regard to what strings are integer expressions as well as to parsing).

The set of *assertions* is **Assn** with typical members $p, q, r, \ldots$. The abstract syntax is as follows:[2]

$$\textbf{Assn:}\quad p, q, r, \ldots$$
$$p ::= e{=}e' \mid \ldots \mid {\sim}p \mid p\&q \mid \ldots \mid \forall X p \mid \exists X p$$

The *boolean expressions* are the quantifier-free assertions. The set of boolean expressions is **Bexp** with typical members $b, b', \ldots$. The abstract syntax is as follows:

$$\textbf{Bexp:}\quad b, b', \ldots$$
$$b ::= e{=}e' \mid \ldots \mid {\sim}b \mid b\&b' \mid \ldots$$

For simplicity, we do not introduce "program variables" of type boolean. Note that because each boolean expression is an assertion, any property that holds true for all assertions also holds true for all boolean expressions.

We now present the grammar of **while** programs. As there are no declarations in our simplified Pascal-like dialect, a *while program* is simply a statement. The set of *statements is* **Stat** with typical members $S, S', \ldots$. The abstract syntax is as follows:

$$\textbf{Stat:}\quad S, S', \ldots$$
$$S ::= \mathbf{d} \mid x{:=}e \mid S;S' \mid \mathbf{if}\ b\ \mathbf{then}\ S\ \mathbf{else}\ S' \mid \mathbf{while}\ b\ \mathbf{do}\ S$$

For our current purposes, we could define the *dummy* statement $\mathbf{d} \equiv x{:=}x$ for some integer variable x. However, for reasons that will become apparent in Chapter 5, we prefer to take **d** as a primitive. The statement $x{:=}e$ is called an *assignment statement;* $S;S'$ a *composition statement;* **if** b **then** S **else** S' a *conditional statement;* and **while** b **do** S a **while** statement. Note that we use the terms '**while** program' (or simply 'program') and 'statement' more or less interchangeably.

Our grammar of **while** programs differs from (standard ISO) Pascal in several ways. First, we have introduced the exponentiation operation symbol '**' into the grammar of integer expressions. Pascal does not have an exponentiation operator. Second, we use the symbol '/' for the integer division operator, whereas the symbol '**div**' is used in Pascal. Third, our statements correspond to statement sequences in Pascal. Fourth, our dummy statement **d** is the empty string in Pascal. Fifth, we use the semicolon ';' as the statement composition operator and not just a statement separator as in Pascal. Sixth, we understand the signs '**begin**' and '**end**' to be punctuation marks for state-

[2] As noted in Chapter 0, our grammar is context-sensitive because, in the final two clauses $\forall Xp$ and $\exists Xp$, we understand that the quantified variable X does not occur in p in either of the contexts . . . $\forall X$ . . . or . . . $\exists X$ . . . . Similarly, in describing the syntax of a typical programming language, one gives a context-free description and lists separately context-sensitive restrictions such as the prohibition against declaring a variable more than once.

ments, much like the signs '(' and ')' are for the integer expressions and assertions. Seventh, although we use the set brackets '{' and '}' to delimit assertions, much as comments are delimited in Pascal, set brackets carry a special significance in certain contexts, as we shall explain in the next paragraph.

We understand an *annotated statement* to be either (1) a dummy, an assignment, a composition, or a conditional statement, or (2) a **while** statement prefixed with an assertion enclosed within set brackets. The set of annotated statements is **Asta** with typical members $A, A', \ldots$. The abstract syntax is as follows:

Asta: $A, A', \ldots$
$A ::= \mathbf{d} \mid x{:=}e \mid A;A' \mid \textbf{if } b \textbf{ then } A \textbf{ else } A' \mid$
$\{p\} \textbf{ while } b \textbf{ do } A$

An assertion occurring in an annotated statement is called an *intermediate assertion.* Finally, we introduce the class of *asserted programs* **Aprg** with typical members $AP, AP', \ldots$, having the following abstract syntax:

Aprg: $AP, AP', \ldots$
$AP ::= \{p\}A\{q\}$

In many contexts, to simplify the exposition, we will ignore any intermediate assertions occurring in an annotated program A. In other words, we deal with the statement S obtained by deleting all intermediate assertions occurring in the annotated statement A. S is called *the statement of* A.

A *specification* for a **while** program is an ordered pair of assertions $\langle p,q \rangle$. Intuitively, the specification requires that program S be written in a manner so that q will hold after execution of S if p holds at the time execution of S begins. The assertion p is called the *precondition* of program S; assertion q is called its *postcondition.* The precondition is the assertion p and the postcondition is the assertion q in the asserted program $AP \equiv \{p\}S\{q\}$. The program S is said to be *the full program* if we do not use S as a constituent of a larger program S'.[3] When S is the full program, we call an integer variable belonging to $\mathfrak{ivar}[p]$ an *input variable* and an integer variable belonging to $\mathfrak{ivar}[q]$-$\mathfrak{ivar}[p]$ an *output variable.* We prohibit assignments to input variables. That is, no input variable can occur on the left side of an assignment statement in S.

To facilitate identification of unrestricted input variables, we introduce the monadic predicate 'I' with the explicit definition

(D.I) $\quad \mathrm{I}(X) \leftrightarrow \exists Y(Y{=}Y)$

[3] Later, in Chapter 4, we shall speak of an annotated program being *the full annotated program* in an entirely similar manner.

which has the intended reading "X is an integer". $I(X)$ does not restrict input variable X because, by the definition of validity in Chapter 0, $\models I(e)$ for any integer expression e.[4]

We define other **while** program statements in terms of the primitives just provided. We have

> **if** b **then** $S \equiv$
>   **if** b **then** S **else** d
> **for** $x{:=}e$ **to** e' **do** $S \equiv$
> $x{:=}e$; **while** $x \leqslant e'$ **do begin** S; $x{:=}x+1$ **end**
> **for** $x{:=}e$ **downto** e' **do** $S \equiv$
> $x{:=}e$; **while** $x \geqslant e'$ **do begin** S; $x{:=}x-1$ **end**

In the **for – to** and **for – downto** statements, we require that the control variable x be foreign to the final expression e' and we prohibit assignments to x and to any integer variable $y \in \mathfrak{ivar}[e']$ in the loop body S. A **for** program is a **while** program composed solely of dummy, assignment, composition, conditional, and **for** statements.[5]

Note that our definitions of the two **for** statements are not in agreement with Pascal. First, Pascal does not prohibit occurrences of the control variable x in the final expression e' because, to speed program execution, Pascal evaluates e' only once (during the initialization of the **for** loop). Our prohibition is motivated by the desire to keep the definitions of the **for** statements (in terms of the **while** and assignment statements) short. A second and more critical difference is that, by the preceding definitions, the control variable x is defined upon completion of the **for** loop, whereas it is not defined in Pascal. However, we will refrain from making use of this feature in our programs and assertions.[6]

Regarding annotated **for** statements, we understand the following to be true:

> $\{p\}$ **for** $x{:=}e$ **to** e' **do** $S \equiv$
> $x{:=}e$; $\{p\}$ **while** $x \leqslant e'$ **do begin** S; $x{:=}x+1$ **end**
> $\{p\}$ **for** $x{:=}$ e **downto** e' **do** $S \equiv$
> $x{:=}e$; $\{p\}$ **while** $x \geqslant e'$ **do begin** S; $x{:=}x-1$ **end**

[4] In Chapter 5, when we revise the logic of Chapter 0 to deal with errors, the predicate 'I' will take on additional significance because an integer expression can be undefined and so $\models I(e)$ does not hold.

[5] The **for** programs are of considerable theoretical interest as they coincide with the primitive recursive functions—it is easy to show that each primitive recursive function can be computed by a **for** program, and Meyer and Ritchie have shown that every **for** program computes a primitive recursive function. Because the **while** programs correspond with the computable or general recursive functions by the Böhm–Jacopini result, the **while** statement is seen to be the counterpart of the unbounded minimization operator of recursive function theory.

[6] A safer treatment of control variables than ours is found in ALGOL 68. In ALGOL 68, the control variable is local to the **for** loop and can be shielded from assignments in the loop body.

In the following sections, we do not give the semantics and proof rules directly for the **for-to** and **for-downto** statements because they can be garnered from the semantics and proof rules for the primitive assignment, composition, and **while** statements. *We prove correct a **for** program by proving correct the primitive **while** program.*

We now give an example of a **while** program that sets z equal to $x**y$ for any $y \geq 0$ using the method of successive multiplications. To increase the readability of our programs, we do not restrict ourselves to the letters $x, \ldots$ for our integer variables.

```
{y≥0 & I(x)}
z := 1;
{z=x**(y−t) & 0≤t≤y}
for t:=y downto 1 do
        z := z*x
{z=x**y}
```

Viewed as an asserted program $AP \equiv \{p\}S\{r\}$, we have the full program

$S \equiv z{:=}1;$ **for** $t{:=}y$ **downto** 1 **do** $z{:=}z*x$
$\quad \equiv z{:=}1; t{:=}y;$ **while** $t \geq 1$ **do begin** $z{:=}z*x; t{:=}t-1$ **end**

the precondition

$$p \equiv y \geq 0 \ \& \ \mathrm{I}(x)$$

and the postcondition

$$r \equiv z = x**y$$

The intermediate assertion

$$q \equiv z = x**(y-t) \ \& \ 0 \leq t \leq y$$

is called a *loop invariant* because it holds (is invariantly true) whenever program control reaches the test $t \geq 1$ in the **while** statement (**while** loop). The loop invariant divides the asserted program AP into two constituent asserted programs AP' and AP'', where

$AP' \equiv \{p\}S'\{q\}$
$\quad \equiv \{y \geq 0 \ \& \ \mathrm{I}(x)\}\ z{:=}1; t{:=}y\ \{z=x**(y-t) \ \& \ 0 \leq t \leq y\}$

and

$AP'' \equiv \{q\}S''\{r\}$
$\quad \equiv \{z=x**(y-t) \ \& \ 0 \leq t \leq y\}$
$\qquad$ **while** $t \geq 1$ **do begin** $z{:=}z*x; t{:=}t-1$ **end**
$\quad \{z=x**y\}$

If we did not prohibit an assignment to the input variable y, a "correct" full program would be, for example,

$$y{:=}0;\ z{:=}1$$

The postcondition $r \equiv z = x{*}{*}y$ would always be satisfied because $1 = x{*}{*}0$ for any value of x, but the program would not behave as intended. Similarly, if an assignment could be made to the input variable x, a "correct" full program would be

$$x{:=}0;\ \textbf{if}\ y=0\ \textbf{then}\ z{:=}1\ \textbf{else}\ z{:=}0$$

We should have $z = x{*}{*}y$ on program termination, where x and y have retained their original values.

1.2. OPERATIONAL SEMANTICS

The semantics of integer variables, integer expressions, and assertions is as in Chapter 0, and the semantics of boolean expressions is given by the semantics of assertions. Here, we need only specify the semantics of **Stat** (the set of **while** programs) and **Aprg** (the set of asserted programs).

We understand the set of states to be **States** with typical members $\mathfrak{s}, \mathfrak{s}', \ldots$. Intuitively, an unextended state $\mathfrak{s}$ describes a memory configuration in which $\mathfrak{s}[x]$ is the integer contained in memory location x. We extend $\mathfrak{s}$ to $S \in \textbf{Stat}$ so that $\mathfrak{s}[S]$ is the new memory configuration (state) reached when S is executed in state $\mathfrak{s}$. The *operational semantics of* **Stat** is defined inductively as shown in Figure 1.1. Note that, for any state $\mathfrak{s}$, $S \equiv$ **while** true **do** S' does not terminate, and $\mathfrak{s}[S']$ is undefined by the preceding definition.

As an example, let $\mathfrak{s}$ be a state such that $\mathfrak{s}[x]=3$, $\mathfrak{s}[y]=2$, and, for example,

$\mathfrak{s}[\textbf{d}] = \mathfrak{s}$
$\mathfrak{s}[x{:=}e] = \mathfrak{s}\{\mathfrak{s}[e]\backslash x\}$
$\mathfrak{s}[S';S''] = \mathfrak{s}[S'][S'']$
$\mathfrak{s}[\textbf{if}\ b\ \textbf{then}\ S'\ \textbf{else}\ S''] = \mathfrak{s}[S']$ if $\mathfrak{s}[b]=\mathrm{t}$,
$= \mathfrak{s}[S'']$ otherwise
$\mathfrak{s}[\textbf{while}\ b\ \textbf{do}\ S'] = \mathfrak{s}{*}$ if there is a finite sequence of states $\langle \mathfrak{s}_0, \mathfrak{s}_1, \ldots, \mathfrak{s}_m \rangle$ $(m \geq 0)$ such that $\mathfrak{s}=\mathfrak{s}_0$, $\mathfrak{s}{*}=\mathfrak{s}_m$, $\mathfrak{s}_m[b]=\mathrm{f}$, and, for each i such that $0 \leq i \leq m-1$, $\mathfrak{s}_i[b]=\mathrm{t}$ and $\mathfrak{s}_{i+1}=\mathfrak{s}_i[S']$.

FIGURE 1.1. The operational semantics of statements.

$\mathscr{s}[t]=\mathscr{s}[z]=0$. That is,

$$\mathscr{s}=\{\langle x,3\rangle,\langle y,2\rangle,\langle t,0\rangle,\langle z,0\rangle, \ldots\}$$

and let S be our exponentiation program. Tracing the execution of S when started up in state $\mathscr{s}$, we have the following finite sequence of states:

State	**Statement**
$\mathscr{s}=\mathscr{s}_0=\{\langle x,3\rangle,\langle y,2\rangle,\langle t,0\rangle,\langle z,0\rangle, \ldots\}$	
	$z:=1$
$\mathscr{s}_1=\{\langle x,3\rangle,\langle y,2\rangle,\langle t,0\rangle,\langle z,1\rangle, \ldots\}$	
	$t:=y$
$\mathscr{s}_2=\{\langle x,3\rangle,\langle y,2\rangle,\langle t,2\rangle,\langle z,1\rangle, \ldots\}$	
	while $t\geq 1$ **do** . . .
	$z:=z*x$
$\mathscr{s}_3=\{\langle x,3\rangle,\langle y,2\rangle,\langle t,2\rangle,\langle z,3\rangle, \ldots\}$	
	$t:=t-1$
$\mathscr{s}_4=\{\langle x,3\rangle,\langle y,2\rangle,\langle t,1\rangle,\langle z,3\rangle, \ldots\}$	
	while $t\geq 1$ **do** . . .
	$z:=z*x$
$\mathscr{s}_5=\{\langle x,3\rangle,\langle y,2\rangle,\langle t,1\rangle,\langle z,9\rangle, \ldots\}$	
	$t:=t-1$
$\mathscr{s}_6=\{\langle x,3\rangle,\langle y,2\rangle,\langle t,0\rangle,\langle z,9\rangle, \ldots\}$	
	while $t\geq 1$ **do** . . .

So, $\mathscr{s}[S]=\mathscr{s}_6$

Notice that if y is initially nonnegative (i.e., $\mathscr{s}_0[y]\geq 0$), the loop invariant $z=x**(y-t)\ \&\ 0\leq t\leq y$ holds each time program control reaches the beginning of the **while** loop body (in states $\mathscr{s}_2$, $\mathscr{s}_4$, and $\mathscr{s}_6$ in our example). It holds in state $\mathscr{s}_2$ because $\mathscr{s}_0[y\geq 0]=\mathrm{t}$, z has been initialized to 1, t has been initialized to y, and $x**0=1$ by the axiom of arithmetic **(**.0)**:

$$\mathscr{s}_2[z=x**(y-t)\ \&\ 0\leq t\leq y]=\mathscr{s}_0[1=x**(y-y)\ \&\ 0\leq y\leq y]=\mathrm{t}$$

Furthermore, when the boolean expression $t\geq 1$ guarding the execution of the **while** statement's body holds, the loop invariant is preserved by the **while's** body because z and t are set to $z*x$ and $t-1$. For example, if we are in state $\mathscr{s}_2$ with $\mathscr{s}_2[t]\geq 1$, and we execute the body of the **while,** we reach state $\mathscr{s}_4$ and have the following:

$$\mathscr{s}_4[z=x**(y-t)\ \&\ 0\leq t\leq y]=\mathscr{s}_2[z*x=x**(y-(t-1))\ \&\ 0\leq t-1\leq y]=\mathrm{t}$$

In the following definitions, we will use *wrt* to abbreviate the phase "with respect to." We understand a state $\mathfrak{s}$ to be *initial* for an asserted program $AP \equiv \{p\}S\{q\}$ and for the statement S (with precondition p) provided that $\mathfrak{s}[p]=t$. A statement S is *partially correct* wrt specification $\langle p,q \rangle$ provided that, for every initial state $\mathfrak{s}$ for S either $\mathfrak{s}[S]$ is undefined or $\mathfrak{s}[S][q]=\mathrm{t}$. Note that S is partially correct wrt a specification $\langle p,q \rangle$ if, for every initial state $\mathfrak{s}$ for S, $\mathfrak{s}[S]$ is undefined (i.e., S does not terminate when started up in initial state $\mathfrak{s}$). We say that S *terminates* (for precondition p) if, for every initial state $\mathfrak{s}$ for S, $\mathfrak{s}[S]$ is defined (i.e., a state $\mathfrak{s}'$ exists such that $\mathfrak{s}'=\mathfrak{s}[S]$). A statement S is *totally correct* wrt specification $\langle p,q \rangle$ provided that, for every initial state $\mathfrak{s}$ for S, $\mathfrak{s}[S]$ is defined and $\mathfrak{s}'[q]=\mathrm{t}$. As an immediate consequence of the above definitions, we have the following theorem:

TOTAL CORRECTNESS THEOREM: A program S is totally correct wrt specification $\langle p,q \rangle$ iff S is partially correct wrt specification $\langle p,q \rangle$ and S terminates for precondition p.

The concepts of partial and total correctness are sometimes understood in terms of the concept of validity, suitably extended. We will use the definition of partial correctness in terms of validity in Section 1.4 when we prove the soundness of the Hoare Axiomatization. In the case of partial correctness, a state $\mathfrak{s}$ is extended so that a truth-value is assigned to each asserted program $AP \equiv \{p\}S\{q\}$. The *operational semantics of* **Aprg** is defined as follows:

$$\begin{aligned} \mathfrak{s}[AP] &= \mathrm{t} \text{ provided that (1) } \mathfrak{s} \text{ is not an initial state for } \\ &\qquad AP, \text{ or (2) } \mathfrak{s}[S] \text{ is undefined, or (3) } \mathfrak{s}[S][q]=\mathrm{t}. \\ &= \mathfrak{f} \text{ otherwise.} \end{aligned}$$

The concept of *validity* is extended to $AP \in$ **Aprg** in the usual manner—$\models AP$ iff $\mathfrak{s}[AP]=\mathrm{t}$ for every state $\mathfrak{s}$. This leads to the next theorem:

PARTIAL CORRECTNESS/VALIDITY THEOREM: Program S is partially correct wrt specification $\langle p,q \rangle$ iff $\models \{p\}S\{q\}$.

The concepts of truth and validity are extended to $AP \in$ **Aprg,** viewed in the context of total correctness, in a similar manner.

To simplify the method of proving program correctness presented in the next section, we will restrict our attention to the Hoare Axiomatization for proving partial correctness, postponing treatment of problems relating to the nontermination of **while** programs until Chapter 4. However, as noted earlier, our sample proofs in this chapter deal for the most part with **for** programs. In light of the **For** Program Total Correctness Theorem, which follows, Hoare's partial correctness axiomatization is seen to be adequate for proving the total correctness of **for** programs. Some of the concepts arising in the following two lemmas leading up to the proof of the **For** Program Total

Correctness Theorem will be developed further in later chapters. However, the remainder of this section can be skipped on the first reading without loss of continuity.

Intuitively, the following lemma states that if no assignment statement of the form $x{:=}e$ occurs in a (primitive) statement S, then execution of S does not set (change the value of) x. (The restriction to (primitive) statements excludes the **for** statements.) We understand that, for any states $\mathfrak{s}$ and $\mathfrak{s}'$ if $\mathfrak{s}'=\mathfrak{s}[S]$, then S terminates when started up in state $\mathfrak{s}$.

SETTING LEMMA: For any states $\mathfrak{s}$ and $\mathfrak{s}'$, any statement S such that $\mathfrak{s}'=\mathfrak{s}[S]$, and any integer variable x, if no assignment to x occurs in S, then $\mathfrak{s}'[x] = \mathfrak{s}[x]$.

Proof: The proof proceeds by Nötherian Induction on the complexity of S. The details are left as an exercise. □

FOR PROGRAM TERMINATION LEMMA: Every **for** program terminates. That is, for every $\mathfrak{s}\in$**States** and every **for** program $S\in$**Stat**, there is a state $\mathfrak{s}*\in$**States** such that $\mathfrak{s}*=\mathfrak{s}[S]$.

Proof: Let $\mathfrak{s}$ be any state. We shall exhibit a state $\mathfrak{s}*=\mathfrak{s}[S]$ in which S terminates when started up in state $\mathfrak{s}$. The construction of $\mathfrak{s}*$ proceeds by Nötherian Induction on the complexity of the **for** program S.

BASIS: S is simple.
Because S is simple, we have either $S\equiv$ **d** or $S\equiv x{:=}e$. If $S\equiv$ **d**, then $\mathfrak{s}[\mathbf{d}]=\mathfrak{s}$ by the operational semantics of the dummy statement, and we take $\mathfrak{s}*$ to be $\mathfrak{s}$. If $S\equiv x{:=}e$, then $\mathfrak{s}[x{:=}e]=\mathfrak{s}\{\mathfrak{s}[e]\backslash x\}$ by the operational semantics of the assignment statement, and we take $\mathfrak{s}*$ to be $\mathfrak{s}\{\mathfrak{s}[e]\backslash x\}$.

INDUCTION STEP: S is complex.

Case: $S\equiv S';S''$
We have $\mathfrak{s}[S';S'']=\mathfrak{s}[S'][S'']$ by the operational semantics of the composition statement. Because S' is simpler than $S\equiv S';S''$, we have by the IH that $\mathfrak{s}[S']$ is defined (i.e., S' terminates when started up in state $\mathfrak{s}$). Applying the IH again, we have that $\mathfrak{s}[S'][S'']$ is defined because S'' is simpler than S. Take $\mathfrak{s}*$ to be $\mathfrak{s}[S'][S'']$.

Case: $S\equiv$ **if** b **then** S' **else** S''
The proof is left as an exercise.

Case: $S\equiv$ **for** $x{:=}e$ **to** e' **do** S''
Let $S'\equiv$ **while** $x\leq e'$ **do begin** S''; $x{:=}x+1$ **end.** We have $S\equiv x{:=}e;S'$ by the definition of the **for – to** statement and $\mathfrak{s}[S]=\mathfrak{s}[x{:=}e][S']$ by the opera-

tional semantics of the composition statement. Let $\mathfrak{s}_0 = \mathfrak{s}[x{:=}e] = \mathfrak{s}\{\mathfrak{s}[e]\backslash x\}$, which is defined by the IH. Suppose $\mathfrak{s}_0[x] > \mathfrak{s}_0[e']$. Then $\mathfrak{s}_0[S'] = \mathfrak{s}_0$ by the operational semantics of the **while** statement. Consequently, we take $\mathfrak{s}*$ to be $\mathfrak{s}_0$. On the other hand, suppose $\mathfrak{s}_0[x] \leqslant \mathfrak{s}_0[e']$. For each $i \geqslant 1$, let $\mathfrak{s}_i = \mathfrak{s}_{i-1}[S'';x{:=}x+1]$. A simple mathematical (inner) induction on i using the operational semantics of the composition and assignment statements, the Setting Lemma, and the IH of the Nötherian (outer) Induction establishes that $\mathfrak{s}_i = \mathfrak{s}_{i-1}[S'']\{\mathfrak{s}_{i-1}[x+1]\backslash x\}$ is defined for every $i \geqslant 1$. The proof now proceeds by another simple mathematical (inner) induction on the quantity $\mathrm{r}(i) = \mathfrak{s}_i[e'] + 1 - \mathfrak{s}_i[x]$ $(i \geqslant 0)$. Intuitively, $\mathrm{r}(i)$ is the number of iterations remaining after i iterations when control reaches the beginning of the **while** loop.

Basis: $\mathrm{r}(i)=0$
Because $\mathrm{r}(i)=0$, $\mathfrak{s}_i[x] = \mathfrak{s}_i[e']+1 > \mathfrak{s}_i[e']$, and so S' terminates in state $\mathfrak{s}_i$. Take $\mathfrak{s}*$ to be $\mathfrak{s}_i$.

Induction Step: $\mathrm{r}(i) \geqslant 1$
By the IH of the mathematical (inner) induction on $\mathrm{r}(i)$, $\mathfrak{s}_{\mathrm{r}(i)-1}$ is defined because $0 \leqslant \mathrm{r}(i)-1 < \mathrm{r}(i)$. Applying the Setting Lemma and the Coincidence Lemma, $\mathfrak{s}_{\mathrm{r}(i)-1}[e'+1-x] = \mathfrak{s}_{\mathrm{r}(i)}[e'+1-x]-1$ by the definitions of $\mathfrak{s}_i$ and $\mathrm{r}(i)$ because no assignment to x or any $y \in \mathfrak{ivar}[e']$ occurs in S'' and $x \notin \mathfrak{ivar}[e']$. Hence, by the definitions of $\mathfrak{s}_i$ and $\mathrm{r}(i)$ again, $\mathfrak{s}_{\mathrm{r}(i)}[S'';x{:=}x+1] = \mathfrak{s}_{\mathrm{r}(i)-1}$. Take $\mathfrak{s}*$ to be $\mathfrak{s}_{\mathrm{r}(i)-1}$ $(=\mathfrak{s}_{\mathrm{r}(i+1)})$.

Case: $S \equiv$ **for** $x{:=}e$ **downto** e' **do** S''
The proof is left as an exercise. □

As an immediate consequence of the Total Correctness Theorem and the **For** Program Termination Lemma, we have the following theorem:

FOR PROGRAM TOTAL CORRECTNESS THEOREM: A **for** program S is totally correct wrt a specification $\langle p,q \rangle$ iff S is partially correct wrt $\langle p,q \rangle$.

1.3. PROVING PARTIAL CORRECTNESS: THE HOARE AXIOMATIZATION

In this section, we present Hoare's method for proving partial correctness. Partial correctness is proved using an axiomatic system and, in Chapter 4, we will modify the axiomatic system to obtain a system for proving total correctness. However, as noted in the preceding section, a partial correctness proof, in the special case of **for** programs, also establishes total correctness. And, because most of this chapter's sample programs are **for** programs, the

Hoare axiomatic system for proving partial correctness generally suffices for proving total correctness.

We supplement the deductive system for arithmetic in Chapter 0 with the *Hoare Axiomatization* for proving the correctness of asserted programs. In this chapter, we follow the usual convention adopted in the Hoare Axiomatization that prohibits a proof of an asserted program from a set of assumptions. (The reasons for this prohibition will be explained in the next section). Due to the fact that the deductive system of Chapter 0 *does* allow proofs from assumptions, we will strictly separate proofs in the Hoare Axiomatization from proofs in arithmetic. To make our proofs of asserted programs more readable, we will break our proofs up into small modules (lemmas), as illustrated shortly. A formal proof can be reconstructed mechanically from such modular proofs. Our rules of inference are of the form

$$\textbf{if}\ \vdash p_1, \ldots, \vdash p_m\ \textbf{and}\ \vdash AP_1, \ldots, \vdash AP_n,\ \textbf{then}\ \vdash AP$$

written more graphically as

$$\frac{p_1, \ldots, p_m, AP_1, \ldots, AP_n}{AP}$$

The p_i are proved using the deductive system of Chapter 0 whereas the AP_j are proved using the Hoare Axiomatization.

The Hoare Partial Correctness Axiomatization has two axioms and four rules of inference. Underneath each axiom or rule of inference, we provide an intuitive reading. The axioms and rules of inference are listed in Figure 1.2.

Let $a_i (1 \leq i \leq n)$ be either an assertion or an asserted program. A *proof* of an asserted program AP (in the Hoare Axiomatization) is a finite sequence of lines $\langle a_1, \ldots, a_n \rangle$ such that $AP \equiv a_n$ and each a_i is either (1) a theorem of arithmetic, (2) a Hoare Axiom, or (3) obtained from one or more preceding lines by an application of one of the four Hoare Rules of Inference. AP is *provable* if there is a proof of AP.

Regarding the premises of the Consequence Rule, proofs of $p \rightarrow p'$ and $q' \rightarrow q$ are obtained using the deductive system for arithmetic in Chapter 0, whereas the proof of $\{p'\}S\{q'\}$ uses the Hoare Axiomatization. The Consequence Rule "glues together" the program part of the proof (the Hoare Axiomatization) and the arithmetic part of the proof (the axiomatization of Chapter 0).

In our proofs of the correctness of **while** programs, we will restrict attention to the program part, leaving aside formal proofs of the arithmetic part. In other words, we shall claim, for example (see the proof of (6), which follows), that

$$\vdash y \geq 0\ \&\ \mathrm{I}(x) \rightarrow 1 = x{*}{*}(y-y)\ \&\ 0 \leq y \leq y$$

1. *The Dummy Axiom*

$\{p\}\mathbf{d}\{p\}$

("p always holds after execution of **d** if p holds before (execution of **d**).")

2. *The Assignment Axiom*

$\{p[e\backslash x]\}x{:=}e\{p\}$

("p always holds after execution of $x{:=}e$ if $p[e\backslash x]$ holds before.")

3. *The Composition Rule*

$$\frac{\{p\}S\{q\},\quad \{q\}S'\{r\}}{\{p\}S;S'\{r\}}$$

("If q always holds after execution of S if p holds before, and r always holds after execution of S' if q holds before, then r always holds after execution of $S;S'$ if p holds before.")

4. *The Conditional Rule*

$$\frac{\{p\&b\}S\{q\},\quad \{p\&{\sim}b\}S'\{q\}}{\{p\}\ \mathbf{if}\ b\ \mathbf{then}\ S\ \mathbf{else}\ S'\{q\}}$$

("If q always holds after execution of S if $p\&b$ holds before, and q also always holds after execution of S' if $p\&{\sim}b$ holds before, then q always holds after execution of **if** b **then** S **else** S' if p holds before.")

5. *The **While** Rule*

$$\frac{\{p\&b\}S\{p\}}{\{p\}\mathbf{while}\ b\ \mathbf{do}\ S\{p\&{\sim}b\}}$$

("If p always holds after execution of S if $p\&b$ holds before execution, then $p\&{\sim}b$ always holds after execution of **while** b **do** S **if** p holds before.")

6. *The Consequence Rule*

$$\frac{p{\to}p',\quad \{p'\}S\{q'\},\quad q'{\to}q}{\{p\}S\{q\}}$$

("If p always implies p', q' always holds after execution of S if p' holds before, and q' always implies q, then q always holds after execution of S if p holds before.")

FIGURE 1.2. The Hoare partial correctness axiomatization.

but we shall not carry out the proof. Using the deductive system of Chapter 0, a relatively short proof can show that this particular assertion is a theorem of arithmetic. However, although most of the theorems of arithmetic needed to apply the Consequence Rule are simple and "intuitively obvious," proofs of some of these theorems can be extremely long.

We illustrate the use of the Hoare Axiomatization with a proof of our asserted exponentiation program $AP \equiv \{p\}S\{r\} \equiv \{p\}S';S''\{r\}$, where

$$\begin{aligned} p &\equiv y \geqslant 0 \ \&\ \mathrm{I}(x), \\ S' &\equiv z{:=}1;\ t{:=}y, \\ S'' &\equiv \textbf{while } t \geqslant 1 \textbf{ do begin } z{:=}z*x;\ t{:=}t-1 \textbf{ end} \end{aligned}$$

and,

$$r \equiv z = x**y$$

Let $q \equiv z = x**(y-t) \ \&\ 0 \leqslant t \leqslant y$ and $b \equiv t \geqslant 1$.

Working in a top-down manner, we break the proof of

(1) $$\begin{aligned} &\{p\}\ S\ \{r\} \\ \equiv\ &\{y \geqslant 0 \ \&\ \mathrm{I}(x)\} \\ &\quad z{:=}1;\ t{:=}y;\ \textbf{while } t \geqslant 1 \textbf{ do begin } z{:=}z*x;\ t{:=}t-1 \textbf{ end} \\ &\{z = x**y\} \end{aligned}$$

into two parts. That is, we show that

(2) $$\begin{aligned} &\{p\}S'\{q\} \\ \equiv\ &\{y \geqslant 0 \ \&\ \mathrm{I}(x)\}\ z{:=}1;\ t{:=}y\ \{z = x**(y-t) \ \&\ 0 \leqslant t \leqslant y\} \end{aligned}$$

and

(3) $$\begin{aligned} &\{q\}S''\{\mathrm{r}\} \\ \equiv\ &\{z = x**(y-t) \ \&\ 0 \leqslant t \leqslant y\} \\ &\quad \textbf{while } t \geqslant 1 \textbf{ do begin } z{:=}z*x;\ t{:=}t-1 \textbf{ end} \\ &\{z = x**y\} \end{aligned}$$

Applying the Composition Rule to (2) and (3), we have (1).

Proof of (2): By the Assignment Axiom we have

(4) $$\begin{aligned} &\{q[y \backslash t]\}\ t{:=}y\ \{q\} \\ \equiv\ &\{z = x**(y-y) \ \&\ 0 \leqslant y \leqslant y\}\ t{:=}y\ \{z = x**(y-t) \ \&\ 0 \leqslant t \leqslant y\} \end{aligned}$$

and,

(5) $\{q[y\backslash t][1\backslash z]\}\ z{:=}1\ \{q[y\backslash t]\}$
$\equiv \{1{=}x{*}{*}(y-y)\ \&\ 0{\leq}y{\leq}y\}\ z{:=}1\ \{z{=}x{*}{*}(y-y)\ \&\ 0{\leq}y{\leq}y\}$

Because $\vdash y{\geq}0\ \&\ \mathrm{I}(x) \rightarrow 1{=}x{*}{*}(y-y)\ \&\ 0{\leq}y{\leq}y$ (and, obviously, $\vdash z{=}x{*}{*}(y-y)\ \&\ 0{\leq}y{\leq}y \rightarrow z{=}x{*}{*}(y-y)\ \&\ 0{\leq}y{\leq}y$), we have

(6) $\{y{\geq}0\ \&\ \mathrm{I}(x)\}\ z{:=}1\ \{z{=}x{*}{*}(y-y)\ \&\ 0{\leq}y{\leq}y\}$

by the Consequence Rule applied to (5). Hence, we have (2) by applying the Composition Rule to (4) ad (6). □

We worked ackwards in our proof of (2), deriving $q[y\backslash t]$, the precondition of (4) and then using $q[y\backslash t]$ as the postcondition of (5). Notice the similarity of the proof of (6) and the proof of (9), which follows shortly.

Proof of (3): By the Assignment Axiom we have

(7) $\{q[t-1\backslash t]\}\ t{:=}t-1\ \{q\}$
$\equiv \{z{=}x{*}{*}(y-(t-1))\ \&\ 0{\leq}t-1{\leq}y\}\ t{:=}t-1$
$\{z{=}x{*}{*}(y-t)\ \&\ 0{\leq}t{\leq}y\}$

and

(8) $\{q[t-1\backslash t][z{*}x\backslash z]\}\ z{:=}z{*}x\ \{q[t-1\backslash t]\}$
$\equiv \{z{*}x{=}x{*}{*}(y-(t-1))\ \&\ 0{\leq}t-1{\leq}y\}$
$z := z{*}x$
$\{z{=}x{*}{*}(y-(t-1))\ \&\ 0{\leq}t-1{\leq}y\}$

Due to the fact that

$$\vdash z{=}x{*}{*}(y-t)\ \&\ 0{\leq}t{\leq}y\ \&\ t{\geq}1 \rightarrow z{*}x{=}x{*}{*}(y-(t-1))\ \&\ 0{\leq}t-1{\leq}y$$

we have

(9) $\{q\&b\}\ z{:=}z{*}x\ \{q[t-1\backslash t]\}$
$\equiv \{z{=}x{*}{*}(y-t)\ \&\ 0{\leq}t{\leq}y\ \&\ t{\geq}1\}$
$z := z{*}x$
$\{z{=}x{*}{*}(y-(t-1))\ \&\ 0{\leq}t-1{\leq}y\}$

by the Consequence Rule applied to (8). Hence, we have

$$(10) \qquad \begin{aligned} &\{q\&b\}\ z{:=}z*x;\ t{:=}t-1\ \{q\} \\ \equiv\ &\{z=x**(y-t)\ \&\ 0\leqslant t\leqslant y\ \&\ t\geqslant 1\} \\ &\quad z{:=}z*x;\ t{:=}t-1 \\ &\{z=x**(y-t)\ \&\ 0\leqslant t\leqslant y\} \end{aligned}$$

by applying the Composition Rule to (7) and (9). Applying the **While** Rule to (10), we have

$$(11) \qquad \begin{aligned} &\{q\}S''\{q\&{\sim}b\} \\ \equiv\ &\{z=x**(y-t)\ \&\ 0\leqslant t\leqslant y\} \\ &\quad \textbf{while}\ t\geqslant 1\ \textbf{do begin}\ z{:=}z*x;\ t{:=}t-1\ \textbf{end} \\ &\{z=x**(y-t)\ \&\ 0\leqslant t\leqslant y\ \&\ {\sim}t\geqslant 1\} \end{aligned}$$

Because $\vdash z=x**(y-t)\ \&\ 0\leqslant t\leqslant y\ \&\ {\sim}t\geqslant 1 \rightarrow z=x**y$, we have (3) by applying the Consequence Rule to (11). □

The structure of (the program part of) our proof is depicted in the *proof tree* shown in Figure 1.3. In the proof tree, the leaf nodes are instances of the Assignment Axiom as indicated by the label A2, and, for example, the root node was derived from lines (2) and (3) by the Composition Rule as indicated by the label R3. To obtain a formal proof, we must work bottom-up through the proof tree—that is, from the leaf nodes up to the root node. Leaving aside formal proofs of theorems of arithmetic needed in applications of the

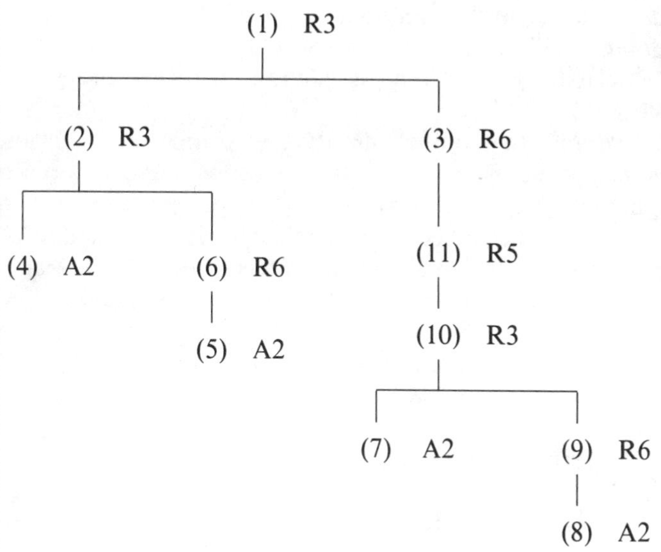

FIGURE 1.3. The proof tree for the asserted exponentiation program.

consequence rule, a completely formal proof of $\vdash AP$ might proceed in the following order:

(4), (5), (6), (2),
(7), (8), (9), (10), (11), (3),
(1)

This is obtained by performing a postorder traversal of the proof tree. The formal proof might be ordered in other ways. Basically, we have a partial order as depicted in the tree. A formal proof can be had by extending this partial order into a total order, for instance, by using the topological sort algorithm. However, some total orders are less comprehensible than others (consider the order (5), (8), (4), . . .). We have already noted that a useful heuristic is to work backward through a statement S composed of a sequence of assignment statements (or dummy statements, or conditional statements, or any combination of these) from the postcondition of S to its precondition.

Consider the second conjunct $0 \leq t \leq y$ in the loop invariant q. The condition that $0 \leq t$ is required so that the Consequence Rule can be applied to (11) to obtain (3); that is, $0 \leq t$ and $b \equiv \sim t \geq 1$ imply that $t=0$, and $t=0$ and $z=x**(y-t)$ imply that $z=x**y$. The condition that $t \leq y$ in the second conjunct of q is required so that the Consequence Rule can be applied to (8) to obtain (9). If we had $t>y$, then $z=x**(y-t)$ would not, in general, imply $z=x**(y-t+1)$. For example, supposing we could have $t>y$, consider the case when $x=5$, $y=1$, and $t=2$. To prevent errors from slipping into our proofs, as would occur had we left out any part of the second conjunct in the loop invariant q, we prefer to make information about the lower and upper bounds of a **for** statement control variable explicit in the loop invariant, even when closer consideration of the proof would reveal that one of the bounds is not essential to the proof. The most economical proof is not always the safest or the clearest.

When we apply the Consequence Rule, we claim that $\vdash p \rightarrow p'$ and $\vdash q' \rightarrow q$ in arithmetic. If they are not theorems, then either our program needs some work or our loop invariants are inadequate. As our policy of not carrying out formal proofs of these theorems bears some risk, we should be at least prepared to produce informal sketches of their proofs. In the relatively simple programs that we will consider, we are relatively (but not entirely!) safe in disregarding the possibility that a valid but unprovable assertion will be needed in an application of the Consequence Rule.

1.4. THE SOUNDNESS OF THE AXIOMATIZATION

The **While** Partial Correctness Soundness Theorem states that, in the Hoare Axiomatization presented in this chapter, we can prove correct an asserted program AP only if AP is valid—that is, if $\vdash AP$, then $\models AP$. In other words, the **While** Partial Correctness Soundness Theorem is a weak soundness theorem. As noted previously, soundness enables us to know that any asserted program we "prove correct" using the Hoare Axiomatization is, in fact, correct. In outline, the proof of (weak) soundness runs as follows. First, we give semantic arguments demonstrating that the Dummy and Assignment Axioms are valid. Next, we prove that each of the four rules of inference preserves validity. Finally, we establish proof of the **While** Partial Correctness Soundness Theorem by mathematical induction on the length of a proof. At the end of this section, we explain why we must have the prohibition, stated in the preceding section, forbidding the proof of an asserted program from a set of assumptions.

We say that a rule of inference

$$\frac{p_1, \ldots, p_m, AP_1, \ldots, AP_n}{AP}$$

is *validity-preserving* and write

$$\begin{array}{|c|}\hline p_1, \ldots, p_m, AP_1, \ldots, AP_n \\ \hline AP \\ \hline \end{array}$$

if $\models p_1, \ldots, \models p_m$ and $\models AP_1, \ldots, \models AP_n$ imply $\models AP$. Our definition of validity-preservation is equivalent to requiring the following sentence of higher-order logic to hold:

$$\forall\mathfrak{s}(\mathfrak{s}[p_1])\& \ldots \&\forall\mathfrak{s}(\mathfrak{s}[p_m])\&\forall\mathfrak{s}(\mathfrak{s}[AP_1])\& \ldots \&\forall\mathfrak{s}(\mathfrak{s}[AP_n]) \rightarrow \forall\mathfrak{s}(\mathfrak{s}[AP])$$

As briefly indicated in the preceding chapter, a rule of inference is said to be *truth-preserving* if

$$\models p_1\& \ldots \&p_m\&AP_1\& \ldots \&AP_n \rightarrow AP$$

or, equivalently phrased in higher-order logic

$$\forall\mathfrak{s}(\mathfrak{s}[p_1\& \ldots \&p_m\&AP_1\& \ldots \&AP_n \rightarrow AP])$$

Every rule of inference that is truth-preserving is also validity-preserving because the distribution law

$$\models\forall\mathfrak{s}(\mathfrak{s}[p\rightarrow q]) \rightarrow (\forall\mathfrak{s}(\mathfrak{s}[p])\rightarrow\forall\mathfrak{s}(\mathfrak{s}[q]))$$

holds in higher-order logic. For example, the rules of the natural deduction system of Chapter 0 are validity-preserving as well as truth-preserving. However, there are rules of inference that are validity-preserving but not truth-preserving because the converse of the distribution law does not hold. As a simple illustration, suppose that a rule of inference states that $x=1$ can be derived from $x=0$. Our rule is validity-preserving because

$$\models \forall \mathfrak{s}(\mathfrak{s}[x]=0) \rightarrow \forall \mathfrak{s}(\mathfrak{s}[x]=1)$$

and because the antecedent $\forall \mathfrak{s}(\mathfrak{s}[x]=0)$ is false. The rule is useless but harmless in the Hoare Axiomatization due to the fact that we can never establish the antecedent. However,

$$\models \forall \mathfrak{s}(\mathfrak{s}[x]=0 \rightarrow \mathfrak{s}[x]=1)$$

is false, and so our rule is not truth-preserving. If we added our rule to the natural deduction system of Chapter 0 (which permits proofs from a set of assumptions), we could derive the contradiction $x=0$ and $\sim x=0$ from the assumption $x=0$ using the axioms **(succ.$\geqslant$)**, **(succ.$\neq$)**, and **(D.1)**.

As indicated in the preceding chapter, the soundness of the Hoare Axiomatization hinges on the Soundness of Arithmetic Theorem. This is because, in the Consequence Rule, the theorems of arithmetic $p \rightarrow p'$ and $q' \rightarrow q$, as well as the Hoare theorem $\{p'\}S\{q'\}$ in the antecedent of the Rule, must be valid to insure that the Hoare theorem $\{p\}S\{q\}$ in the conclusion is also valid. Recall that the Soundness of Arithmetic Theorem is a strong soundness theorem, whereas the **While** Partial Correctness Soundness Theorem is of the weak variety.

DUMMY VALIDITY LEMMA: $\models \{p\}\mathbf{d}\{p\}$

Proof: Let $\mathfrak{s}$ be any state such that $\mathfrak{s}[p]=\mathrm{t}$. By the definition of validity, we must show that $\mathfrak{s}[\mathbf{d}][p]=\mathrm{t}$. Because $\mathfrak{s}[\mathbf{d}]=\mathfrak{s}$ by the operational semantics, we have $\mathfrak{s}[\mathbf{d}][p] = \mathfrak{s}[p] = \mathrm{t}$. □

ASSIGNMENT VALIDITY LEMMA: $\models \{p[e\backslash x]\}x{:=}e\{p\}$

Proof: Let $\mathfrak{s}$ be any state such that $\mathfrak{s}[p[e\backslash x]]=\mathrm{t}$. We must show that $\mathfrak{s}[x{:=}e][p]=\mathrm{t}$. We have $\mathfrak{s}[x{:=}e]=\mathfrak{s}\{\mathfrak{s}[e]\backslash x\}$ by the operational semantics, and, by the Coincidence Lemma, part (d), we have $\mathfrak{s}\{\mathfrak{s}[e]\backslash x\}[p]=\mathfrak{s}[p[e\backslash x]]$. Hence, $\mathfrak{s}[x{:=}e][p] = \mathfrak{s}\{\mathfrak{s}[e]\backslash x\}[p] = \mathfrak{s}[p[e\backslash x]] = \mathrm{t}$. □

COMPOSITION VALIDITY-PRESERVATION LEMMA

$$\frac{\{p\}S\{q\}, \quad \{q\}S'\{r\}}{\{\mathrm{p}\}S;S'\{r\}}$$

Proof: Suppose $\models\{p\}S\{q\}$ and $\models\{q\}S'\{r\}$. We must show that $\models\{p\}S;S'\{r\}$. Let $\mathcal{S}$ be any state such that $\mathcal{S}[p]=\mathrm{t}$ and $\mathcal{S}[S;S']$ is defined. Because $\mathcal{S}[S;S']$ is defined, so are $\mathcal{S}[S]$ and $\mathcal{S}[S][S']$. Let $\mathcal{S}'=\mathcal{S}[S]$ and $\mathcal{S}''=\mathcal{S}'[S']$. $\models\{p\}S\{q\}$, so we have $\mathcal{S}'[q]=\mathrm{t}$ by the assumption on $\mathcal{S}$. Similarly, we have $\mathcal{S}''[r]=\mathrm{t}$ because $\models\{q\}S'\{r\}$. So, for any state $\mathcal{S}$ such that $\mathcal{S}[p]=\mathrm{t}$ and $\mathcal{S}[S;S']$ is defined, $\mathcal{S}[S;S'][r]=\mathrm{t}$. Hence, $\models\{p\}S;S'\{r\}$. □

CONDITIONAL VALIDITY-PRESERVATION LEMMA

$$\frac{\{p\&b\}S\{q\},\quad \{p\&{\sim}b\}S'\{q\}}{\{p\}\ \textbf{if}\ b\ \textbf{then}\ S\ \textbf{else}\ S'\{q\}}$$

Proof: Suppose $\models\{p\&b\}S\{q\}$ and $\models\{p\&{\sim}b\}S'\{q\}$. We must show that $\models\{p\}$ **if** b **then** S **else** $S'\{q\}$. Due to the fact that $\models\{p\&b\}S\{q\}$, by the definition of validity, we have that, for any state $\mathcal{S}$, if $\mathcal{S}[p\&b]=\mathrm{t}$ and if $\mathcal{S}[S]$ is defined, then $\mathcal{S}[S][q]=\mathrm{t}$. Similarly, because $\models\{p\&{\sim}b\}S'\{q\}$, we have that, for any state $\mathcal{S}$, if $\mathcal{S}[p\&{\sim}b]=\mathrm{t}$ and if $\mathcal{S}[S']$ is defined, then $\mathcal{S}[S'][q]=\mathrm{t}$. Let $\mathcal{S}$ be any state such that $\mathcal{S}[p]=\mathrm{t}$ and $\mathcal{S}$[**if** b **then** S **else** S'] is defined. Suppose $\mathcal{S}[b]=\mathrm{t}$. Then $\mathcal{S}[p\&b]=\mathrm{t}$ because $\mathcal{S}[p]=\mathrm{t}$ and $\mathcal{S}[b]=\mathrm{t}$. Furthermore, by the operational semantics, $\mathcal{S}[S]$ is defined because $\mathcal{S}[b]=\mathrm{t}$ and $\mathcal{S}$[**if** b **then** S **else** S']$=\mathcal{S}[S]$ is defined. Hence, $\mathcal{S}[S][q]=\mathrm{t}$ by the assumption that $\models\{p\&b\}S\{q\}$. $\mathcal{S}$[**if** b **then** S **else** S']$=\mathcal{S}[S]$, so we have $\mathcal{S}$[**if** b **then** S **else** S']$[q]=\mathrm{t}$. On the other hand, suppose $\mathcal{S}[b]=\mathrm{f}$. Arguing much as before, we have $\mathcal{S}[S'][q]=\mathrm{t}$ and $\mathcal{S}$[**if** b **then** S **else** S'] $=\mathcal{S}[S']$. Hence, $\mathcal{S}$[**if** b **then** S **else** S']$[q]=\mathrm{t}$. So, in any state $\mathcal{S}$ such that $\mathcal{S}[p]=\mathrm{t}$ and $\mathcal{S}$[**if** b **then** S **else** S'] is defined, $\mathcal{S}$[**if** b **then** S **else** S']$[q]=\mathrm{t}$. Hence, $\models\{p\}$**if** b **then** S **else** $S'\{q\}$ by the definition of validity. □

WHILE VALIDITY-PRESERVATION LEMMA

$$\frac{\{p\&b\}S\{p\}}{\{p\}\textbf{while}\ b\ \textbf{do}\ S\{p\&{\sim}b\}}$$

Proof: Suppose $\models\{p\&b\}S\{p\}$. We must show $\models\{p\}$**while** b **do** $S\{p\&{\sim}b\}$. By the supposition and the definition of validity, we have

(!) for any state $\mathcal{S}$, if $\mathcal{S}[p\&b]=\mathrm{t}$ and $\mathcal{S}[S]$ is defined, then $\mathcal{S}[S][p]=\mathrm{t}$.

Let $\mathcal{S}$ be any state such that $\mathcal{S}[p]=\mathrm{t}$ and $\mathcal{S}$[**while** b **do** S] is defined. Also, let $\mathcal{S}*=\mathcal{S}$[**while** b **do** S]. To establish that $\mathcal{S}*[p\&{\sim}b]=\mathrm{t}$ and hence, that $\models\{p\}$**while** b **do** $S\{p\&{\sim}b\}$, we show that (1) $\mathcal{S}*[{\sim}b]=\mathrm{t}$, and (2) $\mathcal{S}*[p]=\mathrm{t}$. Recall that, by the operational semantics, there is a finite sequence of states $\langle\mathcal{S}_0, \ldots, \mathcal{S}_m\rangle$ ($m\geqslant 0$) such that $\mathcal{S}=\mathcal{S}_0$, $\mathcal{S}*=\mathcal{S}_m$, $\mathcal{S}_m[b]=\mathrm{f}$, and, for each i

such that $0 \leq i \leq m-1$, $\mathfrak{s}_i[b]=\mathrm{t}$ and $\mathfrak{s}_{i+1}=\mathfrak{s}_i[S]$. Hence, (1) $\mathfrak{s}^*[\sim b]=\mathrm{t}$ because $\mathfrak{s}^*=\mathfrak{s}_m$ and $\mathfrak{s}_m[b]=\mathrm{f}$. To establish (2), we prove below that (3) for each i such that $0 \leq i \leq m-1$, $\mathfrak{s}_i[p\&b]=\mathrm{t}$. From (3), it follows, in particular, that $\mathfrak{s}_{m-1}[p\&b]=\mathrm{t}$. Applying (!), we have $\mathfrak{s}_m[p]=\mathfrak{s}^*[p]=\mathrm{t}$. Hence, $\mathfrak{s}^*[p\&\sim b]=\mathrm{t}$.

The proof of (3) proceeds by induction on i. Suppose $0 \leq i \leq m-1$.

BASIS: $i=0$
Because $\mathfrak{s}_0=\mathfrak{s}$ and $\mathfrak{s}[p]=\mathrm{t}$, we have $\mathfrak{s}_0[p]=\mathrm{t}$. And, because $0 \leq i \leq m-1$, $\mathfrak{s}_0[b]=\mathrm{t}$ by the operational semantics. Hence, $\mathfrak{s}_0[p\&b]=\mathrm{t}$.

INDUCTION STEP: $i \geq 1$
By the IH, $\mathfrak{s}_{i-1}[p\&b]=\mathrm{t}$. Since $1 \leq i \leq m-1$, we have that $\mathfrak{s}_i=\mathfrak{s}_{i-1}[S]$ is defined by the operational semantics and the definition of $\mathfrak{s}_i$. Hence, by (!), we have $\mathfrak{s}_i[p]=\mathrm{t}$ because $\mathfrak{s}_{i-1}[p\&b]=\mathrm{t}$ and $\mathfrak{s}_i$ is defined. Because $1 \leq i \leq m-1$, $\mathfrak{s}_i[b]=\mathrm{t}$ by the operational semantics. Hence, $\mathfrak{s}_i[p\&b]=\mathrm{t}$. □

CONSEQUENCE VALIDITY-PRESERVATION LEMMA

$p \rightarrow p', \quad \{p'\}S\{q'\}, \quad q' \rightarrow q$
$\{p\}S\{q\}$

Proof: Suppose $\models p \rightarrow p'$, $\models \{p'\}S\{q'\}$, and $\models q' \rightarrow q$. Let $\mathfrak{s}$ be any state such that $\mathfrak{s}[p]=\mathrm{t}$ and $\mathfrak{s}[S]$ is defined. Since $\mathfrak{s}[p]=\mathrm{t}$, we have $\mathfrak{s}[p']=\mathrm{t}$ by the definition of validity because $\models p \rightarrow p'$. Consequently, for any state $\mathfrak{s}$, $\mathfrak{s}[p \rightarrow p']=\mathrm{t}$. Since $\mathfrak{s}[p']=\mathrm{t}$ and $\mathfrak{s}[S]$ is defined, we have $\mathfrak{s}[S][q']=\mathrm{t}$ because $\models \{p'\}S\{q'\}$. Hence, $\mathfrak{s}[S][q]=\mathrm{t}$ because $\mathfrak{s}[S][q']=\mathrm{t}$ and $\models q' \rightarrow q$. So, for any state $\mathfrak{s}$ such that $\mathfrak{s}[p]=\mathrm{t}$ and $\mathfrak{s}[S]$ is defined, $\mathfrak{s}[S][q]=\mathrm{t}$. Hence, $\models \{p\}S\{q\}$ by the definition of validity. □

WHILE PARTIAL CORRECTNESS SOUNDNESS THEOREM

If $\vdash AP$, then $\models AP$

Proof: Suppose $\vdash \{p\}S\{q\}$. Then, by the definition of a proof, there is a finite sequence $\langle a_1, \ldots, a_n \rangle$ $(n \geq 1)$ of assertions and asserted programs such that $a_n \equiv \{p\}\ S\ \{q\}$, and each $a_i\,(1 \leq i \leq n)$ is (1) a theorem of arithmetic, or (2) one of the two Hoare Axioms, or (3) derived from one or more preceding lines by one of the four Hoare Rules of Inference. By mathematical induction on i, we show that $\models a_i$ for each i such that $1 \leq i \leq n$. Because $\models a_n$ and $a_n \equiv \{p\}S\{q\}$, we have $\models \{p\}S\{q\}$. Hence, $\models \{p\}S\{q\}$ if $\vdash \{p\}S\{q\}$.

BASIS: $i=1$
Since a_1 is the first line in the proof, a_1 is either (1) a theorem of arithmetic, or

(2) one of the two Hoare Axioms. If (1), and so $a_1 \equiv p$, then $\models p$ by the Soundness of Arithmetic Theorem. If (2) and $a_1 \equiv \{p\}\mathbf{d}\{p\}$, then $\models \{p\}\mathbf{d}\{p\}$ by the Dummy Validity Lemma. If (2) and $a_1 \equiv \{p[e \backslash x]\}x:=e\{p\}$, then $\models \{p[e \backslash x]\}x:=e\{p\}$ by the Assignment Validity Lemma.

INDUCTION STEP: $i \geqslant 2$

If a_i is either (1) a theorem of arithmetic, or (2) a Hoare Axiom, the proof is as in the basis. There remains the case (3), however, when $a_i \equiv \{p_i\}S_i\{q_i\}$ was derived from one or more preceding lines by one of the four Hoare Rules of Inference. Suppose a_i was derived from a_j and a_k ($1 \leqslant j < i$, $1 \leqslant k < i$) by the Composition Rule. Then, for instance, $S_i \equiv S_j;S_k$, $a_j \equiv \{p_i\}S_j\{p_k\}$, and $a_k \equiv \{p_k\}S_k\{q_i\}$. Because $1 \leqslant j < i$ and $1 \leqslant k < i$, we have $\models \{p_i\}S_j\{p_k\}$ and $\models \{p_k\}S_k\{q_i\}$ by the IH. Hence, by the Composition Validity Preservation Lemma, we have $\models \{p_i\}S_i\{q_i\}$. The cases when a_i was derived by one of the other three Hoare Rules of Inference are similar. □

The Hoare Axiomatization provides more examples of rules of inference that are validity-preserving but are not truth-preserving. Consider, for example, the Composition Rule. We exhibit a counterexample to the conjecture that the Composition Rule is truth-preserving. Suppose $\mathfrak{s}[x]=0$. Then, by the definition of truth for asserted programs, $\mathfrak{s}[\{x=0\}x:=1\{x=1\}] = \mathfrak{s}[\{x=1\}x:=0\{x=1\}] = \mathfrak{t}$, but $\mathfrak{s}[\{x=0\}x:=1;x:=0\{x=1\}] = \mathfrak{f}$. Hence, the Composition Rule is not truth-preserving. This counterexample reveals one of the reasons behind the prohibition stated in the preceding section forbidding proofs of asserted programs from a set of assumptions.

Failure to appreciate the distinction between truth-preservation and validity-preservation leads to unsound axiomatizations. Moreover, when a programming language (e.g., EUCLID) has been "defined" in terms of a Hoare-style axiomatization, unsoundness undermines the *entire* definitional foundation of the language.

1.5. SOME SAMPLE PROOFS

EXAMPLE 1

The following program computes $z = x**y$, much as the program illustrated in Section 1.3, except that we use a **for-to** instead of a **for-downto** construction. The modifications to the program and the proof are minor: The structure of the proof is the same as depicted in Figure 1.3, and the lines in the proof are numbered in a similar manner. We seek to prove correct the following asserted exponentiation program:

(1) $\{p\}S\{r\} \equiv$

$\{y \geqslant 0 \ \& \ \mathrm{I}(x)\}$

$z:=1;$

$$\{\,q\,\}$$
for t:=1 **to** y **do**
z:=z*x
$\{z=x**y\}$

The reader might try to discover a suitable loop invariant q. We provide some hints in this paragraph and the next. Much as in our previous example, we can take

$b \equiv t \leq y$
$p \equiv y \geq 0$ & I(x)
$q \equiv$ ________________________________
$r \equiv z=x**y$,

and

$S \equiv S';S''$

where

$S' \equiv z$:=1; t:=1
$S'' \equiv$ **while** $t \leq y$ **do begin** z:=$z*x$; t:=t+1 **end**

As before, the proof of (1) is broken into two parts. We derive (1) by applying the Composition Rule to

(2) $\{p\}S'\{q\}$

and

(3) $\{q\}S''\{r\}$

Proofs of (2) and (3) continue as in section 1.3.

Unfortunately, no general algorithm is known for finding a suitable and simple loop invariant. At best, we can only offer some rules of thumb. To find a suitable loop invariant q, the first step is to initialize q to a boolean expression $bounds(t, y)$ giving the lower and upper bounds of the control variable t. Your $bounds(t, y)$ and $\sim b \equiv \sim(t \leq y)$ should imply that the control variable t has reached its final value $t=y+1$. The second step is to add one or more additional conjuncts to q that appear to be true each time control reaches the beginning of the loop, and such that $\vdash q \& \sim b \rightarrow r$ so that line (3) can be derived from line

(11) $\{q\}\ S''\{q \& \sim b\}$

by the Consequence Rule. The third step is to check and see if your q does, in fact, hold the first time control reaches the beginning of the **while** loop by making sure that line

(6) $$\{p\}z{:=}1\{q[1\backslash t]\}$$

can be derived from line

(5) $$\{q[1\backslash t][1\backslash z]\}z{:=}1\{q[1\backslash t]\}$$

by an application of the Consequence Rule. If q does not hold, return to the second step, trying a weaker conjunct or conjuncts (in addition to the conjunct *bounds*(t, y)). If q does hold the first time control reaches the beginning of the **while** loop, you can proceed with the next step. The fourth step is to check and see if the loop body preserves q by making sure that line

(9) $$\{q\&b\}z{:=}z*x\{q[t+1\backslash t]\}$$

can be derived from line

(8) $$\{q[t+1\backslash t][z*x\backslash z]\}z{:=}z*x\{q[t+1\backslash t]\}$$

by an application of the Consequence Rule. If q is not preserved, return to the second step, If q is preserved, you are ready to fill in the details of the proof, which are left as an exercise.

Before reading on, try to find a suitable loop invariant q. If you are stumped, we provide a suitable q at the end of this chapter.

EXAMPLE 2

The following (asserted) **while** program computes the quotient $q = x/y$ and the remainder $r = x \bmod y$ using the method of successive subtractions. Its proof can have the same structure and same number of lines as in our preceding examples. Again, the reader might wish to discover a suitable loop invariant p' before looking ahead to the end of this chapter.

```
{x≥0 & y≥1}
q:=0;
r:=x;
{ p' }
while r≥y do
      begin q:=q+1;
            r:=r−y
      end
{q = x/y & r = x mod y}
```

This program is not a **for** program because, in the loop body, the integer variable r is not decremented by the constant one, but rather r is decremented by the integer variable y. If the incrementation parameter (decrement) in a **for-downto** statement could be any integer expression e'', with the abstract syntax

$$\textbf{for } x{:=}e \textbf{ downto } e' \textbf{ by } e'' \textbf{ do } S$$

and the additional prohibition forbidding assignments to any $y \in \mathfrak{ivar}[e'']$, then nontermination would occur in a state $\mathfrak{s}$ if $\mathfrak{s}[e] \geq \mathfrak{s}[e']$ and $\mathfrak{s}[e''] \leq 0$.[7] If an integer variable $x \in \mathfrak{ivar}[e'']$, then nontermination is not detectable at compile time, and the partial correctness of such **for** programs does not imply their total correctness. For these reasons, we prefer **for** programs without an incrementation parameter, as in Pascal.

Informally previewing the total correctness axiomatization, which we will present in Chapter 4, we will establish total correctness by showing termination (in addition to the above). That is, we shall prove termination by showing that, if the precondition p holds, then r never becomes negative and decreases after each iteration of the body of the **while** statement.

EXAMPLE 3

The binary operation symbols min and max can be introduced into the theory of integers with the explicit definition

(D.min) $\min(X,Y){=}Z \leftrightarrow (X{<}Y \rightarrow Z{=}X) \& (X{\geq}Y {\rightarrow} Z{=}Y)$

and the equational definition

(D.max) $\max(X,Y) = X{+}Y{-}\min(X,Y)$

The following program determines the smallest s of three integer variables x, y, and z. In the postcondition, we have abbreviated $\min(\min(X,Y),Z)$ as $\min(X,Y,Z)$.

(1)

```
{I(x)&I(y)&I(z)}
if x<y then
        s:=x
else
        s:=y;
if z<s then
        s:=z
{s=min(x, y, z)}
```

[7] Essentially this situation arises in FORTRAN 77 when the incrementation parameter of e'' of a **Do** statement evaluates to zero.

As in the preceding examples, we work backwards in our proof from the postcondition to the precondition. By the Assignment Axiom, we have

(2) $\{z=\min(x,y,z)\}\ s:=z\ \{s=\min(x,y,z)\}$

and, by the Dummy Axiom, we have

(3) $\{s=\min(x,y,z)\}$ **d** $\{s=\min(x,y,z)\}$

Because $\vdash s=\min(x,y)\&z<s \rightarrow z=\min(x,y,z)$
and $\vdash s=\min(x,y)\&{\sim}z<s \rightarrow s=\min(x,y,z)$

we can apply the Consequence Rule to (2) and (3) to obtain

(4) $\{s=\min(x,y)\&z<s\} s:=z\ \{s=\min(x,y,z)\}$

and

(5) $\{s=\min(x,y)\&{\sim}z<s\}$ **d** $\{s=\min(x,y,z)\}$

Applying the Conditional Rule to (4) and (5), we obtain

(6) $\{s=\min(x,y)\}$ **if** $z<s$ **then** $s:=z$ **else d** $\{s=\min(x,y,z)\}$

By the Assignment Axiom, we have

(7) $\{x=\min(x,y)\}\ s:=x\ \{s=\min(x,y)\}$

and

(8) $\{y=\min(x,y)\}\ s:=y\ \{s=\min(x,y)\}$

Because $\vdash I(x)\&I(y)\&I(z)\&x<y \rightarrow x=\min(x,y)$
and $\vdash I(x)\&I(y)\&I(z)\&{\sim}x<y \rightarrow y=\min(x,y)$

we can apply the Consequence Rules to (7) and (8) to obtain

(9) $\{I(x)\&I(y)\&I(z)\&x<y\}\ s:=x\ \{s=\min(x,y)\}$

and

(10) $\{I(x)\&I(y)\&I(z)\&{\sim}x<y\}\ s:=y\ \{s=\min(x,y)\}$

Applying the Conditional Rule to (9) and (10), we obtain

(11) $\{I(x)\&I(y)\&I(z)\}$ **if** $x<y$ **then** $s:=x$ **else** $s:=y$ $\{s=\min(x,y)\}$

Applying the Composition Rule to (6) and (11), we have (1).

Note that, instead of using the "intermediate assertion" $s=\min(x,y)$ in lines (6) to (10), we could have used the more complicated $p \equiv (z<x \rightarrow z=\min(x,y,z))$ & $(\sim z<x \rightarrow s=\min(x,y,z))$. As we will see in Chapter 6, for "straight line" programs (those without loops) we can construct mechanically (in not *too* unreasonable a manner) intermediate assertions such as our rather complicated p.

EXAMPLE 4

The following **for** program computes $x**y$ using only the unary operations '$-$' and 'abs' and the binary operation '$+$'. The program contains two **for** statements, one nested inside the other. The inner **for** statement computes $prod=z*\text{abs}(x)$. The precondition is $p \equiv y\geqslant 0 \& I(x)$, and the postcondition is $r \equiv z=x**y$.

```
(1)     {p}S{r} ≡
        {y≥0&I(x)}
        z:=1;
        {z=x**(y−t1) & 0≤t1≤y}
        for t1:=y downto 1 do
            begin
            prod:=0;
            {z=x**(y−t1) & prod=z*(abs(x)−t2) & 1≤t1≤y &
              0≤t2≤abs(x)}
            for t2:=abs(x) downto 1 do
                prod:=prod+z
            if x≥0 then
                z:=prod
            else
                z:=−prod
            end
        {z=x**y}
                ≡
        {y≥0&I(x)}
        z:=1;
        t1:=y;
        {z=x**(y−t1) & 0≤t1≤y}
        while t1≥1 do
            begin
            prod:=0;
            t2:=abs(x);
            {z=x**(y−t1) & prod=z*(abs(x)−t2) & 1≤t1≤y &
              0≤t2≤abs(x)}
            while t2≥1 do
                begin
                prod:=prod+z;
```

```
                t2:=t2-1
                end;
            if x>=0 then
                z:=prod
            else
                z:=-prod;
            t1:=t1-1
            end
        {z=x**y}
```

Let $b1 \equiv t1 \geqslant 1$

$b2 \equiv t2 = 1$

$q1 \equiv z = x**(y-t1)\ \&\ 0 \leqslant t1 \leqslant y$

$q2 \equiv z = x**(y-t1)\ \&\ prod = z*(\text{abs}(x)-t2)\ \&\ 1 \leqslant t1 \leqslant y\ \&$
$0 \leqslant t2 \leqslant \text{abs}(x)$

$S' \equiv z:=1;\ t:=y$

$S2 \equiv$ *prod*:=0; *t*2:=abs(*x*); **while** *b*2 **do begin** . . . ; *t*2:=*t*2−1;
if *x*≥0 . . . ; *t*1:=*t*1−1

$S1 \equiv$ **while** *b*1 **do begin** *S*2 **end**

and

$$S \equiv S';S1$$

Much as in the example in section 1.3, the proof of (1) is obtained by applying the Composition Rule to

(2) $$\{p\}S'\{q1\}$$

and

(3) $$\{q1\}S1\{r\}$$

The proof of (2) is exactly as in section 1.3. To prove (3), it suffices to prove

(4) $$\{q1\&b1\}S2\{q1\}$$

and apply the **While** and Consequence Rules. The proof of (4) involves demonstrating

(5) $$\{q2\&b2\}prod:=prod+z;t2:=t2-1\{q2\}$$

and then applying the **While** Rule. Next, the Assignment Axiom together with the Composition, Conditional, and Consequence Rules are applied to obtain (4) from (5). In applying the Consequence Rule, we can make use of the following theorems of arithmetic:

$$\vdash q1 \& b1 \rightarrow q2[\text{abs}(x)\backslash t2][0\backslash prod]$$
$$\vdash q2 \& {\sim} b2 \& x \geqslant 0 \rightarrow prod = z * x$$

and

$$\vdash q2 \& {\sim} b2 \& {\sim} x \geqslant 0 \rightarrow -prod = z * x$$

The details are left as an exercise.

EXAMPLE 5

The following **while** program computes the greatest common divisor (gcd) of two positive odd integers x and y. The binary operation symbol 'gcd' is introduced into the theory of integers with the explicit definition

(D.gcd)

$$\begin{aligned}\text{gcd}(X,Y)=Z \leftrightarrow\ & (X=0 \ \&\ Y=0 \rightarrow Z=0)\ \&\\ & (X=0 \ \&\ Y\neq 0 \rightarrow Z=Y)\ \&\\ & (X\neq 0 \ \&\ Y=0 \rightarrow Z=X)\ \&\\ & (X\neq 0 \& Y\neq 0 \rightarrow\\ & \quad (\\ & \quad (X \bmod Z)=0 \ \&\ (Y \bmod Z)=0 \ \&\\ & \quad \forall Z'((X \bmod Z')=0 \ \&\ (Y \bmod Z')=0 \rightarrow Z'\leqslant Z)\\ & \quad))\end{aligned}$$

and the 4-ary predicate symbol 'g' with the explicit definition

(D.g) $\text{g}(X,Y,T1,T2) \leftrightarrow 1\leqslant T1 \leqslant X \ \&\ 1 \leqslant T2 \leqslant Y \ \&\ \text{gcd}(X,Y)=\text{gcd}(T1,T2)$

$\text{g}(X,Y,T1,T2)$ has the intended reading "the positive integers $T1$ and $T2$ have the same greatest common divisor as do X and Y". In our proof, we make use of the following laws of the greatest common divisor:

$$\vdash X=\text{gcd}(X,X)$$
$$\vdash \text{gcd}(X,Y)=\text{gcd}(Y,X)$$

and

$$\vdash 1 \leqslant X < Y \rightarrow \text{gcd}(X,Y)=\text{gcd}(X,Y-X)$$

```
{1≤x) & 1≤y}
t1:=x;
t2:=y;
{g(x,y,t1,t2)}
```

```
while t1≠t2 do
   begin
      {g(x,y,t1,t2)}
      while t1>t2 do t1:=t1−t2;
      {g(x,y,t1,t2)}
      while t2>t1 do t2:=t2−t1
   end
{t1=gcd(x,y)}
```

The proof of the full program follows readily from a proof of

(1)
```
{g(x,y,t1,t2)}
while t1≠t2 do
   begin
      {g(x,y,t1,t2)}
      while t1>t2 do t1:=t1−t2;
      {g(x,y,t1,t2)}
      while t2>t1 do t2:=t2−t1
   end
{g(x,y,t1,t2) & ~t1≠t2}
```

We now sketch the proof of (1). By the Assignment Axiom, we have

(2)
```
{g(x,y,t1−t2,t2)}
t1:=t1−t2
{g(x,y,t1,t2)}
```

Because $\vdash g(x,y,t1,t2) \ \& \ t1>t2 \rightarrow g(x,y,t1-t2,t2)$, we have

(3)
```
{g(x,y,t1,t2)}
while t1>t2 do t1:=t1−t2
{g(x,y,t1,t2) & ~t1>t2}
```

by the Consequence and **While** Rules applied to (2). Applying the Consequence Rule again, we have from (3)

(4)
```
{g(x,y,t1,t2) & t1≠t2}
while t1>t2 do t1:=t1−t2
{g(x,y,t1,t2)}
```

because $\vdash g(x,y,t1,t2) \ \& \ t1\neq t2 \rightarrow g(x,y,t1,t2)$

and

$$\vdash g(x,y,t1,t2) \ \& \ \sim t1>t2 \rightarrow g(x,y,t1,t2)$$

Similarly, we have from the Assignment Axiom

(5)
$$\{g(x,y,t1,t2-t1)\}$$
$$t2{:=}t2-t1$$
$$\{g(x,y,t1,t2)\}$$

Because $\vdash g(x,y,t1,t2)\ \&\ t2>t1 \rightarrow g(x,y,t1,t2-t1)$, we have

(6)
$$\{g(x,y,t1,t2)\}$$
$$\textbf{while}\ t2>t1\ \textbf{do}\ t2{:=}t2-t1$$
$$\{g(x,y,t1,t2)\ \&\ {\sim}t2>t1\}$$

by the Consequence and **While** Rules applied to (5). Applying the consequence Rule again, we have

(7)
$$\{g(x,y,t1,t2)\}$$
$$\textbf{while}\ t2>t1\ \textbf{do}\ t2{:=}t2-t1$$
$$\{g(x,y,t1,t2)\}$$

Applying the Composition Rule to (4) and (7), we have

(8)
$$\{g(x,y,t1,t2)\ \&\ t1\neq t2\}$$
$$\textbf{while}\ t1>t2\ \textbf{do}\ t1{:=}t1-t2$$
$$\textbf{while}\ t2>t1\ \textbf{do}\ t2{:=}t2-t1$$
$$\{g(x,y,t1,t2)\}$$

Hence, we have (1) by the **While** Rule applied to (8).

EXERCISES

Proving Programs Correct

1. (a) Write a **for** program to compute $x-y$ using only the unary operation symbols 'succ' and 'pred'. (Neither the unary nor the binary operation symbol '$-$' should occur in your program). The precondition is $p\equiv x\geq 0\ \&\ y\geq 0$ and the postcondition is $r\equiv z=x-y$.

(b) Using the Hoare Axiomatization, prove that your asserted program is totally correct.

2. (a) Write a **for** program to compute $x*y$ using the method of successive additions (The operation symbol '*' should not occur in your program). The precondition is $p\equiv I(x)\ \&\ I(y)$ and the postcondition is $r\equiv z=x*y$.

(b) Using the Hoare Axiomatization, prove that your asserted program is totally correct.

3. (a) Write a straight-line program to determine which integer variable, x or y, has the greatest absolute value. Do not use the 'abs' operation symbol (or the binary operation symbols 'min' and 'max') in your program. The precondition is $p \equiv \mathrm{I}(x)\&\mathrm{I}(y)$ and the postcondition is $r \equiv z=\max(\mathrm{abs}(x),\mathrm{abs}(y))$.

   (b) Using the Hoare Axiomatization, prove that your program is totally correct.

4. (a) Write a **for** program to compute $x+y$ using only the unary operation symbols 'abs', 'pred' and 'succ'. Make your program efficient by using the smaller of abs(x) and abs(y) as the final expression in your **for** statement. The precondition is $p \equiv \mathrm{I}(x)\ \&\ \mathrm{I}(y)$ and the postcondition is $r \equiv z=x+y$.

   (b) Using the Hoare Axiomatization, prove that your asserted program is totally correct.

5. (a) Write a **for** program to compute $x*y$ using only the operation symbols 'pred' and 'succ'. The precondition is $p \equiv x \geqslant 0\ \&\ y \geqslant 0$ and the postcondition is $r \equiv z=x*y$.

   (b) Using the Hoare Axiomatization, prove that your asserted program is totally correct.

6. (a) Write a **while** program to compute x/y using only the operation symbols 'abs', 'pred', and 'succ'. The precondition is $p \equiv \mathrm{I}(x)\ \&\ \mathrm{I}(y)$ and the postcondition is $r \equiv z=x/y$.

   (b) Using the Hoare Axiomatization, prove that your asserted program is partially correct.

7. (a) Write a **for** program to compute $x**y$ using only the operation symbols 'abs', 'pred', and 'succ'. The precondition is $p \equiv x \geqslant 0\ \&\ y \geqslant 0$ and the postcondition is $r \equiv z=x**y$.

   (b) Using the Hoare Axiomatization, prove that your asserted program is totally correct.

8. (a) Write a **while** program to determine whether or not an integer x is prime. The precondition is $p \equiv \mathrm{I}(x)$ and the postcondition is $r \equiv$

$$(\mathrm{prime}(x) \rightarrow xprime=1)\ \&\ (\sim\mathrm{prime}(x) \rightarrow xprime=0)$$

   (b) Using the Hoare Axiomatization, prove that your asserted program is partially correct.

9. (a) Write a **while** program to find the n-th prime number. Let nthprime(X) = X-th prime number. (No simple equational or even explicit definition of the unary operation symbol 'nthprime' is known.) The precondition is $p \equiv n \geqslant 1$ and the postcondition is $r \equiv nthprimen=\mathrm{nthprime}(n)$.

   (b) Using the Hoare Axiomatization, prove that your asserted program is partially correct.

10. (a) Write a **while** program to determine whether or not an integer x is a

perfect number. Let perfect (X) hold provided X is a perfect number. (A perfect number is a positive integer X such that X is the sum of the positive integers less than X that divide X without remainder. For example, 6 (=1+2+3) and 28 (=1+2+4+7+14) are perfect numbers. No simple explicit definition of the unary predicate perfect(X) is known.) The precondition is $p \equiv x \geqslant 1$ and the postcondition is $r \equiv$

$$(\text{perfect}(x) \rightarrow xperfect{=}1) \ \&\ ((\sim\text{perfect}(x) \rightarrow xperfect{=}0)$$

(b) Using the Hoare Axiomatization, prove that your asserted program is partially correct.

11. The following **while** program computes gcd(x,y). Using the Hoare Axiomatization, prove that this program is partially correct wrt the precondition $x \geqslant 1 \& y \geqslant 1$ and the postcondition $t1=\text{gcd}(x,y)$. Begin by finding a suitable loop invariant q.

```
{x≥1&y≥1}
t1:=x;
t2:=y;
{q}
while t1≠t2 do
     if t1>t2 then t1:=t1−t2 else t2:=t2−t1
{t1=gcd(x,y)}
```

12. The following **while** program computes gcd(x,y). Using the Hoare Axiomatization, prove that this program is partially correct wrt the precondition I(x)&I(y) and the postcondition $g=\text{gcd}(x,y)$. Begin by finding a suitable loop invariant q. In your proof, you can make use of the following law of the greatest common divisor:

$$\vdash 1 \leqslant X \leqslant Y \rightarrow \text{gcd}(X,Y)=\text{gcd}(Y \bmod X, X)$$

```
{I(x)&I(y)}
if abs(x)>abs(y) then
     begin
     g:=abs(x);
     s:=abs(y)
     end
else
     begin
     g:=abs(y);
     s:=abs(x)
     end;
{q}
while s≠0 do
     begin
```

```
        t:=s;
        s:=g mod s;
        g:=t
        end
    {g=gcd(x,y)}
```

13. The following **while** program computes sqrt(x), the integer square root of x. The unary operation symbol 'sqrt' can be introduced into arithmetic with the following explicit definition:

(D.sqrt) $\text{sqrt}(X) = Y \leftrightarrow (X<0 \rightarrow Y=0)\ \&$
$(X \geqslant 0 \rightarrow Y{*}{*}2 \leqslant X \,\&\, \forall Z(Z{*}{*}2 \leqslant X \rightarrow Z \leqslant Y))$

Using the Hoare Axiomatization, prove that this program is partially correct wrt the precondition I(x) and the postcondition $sqrtx$=sqrt(x). Begin by finding a suitable loop invariant q.

```
{I(x)}
sqrtx:=0;
sum:=1;
nextodd:=1;
{q}
while sum≤x do
    begin
    sqrtx:=sqrtx+1;
    nextodd:=nextodd+2;
    sum:=sum+nextodd
    end
{sqrtx=sqrt(x)}
```

14. The following **while** program computes $x{*}{*}y$. Using the Hoare Axiomatization, prove that this program is partially correct wrt the precondition I(x)&I(y) and the postcondition $z=x{*}{*}y$. Begin by finding a suitable loop invariant q.

```
{I(x)&I(y)}
if y<0 then
    z:=0
else
    begin
    t1:=x;
    t2:=y;
    z:=1;
    {q}
    while t2≠0 do
        begin
```

```
            if t2 mod 2 = 1 then
                begin
                t2:=t2-1;
                z:=z*t1
                end;
            t1:=t1*t1;
            t2:=t2/2
            end
    end
{z=x**y}
```

Semantics

15. Give the operational semantics of the **if-then** statement by adding a clause for it to the operational semantics of Section 1.2. Your definition should be direct. That is, do not use the conditional **(if-then-else)** or dummy statements in your definition.
16. Give the operational semantics of the **for-to** statement. Your definition should be direct. That is, do not use the **while** statement in your definition.
17. Give the operational semantics of the **repeat-until** statement. Your definition should be direct. That is, do not use the **while** statement in your definition. (The **repeat-until** statement can be defined in terms of the **while** statement as follows: **repeat** S **until** $b \equiv S$; **while** $\sim b$ **do** S.)
18. (a) State a useful proof rule for the **if-then** statement. Prove that your rule is validity-preserving.

    (b) Is your rule of part (a) truth-preserving? If so, prove that it is. If not, exhibit a counterexample.
19. (a) State a useful proof rule for the **for-to** statement. Prove that your rule is validity-preserving.

    (b) Is your rule of part (a) truth-preserving? If so, prove that it is. If not, exhibit a counterexample.
20. (a) State a useful proof rule for the **repeat-until** statement. Prove that your rule is validity-preserving.

    (b) Is your rule of part (a) truth-preserving? If so, prove that it is. If not, exhibit a counterexample.
21. (a) Is the Conditional Rule truth-preserving? If it is, prove that it is. If it is not, exhibit a counterexample.

    (b) Is the **While** Rule truth-preserving? If so, prove that it is. If not, exhibit a counterexample.

    (c) Is the Consequence Rule truth-preserving? If it is, prove that it is. If it is not, exhibit a counterexample.
22. Prove that the following rules of inference are validity-preserving:

(a) Incremental Proof Rule

$$\frac{\{p\}S\{q\},\{p\}S\{q'\}}{\{p\}S\{q\&q'\}}$$

(b) Proof by Cases Rule

$$\frac{\{p\}S\{q\},\{p'\}S\{q\}}{\{p \vee p'\}S\{q\}}$$

Programming Projects

23. In your favorite programming language, write an interpreter for the **while** programs. The input to your program consists of a **while** program and integers to be stored in the input variables. Your output should show a trace of program execution as illustrated in Section 1.2.
24. In your favorite programming language, write a proof-checker for the Hoare Axiomatization. The input file contains an alleged formal proof, including assertions as well as asserted programs. Your output should indicate whether the programming part of the alleged proof is legitimate, and, if it is not, it should display the first line in error and an indication of what the error is. In this exercise, you are not required to check the assertions to see if they are, in fact, theorems of arithmetic.

Suitable Loop Invariants (Section 1.5):

Example 1

$$q \equiv z=x**(t-1) \ \& \ bounds(t,y)$$

where

$$bounds(t,y) \equiv 1 \leqslant t \leqslant y+1$$

The condition $1 \leqslant t$ is essential.

Example 2

$$p' \equiv x=y*q+r \ \& \ bounds(r,x,y) \ \& \ y \geqslant 1$$

where

$$bounds(r,x,y) \equiv 0 \leqslant r \leqslant x$$

Is the condition $y \geqslant 1$ essential?

CHAPTER 2

The Total Correctness of Flowchart Programs

Flowchart programs (or *flowcharts*) can be unstructured in that, when they are written in an undisciplined manner, they appear to be a spaghetti-like tangle of lines and boxes. It is convenient to identify flowchart programs with programs written in a BASIC-like syntax because we can deal with one-dimensional programs (a string of symbols) instead of the two-dimensional objects that are frequently used to represent flowchart programs. Our BASIC-like *FC programs* are so named because they share many of the features of flowchart programs. In particular, the **goto** command in FC programs is the counterpart of a line with an arrow in a flowchart, and undisciplined use of the **goto** leads to the same conceptual tangles frequently found in flowcharts.

In Sections 2.1 and 2.2, we present the syntax and operational semantics of FC programs. To simplify the semantics and conventions presented in the following sections, we will impose restrictions on the syntax of FC programs that are not found in any other dialect of BASIC. By a *structured FC program,* we mean an FC program obtained by translating a **while** program as taught in introductory texts on structured programming in assembly language, BASIC, or FORTRAN.[1] To simplify the explanation of how the proof techniques introduced in this chapter work, we will consider primarily structured FC programs in our examples.

Robert Floyd's method for proving program termination is the principal new proof technique introduced in this chapter. In Section 2.3, we present Floyd's method for proving partial correctness as well as his method for proving termination. Then, we incorporate the two methods into a single method for proving the total correctness of a program with respect to its specification. In Section 2.4, we show that Floyd's methods are sound with respect to the operational semantics developed in Section 2.2.

The programs and proofs presented in Section 2.5 are relatively short. We will postpone longer illustrative proofs regarding, for example, sort programs until we introduce arrays in Chapter 3.

2.1. SYNTAX

The syntax of integer expressions, assertions, and boolean expressions is the same as in Chapter 1, and specifications and input and output variables are also to be understood as before. The set of *FC programs* is **Prog** with typical members *P*, ... An FC program is a finite sequence of *commands.* A command is either a **start,** a **stop,** an **assert,** an *assignment,* an *unconditional* **goto,** or a *conditional* **goto** command. The *intermediate commands* **(Icom)** are the commands that can occur more than once in a program (all commands other than the start and stop commands), and the *command sequences* **(Cseq)** are sequences of intermediate commands. Each **start, stop,** or **assert** command contains an assertion. Each **assert** command can also contain a *k*-tuple of integer expressions $\langle e_1, \ldots, e_k \rangle (k \geq 1)$ to be known as a *Floydian expression.* As we will explain in Section 2.3, the Floydian expressions are used to prove termination. Letting ⓔ be the empty sequence, we have the abstract syntax

```
Prog:        P, . . .
          P ::= 1   Start
                    CS
                n   Stop
Cseq:       CS, . . .
          CS ::=    ⓔ |
                m   IC
                    CS
```

[1] A formal description of the translation of **while** programs into FC programs will be presented in Chapter 4, when we develop a Hoare Total Correctness Axiomatization for **while** programs guided by properties preserved under the translation.

Icom: $IC, \ldots$

$IC ::=$ **assert** $p \mid$ **assert** $p, \langle e_1, \ldots, e_k \rangle \mid$
$x{=}e \mid$ **goto** $m' \mid$ **if** b **goto** m'

Comm: $C, \ldots$

$C ::= Start \mid Stop \mid IC$

Start:

$Start ::=$ **start** p

Stop:

$Stop ::=$ **stop** p

We understand that *FC programs are subject to the following restrictions:*

(1) There are $n \geq 2$ commands in a program, and each command is labeled with a distinct numeral. A command C is said to be *in location* m if C is labeled with the numeral m.
(2) The **start** command is in location 1, the first location, and its assertion is the precondition of the program.
(3) There are no assignments to the input variables.
(4) The **stop** command is in location n, the last location, and its assertion is the postcondition of the program.[2]
(5) Each unconditional **goto** command is of the form

goto m'

where $2 \leq m' \leq n$.
(6) Each conditional **goto** command is of the form

if b **goto** m'

where $2 \leq m' \leq n$ and, if the conditional **goto** is in location m, $m' \neq m+1$.
(7) The arity k of all the Floydian expression k-tuples is the same. That is, in the same program, we do not allow one Floydian expression to be a m-tuple and another to be an n-tuple if $m \neq n$.

In other words, an FC program has one entry (the **start** command) and one exit (the **stop** command), contains no gaps in the numbering (labeling) of the commands, does not allow transfers of control (**gotos**) outside the program, and has a precondition that holds throughout program execution if it holds at the start.

The following structured FC program, which computes $x{*}{*}y$, is the

[2] Recall, from Restriction (1), that there are n commands. It follows that the n commands are in locations 1 through n.

translation of the **for** program presented in Sections 1.1 through 1.3. Notice that the precondition $y \geqslant 0$ & I(x) is written on the **start** command and the postcondition $z = x{*}{*}y$ on the **stop** command.

```
1    start    y≥0 & I(x)
2    z = 1
3    t = y
4    assert   z=x**(y−t) & 0≤t≤y,      t
5    if t<1 goto 9
6        z = z*x
7        t = t−1
8    goto 4
9    stop     z=x**y
```

In the **assert** command, line 4, we have written t as short for the Floydian expression, the 1-tuple $\langle t \rangle$.

As a final addition to our syntax, we introduce the *program counter pc*. Note that we do *not* consider the program counter to be a integer variable, and so *pc* cannot occur in any integer expression, assertion, or FC command. The program counter plays an essential role in the operational semantics of FC programs presented in the next section.

2.2. OPERATIONAL SEMANTICS

The semantics of integer variables, integer expressions, assertions, and boolean expressions is as in Chapter 1. So, here we need only to specify the semantics of *pc* (the program counter), **Comm** (the set of commands), and **Prog** (the set of FC programs). The semantics of *pc* is straightforward. Each state $\mathfrak{s}$ assigns *pc* a positive integer m (i.e., $\mathfrak{s}[pc] = m \geqslant 1$). For the purposes of describing the semantics of FC programs, we understand *pc* to be in the domain of each *unextended* state $\mathfrak{s}$. We understand the notion of a *pc*-variant in the natural manner, so that, for example, $\mathfrak{s}\{m \backslash pc\}$ is the *pc*-variant of $\mathfrak{s}$ such that $\mathfrak{s}\{m \backslash pc\}[pc] = m$.

We understand the set of states to be **States** with typical members $\mathfrak{s}, \mathfrak{s}', \ldots$. Informally, our semantics of commands is much like what one finds in a typical machine-language manual rendered into the terms of mathematical semantics. We extend a state $\mathfrak{s}$ so that it assigns a denotation (an unextended state) to each command C. Letting $\mathfrak{s}[pc] = m$, we understand the *operational semantics* of **Comm** to be as defined in Figure 2.1.

By the preceding definition, the **stop** command works the same way as would an infinitely looping **goto** command,

n **goto** *n*

$$
\begin{array}{lll}
\mathcal{S}[\textbf{start}\ p] & = \mathcal{S}\{m+1\backslash pc\} & \\
\mathcal{S}[\textbf{stop}\ p] & = \mathcal{S} & \\
\mathcal{S}[\textbf{assert}\ p] & = \mathcal{S}\{m+1\backslash pc\} & \\
\mathcal{S}[\textbf{assert}\ p,\langle e_1, \ldots, e_k\rangle] & = \mathcal{S}\{m+1\backslash pc\} & \\
\mathcal{S}[x{=}e] & = \mathcal{S}\{\mathcal{S}[e], m+1\backslash x, pc\} & \\
\mathcal{S}[\textbf{goto}\ m'] & = \mathcal{S}\{m'\backslash pc\} & \\
\mathcal{S}[\textbf{if}\ b\ \textbf{goto}\ m'] & = \mathcal{S}\{m'\backslash pc\} & \text{if } \mathcal{S}[b]=\text{t}, \\
 & = \mathcal{S}\{m+1\backslash pc\} & \text{otherwise}
\end{array}
$$

FIGURE 2.1. The operational semantics of commands.

and, in any extended state $\mathcal{S}$, the **stop** *does* have a denotation (the unextended state $\mathcal{S}$ itself). Unlike the case for the operational semantics of **Stat** in the preceding chapter, the operational semantics of **Comm** extends a state $\mathcal{S}$ to **Comm** in a manner so that $\mathcal{S}$ remains a total function. The FC Infinite Sequence of States Lemma holds because a state $\mathcal{S}$ (as extended so far in our definitions) is total. The Lemma justifies the definition of the operational semantics of FC programs, which follows.

FC INFINITE SEQUENCE OF STATES LEMMA: Let P be a program and $\mathcal{S}$ be a state such that $\mathcal{S}[pc]=1$. Then, there is an infinite sequence of states $\langle \mathcal{S}_0, \mathcal{S}_1, \ldots\rangle$ such that $\mathcal{S}_0=\mathcal{S}$ and, for each $i\geqslant 1$, $\mathcal{S}_i=\mathcal{S}_{i-1}[C_{i-1}]$, where C_i ($i\geqslant 0$) is the command in location $\mathcal{S}_i[pc]$.

Proof: Let P, $\mathcal{S}$, and C_i be as in the statement of the Lemma. We construct the infinite sequence of states $\langle \mathcal{S}_0, \mathcal{S}_1, \ldots\rangle$ using mathematical induction on i, showing that, for each $i\geqslant 0$, $\mathcal{S}_i$ is defined. In the basis of the induction, when $i=0$, we take $\mathcal{S}_0$ to be $\mathcal{S}$, which is defined by assumption. In the induction step, we take $\mathcal{S}_i$ to be $\mathcal{S}_{i-1}[C_{i-1}]$, which is defined by the operational semantics because, from the IH, we have that $\mathcal{S}_{i-1}$ is defined. □

The operational semantics of an FC program P is given in terms of the semantics of commands:

$\mathcal{S}[P] = \mathcal{S}'$ if there is a finite sequence of states $\langle \mathcal{S}_0, \mathcal{S}_1, \ldots, \mathcal{S}_m\rangle$ such that $\mathcal{S}=\mathcal{S}_0$, $\mathcal{S}[pc]=1$, $\mathcal{S}'=\mathcal{S}_m$, $\mathcal{S}'[pc]=n$, and, for each i such i such that $1\leqslant i\leqslant m$, $\mathcal{S}_i=\mathcal{S}_{i-1}[C_{i-1}]$, where C_i is the command in location $\mathcal{S}_i[pc]$.

That is, $\mathcal{S}[P]$ is defined whenever FC program P stops after being started up in state $\mathcal{S}$. We understand $\mathcal{S}[P]$ to be undefined if $\mathcal{S}[pc]\neq 1$.

The following trace of our exponentiation program P illustrates how the operational semantics works. Let $\mathcal{S}$ be a state such that $\mathcal{S}[pc]=1$, $\mathcal{S}[x]=3$,

$\mathfrak{s}[y]=2$, and, say, $\mathfrak{s}[t]=\mathfrak{s}[z]=0$. That is,

$$\mathfrak{s}=\{\langle pc,1\rangle,\langle x,3\rangle,\langle y,2\rangle,\langle t,0\rangle,\langle z,0\rangle,\ \ldots\}$$

Tracing the execution of P when started up in state $\mathfrak{s}$, we have the following infinite sequence:

	Command
$\mathfrak{s}=\mathfrak{s}_0=\{\langle pc,1\rangle,\langle x,3\rangle,\langle y,2\rangle,\langle t,0\rangle,\langle z,0\rangle,\ \ldots\}$	
	1 **start** . . .
$\mathfrak{s}_1=\{\langle pc,2\rangle,\langle x,3\rangle,\langle y,2\rangle,\langle t,0\rangle,\langle z,0\rangle,\ \ldots\}$	
	2 $z=1$
$\mathfrak{s}_2=\{\langle pc,3\rangle,\langle x,3\rangle,\langle y,2\rangle,\langle t,0\rangle,\langle z,1\rangle,\ \ldots\}$	
	3 $t=y$
$\mathfrak{s}_3=\{\langle pc,4\rangle,\langle x,3\rangle,\langle y,2\rangle,\langle t,2\rangle,\langle z,1\rangle,\ \ldots\}$	
	4 **assert** . . .
$\mathfrak{s}_4=\{\langle pc,5\rangle,\langle x,3\rangle,\langle y,2\rangle,\langle t,2\rangle,\langle z,1\rangle,\ \ldots\}$	
	5 **if** $t<1$ **goto** 9
$\mathfrak{s}_5=\{\langle pc,6\rangle,\langle x,3\rangle,\langle y,2\rangle,\langle t,2\rangle,\langle z,1\rangle,\ \ldots\}$	
	6 $z=z*x$
$\mathfrak{s}_6=\{\langle pc,7\rangle,\langle x,3\rangle,\langle y,2\rangle,\langle t,2\rangle,\langle z,3\rangle,\ \ldots\}$	
	7 $t=t-1$
$\mathfrak{s}_7=\{\langle pc,8\rangle,\langle x,3\rangle,\langle y,2\rangle,\langle t,1\rangle,\langle z,3\rangle,\ \ldots\}$	
	8 **goto** 4
$\mathfrak{s}_8=\{\langle pc,4\rangle,\langle x,3\rangle,\langle y,2\rangle,\langle t,1\rangle,\langle z,3\rangle,\ \ldots\}$	
	4 **assert** . . .
$\mathfrak{s}_9=\{\langle pc,5\rangle,\langle x,3\rangle,\langle y,2\rangle,\langle t,1\rangle,\langle z,3\rangle,\ \ldots\}$	
	5 **if** $t<1$ **goto** 9
$\mathfrak{s}_{10}=\{\langle pc,6\rangle,\langle x,3\rangle,\langle y,2\rangle,\langle t,1\rangle,\langle z,3\rangle,\ \ldots\}$	
	6 $z=z*x$
$\mathfrak{s}_{11}=\{\langle pc,7\rangle,\langle x,3\rangle,\langle y,2\rangle,\langle t,1\rangle,\langle z,9\rangle,\ \ldots\}$	
	7 $t=t-1$
$\mathfrak{s}_{12}=\{\langle pc,8\rangle,\langle x,3\rangle,\langle y,2\rangle,\langle t,0\rangle,\langle z,9\rangle,\ \ldots\}$	
	8 **goto** 4
$\mathfrak{s}_{13}=\{\langle pc,4\rangle,\langle x,3\rangle,\langle y,2\rangle,\langle t,0\rangle,\langle z,9\rangle,\ \ldots\}$	
	4 **assert** . . .
$\mathfrak{s}_{14}=\{\langle pc,5\rangle,\langle x,3\rangle,\langle y,2\rangle,\langle t,0\rangle,\langle z,9\rangle,\ \ldots\}$	
	5 **if** $t<1$ **goto** 9
$\mathfrak{s}'=\mathfrak{s}_{15}=\{\langle pc,9\rangle,\langle x,3\rangle,\langle y,2\rangle,\langle t,0\rangle,\langle z,9\rangle,\ \ldots\}$	
	9 **stop**
$\mathfrak{s}_{16+i}=\mathfrak{s}'\ (i\geqslant 0)$	
	9 **stop**

So, $\mathfrak{s}[P]=\mathfrak{s}'$.

Notice that the operational semantics of FC programs is inherently more complicated than the operational semantics of **while** programs. A **while** program S is *referentially transparent* in that we can determine the denotation of S from the denotations of its constituents. For example, if $S \equiv S';S''$, we understand $\mathcal{S}[S]$, the denotation of S in state $\mathcal{S}$, to be $\mathcal{S}[S'][S'']$, the denotation of S'' in the state $\mathcal{S}[S']$. A **while** program is simply a statement, but an FC program is not a command. Without complicating our definitions considerably, the operational semantics of FC programs cannot be given in such a referentially transparent manner. The operational semantics of FC commands and programs must be given separately.[3]

The definitions of partial and total correctness for FC programs are similar to those for **while** programs except that the presence of the program counter slightly complicates the definition of an initial state. At the risk of some repetition, we state the definitions in full to avoid any misunderstanding. We understand a state $\mathcal{S}$ to be *initial* for an FC program P (having a precondition p) provided $\mathcal{S}[pc]=1$ and $\mathcal{S}[p]=\mathrm{t}$. An FC program P is *partially correct* with respect to specification $\langle p,q \rangle$ if (1) $\mathcal{S}[P]$ is undefined, or (2) $\mathcal{S}[P][q]=\mathrm{t}$ for every initial state $\mathcal{S}$ for P. We say that P *terminates* (for precondition p) if, for every initial state $\mathcal{S}$ for P, there is a state $\mathcal{S}'$ such that $\mathcal{S}'=\mathcal{S}[P]$. An FC program P is *totally correct* with respect to specification $\langle p,q \rangle$ provided that, for every initial state $\mathcal{S}$ for P, there is a state $\mathcal{S}'$ such that $\mathcal{S}'=\mathcal{S}[P]$ and $\mathcal{S}'[q]=\mathrm{t}$.

2.3. FLOYD'S METHOD FOR PROVING PROGRAM CORRECTNESS

In this section, we present Floyd's method for proving total correctness. Partial correctness is proved by the *method of inductive assertions,* and termination is proved by the *well-founded sets method.* We present the two methods separately initially, then we combine them to obtain a method of proving total correctness. Combining the methods of inductive assertions and well-founded sets is justified by the Total Correctness Theorem.

2.3.1. Partial Correctness: The Method of Inductive Assertions

In an FC program, understand a *cutpoint* to be either a **start** command, a **stop** command, or an **assert** command. An *inductive assertion* is the asser-

[3] In denotational semantics, the referential transparency of FC programs is preserved by introducing an additional semantic function known as a *continuation.* Roughly, a continuation models, at a given point in a program, "the rest of the program". The reader is referred to Gordon, Stoy, and de Bakker for details. The latter two texts are advanced, but they should be understandable after the reader has completed this text.

tion on a cutpoint. Intuitively, a *path* is a sequence of locations between two adjacent cutpoints in the flow of control. (A more formal definition follows in the next paragraph.) The two adjacent cutpoints on the path need not be distinct. Paths in the flow of program control must be defined in a manner so that, for each path, cutpoints occur at both the beginning and the end of the path, and at no intermediate points on the path. For example, in the program fragment

```
         :
17    assert . . .
18    if x>x goto 20
19       z=x+y
20    assert . . .
         :
```

we consider there to be two paths from cutpoint 17 to cutpoint 20; one that passes through line 19 and one that does not, even though the latter path would never be executed. If no loops occur in a program, we do not need to add any cutpoints (**assert** commands), as a cutpoint is sure to occur at the beginning (the **start** command) and the end (the **stop** command) of each path. Even if there are no loops in a program, we will sometimes add an **assert** command (one containing no Floydian expression) to simplify our proof, as illustrated in Example 2 in Section 2.5.

Let C_i be the command in location i. We say that there is a *route* from location i to location j ($1 \leq i < n$, $1 < j \leq n$) if (1) $j = i+1$ and C_i is not an unconditional **goto** k, where $k \neq j$, or (2) $j = k$ and C_i is a conditional or an unconditional **goto** k, or (3) there is a location k such that there is a route from i to k and a route from k to j. Location i is *contained on a loop* if there is a route from i to i. We say that α is a *path* and that cutpoint j is *adjacent* to cutpoint i on path α provided that path α is a route from cutpoint i to cutpoint j, and that there is no other cutpoint k between i and j on route α. A path α from cutpoint i to cutpoint j is *part of a loop* if there is a route from j to i. Note that cutpoints i and j need not be distinct—generally, cutpoints i and j will be the same when the cutpoint occurs at the beginning of a loop containing no nested loops. We identify a path α with the sequence of h numerals used to label the FC commands occurring on path α. That is, we shall write $\alpha = \langle l_1, l_2, \ldots, l_h \rangle$ from $i = l_1$ to $j = l_h$. For example, there are three paths in our exponentiation program: $a = \langle 1,2,3,4 \rangle$, $b = \langle 4,5,6,7,8,4 \rangle$, and $c = \langle 4,5,9 \rangle$.

If there are loops in the program, we must insure that each loop contains a cutpoint. We accomplish this by adding a *loop cutpoint* (an **assert** command) to the loop body, renumbering the commands as needed. In practice, we will deal primarily with structured programs, and in this case we will usually (but not always!) place a loop cutpoint at the beginning of each loop.

To establish the partial correctness of an FC program using *the method of inductive assertions,* carry out the following steps:

(1) Write down the specification. That is,
  (a) Make the precondition the assertion on the **start** command, and
  (b) Make the postcondition the assertion on the **stop** command.
(2) (a) Insert one or more **assert** commands so that each loop contains at least one cutpoint, renumbering the commands as necessary.
  (b) Create adequate inductive assertions for all **assert** commands occurring in your program. The inductive assertions are *adequate (for the method of inductive assertions)* if they can be used to carry out Steps (3) and (4).
(3) For each path between adjacent cutpoints, construct the verification condition (for the method of inductive assertions). This will be described shortly.
(4) Prove that all the verification conditions hold.

Step (1) is straightforward. Step (2) may require ingenuity. If the FC program is the translation of a **for** program, the rules of thumb offered in the preceding chapter (Section 1.5, Example 1) can be followed. Step (3) requires the construction of a verification condition for each path between adjacent cutpoints. The algorithm that we will sketch is called a *Verification Condition Generator (VCG).* Step (4) requires that we prove the verification condition in arithmetic (i.e., using the deductive system explained in Chapter 0).

We now explain informally the algorithm to be used in constructing the verification condition required in Step (3). This informal description is intended to facilitate application of the algorithm by the human hand. A formal description of the algorithm can be found in Section 2.4.

In explaining the algorithm, some additional notational conventions are useful. We understand $\langle e_1, \ldots, e_m\rangle[e\backslash x] \equiv \langle e_1[e\backslash x], \ldots, e_m[e\backslash x]\rangle$. When $m=0$, we have the *empty substitution* $\in$, which has the property that, for any integer expression e, $e\in\equiv e$, and for any assertion p, $p\in\equiv p$. The main step is to construct a *path substitution* $\theta_\alpha \equiv [e_1, \ldots, e_m\backslash x_1, \ldots, x_m]$ and a *boolean path expression* b_α for path $\alpha=\langle i=l_1, l_2, \ldots, l_h=j\rangle$. Intuitively, each e_i in θ_α is the value of x_i, (after executing the commands in path α), expressed in terms of the values of the integer variables before executing path α, and each e_i in θ_α is to be substituted for the corresponding x_i $(1\leqslant i\leqslant m)$. The substitutions of the e_i's for the x_i's are performed simultaneously. The boolean expression b_α indicates when path α will be traversed, and is expressed in terms of the values of the integer variables before executing path α. We construct the $\langle e_1, \ldots, e_m\rangle$ of θ_α and b_α as described in Figure 2.2.

To illustrate the construction of path substitutions and boolean path expressions, we consider the exponentiation program on page 93. The three paths in our program are: $a=\langle 1,2,3,4\rangle$, $b=\langle 4,5,6,7,8,4\rangle$, and $c=\langle 4,5,9\rangle$. We

(a) For each g from 1 to h, write down the command labeled l_g (one command per line) if it is an assignment command or a conditional **goto** command. **Start, stop, assert,** and unconditional **goto** commands need not be written down.

(b) Under and to the left of the list of commands generated in Step (a), write down all integer variables $\langle x_1, \ldots, x_m \rangle$ ($m \geqslant 0$) to which assignments occur on path α. The values $\langle x_1, \ldots, x_m \rangle$ are to be the initial values used in the construction of the $\langle e_1, \ldots, e_m \rangle$ in the path substitution θ_α. If no assignments occur on path α (in which case $m=0$), then θ_α will be the empty substitution $\in$.

(c) Under and to the right of the list of commands, write down true. True is the initial value used in the construction of the boolean path expression b_α.

(d) Working from the bottom of the list of commands to the top, construct from the old $\langle e_1, \ldots, e_m \rangle$ and b_α new values, as given in the following steps:

(i) If the command passed through is an assignment command, we schematize the construction of the new values as follows:

new $\langle e_1, \ldots, e_m \rangle[e \backslash x]$ $\qquad$ $\mathrm{b}_\alpha[e \backslash x]$

$m \quad x = e$

old $\langle e_1, \ldots, e_m \rangle$ $\qquad$ b_α

In other words, we obtain our new values by substituting e for every occurrence of x in our old values.

(ii) If the command passed through is a conditional **goto,** we schematize the construction of the new values as follows:

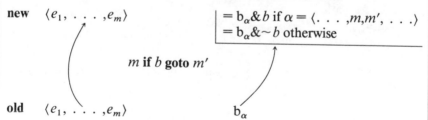

new $\langle e_1, \ldots, e_m \rangle$ $\qquad$ $= \mathrm{b}_\alpha \& b$ if $\alpha = \langle \ldots, m, m', \ldots \rangle$
$= \mathrm{b}_\alpha \& {\sim} b$ otherwise

m **if** b **goto** m'

old $\langle e_1, \ldots, e_m \rangle$ $\qquad$ b_α

In other words, only the boolean path expression b_α can change when we pass through a conditional **goto.** If there is a transfer of control on path α from m to m', then the boolean expression b must be true, so we obtain our new value for the boolean path expression by conjoining b to the old value. Otherwise, control flows to $m+1$ because b is false. As a result, we obtain our new value by conjoining ${\sim}b$ to our old value.

FIGURE 2.2. Construction of a path substitution and a boolean path expression.

step through the construction of the path substitution θ_b and boolean path expression b_b for path b. Following Step (a), we write down lines 5 (the conditional **goto**), 6 (the assignment to z), and 7 (the assignment to t). Following Steps (b) and (c), we write down underneath the list of commands $\langle t,z\rangle$ and **true.** Now we follow Step (d), working from the bottom of the list of commands to the top.

θ_b		b_b
$\langle t-1,z*x\rangle$		true & $\sim t<1$
$\uparrow$	**if** $t<1$ **goto** . . .	$\uparrow$
$\langle t-1,z*x\rangle$		true
$\uparrow$	$z=z*x$	$\uparrow$
$\langle t-1,z\rangle$		true
$\uparrow$	$t=t-1$	$\uparrow$
$\langle t,z\rangle$		true

From here on, for any assertion p, we shall abbreviate true&p as p. So

$$\theta_b \equiv [t-1,z*x\backslash t,z] \text{ and } \mathrm{b}_b \equiv \sim t<1$$

Similarly, we have

$$\theta_a \equiv [y,1\backslash t,z],\ \mathrm{b}_a \equiv \text{true},$$
$$\theta_c \equiv \in, \text{ and } \mathrm{b}_c \equiv t<1.$$

We understand b_α to be as constructed in Steps (a) to (d), and θ_α to be $[e_1, \ldots ,e_m\backslash x_1, \ldots ,x_m]$, where the x_i's are as in Step (b) and the e_i's are constructed as in Steps (a) through (d). If $m=0$, then θ_α is the empty substitution $\in$. Let p_i (p_j) be the inductive assertion at cutpoint i (j). *The verification condition* for path α is

$$(VC_\alpha) \qquad p_1,p_i,\mathrm{b}_\alpha \vdash p_j\theta_\alpha$$

For example, the verification conditions for paths a, b, and c in our exponentiation program are as follows:

$$(\mathrm{VC}_a) \qquad p_1,\mathrm{b}_a \vdash p_4\theta_a$$
$$y\geqslant 0 \,\&\, \mathrm{I}(x), \text{ true}$$
$$\vdash (z=x**(y-t)\&0\leqslant t\leqslant y)[y,1\backslash t,z]$$

That is,

$$y\geqslant 0 \,\&\, \mathrm{I}(x), \text{ true}$$
$$\vdash 1=x**(y-y)\&0\leqslant y\leqslant y$$

$$(\mathrm{VC}_b) \quad p_1,p_4,\mathrm{b}_b \vdash p_4\theta_b$$
$$y\geqslant 0 \,\&\, \mathrm{I}(x),\ z=x**(y-t)\&0\leqslant t\leqslant y,\ \sim t<1$$
$$\vdash (z=x**(y-t)\&0\leqslant t\leqslant y)[t-1,z*x\backslash t,z]$$

That is, $y \geqslant 0$ & $I(x)$, $z = x**(y-t)\&0 \leqslant t \leqslant y$, $\sim t<1$
$\vdash z*x = x**(y-(t-1))\&0 \leqslant t-1 \leqslant y$

(VC_c) $p_1, p_4, b_c \vdash p_9\theta_c$
$y \geqslant 0$ & $I(x)$, $z = x**(y-t)\&0 \leqslant t \leqslant y$, $t<1$
$\vdash (z = x**y)\in$

That is, $y \geqslant 0$ & $I(x)$, $z = x**(y-t)\&0 \leqslant t \leqslant y$, $t<1$
$\vdash z = x**y$

2.3.2. Termination: The Well-Founded Sets Method

To carry out Floyd's method of proving program termination, we require that *all assert commands used as loop cutpoints must contain a Floydian expression.* To establish termination using *the well-founded sets method,* carry out the following steps in addition to Steps (1a) and (2a) of the method of inductive assertions:

(2) (b) Create adequate inductive assertions and Floydian expressions for all **assert** commands occurring in your program. The inductive assertions and Floydian expressions are *adequate (for the well-founded sets method)* if they can be used to carry out Steps (3) and (4).

(3) (a) For each path ending with an **assert** command, construct the verification condition as described in the preceding section.

(b) For each loop cutpoint, construct the well-foundedness condition as described in the text that follows.

(c) On each path that is part of a loop, construct the termination condition as described in the text that follows.

(4) Prove that all the well-foundedness and termination conditions hold.

In our exponentiation program, an adequate inductive assertion for the **assert** command (loop cutpoint) at line 4 is $0 \leqslant t$. In keeping with our policy in Chapter 1, we prefer the longer inductive assertion $0 \leqslant t \leqslant y$ (the second conjunct of the **assert** command at line 4), which is also adequate. The entire assertion on line 4 is also adequate, and we will use it because we will combine the methods of inductive assertions and well-founded sets in Section 2.3.3. An adequate Floydian expression is $t (\equiv \langle t \rangle)$ because, when t counts down to 0, the program will terminate.

We have already described Step (3a) in the preceding section. As for Step (3b), let p_i be the inductive assertion on loop cutpoint i, k be the arity of the Floydian expressions, $E_i \equiv \langle e_{i,1}, \ldots, e_{i,k} \rangle$ be the Floydian expression on loop cutpoint i, $\langle 0 \rangle$ be a k-tuple of 0's, and $\not\geqslant$ be the direct product ordering induced by $\geqslant$. *The well-foundedness condition* for cutpoint i is

$$(WC_i) \qquad p_1, p_i \vdash E_i \mathrel{\dot{\geqslant}} \langle 0 \rangle$$

That is, $\quad p_1, p_i \vdash e_{i,1} \geqslant 0 \;\&\; . \; . \; . \;\&\; e_{i,k} \geqslant 0$

For our exponentiation program, because $k=1$, $\langle 0 \rangle$ is 0 and $\dot{\geqslant}$ is the usual $\geqslant$ relation on the integers.

As for Step (3c), let loop cutpoint i be adjacent to loop cutpoint j, $E_i \equiv \langle e_{i,1}, \; . \; . \; . \; , e_{i,k} \rangle$ ($E_j \equiv \langle e_{j,1}, \; . \; . \; . \; , e_{j,k} \rangle$) be the Floydian expression contained on loop cutpoint i (j), α be a path from i to j, θ_α and b_α be the path substitution and boolean path expression as described in the previous section, and $\succ$ be the lexicographic ordering relation. Then, *the termination condition* for path α is as follows:

$$(TC_\alpha) \qquad p_1, p_i, \mathrm{b}_\alpha \vdash E_i \succ E_j\theta_\alpha$$

That is,

$$\begin{aligned} p_1, p_i, \mathrm{b}_\alpha \vdash\; & e_{i,1} > e_{j,1}\theta_\alpha \lor \\ & e_{i,1} = e_{j,1}\theta_\alpha \& e_{i,2} > e_{j,2}\theta_\alpha \lor \\ & . \; . \; . \lor \\ & e_{i,1} = e_{j,1}\theta_\alpha \& e_{i,2} = e_{j,2}\theta_\alpha \& \; . \; . \; . \; \& e_{i,k} > e_{j,k}\theta_\alpha \end{aligned}$$

For our exponentiation program, $\succ$ is the usual $>$ relation on the integers.

In our exponentiation program, the only well-foundedness condition is for the **assert** command labeled 4. It is

$$(\mathrm{WC}_4) \qquad p_1, p_4 \vdash E_4 \mathrel{\dot{\geqslant}} \langle 0 \rangle$$

$$y \geqslant 0 \;\&\; \mathrm{I}(x), z = x{*}{*}(y-t) \& 0 \leqslant t \leqslant y \vdash t \geqslant 0$$

and the only termination condition is the one for path b:

$$(\mathrm{TC}_b) \qquad p_1, p_4, \mathrm{b}_b \vdash E_4 \succ E_4\theta_b$$

$$y \geqslant 0 \;\&\; \mathrm{I}(x),\; z = x{*}{*}(y-t) \& 0 \leqslant t \leqslant y,\; {\sim} t < 1 \vdash t > t[t-1 \backslash t]$$

That is,

$$y \geqslant 0 \;\&\; \mathrm{I}(x),\; z = x{*}{*}(y-t) \& 0 \leqslant t \leqslant y,\; {\sim} t < 1 \vdash t > t-1$$

The well-foundedness and termination conditions obviously hold.

The reader might find a further word on the intuition underlying Floydian expressions useful as this point. Roughly, the Floydian expressions in a program are intended to represent the members of a well-founded set (the set of k-tuples of natural numbers under the direct product ordering). The members of the well-founded set become smaller and smaller (under the lexicographic ordering) as program execution proceeds. It is a bit like the countdown at a race: ". . . ,4,3,2,1,0, and they're off!" In our example program, the countdown of the Floydian expression t always occurs in steps of 1 because our program is the translation of a **for-downto** statement. However, in other programs, the countdown can vary and can be in leaps of greater than 1. Eventually, the countdown must end, and the program terminates. The lexicographic ordering is used to judge when one member of the well-founded set is smaller than another because it extends the direct product ordering. As a result, it is easier to use in some cases than the direct product ordering, as will be illustrated in Example 3 of Section 2.5. However, to insure that a Floydian expression is a member of our well-founded set, the direct product ordering must be used because, for example, we have that $\langle 1,-1 \rangle \succ \langle 0,0 \rangle$, but $\langle 1,-1 \rangle$ is not a member of our well-founded set.[4]

2.3.3. Total Correctness: Combining the Two Methods

To prove total correctness, we simply combine the methods of inductive assertions and well-founded sets as summarized in Figure 2.3.

We shall provide some additional sample proofs of total correctness using the combined method in Section 2.5.

2.4. THE SOUNDNESS OF FLOYD'S METHOD

In outline, the proofs of the soundness of Floyd's methods run as follows. First, we give a semantic argument to show that backward substitution preserves "denotations" as we move backwards from the end of a path to its beginning. The proof makes use of the Coincidence Lemma, much as proof of the validity of the assignment axiom did in Chapter 1. Second, another semantic argument establishes that if the precondition holds when execution begins and the inductive assertions are adequate, then each time control reaches a cutpoint the inductive assertion at the cutpoint will be true. We prove both of these arguments using simple mathematical induction. So, if the method of inductive assertions can be carried out, we do indeed have partial correctness. This follows immediately from the second argument because the postcondition on the **stop** command must be true if it is ever reached. Third, we sketch a Nötherian Induction showing that each loop must eventually terminate if the well-founded sets method can be carried out. So, if we can carry out the combined method, then we do indeed have total correctness = partial correctness + termination.

Let $\alpha'=\langle l'_1, \ldots, l'_m \rangle$ $(m \geqslant 0)$ and $\alpha''=\langle l''_1, \ldots, l''_n \rangle$ $(n \geqslant 0)$ be (finite) sequences of locations. We write $\langle\,\rangle$ for the empty sequence, and we use the

[4] We note that orderings other than those we have chosen can be useful in proving termination. We have fixed on the direct product and lexicographic orderings for three reasons. First, they are easy to use in proving the termination of a wide variety of programs. Second, we wish to standardize our FC language (so that, for example, we do not have to state what the ordering is each time we write a program). Third, the concept of being a well-founded ordering is not definable in first-order logic.

(1) Write down the specification. That is,
   (a) Make the precondition the assertion on the **start** command, and
   (b) Make the postcondition the assertion on the **stop** command.

(2) (a) Insert one or more **assert** commands so that each loop contains at least one loop cutpoint, renumbering the commands as necessary.
   (b) Create adequate inductive assertions for all **assert** commands and adequate Floydian expressions for all loop cutpoints. The inductive assertions and Floydian expressions are *adequate* if they can be used to carry out Steps (3) and (4).

(3) (a) On each path α between adjacent cutpoints i and j, construct the verification condition.

$$(\mathrm{VC}_\alpha) \qquad p_1, p_i, \mathrm{b}_\alpha \vdash p_j\theta_\alpha$$

   (b) For each loop cutpoint i, construct the well-foundedness condition.

$$(\mathrm{WC}_i) \qquad p_1, p_i \vdash E_i \succcurlyeq \langle 0 \rangle$$

   (c) On each path α that is part of a loop, construct the termination condition.

$$(\mathrm{TC}_\alpha) \qquad p_1, p_i, \mathrm{b}_\alpha \vdash E_i \succ E_j\theta_\alpha$$

(4) Prove that all the verification, well-foundedness, and termination conditions hold.

FIGURE 2.3. Floyd's method for proving total correctness.

sign '#' to indicate the concatenation of two sequences. For example, $\alpha'\#\alpha''=\langle l_1, \ldots, l_{m+n}\rangle$, where $l_i=l_i'$ $(1\leqslant i\leqslant m)$ and $l_{j+m}=l_j''$ $(1\leqslant j\leqslant n)$. It follows that for any finite sequence α we have $\alpha=\langle\rangle\#\alpha=\alpha\#\langle\rangle$.

As promised in the preceding section, we shall now define more formally the path substitution θ_α and the boolean path expression b_α. Let $n\geqslant 2$, $1\leqslant i\leqslant n$, $\alpha=\langle l_1, \ldots, l_n\rangle$ be a sequence of locations, $\alpha_i=\langle l_1, \ldots l_i\rangle$ be an initial segment of α, and $\alpha -_i = \langle l_{n-i}, \ldots, l_n\rangle$ be a final segment of α. We have $\alpha=\alpha_n=\alpha -_{n-1}$, and we call n the *length* of α. First, we define inductively $X[\alpha_i]$, *the sequence of variables that are assigned values on path* α_i:

$X[\alpha_1] = \langle\rangle$

$X[\alpha_{i+1}] = x\#X[\alpha_i]$ if the command in location l_i is the assignment command $x{:=}e$, and

$X[\alpha_{i+1}] = X[\alpha_i]$ if the command in location l_i is *not* an assignment command.

Next, we define $F[\alpha,i]$, the *assignment function for the final segment* $\alpha{-}_i$, inductively (working backwards through the path):

$F[\alpha,1] \quad = X[\alpha]$	
$F[\alpha,i+1] = F[\alpha,i][e\backslash x]$	if the command in location l_i is the assignment command $x{:=}e$, and
$F[\alpha,i+1] = F[\alpha,i]$	if the command in location l_i is *not* an assignment command.

Then, the *path substitution* θ_α is $[F[\alpha,n]\backslash X[\alpha]]$.

The boolean path expression is defined in a similar manner. To this end, we define $B[\alpha,i]$, the *boolean path expression for the final segment* $\alpha{-}_i$ as follows:

$B[\alpha,1] \quad = \text{true}$	
$B[\alpha,i+1] = B[\alpha,i][e\backslash x]$	if the command in location l_i is the assignment command $x{:=}e$,
$B[\alpha,i+1] = B[\alpha,i]\ \&\ b$	if the command in location l_i is the conditional **goto** command **if** b **goto** l' and $l'=l_{i+1}$,
$B[\alpha,i+1] = B[\alpha,i]\ \&\ {\sim}b$	if the command in location l_i is the conditional **goto** command **if** b **goto** l' and $l_{i+1}=l_i+1$, and
$B[\alpha,i+1] = B[\alpha,i]$	if the command in location l_i is neither an assignment nor a conditional **goto** command.

The *boolean path expression* b_α is $B[\alpha,n]$.

Before proceeding with the proofs of our main results, we need to establish a somewhat innocuous but messy lemma for which there is no analog in Chapter 1.[5] Let α be as before, let $i=l_1$, $j=l_n$, and C_i be the command in location l_i on path α.

PATH LEMMA: If $\mathfrak{s}[pc]=i$, $\mathfrak{s}[\mathrm{b}_\alpha]$ iff $\mathfrak{s}[C_1]\ \ldots\ [C_{n-1}][pc]=j$

Proof: Let $\mathfrak{s}$ be any state such that $\mathfrak{s}[pc]=i$. The proof proceeds by induction on the path length n and is entirely similar in structure to the proof of the (VCG) Correctness Lemma, which we give in detail in the text that follows. In the basis, we have $n=2$, C_1 is either a **start** of an **assert** command, and $\mathfrak{s}[\mathrm{b}_\alpha]=\mathfrak{s}[\text{true}]$ and $\mathfrak{s}[C_1][pc]=l_1+1=l_2$ by the operational semantics and the definition of a path. The induction step is left as an exercise. □

[5] This is because the meaning of a **while** statement can be analyzed solely in terms of its immediate constituents, whereas FC programs cannot be so analyzed.

The (VCG) Correctness Lemma has the following import. Suppose that we can successfully carry out the method of inductive assertions on path α by demonstrating that (VC_α) holds. The (VCG) Correctness Lemma assures us that if we are at cutpoint i and its inductive assertion p_i and the boolean path expression b_α hold and program control follows path α, then, when control reaches cutpoint j, its inductive assertion p_j will hold. (The Path Lemma guarantees that under these conditions, program control will indeed follow path α.) We have the following:

(VCG) CORRECTNESS LEMMA: If

$$p_1, p_i, b_\alpha \vdash p_j\theta_\alpha$$

then, for every state $\mathcal{S}$ such that $\mathcal{S}[pc]=i$,

$$\mathcal{S}[p_1] \& \mathcal{S}[p_i] \& \mathcal{S}[b_\alpha] \rightarrow \mathcal{S}[C_1] \ldots [C_{n-1}][p_j]$$

Proof: Assume $p_1, p_i, b_\alpha \vdash p_j\theta_\alpha$. Let $\mathcal{S}$ be any state such that $\mathcal{S}[pc]=i$ and $\mathcal{S}[p_1]\&\mathcal{S}[p_i]\&\mathcal{S}[b_\alpha]$, and let $\mathcal{S}'' = \mathcal{S}[C_1] \ldots [C_{n-1}]$. By the Soundness of Arithmetic Theorem, we have $p_1, p_i, b_\alpha \models p_j\theta_\alpha$. And, so it follows that $\mathcal{S}[p_j\theta_\alpha]$. Proof that $\mathcal{S}''[p_j]$ proceeds by induction on $n \geq 2$, the length of path α.

BASIS: $n=2$.
Because $n=2$, $\alpha=\langle l_1, l_2\rangle$, C_1 is either a **start** or an **assert** command, $i=l_1$, $\theta_\alpha=\in$, and b_α=true. We have, therefore,

$$\begin{aligned} \mathcal{S}[C_1][p_j] &= \mathcal{S}\{i+1 \backslash pc\}[p_j] \text{ by the operational semantics} \\ &= \mathcal{S}[p_j] \text{ by the Coincidence Lemma, part (b)} \\ &= \mathcal{S}[p_j\theta_\alpha] \text{ because } \theta_\alpha=\in \\ &= \mathrm{t} \end{aligned}$$

INDUCTION STEP: $n \geq 3$.
Let $\alpha'=\alpha_{n-1}$, $\alpha''=\alpha_{-1}$, and $\mathcal{S}'=\mathcal{S}[C_1] \ldots [C_{n-2}]$. Note that $p_j\theta_\alpha \equiv [p_j\theta_{\alpha''}]\theta_{\alpha'}$. The IH states that if

$$p_1, p_i \& b_{\alpha''}\theta_{\alpha'}, b_{\alpha'} \vdash [p_j\theta_{\alpha''}]\theta_{\alpha'}$$

then, for every state $\mathcal{S}$ such that $\mathcal{S}[pc]=i$ and $\mathcal{S}[p_1]\&\mathcal{S}[p_i\&b_{\alpha''}\theta_{\alpha'}]\&\mathcal{S}[b_{\alpha'}]$, we have $\mathcal{S}'[p_j\theta_{\alpha''}]$. Under our assumptions, we must show that $\mathcal{S}''[p_j]$. The proof proceeds by cases, depending on the form of the command C_{n-1} in location l_{n-1}.

Case: $C_{n-1} \equiv x := e$
Because $b_\alpha \equiv b_{\alpha'}$, we have

$$p_1, p_i \& b_{\alpha''}\theta_{\alpha'}, b_{\alpha'} \vdash [p_j\theta_{\alpha''}]\theta_{\alpha'}$$

because

$$p_1, p_i, \mathrm{b}_\alpha \vdash p_j\theta_\alpha$$

$\mathrm{b}_\alpha \equiv \mathrm{true}\&\mathrm{b}_{\alpha'}$, and $p_j\theta_\alpha \equiv [p_j\theta_{\alpha''}]\theta_{\alpha'}$. Applying the IH, we have $\mathcal{s}'[p_j\theta_{\alpha''}]$ because $\mathrm{b}_{\alpha''}\theta_{\alpha'} \equiv \mathrm{true}$. Consequently,

$$\begin{aligned}\mathcal{s}''[p_j] &= \mathcal{s}'[x{:=}e][p_i]\\ &= \mathcal{s}'\{\mathcal{s}'[e]\backslash x\}[p_j] \text{ by the operational semantics}\\ &= \mathcal{s}'[p_j[e\backslash x]] \text{ by the Coincidence Lemma, part (d)}\\ &= \mathcal{s}'[p_j\theta_{\alpha''}] \text{ because } \theta_{\alpha''} \equiv [e\backslash x]\\ &= \mathrm{t} \text{ by the IH}\end{aligned}$$

Case: $C_{n-1} \equiv$ **if** b **goto** l'

We have $\mathrm{b}_{\alpha'} \equiv \mathrm{true}\&\mathrm{b}'_{\alpha'}$ for some $\mathrm{b}'_{\alpha'}$. Furthermore, we have $\theta_{\alpha''} \equiv \in$ and $\theta_\alpha \equiv \theta_{\alpha'}$. Hence,

$$p_1, p_i\&\mathrm{b}_{\alpha''}\theta_{\alpha'}, \mathrm{b}_{\alpha'} \vdash [p_j\theta_{\alpha''}]\theta_{\alpha'}$$

because

$$\vdash \mathrm{b}_{\alpha''}\theta_{\alpha'}\&\mathrm{b}_{\alpha'} \leftrightarrow \mathrm{b}_\alpha.$$

Because $\mathcal{s}[\mathrm{b}_\alpha]$, we have $\mathcal{s}[\mathrm{b}_{\alpha''}\theta_{\alpha'}]$ and $\mathcal{s}[\mathrm{b}_{\alpha'}]$. Applying the IH, we have $\mathcal{s}'[p_j\theta_{\alpha''}]$ because $\mathcal{s}[\mathrm{b}_{\alpha''}\theta_{\alpha'}]$ by the Path Lemma. And, because $\theta_\alpha \equiv \in$, we have $\mathcal{s}''[p_j]$ due to the fact that $\mathcal{s}''[p_j] = \mathcal{s}[p_j]$ by the operational semantics and the Coincidence Lemma, part (b).

The other cases are similar and are left as exercises. □

METHOD OF INDUCTIVE ASSERTIONS SOUNDNESS THEOREM: Let P be an FC program, the **stop** command be in location n, and $\mathcal{s}$ be any initial state for P. If, for every path α in P we can demonstrate (VC_α), then P is partially correct wrt the specification $\langle p_1, p_n \rangle$.

Proof: We show that the assertion on a cutpoint is true each time the flow of control reaches it. It follows immediately that, if control reaches the **stop** command in, for instance, state $\mathcal{s}*$, we have $\mathcal{s}*[p_n]$. The proof is by induction on $m \geq 1$, the number of times the flow of control reaches a cutpoint. We shall say that we are *at time m* if the flow of control has reached m (not necessarily distinct) cutpoints.

BASIS: $m=1$

The first cutpoint reached (at time 1) is the **start** command in location 1 when execution is begun in state $\mathcal{s}$, and, by the assumption that $\mathcal{s}$ is an initial state for P, we have $\mathcal{s}[p_1]$.

INDUCTION STEP: $m \geqslant 2$
Let $\mathfrak{s}'$ be the state at time $m-1$ with $\mathfrak{s}'[pc]=i$, $\mathfrak{s}''$ be the state at time m with $\mathfrak{s}''[pc]=j$, and α be the execution path from cutpoint i to cutpoint j. By assumption, we can demonstrate the following:

$$(\mathrm{VC}_\alpha) \qquad p_1, p_i, \mathrm{b}_\alpha \vdash p_j \theta_\alpha$$

We have $\mathfrak{s}''[p_1]$ by an analog of the Setting Lemma. By the IH, we have $\mathfrak{s}'[p_i]$. By the Path Lemma, we have $\mathfrak{s}[\mathrm{b}_\alpha]$. Hence, $\mathfrak{s}''[p_j]$ by the (VCG) Correctness Lemma. □

We now show that if the well-founded sets method can be carried out for an FC program, then the program will terminate. For brevity's sake, our proof will be informal.

METHOD OF WELL-FOUNDED SETS SOUNDNESS THEOREM: Let P be an FC program as before, and $\mathfrak{s}$ be any initial state for P. If, for every loop cutpoint i we can demonstrate (WC_i), for every path α ending with an **assert** command we can demonstrate (VC_α), and for every path α that is part of a loop we can demonstate (TC_α), then P terminates for precondition p_1.

Proof Sketch: Because every FC program P contains only a finite number of loops, if every loop in P terminates, then P must terminate as well. Suppose that the well-founded sets method can be carried out—that is, that we can demonstrate (VC_α) for each path α ending with an **assert** command, (WC_i) for each loop cutpoint i, and (TC_α) for each path α that is part of a loop. Consider any path α that is part of a loop, let $\mathfrak{s}$ be any state such that $\mathfrak{s}[p_1]\&\mathfrak{s}[p_i]\&\mathfrak{s}[\mathrm{b}_\alpha]$, and let $\mathfrak{s}''=\mathfrak{s}[C_1]\ \ldots\ [C_{n-1}]$. By an inductive argument similar to that used in the proofs of the (VCG) Correctness Lemma and the Method of Inductive Assertions Soundness Theorem, we have $\mathfrak{s}[E_i] \succ \mathfrak{s}''[E_j]$ because (VC_α) and (TC_α) hold. Similarly, we have $\mathfrak{s}[E_i]$ and $\mathfrak{s}''[E_j]$ as members of a well-founded set because (VC_α), (WC_i), and (WC_j) hold. Since α was chosen arbitrarily, the total number of times the paths in the loop can be executed must be finite. Hence, each loop must terminate, and so P must terminate. □

As an immediate consequence of the Soundness Theorems for the Methods of Inductive Assertions and Well-Founded Sets, we have the following theorem:

COMBINED FLOYD-METHOD SOUNDNESS THEOREM: Let P be an FC program as before, and $\mathfrak{s}$ be any initial state for P. If, for every loop cutpoint i we can demonstrate (WC_i), for every path α we can demonstrate (VC_α), and for every path α that is part of a loop we can demonstrate (TC_α), then P is totally correct wrt the specification $\langle p_1, p_n \rangle$.

2.5. SOME SAMPLE PROOFS

EXAMPLE 1

The following FC program is the translation of the **while** program presented in Example 2 of Section 1.5. It computes the quotient $q=x/y$ and the remainder $r=x \bmod y$ $(x\geqslant 0, y\geqslant 1)$ using the method of successive subtractions. Try to discover an adequate Floydian expression E_4. Hint: Adequate Floydian expressions in the case of (the translation of) **for** programs containing no nested loops and being of the form

for $x{:=}e$ **downto** e' **do** . . .

and

for $x{:=}e$ **to** e' **do** . . .

are $x-e'$ (or simply x if e' cannot be negative) and $e'-x$, respectively. We provide an adequate Floydian expression at the end of this chapter.

```
1    start     x≥0 & y≥1
2    q=0
3    r=x
4    assert    x=y*q+r & 0≤r≤x,        E4
5    if r<y goto 9
6        q=q+1
7        r=r−y
8    goto 4
9    stop      q=x/y & r=x mod y
```

The paths are $a=\langle 1,2,3,4\rangle$, $b=\langle 4,5,6,7,8,4\rangle$, and $c=\langle 4,5,9\rangle$, and the path substitutions and boolean path expressions are as follows:

$$\theta_a \equiv [0,x\backslash q,r],\ \mathrm{b}_a \equiv \text{true},$$

$$\theta_b \equiv [q+1,r-y\backslash q,r],\ \mathrm{b}_b \equiv {\sim} r<y$$

$$\theta_c \text{ is } \in, \text{ and } \mathrm{b}_c \equiv r<y$$

The verification conditions are as follows:

(VC_a) $\quad p_1, \mathrm{b}_a \vdash p_4\theta_a$

$x\geqslant 0 \& y\geqslant 1, \text{true} \vdash (x=y*q+r \& 0\leqslant r\leqslant x)[0,x\backslash q,r]$

That is, $\quad x\geqslant 0 \& y\geqslant 1, \text{true} \vdash x=y*0+x \& 0\leqslant x\leqslant x$

(VC_b) $\quad p_1, p_4, \mathrm{b}_b \vdash p_4\theta_b$

$x\geqslant 0 \& y\geqslant 1,\ x=y*q+r \& 0\leqslant r\leqslant x,\ {\sim} r<y$

$\qquad \vdash (x=y*q+r \& 0\leqslant r\leqslant x)[q+1,r-y\backslash q,r]$

That is, $x \geq 0 \& y \geq 1,\ x = y * q + r \& 0 \leq r \leq x,\ \sim r < y$
$$\vdash x = y*(q+1) + r - y \ \&\ 0 \leq r - y \leq x$$

(VC$_c$) $p_1, p_4, \mathrm{b}_c \vdash p_9 \theta_c$
$$x \geq 0 \& y \geq 1,\ x = y*q + r \& 0 \leq r \leq x,\ r < y$$
$$\vdash (q = x/y \ \&\ r = x \bmod y) \in$$

That is, $x \geq 0 \& y \geq 1,\ x = y*q + r \& 0 \leq r \leq x,\ r < y$
$$\vdash q = x/y \ \&\ r = x \bmod y$$

The only well-foundedness condition is the one for the assert command at line 4.

(WC$_4$) $p_1, p_4 \vdash E_4 \succcurlyeq \langle 0 \rangle$
$$x \geq 0 \& y \geq 1,\ x = y*q + r \ \&\ 0 \leq r \leq x \vdash E_4 \geq 0$$

The only termination condition is the one for path b.

(TC$_b$) $p_1, p_4, \mathrm{b}_b \vdash E_4 \succ E_4 \theta_b$
$$x \geq 0 \& y \geq 1,\ x = y*q + r \& 0 \leq r \leq x,\ \sim r < y$$
$$\vdash E_4 > E_4[q+1, r-y \backslash q, r]$$

In (TC$_b$), we need $y \geq 1$ in the antecedent to insure that $E_4 > E_4[q+1, r-y \backslash q, r]$ in the consequent. However, the conjunct $y \geq 1$ is not required in p_4, as it was in the similar example in Chapter 1, because it is a conjunct of p_1. In the Hoare Axiomatization, we are forced to carry essential conjuncts in the precondition along into the intermediate assertions. Analogous conjuncts are not required in **for** programs because the control variable is always incremented (decremented) by one on completion of the loop body.

EXAMPLE 2

The following FC straight-line program, which determines the smaller of the integer variables x, y, and z, is similar to Example 3 in Section 1.5.

```
1   start    I(x)&I(y)&I(z)
2   if x≥y goto 5
3       s=x
4   goto 6
5       s=y
6   assert   s=min(x,y)
7   if z≥s goto 9
8       s=z
9   stop     s=min(x,y,z)
```

There are four paths: $a = \langle 1,2,3,4,6 \rangle$, $b = \langle 1,2,5,6 \rangle$, $c = \langle 6,7,8,9 \rangle$, and $d = \langle 6,7,9 \rangle$. The path substitutions and boolean path expressions are as follows:

$$
\begin{array}{ll}
\theta_a \equiv [x\backslash s] & \mathrm{b}_a \equiv {\sim}x \geqslant y \\
\theta_b \equiv [y\backslash s] & \mathrm{b}_b \equiv x \geqslant y \\
\theta_c \equiv [z\backslash s] & \mathrm{b}_c \equiv {\sim}z \geqslant s \\
\theta_d \equiv \in & \mathrm{b}_d \equiv z \geqslant s
\end{array}
$$

After making all substitutions, the verification conditions are as follows:

$$
\begin{array}{ll}
(\mathrm{VC}_a) & \mathrm{I}(x)\&\mathrm{I}(y)\&\mathrm{I}(z),\ {\sim}x \geqslant y \vdash x=\min(x,y) \\
(\mathrm{VC}_b) & \mathrm{I}(x)\&\mathrm{I}(y)\&\mathrm{I}(z),\ x \geqslant y \vdash y=\min(x,y) \\
(\mathrm{VC}_c) & \mathrm{I}(x)\&\mathrm{I}(y)\&\mathrm{I}(z),\ s=\min(x,y),\ {\sim}z \geqslant s \vdash z=\min(x,y,z) \\
(\mathrm{VC}_d) & \mathrm{I}(x)\&\mathrm{I}(y)\&\mathrm{I}(z),\ s=\min(x,y),\ z \geqslant s \vdash s=\min(x,y,z)
\end{array}
$$

There are no well-foundedness and termination conditions because there are no loops. The **assert** command on line 6 does not contain a Floydian expression because it is not a loop cutpoint. If we dispensed with line 6, we would still have four paths. That is, if we changed line 6 to

6 **goto** 7

one of the four paths would be $a'=\langle 1,2,3,4,6,7,8,9\rangle$ and would have the following verification condition:

$$
(\mathrm{VC}_{a'}) \quad \mathrm{I}(x)\&\mathrm{I}(y)\&\mathrm{I}(z),\ {\sim}z \geqslant x,\ {\sim}x \geqslant y \vdash z=\min(x,y,z)
$$

In this particular example, no significant advantage is gained by adding the **assert** statement. However, suppose we had a fourth integer variable w. Our precondition is now $\mathrm{I}(x)\&\mathrm{I}(y)\&\mathrm{I}(z)\&\mathrm{I}(w)$ and our postcondition becomes $s=\min(x,y,z,w)$. We modify the program by adding the conjunct $\mathrm{I}(w)$ to the assertion on the **start** command and replace line 9 with the following lines:

```
 9    assert    s=min(x,y,z)
10    if w≥s goto 12
11        s=w
12    stop      s=min(x,y,z,w)
```

With the two **assert** commands on lines 6 and 9, there are $6=2*3$ paths. However, if we dispensed with lines 6 and 9, we would have $8=2**3$ paths. Judicious placement of **assert** commands can significantly simplify proofs for long programs.

EXAMPLE 3

The following **for** program, which computes $x**y$ using only the unary operation symbols '—' and 'abs' and the binary operation symbols '—' and

'+', is similar to Example 4 in Section 1.5. The precondition is $I(x)\&y\geq 0$, and the postcondition is $z=x{**}y$. Try to find an adequate Floydian expression for the loop cutpoints on lines 4 and 8 before turning to the end of this chapter.

```
 1   start        I(x)&y≥0
 2   z=1
 3   t1=y
 4   assert       z=x**(y−t1) & 0≤t1≤y, E4
 5   if t1<1 goto 19
 6        p=0
 7        t2=abs(x)
 8        assert          z=x**(y−t1) & p=z*(abs(x)−t2) &
                          1≤t1≤y & 0≤t2≤abs(x), E8
 9        if t2<1 goto 13
10             p=p+z
11             t2=t2−1
12             goto 8
13        if x<0 goto 16
14             z=p
15             goto 17
16             z=−p
17        t1=t1−1
18        goto 4
19   stop         z=x**y
```

As paths, path substitutions, and boolean path expressions, we have the following:

α Path	θ_α Path Substitution	b_α Boolean Path Expression
$a=\langle 1,2,3,4\rangle$	$[y,1\backslash t1,z]$	true
$b=\langle 4,5,6,7,8\rangle$	$[abs(x),0\backslash t2,p]$	$\sim t1<1$
$c=\langle 4,5,19\rangle$	$\in$	$t1<1$
$d=\langle 8,9,10,11,12,8\rangle$	$[t2-1,p+z\backslash t2,p]$	$\sim t2<1$
$e=\langle 8,9,13,14,15,17,18,4\rangle$	$[p,t1-1\backslash z,t1]$	$\sim x<0\&t2<1$
$f=\langle 8,9,13,16,17,18,4\rangle$	$[-p,t1-1\backslash z,t1]$	$x<0\&t2<1$

The verification conditions are as follows:

(VC_a) $p_1, b_a \vdash p_4\theta_a$
$I(x)\&y\geq 0,\ \text{true} \vdash 1=x{**}(y-y)\ \&\ 0\leq y\leq y$

(VC_b) $p_1, p_4, b_b \vdash p_8\theta_b$
$I(x)\&y\geq 0,\ z=x{**}(y-t1)\&0\leq t1\leq y,\ \sim t1<1$

$\vdash z{=}x{*}{*}(y{-}t1)\ \&\ 0{=}z{*}(\text{abs}(x){-}\text{abs}(x))\ \&$
$\quad 1{\leqslant}t1{\leqslant}y\ \&\ 0{\leqslant}\text{abs}(x){\leqslant}\text{abs}(x)$

(VC_c) $p_1, p_4, b_c \vdash p_{19}\theta_c$
$I(x)\&y{\geqslant}0,\ z{=}x{*}{*}(y{-}t1)\&0{\leqslant}t1{\leqslant}y,\ t1{<}1 \vdash z{=}x{*}{*}y$

(VC_d) $p_1, p_8, b_d \vdash p_8\theta_d$
$I(x)\&y{\geqslant}0,\ z{=}x{*}{*}(y{-}t1)\&p{=}z{*}(\text{abs}(x){-}t2)\&1{\leqslant}t1{\leqslant}y\ \&$
$\quad 0{\leqslant}t2{\leqslant}\text{abs}(x),\ {\sim}t2{<}1$
$\vdash z{=}x{*}{*}(y{-}t1)\ \&\ p{+}z{=}z{*}(\text{abs}(x){-}(t2{-}1))\ \&$
$\quad 1{\leqslant}t1{\leqslant}y\ \&\ 0{\leqslant}t2{-}1{\leqslant}\text{abs}(x)$

(VC_e) $p_1, p_8, b_e \vdash p_4\theta_e$
$I(x)\&y{\geqslant}0,\ z{=}x{*}{*}(y{-}t1)\&p{=}z{*}(\text{abs}(x){-}t2)\&1{\leqslant}t1{\leqslant}y\ \&$
$\quad 0{\leqslant}t2{\leqslant}\text{abs}(x),\ {\sim}x{<}0\&t2{<}1$
$\vdash p{=}x{*}{*}(y{-}(t1{-}1))\ \&\ 0{\leqslant}t1{-}1{\leqslant}y$

(VC_f) $p_1, p_8, b_f \vdash p_4\theta_f$
$I(x)\&y{\geqslant}0,\ z{=}x{*}{*}(y{-}t1)\&p{=}z{*}(\text{abs}(x){-}t2)\&1{\leqslant}t1{\leqslant}y\ \&$
$\quad 0{\leqslant}t2{\leqslant}\text{abs}(x),\ x{<}0\&t2{<}1$
$\vdash {-}p{=}x{*}{*}(y{-}(t1{-}1))\ \&\ 0{\leqslant}t1{-}1{\leqslant}y$

The well-foundedness conditions are as follows:

(WC_4) $p_1, p_4 \vdash E_4 \dot{\succcurlyeq} \langle 0 \rangle$
$I(x)\&y{\geqslant}0,\ z{=}x{*}{*}(y{-}t1)\&0{\leqslant}t1{\leqslant}y \vdash E_4 \dot{\succcurlyeq} \langle 0 \rangle$

(WC_8) $p_1, p_8 \vdash E_8 \dot{\succcurlyeq} \langle 0 \rangle$
$I(x)\&y{\geqslant}0,\ z{=}x{*}{*}(y{-}t1)\&p{=}z{*}(\text{abs}(x){-}t2)\&1{\leqslant}t1{\leqslant}y\ \&$
$\quad 0{\leqslant}t2{\leqslant}\text{abs}(x)$
$\vdash E_8 \dot{\succcurlyeq} \langle 0 \rangle$

The termination conditions are as follows:

(TC_b) $p_1, p_4, b_b \vdash E_4 \succ E_8\theta_b$
$I(x)\&y{\geqslant}0,\ z{=}x{*}{*}(y{-}t1)\&0{\leqslant}t1{\leqslant}y,\ {\sim}t1{<}1 \vdash E_4 \succ E_8\theta_b$

(TC_d) $p_1, p_8, b_d \vdash E_8 \succ E_8\theta_d$
$I(x)\&y{\geqslant}0,\ z{=}x{*}{*}(y{-}t1)\&p{=}z{*}(\text{abs}(x){-}t2)\&1{\leqslant}t1{\leqslant}y\ \&$
$\quad 0{\leqslant}t2{\leqslant}\text{abs}(x),\ {\sim}t2{<}1$
$\vdash E_8 \succ E_8\theta_d$

(TC_e) $p_1, p_8, b_e \vdash E_8 \succ E_4\theta_e$
$I(x)\&y{\geqslant}0,\ z{=}x{*}{*}(y{-}t1)\&p{=}z{*}(\text{abs}(x){-}t2)\&1{\leqslant}t1{\leqslant}y\ \&$
$\quad 0{\leqslant}t2{\leqslant}\text{abs}(x),\ {\sim}x{<}0\&t2{<}1$
$\vdash E_8 \succ E_4\theta_e$

(TC_f) $p_1, p_8, b_f \vdash E_8 \succ E_4\theta_f$
$I(x)\&y{\geqslant}0,\ z{=}x{*}{*}(y{-}t1)\&p{=}z{*}(\text{abs}(x){-}t2)\&1{\leqslant}t1{\leqslant}y\ \&$
$\quad 0{\leqslant}t2{\leqslant}\text{abs}(x),\ x{<}0\&t2{<}1$
$\vdash E_8 \succ E_4\theta_f$

EXAMPLE 4

The following unstructured program computes the greatest common divisor g of two positive odd integers x and y. The unary predicate symbols 'odd' and 'even' can be introduced into the theory of integers with the following explicit definitions:

(D.odd) $\quad \text{odd}(X) \leftrightarrow X \bmod 2 \neq 0$

and

(D.even) $\quad \text{even}(X) \leftrightarrow {\sim}\text{odd}(X)$[6]

```
1    start     x≥1 & y≥1 & odd(x) & odd(y)
2    s = x
3    g = y
4    assert    s≥1 & g≥1 & odd(s) & odd(g) &
               gcd(s,g)=gcd(x,y),        E4
5    if s≤g goto 9
6         t1 = s
7         s = g
8         g = t1
9    if s=g goto 16
10   t2 = g−s
11   assert    1≤s≤g & 1≤t2≤g & odd(s) & even(t2) &
               gcd(t2,s)=gcd(x,y),       E11
12        t2 = t2/2
13        if even(t2) goto 11
14   g = t2
15   goto 4
16   stop g=gcd(x,y)
```

We have added two loop cutpoints (lines 4 and 11), but only the one at line 11 is essential as it cuts both the inner and outer loops. Before reading on, the reader might wish to discover adequate Floydian expressions E_4 and E_{11}.

The paths are $a=\langle 1,2,3,4\rangle$, $b=\langle 4,5,6,7,8,9,10,11\rangle$, $c=\langle 4,5,9,10,11\rangle$, $d=\langle 11,12,13,11\rangle$, $e=\langle 11,12,13,14,15,4\rangle$, $f=\langle 4,5,6,7,8,9,16\rangle$, and $g=\langle 4,5,9,16\rangle$. The path substitutions and boolean path expressions are as

[6] The reader will notice that in the following program the defined predicate even occurs in a boolean expression on line 13. The virtual machine executing this program can evaluate even ($t2$) in a finite amount of time. In general, we place no syntactic restriction on predicates occurring within programs. This is due to the fact that different predicates are native to different virtual machines. However, we do require that each predicate native to a virtual machine be decidable. For more on decidable predicates, see Boolos and Jeffrey or Lewis and Papadimitriou.

follows:

$$\theta_a \equiv [x,y \backslash s,g] \qquad \mathrm{b}_a \equiv \text{true}$$
$$\theta_b \equiv [s,g,s,s-g \backslash t1,s,g,t2] \qquad \mathrm{b}_b \equiv {\sim}g{=}s \& {\sim}s{\leq}g$$
$$\theta_c \equiv [g-s \backslash t2] \qquad \mathrm{b}_c \equiv {\sim}s{=}g \& s{\leq}g$$
$$\theta_d \equiv [t2/2 \backslash t2] \qquad \mathrm{b}_d \equiv \text{even}(t2/2)$$
$$\theta_e \equiv [t2/2,t2/2 \backslash t2,g] \qquad \mathrm{b}_e \equiv {\sim}\text{even}(t2/2)$$
$$\theta_f \equiv [s,g,s \backslash t1,s,g] \qquad \mathrm{b}_f \equiv s{=}g \& {\sim}s{\leq}g$$
$$\theta_g \equiv \in \qquad \mathrm{b}_g \equiv s{=}g \& s{\leq}g$$

Notice that path f can never be executed, as reflected in the inconsistency of b_f.

The seven verification conditions are as follows:

(VC$_a$) $p_1,\mathrm{b}_a \vdash p_4\theta_a$
$x{\geq}1 \& y{\geq}1 \& \text{odd}(x) \& \text{odd}(y)$, true
$\vdash x{\geq}1 \& y{\geq}1 \& \text{odd}(x) \& \text{odd}(y) \ \& \ \text{gcd}(x,y){=}\text{gcd}(x,y)$

(VC$_b$) $p_1,p_4,\mathrm{b}_b \vdash p_{11}\theta_b$
$x{\geq}1 \& y{\geq}1 \& \text{odd}(x) \& \text{odd}(y)$, $s{\geq}1 \& g{\geq}1 \& \text{odd}(s) \& \text{odd}(g)$ &
$\text{gcd}(s,g){=}\text{gcd}(x,y)$, ${\sim}g{=}s \& {\sim}s{\leq}g$
$\vdash 1{\leq}g{\leq}s \& 1{\leq}s-g{\leq}s \& \text{odd}(g) \& \text{even}(s-g) \& \text{gcd}(s-g,g){=}$
$\text{gcd}(x,y)$

(VC$_c$) $p_1,p_4,\mathrm{b}_c \vdash p_{11}\theta_c$
$x{\geq}1 \& y{\geq}1 \& \text{odd}(x) \& \text{odd}(y)$, $s{\geq}1 \& g{\geq}1 \& \text{odd}(s) \& \text{odd}(g)$ &
$\text{gcd}(s,g){=}\text{gcd}(x,y)$, ${\sim}s{=}g \& s{\leq}g$
$\vdash 1{\leq}s{\leq}g \& 1{\leq}g-s{\leq}g \& \text{odd}(s) \& \text{even}(g-s) \& \text{gcd}(g-s,s){=}$
$\text{gcd}(x,y)$

(VC$_d$) $p_1,p_{11},\mathrm{b}_d \vdash p_{11}\theta_d$
$x{\geq}1 \& y{\geq}1 \& \text{odd}(x) \& \text{odd}(y)$, $1{\leq}s{\leq}g \& 1{\leq}t2{\leq}g$ &
$\text{odd}(s) \& \text{even}(t2) \& \text{gcd}(t2,s){=}\text{gcd}(x,y)$, $\text{even}(t2/2)$
$\vdash 1{\leq}s{\leq}g \& 1{\leq}t2/2{\leq}g \& \text{odd}(s) \& \text{even}(t2/2)$ &
$\text{gcd}(t2/2,s){=}\text{gcd}(x,y)$

(VC$_e$) $p_1,p_{11},\mathrm{b}_e \vdash p_4\theta_e$
$x{\geq}1 \& y{\geq}1 \& \text{odd}(x) \& \text{odd}(y)$, $1{\leq}s{\leq}g \& 1{\leq}t2{\leq}g$ &
$\text{odd}(s) \& \text{even}(t2) \& \text{gcd}(t2,s){=}\text{gcd}(x,y)$, ${\sim}\text{even}(t2/2)$
$\vdash s{\geq}1 \& t2/2{\geq}1 \& \text{odd}(s) \& \text{odd}(t2/2) \& \text{gcd}(s,t2/2){=}\text{gcd}(x,y)$

(VC$_f$) $p_1,p_4,\mathrm{b}_f \vdash p_{16}\theta_f$
$x{\geq}1 \& y{\geq}1 \& \text{odd}(x) \& \text{odd}(y)$, $s{\geq}1 \& g{\geq}1 \& \text{odd}(s) \& \text{odd}(g)$ &
$\text{gcd}(s,g){=}\text{gcd}(x,y)$, $s{=}g \& {\sim}s{\leq}g$
$\vdash s{=}\text{gcd}(x,y)$

(VC$_g$) $p_1, p_4, b_g \vdash p_{16}\theta_g$
$x \geqslant 1 \& y \geqslant 1 \& odd(x) \& odd(y),\ s \geqslant 1 \& g \geqslant 1 \& odd(s) \& odd(g)\ \&$
$gcd(s,g) = gcd(x,y),\ s = g \& s \leqslant g$
$\vdash g = gcd(x,y)$

The two well-foundedness conditions are as follows:

(WC$_4$) $p_1, p_4 \vdash E_4 \dot{\geqslant} \langle 0 \rangle$
$x \geqslant 1 \& y \geqslant 1 \& odd(x) \& odd(y),\ s \geqslant 1 \& g \geqslant 1 \& odd(s) \& odd(g)\ \&$
$gcd(s,g) = gcd(x,y)$
$\vdash E_4 \dot{\geqslant} \langle 0 \rangle$

(WC$_{11}$) $p_1, p_{11} \vdash E_{11} \dot{\geqslant} \langle 0 \rangle$
$x \geqslant 1 \& y \geqslant 1 \& odd(x) \& odd(y),\ 1 \leqslant s \leqslant g \& 1 \leqslant t2 \leqslant g\ \&$
$odd(s) \& even\ (t2) \& gcd(t2,s) = gcd(x,y)$
$\vdash E_{11} \dot{\geqslant} \langle 0 \rangle$

The four termination conditions are as follows:

(TC$_b$) $p_1, p_4, b_b \vdash E_4 \succ E_{11}\theta_b$
$x \geqslant 1 \& y \geqslant 1 \& odd(x) \& odd(y),\ s \geqslant 1 \& g \geqslant 1 \& odd(s) \& odd(g)\ \&$
$gcd(s,g) = gcd(x,y),\ \sim g = s \& \sim s \leqslant g$
$\vdash E_4 \succ E_{11}\theta_b$

(TC$_c$) $p_1, p_4, b_c \vdash E_4 \succ E_{11}\theta_c$
$x \geqslant 1 \& y \geqslant 1 \& odd(x) \& odd(y),\ s \geqslant 1 \& g \geqslant 1 \& odd(s) \& odd(g)\ \&$
$gcd(s,g) = gcd(x,y),\ \sim s = g \& s \leqslant g$
$\vdash E_4 \succ E_{11}\theta_c$

(TC$_d$) $p_1, p_{11}, b_d \vdash E_{11} \succ E_{11}\theta_d$
$x \geqslant 1 \& y \geqslant 1 \& odd(x) \& odd(y),\ 1 \leqslant s \leqslant g \& 1 \leqslant t2 \leqslant g\ \&$
$odd(s) \& even(t2) \& gcd(t2,s) = gcd(x,y),\ even(t2/2)$
$\vdash E_{11} \succ E_{11}\theta_d$

(TC$_e$) $p_1, p_{11}, b_e \vdash E_{11} \succ E_4\theta_e$
$x \geqslant 1 \& y \geqslant 1 \& odd(x) \& odd(y),\ 1 \leqslant s \leqslant g \& 1 \leqslant t2 \leqslant g\ \&$
$odd(s) \& even(t2) \& gcd(t2,s) = gcd(x,y),\ \sim even(t2/2)$
$\vdash E_{11} \succ E_4\theta_e$

Notice that (VC$_f$) holds because b_f is inconsistent.

EXAMPLE 5

The following FC program is the translation of the **while** program presented in Example 5 of Section 1.5. The complexity of the inductive assertions and the Floydian expressions results from a hypothetical requirement (which we assume for the moment for the sake of making a point) that a loop cutpoint be placed at the beginning of each loop. Before presenting the program, we introduce some predicate and operation symbols into the theory of integers. Intuitively, the predicate 'first' expresses the fact that this is the first time program control has reached loop cutpoint 4 (more accurately, that the variables $t1$ and $t2$ still have their initial values of x and y). The operation symbols '$e_{4,i}$', '$e_{6,i}$', and '$e_{10,i}$' (i=1,2) are to be used as (ordered pairs in) Floydian expressions and, outside of this program, they have no intuitive reading. In this program, their role can be understood by studying either (formally) the termination conditions or (informally) the relationships that hold the first and subsequent times the flow of control reaches the loop cutpoints on which they are placed. The introduction of these operation symbols illustrates the point that, to simplify program proving, we sometimes find it convenient to introduce symbols into arithmetic (using explicit definitions when possible) that are, for arithmetic itself, devoid of significance. We have the following:

$$\text{first}(X,Y,T1,T2) \leftrightarrow T1=X \;\&\; T2=Y$$

$$e_{4,1}(X,Y,T1,T2)=Z \leftrightarrow (\text{first}(X,Y,T1,T2) \rightarrow Z=T1+T2) \;\&\; ({\sim}\text{first}(X,Y,T1,T2) \rightarrow Z=T1)$$

$$e_{4,2}(X,Y,T1,T2)=Z \leftrightarrow (\text{first}(X,Y,T1,T2) \rightarrow Z=1) \;\&\; ({\sim}\text{first}(X,Y,T1,T2) \rightarrow Z=T2)$$

$$e_{6,1}(X,Y,T1,T2)=Z \leftrightarrow (\text{first}(X,Y,T1,T2) \rightarrow Z=T1+T2) \;\&\; ({\sim}\text{first}(X,Y,T1,T2) \rightarrow Z=T2)$$

$$e_{6,2}(X,Y,T1,T2)=Z \leftrightarrow (\text{first}(X,Y,T1,T2) \rightarrow Z=0) \;\&\; ({\sim}\text{first}(X,Y,T1,T2) \rightarrow Z=T1+2)$$

$$e_{10,1}(X,Y,T1,T2) = T1$$

$$e_{10,2}(X,Y,T1,T2) = T2+1$$

We write $E_i(X,Y,T1,T2)$ (i=4,6,10) as an abbreviation for $\langle e_{i,1}(X,Y,T1,T2), e_{i,2}(X,Y,T1,T2)\rangle$. The 4-ary predicate 'g' is the loop invariant of Example 5 in Section 1.5.

```
1    start   x≥1 & y≥1
2    t1 = x
3    t2 = y
4    assert  g(x,y,t1,t2) & (~first(x,y,t1,t2)→t1≥t2),
             E4(x,y,t1,t2)
5    if t1=t2 goto 15
6        assert     g(x,y,t1,t2) & (t1=t2→~first(x,y,t1,t2)),
             E6(x,y,t1,t2)
7        if t1≤t2 goto 10
8            t1 = t1−t2
```

```
 9        goto 6
10        assert    g(x,y,t1,t2) & (t2≤t1→~first(x,y,t1,t2)),
                E10(x,y,t1,t2)
11        if t2≤t1 goto 14
12              t2 = t2−t1
13        goto 10
14    goto 4
15    stop t1=gcd(x,y)
```

The paths, path substitutions, and boolean path expressions are as follows:

α Path	θ_α Path Substitution	$\mathbf{b}_\alpha$ Boolean Path Expression
$a=\langle 1,2,3,4\rangle$	$[x,y\backslash t1,t2]$	true
$b=\langle 4,5,6\rangle$	$\in$	$\sim t1=t2$
$c=\langle 6,7,8,9,6\rangle$	$[t1-t2\backslash t1]$	$\sim t1\leq t2$
$d=\langle 6,7,10\rangle$	$\in$	$t1\leq t2$
$e=\langle 10,11,12,13,10\rangle$	$[t2-t1\backslash t2]$	$\sim t2\leq t1$
$f=\langle 10,11,14,4\rangle$	$\in$	$t2\leq t1$
$g=\langle 4,5,15\rangle$	$\in$	$t1=t2$

The seven verification conditions are as follows:

(VC$_a$) $p_1, \mathrm{b}_a \vdash p_4\theta_a$

$x\geq 1 \& y\geq 1$, true $\vdash \mathrm{g}(x,y,x,y) \& (\sim\mathrm{first}(x,y,x,y)\rightarrow x\geq y)$

(VC$_b$) $p_1, p_4, \mathrm{b}_b \vdash p_6\theta_b$

$x\geq 1 \& y\geq 1$, $\mathrm{g}(x,y,t1,t2) \& (\sim\mathrm{first}(x,y,t1,t2)\rightarrow t1\geq t2)$,
$\sim t1=t2$
$\vdash \mathrm{g}(x,y,t1,t2) \& (t1=t2\rightarrow\sim\mathrm{first}(x,y,t1,t2))$

(VC$_c$) $p_1, p_6, \mathrm{b}_c \vdash p_6\theta_c$

$x\geq 1 \& y\geq 1$, $\mathrm{g}(x,y,t1,t2) \& (t1=t2\rightarrow\sim\mathrm{first}(x,y,t1,t2))$
$\sim t1\leq t2$
$\vdash \mathrm{g}(x,y,t1-t2,t2) \& (t1-t2=t2\rightarrow\sim\mathrm{first}(x,y,t1-t2,t2))$

(VC$_d$) $p_1, p_6, \mathrm{b}_d \vdash p_{10}\theta_d$

$x\geq 1 \& y\geq 1$, $\mathrm{g}(x,y,t1,t2) \& (t1=t2\rightarrow\sim\mathrm{first}(x,y,t1,t2))$,
$t1\leq t2$
$\vdash \mathrm{g}(x,y,t1,t2) \& (t2\leq t1\rightarrow\sim\mathrm{first}(x,y,t1,t2))$

(VC$_e$) $p_1, p_{10}, \mathrm{b}_e \vdash p_{10}\theta_e$

$x\geq 1 \& y\geq 1$, $\mathrm{g}(x,y,t1,t2) \& (t2\leq t1\rightarrow\sim\mathrm{first}(x,y,t1,t2))$,
$\sim t2\leq t1$
$\vdash \mathrm{g}(x,y,t1,t2-t1) \& (t2-t1\leq t1\rightarrow\sim\mathrm{first}(x,y,t1,t2-t1))$

$$(\mathrm{VC}_f)\quad p_1, p_{10}, \mathrm{b}_f \vdash p_4\theta_f$$
$$x \geqslant 1 \,\&\, y \geqslant 1,\ \mathrm{g}(x,y,t1,t2) \,\&\, (t2 \leqslant t1 \rightarrow \sim\mathrm{first}(x,y,t1,t2)),\ t2 \leqslant t1$$
$$\vdash \mathrm{g}(x,y,t_1,t2) \,\&\, (\sim\mathrm{first}(x,y,t1,t2) \rightarrow t1 \geqslant t2)$$

$$(\mathrm{VC}_g)\quad p_1, p_4, \mathrm{b}_g \vdash p_{15}\theta_g$$
$$x \geqslant 1 \,\&\, y \geqslant 1,\ \mathrm{g}(x,y,t1,t2) \,\&\, (\sim\mathrm{first}(x,y,t1,t2) \rightarrow t1 \geqslant t2),\ t1 = t2$$
$$\vdash t1 = \mathrm{gcd}(x,y)$$

The three well-foundedness conditions are as follows:

$$(\mathrm{WC}_4)\quad p_1, p_4 \vdash \mathrm{E}_4(x,y,t1,t2) \succcurlyeq \langle 0 \rangle$$
$$x \geqslant 1 \,\&\, y \geqslant 1,\ \mathrm{g}(x,y,t1,t2) \,\&\, (\sim\mathrm{first}(x,y,t1,t2) \rightarrow t1 \geqslant t2)$$
$$\vdash \mathrm{E}_4(x,y,t1,t2) \succcurlyeq \langle 0,0 \rangle$$

$$(\mathrm{WC}_6)\quad p_1, p_6 \vdash \mathrm{E}_6(x,y,t1,t2) \succcurlyeq \langle 0 \rangle$$
$$x \geqslant 1 \,\&\, y \geqslant 1,\ \mathrm{g}(x,y,t1,t2) \,\&\, (t1 = t2 \rightarrow \sim\mathrm{first}(x,y,t1,t2))$$
$$\vdash \mathrm{E}_6(x,y,t1,t2) \succcurlyeq \langle 0,0 \rangle$$

$$(\mathrm{WC}_{10})\quad p_1, p_{10} \vdash \mathrm{E}_{10}(x,y,t1,t2) \succcurlyeq \langle 0 \rangle$$
$$x \geqslant 1 \,\&\, y \geqslant 1,\ \mathrm{g}(x,y,t1,t2) \,\&\, (t2 \leqslant t1 \rightarrow \sim\mathrm{first}(x,y,t1,t2))$$
$$\vdash \langle t1, t2+1 \rangle \succcurlyeq \langle 0,0 \rangle$$

The five termination conditions are as follows:

$$(\mathrm{TC}_b)\quad p_1, p_4, \mathrm{b}_b \vdash \mathrm{E}_4(x,y,t1,t2) \succ \mathrm{E}_6(x,y,t1,t2)\theta_b$$
$$x \geqslant 1 \,\&\, y \geqslant 1,\ \mathrm{g}(x,y,t1,t2) \,\&\, (\sim\mathrm{first}(x,y,t1,t2) \rightarrow t1 \geqslant t2),\ \sim t1 = t2$$
$$\vdash \mathrm{E}_4(x,y,t1,t2) \succ \mathrm{E}_6(x,y,t1,t2)$$

$$(\mathrm{TC}_c)\quad p_1, p_6, \mathrm{b}_c \vdash \mathrm{E}_6(x,y,t1,t2) \succ \mathrm{E}_6(x,y,t1,t2)\theta_c$$
$$x \geqslant 1 \,\&\, y \geqslant 1,\ \mathrm{g}(x,y,t1,t2) \,\&\, (t1 = t2 \rightarrow \sim\mathrm{first}(x,y,t1,t2)),\ \sim t1 \leqslant t2$$
$$\vdash \mathrm{E}_6(x,y,t1,t2) \succ \mathrm{E}_6(x,y,t1-t2,t2)$$

$$(\mathrm{TC}_d)\quad p_1, p_6, \mathrm{b}_d \vdash \mathrm{E}_6(x,y,t1,t2) \succ \mathrm{E}_{10}(x,y,t1,t2)\theta_d$$
$$x \geqslant 1 \,\&\, y \geqslant 1,\ \mathrm{g}(x,y,t1,t2) \,\&\, (t1 = t2 \rightarrow \sim\mathrm{first}(x,y,t1,t2)),\ t1 \leqslant t2$$
$$\vdash \mathrm{E}_6(x,y,t1,t2) \succ \langle t1, t2+1 \rangle$$

$$(\mathrm{TC}_e)\quad p_1, p_{10}, \mathrm{b}_e \vdash \mathrm{E}_{10}(x,y,t1,t2) \succ \mathrm{E}_{10}(x,y,t1,t2)\theta_e$$
$$x \geqslant 1 \,\&\, y \geqslant 1,\ \mathrm{g}(x,y,t1,t2) \,\&\, (t2 \leqslant t1 \rightarrow \sim\mathrm{first}(x,y,t1,t2)),\ \sim t2 \leqslant t1$$
$$\vdash \langle t1, t2+1 \rangle \succ \langle t1, t2-t1+1 \rangle$$

$$(\mathrm{TC}_f)\quad p_1, p_{10}, \mathrm{b}_f \vdash \mathrm{E}_{10}(x,y,t1,t2) \succ \mathrm{E}_4(x,y,t1,t2)\theta_f$$
$$x \geqslant 1 \,\&\, y \geqslant 1,\ \mathrm{g}(x,y,t1,t2) \,\&\, (t2 \leqslant t1 \rightarrow \sim\mathrm{first}(x,y,t1,t2)),\ t2 \leqslant t1$$
$$\vdash \langle t1, t2+1 \rangle \succ \mathrm{E}_4(x,y,t1,t2)$$

The reader who has carefully followed the details of this proof will appreciate its complexity. By dropping the requirement that a loop cutpoint must be placed at the beginning of a loop, a simpler proof can be had. See Exercise 15. We will discuss this example further in Chapter 4, when we compare the methods of Floyd and Hoare.

EXERCISES

Proving Programs Correct

1. (a) Write an FC program to compute $x-y$ using only the unary operation symbols 'succ' and 'pred'. (Neither the unary nor the binary operation symbol '$-$' should occur in your program). The precondition is $p \equiv x \geqslant 0$ & $y \geqslant 0$, and the postcondition is $r \equiv z = x - y$.

   (b) Using the Floyd method, prove that your program is totally correct.

2. (a) Write an FC program to compute $x*y$ using the method of successive additions (the operation symbol '*' should not occur in your program). The precondition is $p \equiv \mathrm{I}(x)$ & $\mathrm{I}(y)$, and the postcondition is $r \equiv z = x*y$.

   (b) Using the Floyd method, prove that your program is totally correct.

3. (a) Write an FC program to determine which integer variable, x or y, has the greatest absolute value. Do not use the 'abs' operation symbol (or the binary operation symbols 'min' and 'max') in your program. The precondition is $p \equiv \mathrm{I}(x)\&\mathrm{I}(y)$, and the postcondition is $r \equiv z = \max(\mathrm{abs}(x), \mathrm{abs}(y))$.

   (b) Using the Floyd method, prove that your program is totally correct.

4. (a) Write an FC program to compute $x+y$ using only the unary operation symbols 'abs', 'pred' and 'succ'. Make your program efficient by using the smaller of abs(x) and abs(y) as the final expression for your loop control variable. The precondition is $p \equiv \mathrm{I}(x)$ & $\mathrm{I}(y)$, and the postcondition is $r \equiv z = x + y$.

   (b) Using the Floyd method, prove that your program is totally correct.

5. (a) Write an FC program to compute $x*y$ using only the operation symbols 'pred' and 'succ'. The precondition is $p \equiv x \geqslant 0$ & $y \geqslant 0$, and the postcondition is $r \equiv z = x*y$.

   (b) Using the Floyd method, prove that your program is totally correct.

6. (a) Write an FC program to compute x/y using only the operation symbols 'abs', 'pred', and 'succ'. The precondition is $p \equiv \mathrm{I}(x)$ & $\mathrm{I}(y)$, and the postcondition is $r \equiv z = x/y$.

   (b) Using the Floyd method, prove that your program is totally correct.

7. (a) Write an FC program to compute $x**y$ using only the operation symbols 'abs', 'pred', and 'succ'. The precondition is $p \equiv x \geqslant 0$ & $y \geqslant 0$, and the postcondition is $r \equiv z = x**y$.

(b) Using the Floyd method, prove that your program is totally correct.

8. (a) Write an FC program to determine if an integer x is prime. The precondition is $p \equiv \mathrm{I}(x)$, and the postcondition is $r \equiv$

$$(\mathrm{prime}(x) \rightarrow xprime=1)\ \&\ ((\sim\mathrm{prime}(x) \rightarrow xprime=0)$$

(b) Using the Floyd method, prove that your program is totally correct.

9. (a) Write an FC program to find the n-th prime number. Let nthprime(X) be the X-th prime number. The precondition is $p \equiv n \geqslant 1$, and the postcondition is $r \equiv nthprimen = \mathrm{nthprime}(n)$.

(b) Using the Floyd method, prove that your program is totally correct.

10. (a) Write an FC program to determine if an integer x is a perfect number. (See Exercise 10 in Chapter 1 for examples of perfect numbers.) The precondition is $p \equiv x \geqslant 1$, and the postcondition is $r \equiv$

$$(\mathrm{perfect}(x) \rightarrow xperfect=1)\ \&\ ((\sim\mathrm{perfect}(x) \rightarrow xperfect=0)$$

(b) Using the Floyd method, prove that your program is totally correct.

11. The following FC program finds the largest integer stored in $m1$, $m2$, or $m3$:

```
1    start          true
2    if m1<m2 goto 8
3         if m1<m3 goto 6
4              g = m1
5         goto 12
6              g = m3
7    goto 12
8         if m2<m3 goto 11
9              g = m2
10        goto 12
11             g = m3
12   stop      g = max(m1,m2,m3)
```

Note: Understand $\max(m1,m2,m3) = \max(\max(m1,m2),m3)$
$= \max(m1,\max(m2,m3))$.

Let path $a = \langle 1,2,3,4,5,12 \rangle$.

(a) List the other paths in the program.

(b) For each path α, list θ_α, b_α, and (VC_α).

12. The following FC program computes $z=x+y$. Using the Floyd method, prove that this program is totally correct wrt the precondition $\mathrm{I}(x)\&\mathrm{I}(y)$ and the postcondition $z=x+y$. Begin by finding a suitable loop invariant p_4 and a suitable Floydian expression E_4.

```
1    start     I(x)&I(y)
2    z = x
```

```
3     t = y
4     assert   p4,E4
5     if t=0 goto 13
6         if t<0 goto 10
7             z = succ(z)
8             t = pred(r)
9         goto 12
10            z = pred(z)
11            t = succ(t)
12    goto 4
13    stop z=x+y
```

13. The following FC program computes $t1=\text{gcd}(x,y)$. Using the Floyd method, prove that this program is totally correct wrt the precondition $x \geq 1 \& y \geq 1$ and the postcondition $t1=\text{gcd}(x,y)$. Begin by finding a suitable loop invariant p_4 and a suitable Floydian expression E_4.

```
1     start  x≥1&y≥1
2     t1 = x
3     t2 = y
4     assert p4,E4
5     if t1=t2 goto 11
6       if t1≤t2 goto 9
7           t1 = t1−t2
8       goto 10
9           t2 = t2−1
10    goto 4
11    stop   t1=gcd(x,y)
```

14. The following FC program computes $g=\text{gcd}(x,y)$. Using the Floyd method, prove that this program is totally correct wrt the precondition $I(x)\&I(y)$ and the postcondition $g=\text{gcd}(x,y)$. Begin by finding a suitable loop invariant p_8 and a suitable Floydian expression E_8.

```
1     start       I(x)&I(y)
2     if abs(x)≤abs(y) goto 6
3         g = abs(x)
4         s = abs(y)
5     goto 8
6         g = abs(y)
7         s = abs(x)
8     assert     p8,E8
9     if s=0 goto 14
10        t = s
11        s = g mod s
```

```
12          g = t
13      goto 8
14      stop        g=gcd(x,y)
```

15. The following program computes $t1$=gcd(x,y). Write out the paths, the path substitutions, the boolean path expressions, as well as the verification, well-foundedness, and termination conditions. Notice that each loop contains a cutpoint, but that the outer loop is not cut at the beginning. (Compare Example 5 in Section 2.5.)

```
 1      start     x≥1 & y≥1
 2      t1 = x
 3      t2 = y
 4      if t1=t2 goto 14
 5          assert      g(x,y,t1,t2), ⟨t2,t1+1⟩
 6          if t1≤t2 goto 9
 7              t1 = t1−t2
 8          goto 5
 9          assert      g(x,y,t1,t2), ⟨t1,t2⟩
10          if t2≤t1 goto 13
11              t2 = t2−t1
12          goto 9
13      goto 4
14      stop t1=gcd(x,y)
```

16. The following FC program computes sqrt(x), the integer square root of x. Using the Floyd method, prove that this program is totally correct wrt the precondition I(x) and the postcondition *sqrtx*=sqrt(x). Begin by finding a suitable loop invariant p_5 and a suitable Floydian expression E_5.

```
 1      start     I(x)
 2      sqrtx = 0
 3      sum = 1
 4      nextodd = 1
 5      assert    p5,E5
 6      if sum>x goto 11
 7          sqrtx = sqrtx+1
 8          nextodd = nextodd+2
 9          sum = sum+nextodd
10      goto 5
11      stop      sqrtx=sqrt(x)
```

17. The following FC program computes $x{*}{*}y$. Using the Floyd method, prove that this program is totally correct wrt the precondition I(x)&I(y)

and the postcondition $z{=}x{**}y$. Begin by finding a suitable loop invariant p_8 and a suitable Floydian expression E_8.

```
1    start   I(x)&I(y)
2    if y≥0 goto 5
3        z = 0
4    goto 16
5        t1 = x
6        t2 = y
7        z = 1
8        assert  p8,E8
9        if t2=0 goto 16
10           if t2 mod 2 ≠ 1 goto 13
11               t2 = t2−1
12               z = z*t1
13           t1 = t1*t1
14           t2 = t2/2
15       goto 8
16   stop    z=x**y
```

18. McCarthy's 91 function M91 can be introduced into the theory of integers with the explicit definition

$$\textbf{(D.M91)}\qquad M91(X){=}Y \leftrightarrow (X{>}100 \rightarrow Y{=}X{-}10)\ \&\ (X{\leq}100 \rightarrow Y{=}91)$$

Using the methods of inductive assertions and well-founded sets, prove that the following FC program is totally correct with respect to the specification indicated on the **start** and **stop** commands. Add cutpoints and renumber lines as necessary.

```
1    start   I(x)
2    y = x
3    z = 1
4    if y>100 goto 8
5        y = y+11
6        z = z+1
7    goto 4
8    if z=1 goto 12
9        y = y−10
10       z = z−1
11   goto 4
12   y = y−10
13   stop    y=M91(x)
```

Semantics

19. In the style of Section 2.2, give the operational semantics of

(a) the

clear x

command, which sets the value of x to 0.

(b) the

bump x

command, which increments the value of x by 1.

(c) the

swap x,y

command, which exchanges the values of x and y.

(d) the

skip x

command, which skips the next command if the value of x is 0.

20. Let $E=\langle x_1, \ldots ,x_n\rangle$ and $E'=\langle x_1', \ldots ,x_n'\rangle$. Give integer expressions e and e' such that $e>e'$ iff $E > E'$.

21. Suppose that an FC program could (1) have more than one **stop** command, (2) have the **start** command and the **stop** commands in any location, and (3) have gaps in the numbering (labeling) of the commands. For example, with our previous restrictions removed, the following program counts as a syntactically legal FC program that is totally correct wrt the specification $\langle \mathrm{I}(x)\&\mathrm{I}(y), s=\min(x,y)\rangle$:

5	**start**	$\mathrm{I}(x)\&\mathrm{I}(y)$
6	**if** $x<y$ **goto** 1	
7		$s=y$
8	**stop**	$s=\min(x,y)$
1		$s=x$
2	**stop**	$s=\min(x,y)$

In this context, define in the style illustrated on page 96 the following (italicized) predicates:

(a) An FC program P is *partially correct* wrt specification $\langle p,q\rangle$

(b) An FC program P *terminates* for precondition p.

(c) An FC program P is *totally correct* wrt specification $\langle p,q\rangle$.

22. Recall that Restriction (6) on the syntax of FC programs bars a conditional **goto** from going to the next location. Suppose Restriction (6) was dropped. Restate Step (dii) in the part of the VCG algorithm (Section 2.3), in which θ_α and b_α are constructed to handle this change in the syntax. Prove that your new Step (dii) preserves the soundness theorem in Section 2.4. (Such uses of the conditional **goto** make no sense, and a compiler with reasonable diagnostic facilitates should flag them.)

23. Give an example of the following:

(a) An FC program that can be proven to be totally correct.

(b) A totally correct FC program that cannot be proven totally correct.

(c) A partially but not totally correct FC program that can be proven to be partially correct.

(d) A partially but not totally correct FC program that cannot be proven to be partially correct.

(e) An FC program that is not partially correct.

HINT: Recall that arithmetic is incomplete and that the halting problem is unsolvable. In your answer to (b), for example, you might let g be any true but unprovable sentence of arithmetic.

Programming Projects

24. In your favorite programming language, write an interpreter for the FC programs. The input for your program consists of an FC program and integers to be stored in the input variables. Your output should show a trace of program execution.

25. In your favorite programming language, write a program to find all the paths in an FC program. The input for your program is an FC program, and the output is a list of the paths in the program. Use the format illustrated in the text, in which each path is a sequence of locations with the first path labeled a, the second labeled b, and so on.

26. In your favorite programming language, implement the VCG algorithm. The input for your program is a sequence of commands along a path in an FC program, and the output is the verification condition for that path.

Adequate Floydian Expressions (Section 2.5):

Example 1

Take $E_4 \equiv r$. The well-foundedness and termination conditions are

$$(WC_4) \qquad x \geqslant 0 \& y \geqslant 1,\ x = y * q + r \& 0 \leqslant r \leqslant x \vdash r \geqslant 0$$

$$(TC_b) \qquad x \geqslant 0 \& y \geqslant 1,\ x = y * q + r \& 0 \leqslant r \leqslant x,\ \sim r < y \vdash r > r - y$$

Example 3

Take $E_4 \equiv \langle t1, \text{abs}(x)+1\rangle$ and $E_8 \equiv \langle t1,t2\rangle$. The well-foundedness and termination conditions are as follows:

(WC$_4$) $\text{I}(x)\&y\geqslant 0,\ z=x**(y-t1)\&0\leqslant t1\leqslant y \vdash \langle t1,\text{abs}(x)+1\rangle \succcurlyeq \langle 0,0\rangle$

(WC$_8$) $\text{I}(x)\&y\geqslant 0,\ z=x**(y-t1)\&p=z*(\text{abs}(x)-t2)\&1\leqslant t1\leqslant y\ \&$
$0\leqslant t2\leqslant \text{abs}(x)$
$\vdash \langle t1,t2\rangle \succcurlyeq \langle 0,0\rangle$

(TC$_b$) $\text{I}(x)\&y\geqslant 0,\ z=x**(y-t1)\&0\leqslant t1\leqslant y,\ \sim t1<1$
$\vdash \langle t1,\text{abs}(x)+1\rangle \succ \langle t1,\text{abs}(x)\rangle$

(TC$_d$) $\text{I}(x)\&y\geqslant 0,\ z=x**(y-t1)\&p=z*(\text{abs}(x)-t2)\&1\leqslant t1\leqslant y\ \&$
$0\leqslant t2\leqslant \text{abs}(x),\ \sim t2<1$
$\vdash \langle t1,t2\rangle \succ \langle t1,t2-1\rangle$

(TC$_e$) $\text{I}(x)\&y\geqslant 0,\ z=x**(y-t1)\&p=z*(\text{abs}(x)-t2)\&1\leqslant t1\leqslant y\ \&$
$0\leqslant t2\leqslant \text{abs}(x),\ \sim x<0\&t2<1$
$\vdash \langle t1,t2\rangle \succ \langle t1-1,\text{abs}(x)+1\rangle$

(TC$_f$) $\text{I}(x)\&y\geqslant 0,\ z=x**(y-t1)\&p=z*(\text{abs}(x)-t2)\&1\leqslant t1\leqslant y\ \&$
$0\leqslant t2\leqslant \text{abs}(x),\ x<0\&t2<1$
$\vdash \langle t1,t2\rangle \succ \langle t1-1,\text{abs}(x)+1\rangle$

Example 4

Take $E_4 \equiv s+g$ and $E_{11} \equiv s+t2$. The well-foundedness and termination conditions are as follows:

(WC$_4$) $x\geqslant 1\&y\geqslant 1\&\text{odd}(x)\&\text{odd}(y),\ s\geqslant 1\&g\geqslant 1\&\text{odd}(s)\&\text{odd}(g)\ \&$
$\text{gcd}(s,g)=\text{gcd}(x,y)$
$\vdash s+g\geqslant 0$

(WC$_{11}$) $x\geqslant 1\&y\geqslant 1\&\text{odd}(x)\&\text{odd}(y),\ 1\leqslant s\leqslant g\&1\leqslant t2\leqslant g\ \&$
$\text{odd}(s)\&\text{even}(t2)\&\text{gcd}(t2,s)=\text{gcd}(x,y)$
$\vdash s+t2\geqslant 0$

(TC$_b$) $x\geqslant 1\&y\geqslant 1\&\text{odd}(x)\&\text{odd}(y),\ s\geqslant 1\&g\geqslant 1\&\text{odd}(s)\&\text{odd}(g)\ \&$
$\text{gcd}(s,g)=\text{gcd}(x,y),\ \sim g=s\&\sim s\leqslant g$
$\vdash s+g>g+s-g$

(TC$_c$) $x\geqslant 1\&y\geqslant 1\&\text{odd}(x)\&\text{odd}(y),\ s\geqslant 1\&g\geqslant 1\&\text{odd}(s)\&\text{odd}(g)\ \&$
$\text{gcd}(s,g)=\text{gcd}(x,y),\ \sim s=g\&s\leqslant g$
$\vdash s+g>s+g-s$

(TC$_d$) $x\geqslant 1\&y\geqslant 1\&\text{odd}(x)\&\text{odd}(y),\ 1\leqslant s\leqslant g\&1\leqslant t2\leqslant g\ \&$
$\text{odd}(s)\&\text{even}(t2)\&\text{gcd}(t2,s)=\text{gcd}(x,y),\ \text{even}\ (t2/2)$
$\vdash s+t2>s+t2/2$

(TC$_e$) $x\geqslant 1\&y\geqslant 1\&\text{odd}(x)\&\text{odd}(y),\ 1\leqslant s\leqslant g\&1\leqslant t2\leqslant g\ \&$
$\text{odd}(s)\&\text{even}(t2)\&\text{gcd}(t2,s)=\text{gcd}(x,y),\ \sim\text{even}(t2/2)$
$\vdash s+t2>s+t2/2$

CHAPTER 3

The Total Correctness of Flowchart Programs with Arrays and Input and Output

In this chapter, we study the programming language FC+, obtained by extending the syntax and semantics of FC programs to encompass referencing subscripted variables in one-dimensional arrays, reading from the standard input file, and writing to the standard output file. Our principal occupation in this chapter will be with using Floyd's method to prove the total correctness of longer and more interesting algorithms than those we have already seen. Using the methods of inductive assertions and well-founded sets, we will be able to prove the total correctness of, for example, searching, sorting, and merging algorithms. To simplify our proofs, we will ignore such problems as reading past the end-of-file and violating array bounds. We will treat these problems in Chapter 5, where we present a more adequate formalism for dealing with execution-time errors.

To simplify our proofs even further, we will, for example, restrict the syntax of subscripted variables. In the subscripted variable $a(se)$, we prohibit occurrences of an array variable in the subscript expression *se*. Even with this restriction, the verification conditions that we will generate with the VCG algorithm will be more complicated than those in Chapter 2. Regarding the semantics, we understand the standard input and output files to be sequential files of infinite length (in both directions). Similarly, we consider any numeral m to be a legitimate index for the one-dimensional array a. The two factors that call for this somewhat unrealistic semantics are (1) our wish to ignore execution-time errors in our proofs of program correctness, and (2) the necessity of preserving the soundness of the Floyd method with respect to the semantics.

The organization of this chapter is similar to that of the two preceding chapters except that we include a brief discussion in Section 3.6 of the possible advantage of using higher-order specifications (e.g., using assertions of second-order arithmetic to express specifications).

3.1. SYNTAX

The syntax of FC+ is designed to eliminate the nesting of both array variables in subscript expressions and the file name *out* in integer expressions naming an output file record number. For example, neither $a(a(1))$ nor $out(out(1))$ are well-formed by our syntax.[1] By eliminating such nesting from our programs and assertions, we can simplify significantly Floyd's method for proving program correctness as well as proof of the method's soundness.

The set of *subscript variables* is **Svar.** Subscript variables are the only variables that can occur in an array *subscript expression* **(Sexp).** The set of *simple variables* (called integer variables in preceding chapters) is **Simp.** The set of (one-dimensional) *array variables* is **Array** with typical members $a, \ldots$. A *subscripted variable* is of the form $a(se)$, where *se* is a subscript expression. The simple and subscripted variables constitute the *integer variables* **(Ivar),** which can occur in our programs and assertions in the usual contexts except that they cannot occur in subscript expressions. Subscript variables as well as integer variables can occur in the integer expressions **(Iexp)** and boolean expressions **(Bexp)** of our programs. The abstract syntax is as follows:

Svar: $j, \ldots$

Sexp: $se, \ldots$

$$se ::= m \mid j \mid \text{succ}(se) \mid \ldots \mid se{+}se' \mid \ldots$$

[1] Somewhat curiously, $out(a(1))$ is well-formed.

Simp: $x, \ldots$
Array: $a, \ldots$
Ivar: $i, \ldots$
$i ::= x \mid a(se)$
Iexp: $e, \ldots$
$e ::= m \mid j \mid i \mid \mathrm{succ}(e) \mid \ldots \mid e{+}e' \mid \ldots$
Bexp: $b, \ldots$
$b ::= e{=}e' \mid \ldots \mid {\sim}b \mid b\&b' \mid \ldots$

The *input file* (*in*) with its *current input record number* (*cin*) and the *output file* (*out*) with its *current output record number* (*cout*) have the following intended meaning: *in*(m) is the integer contained on the m-th *input record* of file *in*, and *in*(*cin*) is *the next record to be read* from the sequential file *in*. Similarly, *out*(m) is the integer contained on the m-th *output record* of *out*, and *out*(*cout*) is *the next record to be written* on the sequential file *out*. Whereas program execution cannot alter the contents of any input record, the contents of an output record can be altered (by a **print** command).[2] Because program execution can change the value of *cin, cout,* and the output records, we have *cin, cout,* and the output records together with the subscript and integer variables constituting the *assertion variables* **(Avar).** Although *cin, cout,* and input and output records cannot be explicitly referenced in the integer expressions of our programs, they can be in the *assertion expressions* **(Aexp)** of our *assertions* **Assn.** The abstract syntax is as follows:

Avar: $v, \ldots$
$v ::= j \mid i \mid cin \mid cout \mid out(e)$
Aexp: $t, \ldots$
$t ::= m \mid v \mid in(t) \mid \mathrm{succ}(t) \mid \ldots \mid t{+}t' \mid \ldots$
Assn: $p, \ldots$
$p ::= t{=}t' \mid \ldots \mid {\sim}p \mid p\&p' \mid \ldots \mid \forall Xp \mid \exists Xp$

The syntax of assertion expressions and assertions governs the Floydian expressions and inductive assertions (occurring on the **start, stop,** and **assert** commands), prohibiting nested subscripts and nested occurrences of the file name *out*.[3] Without this prohibition, our version of the Coincidence Lemma

[2] The file *in* is "read-only", and the file *out* is "write-only". An output record can be written at most once because *cout* is advanced automatically when a record is written, and *cout* cannot be reset during program execution.

[3] From a logical point of view, outside of our programs and the assertions contained within them, the language of arithmetic is as described in Chapter 0 except that we have added the 0-ary operation symbols *cin* and *cout,* as well as the unary operation symbols *in, out,* and the array variables. These new operation symbols are introduced into the syntax but are unaccompanied by axioms, which makes them serve the role of "parameters" (in the sense of logic). As long as we do not mix in the arithmetic part of a proof (Chapter 0) with the programming part of the proof (Section 3.3), we can have, for example, $a(out(out(a(1)))) = 0$ occurring as a line in the arithme-

to be stated in Section 3.4 would not hold, and our version of Floyd's method for proving program correctness (the "programming part" of program verification, to be presented in Section 3.3) would not be sound.[4]

The syntax of FC+ programs **Prog** is to be understood as in Chapter 2 except that, to accommodate input and output, we extend the syntax of intermediate commands **(Icom).** In the assignment command, a subscript variable can be assigned a subscript expression but not an integer expression. Without this restriction, the *VCG* algorithm (Section 3.3) could generate nested subscripts in verification and well-foundedness conditions, and we would lose soundness for essentially the same reasons as just mentioned. The abstract syntax is as follows:

Icom: $IC, \ldots$

$IC ::= \textbf{assert}\ p \mid \textbf{assert}\ p,\langle t_1, \ldots, t_k\rangle \mid$
$j{=}se \mid i{=}e \mid \textbf{input}\ j \mid \textbf{input}\ i \mid \textbf{print}\ e \mid$
$\textbf{goto}\ m' \mid \textbf{if}\ b\ \textbf{goto}\ m'$

The file names (and *cin* and *cout*) are permitted to occur only in inductive assertions, which are not executable. The file names are not permitted to occur in any executable command because our files are sequential and there is no way to access, for example, $out(1)$ if $cout \geq 2$.[5]

We now illustrate our new syntax of FC+ programs. In the input file *in*, the first record gives the length of the input file (i.e., $in(1)$ tells us how many more records to input). The following structured FC+ program inputs the first $in(1)$ records $in(2), \ldots, in(in(1)+1)$, and then prints them in reverse order (i.e., in the order $in(in(1)+1), \ldots, in(2)$). The array a is used for intermediate storage. The subscript variables occurring in the program are j and n, and the only integer variables are the subscripted variables $a(j)$.[6]

1 **start** $in(1) \geq 0\ \&\ \forall X(2 \leq X \leq in(1)+1 \rightarrow \mathrm{I}(in(X)))$
2 **input** n
3 $j=1$
4 **assert** $\forall X(1 \leq X < j \rightarrow a(X)=in(X+1))\ \&\ 1 \leq j \leq n+1\ \&$
$n=in(1)\ \&\ j=cin-1\ \&\ cout=1,\ n+1-j$

---

tic part of a proof. As mentioned in Chapter 0, the introduction of these new symbols make no parameter-free assertion (an assertion restricted to the symbols of Chapter 0) provable that was not already provable in Chapter 0. For this reason, the theory of integers of the present chapter is a conservative extension of the theory of Chapter 0.

[4] To make the syntax of subscripted variables more representative of languages such as Pascal, the definition of substitution in Section 3.3 must be amended, as described in Example 4, Section 3.5 ("the second, more general, approach"). The amended definition of substitution is more complex and results in considerably more complicated program proofs.

[5] See Exercise 23, which treats the problem of executable inductive assertions.

[6] For the program to be syntactically correct, j must be a subscript variable, but n could be an integer variable instead of a subscript variable.

```
5     if j>n goto 9
6          input a(j)
7          j=j+1
8          goto 4
9     j=n
10     assert  ∀X(1≤X≤n → a(X)=in(X+1)) &
               ∀X(j<X≤n → in(X+1)=out(n+1−X)) &
               0≤j≤n=in(1) & cout=n+1−j, j
11    if j<1 goto 15
12         print a(j)
13         j=j−1
14         goto 10
15    stop  ∀X(1≤X≤in(1) → in(X+1)=out(in(1)+1−X))
```

The presence of array variables and output records in our integer expressions forces us to redefine the syntactic notion of substitution. We will postpone that definition until Section 3.3, where we present the modified VCG algorithm and the definition can be better motivated.

3.2. OPERATIONAL SEMANTICS

We augment an unextended state $\mathcal{S}$ so that $\mathcal{S}$ assigns values to subscript and subscripted variables and file records, as well as to simple variables and the program counter as in Chapter 2. An unextended state $\mathcal{S}$ assigns an integer to each subscript variable and to each array variable indexed by an integer —that is, $\mathcal{S}[j]$ and $\mathcal{S}[a(m)]$ are integers. Similarly, $\mathcal{S}[in(m)]$ and $\mathcal{S}[out(m)]$ are integers. Further, $\mathcal{S}$ assigns a positive integer to *cin,* the current input record number, and *cout,* the current output record number —that is, $\mathcal{S}[cin] \geq 1$ and $\mathcal{S}[cout] \geq 1$. We then extend $\mathcal{S}$ to the subscripted variables with the addition of the clause

$$\mathcal{S}[a(se)] = \mathcal{S}[a(\mathcal{S}[se])]^{7}$$

[7] For example, suppose $\mathcal{S}[j1]=3$, $\mathcal{S}[j2]=5$, and $\mathcal{S}[a(8)]=11$. Then

$$\begin{aligned}\mathcal{S}[a(j1+j2)] &= \mathcal{S}[a(\mathcal{S}[j1+j2])] \qquad (*)\\ &= \mathcal{S}[a(\mathcal{S}[j1]+\mathcal{S}[j2])]\\ &= \mathcal{S}[a(3+5)]\\ &= \mathcal{S}[a(8)]\\ &= 11\end{aligned}$$

The notation in this chain of equations continues an "abuse" of notation, common in the computer science literature, that we began in Chapter 0. On the first line, marked (*), the plus sign '+' denotes a syntactic object. On the second and third lines, '+' denotes the addition operator (that adds two integers). If we were to adopt notational conventions more in keeping with the logic literature, we might "interpret" a numeral '*m*' as the integer [*m*], '*a*' as a unary

and to the file records with the addition of the clauses

$$\mathcal{S}[in(t)] = \mathcal{S}[in(\mathcal{S}[t])]$$

$$\mathcal{S}[out(e)] = \mathcal{S}[out(\mathcal{S}[e])]$$

Finally, $\mathcal{S}$ is extended to the subscript expressions, integer expressions, boolean expressions, assertion expressions, and assertions in an entirely similar manner to the way it was extended in preceding chapters.

Let $\mathcal{S}$ and $\mathcal{S}'$ be states, and let v be a variable. We define the concept of a *v-variant* by cases, depending on the form of v. We state the definition in detail so that there will be no possibility for misunderstanding.

(1) v is a subscript variable j.
The state $\mathcal{S}'$ is a j-variant of $\mathcal{S}$ provided that
   (a) $\mathcal{S}'[cin]=\mathcal{S}[cin]$ and $\mathcal{S}'[\text{cout}]=\mathcal{S}[cout]$,
   (b) For every subscript variable j' distinct from j, $\mathcal{S}'[j'] = \mathcal{S}[j']$,
   (c) For every simple variable x, $\mathcal{S}'[x] = \mathcal{S}[x]$,
   (d) For every array variable a and for every integer m, $\mathcal{S}'[a(m)] = \mathcal{S}[a(m)]$,
   (e) For every integer m, $\mathcal{S}'[in(m)] = \mathcal{S}[in(m)]$, and
   (f) For every integer m, $\mathcal{S}'[out(m)] = \mathcal{S}[out(m)]$.

(2) v is a simple variable x.
The state $\mathcal{S}'$ is a x-variant of $\mathcal{S}$ provided that
   (a) $\mathcal{S}'[cin]=\mathcal{S}[cin]$ and $\mathcal{S}'[cout]=\mathcal{S}[cout]$,
   (b) For every subscript variable j, $\mathcal{S}'[j]=\mathcal{S}[j]$,
   (c) For every simple variable y distinct from x, $\mathcal{S}'[y] = \mathcal{S}[y]$, and
   (d) through (f) Same as clauses (1d) through (1f).

(3) v is the current input record number *cin*.
The state $\mathcal{S}'$ is a *cin*-variant of $\mathcal{S}$ provided that
   (a) $\mathcal{S}'[cout]=\mathcal{S}[cout]$,
   (b) For every subscript variable j, $\mathcal{S}'[j] = \mathcal{S}[j]$,
   (c) through (f) Same as clauses (lc) through (lf).

---

function (i.e., $\mathcal{S}[a] \in Z \rightarrow Z$), and '+' as the addition operator [+]. We might then write $\mathcal{S}[a] = \mathcal{S}[a](\mathcal{S}[se])$, and the preceding chain of equations would read as follows:

$$\begin{aligned}\mathcal{S}[a(j1+j2)] &= \mathcal{S}[a](\mathcal{S}[j1+j2]) \\ &= \mathcal{S}[a](\mathcal{S}[j1]\ [+]\ \mathcal{S}[j2]) \\ &= \mathcal{S}[a]([3]\ [+]\ [5]) \\ &= \mathcal{S}[a]([8]) \\ &= [11]\end{aligned}$$

The notation in the computer science literature is less cluttered than the notation in the logic literature, but the computer science notation can lead to confusion.

(4) v is the current output record number *cout*.
The state $\mathcal{S}'$ is a *cout*-variant of $\mathcal{S}$ provided that
(a) $\mathcal{S}'[cin]=\mathcal{S}[cin]$, and
(b) through (f) Same as clauses (3b) through (3f).

(5) v is a subscripted variable $a(se)$.
The state $\mathcal{S}'$ is an $a(se)$-variant of $\mathcal{S}$ provided that
(a) $\mathcal{S}'[cin]=\mathcal{S}[cin]$ and $\mathcal{S}'[cout]=\mathcal{S}[out]$,
(b) For every subscript variable j, $\mathcal{S}'[j]=\mathcal{S}[j]$,
(c) For every simple variable x, $\mathcal{S}'[x]=\mathcal{S}[x]$,
(d) For every integer m such that $m\neq\mathcal{S}[se]$, $\mathcal{S}'[a(m)] = \mathcal{S}[a(m)]$,
(e) For every array variable a' distinct from a, and for every integer m, $\mathcal{S}'[a'(m)] = \mathcal{S}[a'(m)]$, and
(f) through (g) Same as clauses (1e) through (1f).

(6) v is an output record $out(e)$.
The state $\mathcal{S}'$ is an $out(e)$-variant of $\mathcal{S}$ provided that
(a) through (c) Same as clauses (5a) through (5c),
(d) through (e) Same as clauses (1d) through (1e), and
(f) For every integer m such that $m\neq\mathcal{S}[e]$, $\mathcal{S}'[out(m)] = \mathcal{S}[out(m)]$.

We understand $\mathcal{S}\{m\backslash a(se)\}$ to be $\mathcal{S}\{m\backslash a(\mathcal{S}[se])\}$, and $\mathcal{S}\{m\backslash out(e)\}$ to be $\mathcal{S}\{m\backslash out(\mathcal{S}[e])\}$. Much as in Chapter 0, the state $\mathcal{S}\{m\backslash v\}$ is the v-variant of $\mathcal{S}$ such that $\mathcal{S}\{m\backslash v\}(v) = m$, and the state $\mathcal{S}\{m_1, \ldots, m_n\backslash v_1, \ldots, v_n\}$ is to

$\mathcal{S}$[**start** p]	$= \mathcal{S}\{m+1\backslash pc\}$	
$\mathcal{S}$[**stop** p]	$= \mathcal{S}$	
$\mathcal{S}$[**assert** p]	$= \mathcal{S}\{m+1\backslash pc\}$	
$\mathcal{S}$[**assert** $p,\langle e_1, \ldots, e_k\rangle$]	$= \mathcal{S}\{m+1\backslash pc\}$	
$\mathcal{S}[j{=}se]$	$= \mathcal{S}\{\mathcal{S}[se],\mathcal{S}[pc]+1\backslash j,pc\}$	
$\mathcal{S}[x{=}e]$	$= \mathcal{S}\{\mathcal{S}[e],m+1\backslash x,pc\}$	
$\mathcal{S}[a(se){=}e]$	$= \mathcal{S}\{\mathcal{S}[e],\mathcal{S}[pc]+1\backslash a(\mathcal{S}[se]),pc\}$	
$\mathcal{S}$[**input** j]	$= \mathcal{S}\{\mathcal{S}[in(\mathcal{S}[cin])], \mathcal{S}[cin]+1, \mathcal{S}[pc]+1\backslash j,cin,pc\}$	
$\mathcal{S}$[**input** x]	$= \mathcal{S}\{\mathcal{S}[in(\mathcal{S}[cin])], \mathcal{S}[cin]+1, \mathcal{S}[pc]+1\backslash x,cin,pc\}$	
$\mathcal{S}$[**input** $a(se)$]	$= \mathcal{S}\{\mathcal{S}[in(\mathcal{S}[cin])], \mathcal{S}[cin]+1, \mathcal{S}[pc]+1\backslash a(\mathcal{S}[se]),cin,pc\}$	
$\mathcal{S}$[**print** e]	$= \mathcal{S}\{\mathcal{S}[e], \mathcal{S}[cout]+1,\mathcal{S}[pc]+1\backslash out(\mathcal{S}[cout]), cout,pc\}$	
$\mathcal{S}$[**goto** m']	$= \mathcal{S}\{m'\backslash pc\}$	
$\mathcal{S}$[**if** b **goto** m']	$= \mathcal{S}\{m'\backslash pc\}$	if $\mathcal{S}[b]$=t,
	$= \mathcal{S}\{m+1\backslash pc\}$	otherwise

FIGURE 3.1. The operational semantics of FC+ commands.

be understood in an entirely similar manner. A *pc-variant* is as defined in Chapter 2.

The operational semantics of **Comm** is much the same as in Chapter 2, with the addition of clauses for assigning values to subscript and subscripted variables, inputting subscript and integer variables, and printing integer expressions. The semantic clauses are listed in Figure 3.1.

Aside from the additions indicated in Figure 3.1, the operational semantics of an FC+ program $P \in$ **Prog** is the same as in Chapter 2. The definitions of termination and of partial and total correctness are also as in Chapter 2, except that the presence of the sequential input and output files *in* and *out* requires a modification of the definition of an initial state. In the previous chapter, we required that, at the start of program execution, the precondition p hold and the program counter point to the first command in the program. In this chapter, we also require that, initially, the files *in* and *out* be positioned at their beginnings as indicated by the current input and output record numbers *cin* and *cout*. So, we now understand a state $\mathfrak{s}$ to be *initial* for an FC+ program P (having precondition p) provided that $\mathfrak{s}[pc] = \mathfrak{s}[cin] = \mathfrak{s}[cout] = 1$ and $\mathfrak{s}[p] = \mathrm{t}$.

3.3. PROVING TOTAL CORRECTNESS

We are now prepared to discuss the final modification to our syntax mentioned at the end of Section 3.1, which is necessitated by the problem of *array element name aliasing.* Suppose we are in a state $\mathfrak{s}$ such that $\mathfrak{s}[x] = \mathfrak{s}[y] = \mathfrak{s}[a(1)] = 1$. Clearly, the assertion

(?) $\quad 0+1 = a(y)$

is true. Now we execute the assignment command

$$a(x) = 0$$

After execution, a naive application of the Coincidence Lemma of Chapter 0 might lead us to believe that, at this point, the assertion

(*) $\quad a(x)+1 = a(y)$

is true. After all, the string '$0+1 = a(y)$' is obtained by substituting the string '0' for every occurrence of the string '$a(x)$' in the string '$a(x)+1 = a(y)$'. A moment of reflection reveals, however, that the assertion (*) cannot be true because $a(1)$ has been set to 0, and $a(x)$ and $a(y)$ are aliases for $a(1)$. If the assertion (?) could be obtained from the assertion (*) by our *VCG* algorithm, then the Floyd method would be unsound.

We must preserve the soundness of Floyd's method for proving program correctness, but our naive substitution method undermines the Coincidence Lemma and, hence, soundness. In Section 3.4, we will state and sketch a proof of an appropriately modified version of the Coincidence Lemma. By essentially the same argument as in Chapter 2, the soundness of Floyd's method readily follows from the modified Coincidence Lemma. In our new version of the Lemma, the presence of subscripted variables and output records, as well as the accompanying problems of array element and output record name aliasing, makes it impossible for us to consider $t[e\backslash a(se)]$ as simply the result of replacing the string $a(se)$ with the string e in the string t as we did in preceding chapters.

Our first step in arriving at an adequate concept of substitution is to introduce the binary equality operation symbol eq(X,X') and the trinary arithmetic if-then-else operation symbol cond(X,Y,Y') into the theory of integers. Think of a value of 1 as meaning $\mathfrak{t}$, and a value of 0 as meaning $\mathfrak{f}$. We have the following explicit definitions:

(D.eq) $\mathrm{eq}(X,X')=Y \leftrightarrow (X=X' \rightarrow Y=1)\&(X \neq X' \rightarrow Y=0)$
(D.cond) $\mathrm{cond}(X,Y,Y')=Z \leftrightarrow (X=1 \rightarrow Z=Y)\&(X \neq 1 \rightarrow Z=Y')$

Substitution is handled as in preceding chapters except when we substitute for a variable v, and v is either a subscripted variable or an output record. In particular, if we substitute an integer expression e for the subscripted variable $v \equiv a(se)$ in an assertion expression t in which the subscripted variable $a(se')$ occurs, we must provide a check in our substitution. This check must insure that, in a state $\mathfrak{s}$, $a(se')$ is "replaced" with e if $\mathfrak{s}[se'] = \mathfrak{s}[se]$, and, if $\mathfrak{s}[se'] \neq \mathfrak{s}[se]$, $a(se')$ is not replaced. Our definition of substitution must be a bit more general than suggested by the preceding remarks because we need to be able to handle the case when the "subscript expression" se' (renamed qse in the text that follows) may contain one or more quantified variables. So, understanding a *quasi-subscript expression* qse to be of the form $se[X_1, \ldots, X_n \backslash j_1, \ldots, j_n]$ $(n \geqslant 0)$ and a *quasi-subscripted variable* to be of the form $a(qse)$, we define substitution into quasi-subscripted variables as follows:

$$a(qse)[e\backslash a(se)] \equiv \mathrm{cond}(\mathrm{eq}(qse,se),e,a(qse))$$
$$(e \text{ if } qse=se, \text{ and } a(qse) \text{ otherwise})$$

The situation with output records is entirely similar. Understanding a *quasi-integer expression* qe to be of the form $e[X_1, \ldots, X_n \backslash j_1, \ldots, j_n]$, we have

$$out(qe)[e\backslash out(e')] \equiv \mathrm{cond}(\mathrm{eq}(qe,e'),e,out(qe))$$
$$(e \text{ if } qe=e', \text{ and } out(qe) \text{ otherwise})$$

For example, when we substitute 0 for $a(x)$ in the assertion (*), we do not obtain the assertion (?), but rather we have the following:

$$[a(x)+1=a(y)][0\backslash a(x)] \equiv$$
$$\mathrm{cond}(\mathrm{eq}(x,x),0,a(x))+1 = \mathrm{cond}(\mathrm{eq}(x,y),0,a(y))$$

and, if

$$\mathcal{s}[x] = \mathcal{s}[y] = \mathcal{s}[a(1)] = 1,$$

we have the following:

$$\begin{aligned}\mathcal{s}[&\text{cond}(\text{eq}(x,x),0,a(x))+1 = \text{cond}(\text{eq}(x,y),0,a(y))]\\ &= 0+1 = 0\\ &= \mathsf{f}\end{aligned}$$

We will now turn to the modifications to the VCG algorithm of Chapter 2. The construction of the boolean path expression b_α proceeds much as in Chapter 2. However, due to the substitution conventions for subscripted variables and output records, it is no longer convenient to construct the path substitution θ_α separately. Instead, we construct the *verification condition consequent* (what was $p_j\theta_\alpha$ in Chapter 2) and the *termination condition floor* (what was $E_j\theta_\alpha$ in Chapter 2) directly.

Much as in Chapter 2, let $\alpha = \langle m = l_1, \ldots, l_h = n\rangle$ be a path from cutpoint m to cutpoint n, and p_m (p_n) be the inductive assertion on cutpoint m (n). If m (n) is a loop cutpoint, let E_m (E_n) be the Floydian expression on cutpoint m (n). We understand that substitution associates to the left so that, for example, $p[cin+1\backslash cin][in(cin)\backslash x] \equiv [p[cin+1\backslash cin]][in(cin)\backslash x]$. We construct the boolean path expression b_α, the verification condition consequent $p_{n,\alpha}$, and the termination condition floor $E_{n,\alpha}$ following Steps (a) to (e), schematized in Figure 3.2. We understand that the termination condition floor $E_{n,\alpha}$ is to be constructed only if path α requires a termination condition (TC_α) (i.e., only if path α is part of a loop).

The form of the *verification condition* for path α depends on whether path α begins at the **start** command (i.e., if $m{=}l_1{=}1$). If path α begins at the **start** command, the verification condition is as follows:

$$(VC_\alpha) \qquad cin = cout = 1, p_1, b_\alpha \vdash p_{n,\alpha}$$

And, if path α does not begin at the **start** command, it is as follows:

$$(VC_\alpha) \qquad p_1, p_m, b_\alpha \vdash p_{n,\alpha}$$

If cutpoint m is a loop cutpoint, the well-foundedness condition is exactly as in Chapter 2.

$$(WC_m) \qquad p_1, p_m \vdash E_m \succcurlyeq \langle 0\rangle$$

Recall from Chapter 2 that a *termination condition* (TC_α) is required for path α when, and only when, both cutpoints m and n are loop cutpoints. In this case, we cannot have $m{=}1$ (because the **start** command is never part of a loop), so the termination condition always takes the following form:

$$(TC_\alpha) \qquad p_1, p_m, b_\alpha \vdash E_m \succ E_{n,\alpha}$$

As an example, consider our program in Section 3.1 that prints out the input file in reverse order. We have the following five paths:

$$a = \langle 1,2,3,4\rangle \qquad d = \langle 10,11,12,13,14,10\rangle$$
$$b = \langle 4,5,6,7,8,4\rangle \qquad e = \langle 10,11,15\rangle$$
$$c = \langle 4,5,9,10\rangle$$

We illustrate the application of our revised VCG algorithm along path b. First, we construct the verification condition consequent $p_{4,b}$, the boolean path expression b_b, and the termination condition floor $E_{4,b}$. The initial values of $p_{4,b}$, b_b, and $E_{4,b}$ are as follows:

For $p_{4,b}$: $p_4 \equiv \forall X(1 \leqslant X < j \rightarrow a(X) = in(X+1))\ \&\ 1 \leqslant j \leqslant n+1\ \&$
$n = in(1)\ \&\ j = cin-1\ \&\ cout = 1$

For b_b: true

For $E_{4,b}$: $E_4 \equiv n+1-j$

Tracing Steps (a)–(e) in Figure 3.2, we have:

$\forall X(1 \leqslant X < j+1 \rightarrow$
$\quad cond(eq(X,j), in(cin), a(X)) = in(X+1))$
$\&\ 1 \leqslant j+1 \leqslant n+1\ \&\ n = in(1)\ \&\ j+1 = cin+1-1\ \&$
$cout = 1$

true & $\sim j > n$ $\qquad$ $n+1-(j+1)$

if $j>n$ **goto** . . .

$\forall X(1 \leqslant X < j+1 \rightarrow$
$\quad cond(eq(X,j), in(cin), a(X)) = in(X+1))$
$\&\ 1 \leqslant j+1 \leqslant n+1\ \&\ n = in(1)\ \&\ j+1 = cin+1-1\ \&$
$cout = 1$

true $\qquad$ $n+1-(j+1)$

input($a(j)$)

$\forall X(1 \leqslant X < j+1 \rightarrow a(X) = in(X+1))\ \&$
$1 \leqslant j+1 \leqslant n+1\ \&\ n = in(1)\ \&\ j+1 = cin-1\ \&$
$cout = 1$

true $\qquad$ $n+1-(j+1)$

$j = j+1$

$\forall X(1 \leqslant X < j \rightarrow a(X) = in(X+1))\ \&\ 1 \leqslant j \leqslant n+1$
$\&\ n = in(1)\ \&\ j = cin-1\ \&\ cout = 1$

true $\qquad$ $n+1-j$

(a) For each g from 1 to h, write down the command labeled l_g if it is either an assignment, an **input**, a **print**, or a conditional **goto** command. (**Start, stop, assert,** and unconditional **goto** commands need not be written down.)

(b) Under and to the left of the list of commands generated in Step (a), write down the inductive assertion p_n occurring on cutpoint n. p_n is the initial value used in the construction of the verification condition consequent $p_{n,\alpha}$.

(c) Directly under the list of commands, write down true. True is the initial value used in the construction of the boolean path expression b_α.

(d) Step (d) is to be carried out when, and only when, path α requires a termination condition. Under and to the right of the list of commands, write down the Floydian expression E_n occurring on cutpoint n. E_n is the initial value used in the construction of the termination condition floor $E_{n,\alpha}$.

(e) Working from the bottom of the list of commands to the top, construct from the old $p_{n,\alpha}$ and b_α (and $E_{n,\alpha}$ if required) new values, as follows:

> (i) If the command passed through is an assignment to a subscript variable j, new values are created as follows:

new $\quad p_{n,\alpha}[se\backslash j] \qquad b_\alpha[se\backslash j] \quad E_{n,\alpha}[se\backslash j]$

$$\left(\begin{array}{c} \\ k \quad j = se \\ \end{array} \right)$$

old $\qquad p_{n,\alpha} \qquad\qquad b_\alpha \qquad\quad E_{n,\alpha}$

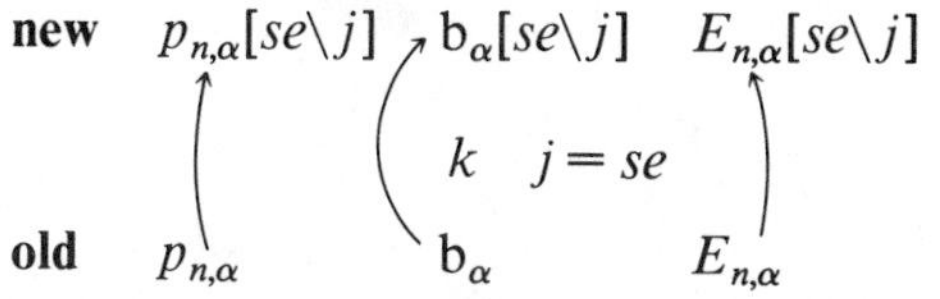

> (ii) If the command passed through is an assignment to an integer variable i, new values are created as follows:

new $\quad p_{n,\alpha}[e\backslash i] \qquad b_\alpha[e\backslash i] \quad E_{n,\alpha}[e\backslash i]$

$$\left(\begin{array}{c} \\ k \quad i = e \\ \end{array} \right)$$

old $\qquad p_{n,\alpha} \qquad\qquad b_\alpha \qquad\quad E_{n,\alpha}$

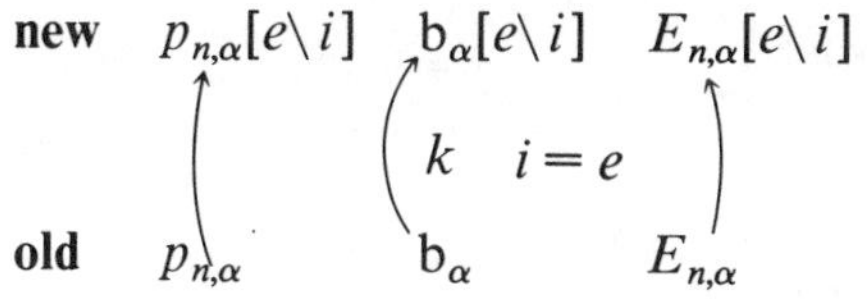

> (iii) If the command passed through is an **input** to a subscript variable j, new values are created as follows:

FIGURE 3.2. Construction of a boolean path expression, a verification condition consequent, and a termination condition floor.

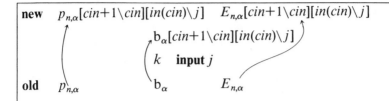

new $p_{n,\alpha}[cin+1\backslash cin][in(cin)\backslash j]$ $E_{n,\alpha}[cin+1\backslash cin][in(cin)\backslash j]$

$b_\alpha[cin+1\backslash cin][in(cin)\backslash j]$

k **input** j

old $p_{n,\alpha}$ b_α $E_{n,\alpha}$

(iv) If the command passed through is an **input** to an integer variable i, new values are created as follows:

new $p_{n,\alpha}[cin+1\backslash cin][\mathrm{in}(cin)\backslash i]$ $E_{n,\alpha}[cin+1\backslash cin][in(cin)\backslash i]$

$b_\alpha[cin+1\backslash cin][in(cin)\backslash i]$

k **input** i

old $p_{n,\alpha}$ b_α $E_{n,\alpha}$

(v) If the command passed through is a **print** of the integer expression e, new values are created as follows:

new $p_{n,\alpha}[cout+1\backslash cout][\mathrm{e}\backslash out(cout)]$ $E_{n,\alpha}[cout+1\backslash cout][e\backslash out(cout)]$

$b_\alpha[cout+1\backslash cout][e\backslash out(cout)]$

k **print** e

old $p_{n,\alpha}$ b_α $E_{n,\alpha}$

(vi) If the command passed through is a conditional **goto**, new values are created as follows:

new $p_{n,\alpha}$ $E_{n,\alpha}$

$= b_\alpha \& b$ if $\alpha = \langle \ldots, k, k', \ldots \rangle$
$= b_\alpha \& \sim b$ otherwise

k **if** b **goto** k'

old $p_{n,\alpha}$ b_α $E_{n,\alpha}$

FIGURE 3.2. *(Continued)*

Consequently, we have the following verification and termination conditions for path b and the well-foundedness condition for loop cutpoint 4:

(VC$_b$) $p_1, p_4, \mathrm{b}_b \vdash p_{4,b}$

$in(1) \geq 0 \;\&\; \forall X(2 \leq X \leq in(1)+1 \rightarrow \mathrm{I}(in(X)))$,
$\forall X(1 \leq X < j \rightarrow a(X) = in(X+1)) \;\&$
$1 \leq j \leq n+1 \;\&\; n = in(1) \;\&\; j = cin-1 \;\&\; cout = 1, \sim j > n$
$\vdash \forall X(1 \leq X < j+1 \rightarrow \mathrm{cond}(\mathrm{eq}(X,j), in(cin), a(X)) = in(X+1))$
$\&\; 1 \leq j+1 \leq n+1 \;\&\; n = in(1) \;\&$
$j+1 = cin+1-1 \;\&\; cout = 1$

(TC$_\mathrm{b}$) $p_1, p_4, \mathrm{b}_b \vdash E_4 \succ E_4, b$

$in(1) \geq 0 \;\&\; \forall X(2 \leq X \leq in(1)+1 \rightarrow \mathrm{I}(in(X)))$,
$\forall X(1 \leq X < j \rightarrow a(X) = in(X+1)) \;\&$
$1 \leq j \leq n+1 \;\&\; n = in(1) \;\&\; j = cin-1 \;\&\; cout = 1, \sim j > n$
$\vdash \quad n+1-j > n+1-(j+1)$

(WC$_4$) $p_1, p_4 \vdash E_4 \succcurlyeq \langle 0 \rangle$

$in(1) \geq 0 \;\&\; \forall X(2 \leq X \leq in(1)+1 \rightarrow \mathrm{I}(in(X)))$,
$\forall X(1 \leq X < j \rightarrow a(X) = in(X+1)) \;\&$
$1 \leq j \leq n+1 \;\&\; n = in(1) \;\&\; j = cin-1 \;\&\; cout = 1$
$\vdash \quad n+1-j \geq 0$

The other verification conditions are as follows:

(VC$_a$) $cin = cout = 1, p_1, \mathrm{b}_a \vdash p_{4,a}$

$cin = cout = 1, in(1) \geq 0 \;\&$
$\forall X(2 \leq X \leq in(1)+1 \rightarrow \mathrm{I}(in(X)))$, true
$\vdash \forall X(1 \leq X < 1 \rightarrow a(X) = in(X+1)) \;\&\; 1 \leq 1 \leq in(cin)+1 \;\&$
$in(cin) = in(1) \;\&\; 1 = cin+1-1 \;\&\; cout = 1$

(VC$_c$) $p_1, p_4, \mathrm{b}_c \vdash p_{10,c}$

$in(1) \geq 0 \;\&\; \forall X(2 \leq X \leq in(1)+1 \rightarrow \mathrm{I}(in(X)))$,
$\forall X(1 \leq X < j \rightarrow a(X) = in(X+1)) \;\&$
$1 \leq j \leq n+1 \;\&\; n = in(1) \;\&\; j = cin-1 \rightarrow cout = 1, j > n$
$\vdash \quad \forall X(1 \leq X \leq n \rightarrow a(x) = in(X+1)) \;\&$
$\forall X(n < X \leq n \rightarrow \mathrm{in}(X+1) = out(n+1-X)) \;\&$
$0 \leq n \leq n = in(1) \;\&\; cout = n+1-n$

(VC$_d$) $p_1, p_{10}, \mathrm{b}_d \vdash p_{10,d}$

$in(1) \geq 0 \;\&\; \forall X(2 \leq X \leq in(1)+1 \rightarrow \mathrm{I}(in(X)))$,
$\forall X(1 \leq X \leq n \rightarrow a(X) = in(X+1)) \;\&$
$\forall X(j < X \leq n \rightarrow in(X+1) = out(n+1-X)) \;\&$
$0 \leq j \leq n = in(1) \;\&\; cout = n+1-j, \sim j < 1$
$\vdash$
$\forall X(1 \leq X \leq n \rightarrow a(X) = in(X+1)) \;\&$

$$\forall X(j-1<X\leq n\rightarrow$$
$$in(X+1)=\text{cond}(\text{eq}(n+1-X,cout),\ a(j),out(n+1-X)))\ \&$$
$$0\leq j-1\leq n=in(1)\ \&\ cout+1=n+1-(j-1)$$

(VC$_e$) $p_1, p_{10}, b_e \vdash p_{15,e}$

$$in(1)\geq 0\ \&\ \forall X(2\leq X\leq in(1)+1\rightarrow \text{I}(in(X))),$$
$$\forall X(1\leq X\leq n\rightarrow a(X)=in(X+1))\ \&$$
$$\forall X(j<X\leq n\rightarrow in(X+1)=out(n+1-X))\ \&$$
$$0\leq j\leq n=in(1)\ \&\ cout=n+1-j,\ j<1$$
$$\vdash\ \forall X(1\leq X\leq in(1)\rightarrow in(X+1)=out(in(1)+1-X))$$

The only other termination condition is for path d:

(TC$_d$) $p_1, p_{10}, b_d \vdash E_{10} \succ E_{10,d}$

$$in(1)\geq 0\ \&\ \forall X(2\leq X\leq in(1)+1\rightarrow \text{I}(in(X))),$$
$$\forall X(1\leq X\leq n\rightarrow a(X)=in(X+1))\ \&$$
$$\forall X(j<X\leq n\rightarrow in(X+1)=out(n+1-X))\ \&$$
$$0\leq j\leq n=in(1)\ \&\ cout=n+1-j,\ \sim j<1$$
$$\vdash\ \ j>j-1$$

And, the only other well-foundedness condition is for loop cutpoint 10:

(WC$_{10}$) $p_1, p_{10} \vdash E_{10} \succcurlyeq 0$

$$in(1)\geq 0\ \&\ \forall X(2\leq X\leq in(1)+1\rightarrow \text{I}(in(X))),$$
$$\forall X(1\leq X\leq n\rightarrow a(X)=in(X+1))\ \&$$
$$\forall X(j<X\leq n\rightarrow in(X+1)=out(n+1-X))\ \&$$
$$0\leq j\leq n=in(1)\ \&\ cout=n+1-j,$$
$$\vdash\ \ j\geq 0$$

3.4. SOUNDNESS

Proof of the soundness of Floyd's method for proving program correctness follows the same lines as in the preceding chapter. However, for the proof in Section 2.4 to carry over to the present chapter, we must revise the Coincidence Lemma. This is necessary because the Coincidence Lemma of Section 0.6 addresses only (in the terminology of the present chapter) variants involving subscript variables (j-variants), simple variables (x-variants), *cin* (*cin*-variants), and *cout* (*cout*-variants). It does not address subscripted variables ($a(se)$-variants) and output records ($out(e)$-variants). We must revise the Coincidence Lemma so that it covers all assertion variables.

Let v be an assertion variable, and $\mathfrak{s}$ and $\mathfrak{s}'$ be states such that $\mathfrak{s}'$ is a v-variant of $\mathfrak{s}$. As in Chapter 0, the Coincidence Lemma expresses the equivalence of semantic and syntactic substitutions for v. For our current purpose the Lemma takes on six different forms depending on the form of v. We state it in a manner that reflects its role in a soundness proof for Floyd's method (as presented in this chapter) that can be readily had by following the outline of the proof in Section 2.4. The Coincidence Lemma covers all forms of *v*-variants that can result from executing an intermediate command IC—*j*-variants, *x*-variants, and *a*(*se*)-variants arising from assignment and input commands, *cin*-variants arising from input commands, and *cout*-variants and *out*(*e*)-variants arising from **print** commands. Details regarding the adaptation of the soundness proof in Section 2.4 to suit the present chapter are left as an exercise. We have stated the Lemma in a more detailed and less general form than it could be stated, hoping to make its role in the soundness proof more apparent.

COINCIDENCE LEMMA (WITH ARRAYS AND INPUT/OUTPUT)

(1) *Coincidence Lemma for Subscript Variables.* Let $\mathscr{S}' = \mathscr{S}\{\mathscr{S}[se]\backslash j\}$:
   (a) If j does not occur in t, then $\mathscr{S}'[t] = \mathscr{S}[t]$
   (b) If j does not occur in p, then $\mathscr{S}'[p] = \mathscr{S}[p]$
   (c) $\mathscr{S}'[t] = \mathscr{S}[t[se\backslash j]]$
   (d) $\mathscr{S}'[p] = \mathscr{S}[p[se\backslash j]]$

(2) *Coincidence Lemma for Simple Variables.* Let $\mathscr{S}' = \mathscr{S}\{\mathscr{S}[e]\backslash x\}$:
   (a) If x does not occur in t, then $\mathscr{S}'[t] = \mathscr{S}[t]$
   (b) If x does not occur in p, then $\mathscr{S}'[p] = \mathscr{S}[p]$
   (c) $\mathscr{S}'[t] = \mathscr{S}[t[e\backslash x]]$
   (d) $\mathscr{S}'[p] = \mathscr{S}[p[e\backslash x]]$

(3) *Coincidence Lemma for Subscripted Variables.* Let $\mathscr{S}' = \mathscr{S}\{\mathscr{S}[e]\backslash a(se)\}$:
   (a) If a does not occur in t, then $\mathscr{S}'[t] = \mathscr{S}[t]$
   (b) If a does not occur in p, then $\mathscr{S}'[p] = \mathscr{S}[p]$
   (c) $\mathscr{S}'[t] = \mathscr{S}[t[e\backslash a(se)]]$
   (d) $\mathscr{S}'[p] = \mathscr{S}[p[e\backslash a(se)]]$

(4) *Coincidence Lemma for the Current Input Record Number cin.* Let $\mathscr{S}' = \mathscr{S}\{\mathscr{S}[cin]+1\backslash cin\}$:
   (a) If cin does not occur in t, then $\mathscr{S}'[t] = \mathscr{S}[t]$
   (b) If cin does not occur in p, then $\mathscr{S}'[p] = \mathscr{S}[p]$
   (c) $\mathscr{S}'[t] = \mathscr{S}[t[cin+1\backslash cin]]$
   (d) $\mathscr{S}'[p] = \mathscr{S}[p[cin+1\backslash cin]]$

(5) *Coincidence Lemma for the Current Output Record Number cout.* Let $\mathscr{S}' = \mathscr{S}\{\mathscr{S}[cout]+1\backslash cout\}$:
   (a) If $cout$ does not occur in t, then $\mathscr{S}'[t] = \mathscr{S}[t]$
   (b) If $cout$ does not occur in p, then $\mathscr{S}'[p] = \mathscr{S}[p]$

(c) $\mathfrak{s}'[t] = \mathfrak{s}[t[cout{+}1\backslash cout]]$
(d) $\mathfrak{s}'[p] = \mathfrak{s}[p[cout{+}1\backslash cout]]$

(6) *Coincidence Lemma for Output Records.* Let $\mathfrak{s}' = \mathfrak{s}\{\mathfrak{s}[e]\backslash out(cout)\}$:
(a) If *out* does not occur in t, then $\mathfrak{s}'[t] = \mathfrak{s}[t]$
(b) If *out* does not occur in p, then $\mathfrak{s}'[p] = \mathfrak{s}[p]$
(c) $\mathfrak{s}'[t] = \mathfrak{s}[t[e\backslash out(cout)]]$
(d) $\mathfrak{s}'[p] = \mathfrak{s}[p[e\backslash out(cout)]]$

Proof: We prove a few representative cases, leaving the other cases as exercises.

(3a) CASE IN THE INDUCTION STEP: $t \equiv a'(se')$, $a \not\equiv a'$.
The proof is proceeding by induction on the complexity of t. We have $\mathfrak{s}' = \mathfrak{s}\{\mathfrak{s}[e]\backslash a(se)\}$ and, by the IH, $\mathfrak{s}'[se'] = \mathfrak{s}[se']$. So, we have the following:

$$\begin{aligned}
\mathfrak{s}'[a'(se')] &= \mathfrak{s}'[a'(\mathfrak{s}'[se'])] && \text{by the definition of a state}\\
&= \mathfrak{s}'[a'(\mathfrak{s}[se'])] && \text{by the IH}\\
&= \mathfrak{s}[a'(\mathfrak{s}[se'])] && \text{by the definition of an}\\
& && a(se)\text{-variant because } a \not\equiv a'\\
&= \mathfrak{s}[a'(se')] && \text{by the definition of a state}
\end{aligned}$$

(3c) CASE IN THE BASIS: $t \equiv a(se')$
The proof is proceeding by induction on the complexity of t. We have $\mathfrak{s}'[a(se')] = \mathfrak{s}'[a(\mathfrak{s}'[se'])]$, by the definition of a state, and $\mathfrak{s}'[se'] = \mathfrak{s}[se']$ by Part (3a) because no array variable (in particular, a) can occur in a subscript expression (in particular, se'). We must show that $\mathfrak{s}'[a(\mathfrak{s}'[se'])] = \mathfrak{s}[\text{cond}(\text{eq}(se',se),e,a(se'))]$. Suppose $\mathfrak{s}[se'] = \mathfrak{s}[se]$. We have $\mathfrak{s}'[se'] = \mathfrak{s}[se]$ because $\mathfrak{s}'[se'] = \mathfrak{s}[se']$. Hence,

$$\begin{aligned}
\mathfrak{s}'[a(\mathfrak{s}'[se'])] &= \mathfrak{s}\{\mathfrak{s}[e]\backslash a(\mathfrak{s}[se])\}[a(\mathfrak{s}'[se'])] && \text{by the definition of } \mathfrak{s}'\\
&= \mathfrak{s}\{\mathfrak{s}[e]\backslash a(\mathfrak{s}[se])\}[a(\mathfrak{s}[se])] && \text{because } \mathfrak{s}'[se']{=}\mathfrak{s}[se]\\
&= \mathfrak{s}[e] && \text{by the definition of an}\\
& && a(se)\text{-variant.}\\
&= \mathfrak{s}[\text{cond}(\text{eq}(se',se),e,a(se')] && \text{because } \mathfrak{s}[se']{=}\mathfrak{s}[se]\\
&= \mathfrak{s}[a(se')[e\backslash a(se)]] && \text{by the definition of substitution}
\end{aligned}$$

On the other hand, suppose $\mathfrak{s}[se'] \neq \mathfrak{s}[se]$. Because $\mathfrak{s}'[se'] = \mathfrak{s}[se']$, we have $\mathfrak{s}'[se'] \neq \mathfrak{s}[se]$. Hence,

$$\begin{aligned}
\mathfrak{s}'[a(\mathfrak{s}'[se'])] &= \mathfrak{s}\{\mathfrak{s}[e]\backslash a(\mathfrak{s}[se])\}[a(\mathfrak{s}'[se'])] && \text{by the definition of } \mathfrak{s}'\\
&= \mathfrak{s}[a(\mathfrak{s}'[se'])] && \text{by the definition of an } a(se)\text{-}\\
& && \text{variant because } \mathfrak{s}'[se'] \neq \mathfrak{s}[se]\\
&= \mathfrak{s}[a(\mathfrak{s}[se'])] && \text{because } \mathfrak{s}'[se'] = \mathfrak{s}[se']
\end{aligned}$$

$= \mathfrak{s}[a(se')]$	by the definition of a state
$= \mathfrak{s}[\text{cond}(\text{eq}(se',se),e,a(se')]$	because $\mathfrak{s}[se'] \neq \mathfrak{s}[se]$
$= \mathfrak{s}[a(se')[e\backslash a(se)]]$	by the definition of substitution □

Note that the last case could be placed in the induction step instead of the basis because $a(se')$ is complex. We placed it in the basis because we did not use the IH and wanted to underline the critical role of the syntactic restriction prohibiting array variables in subscript expressions. Without this restriction (given our definition of substitution), our proof does not work, and the Lemma as we have stated it is, in fact, false, as the following example illustrates. Let $\mathfrak{s}$ be a state such that $\mathfrak{s}[a(0)] = 1$, $\mathfrak{s}[a(1)] = 2$, and $\mathfrak{s}[a(2)] = 0$, and let $\mathfrak{s}' = \mathfrak{s}\{0\backslash a(1)\}$. Now

$$\mathfrak{s}[a(a(a(a(1))))[0\backslash a(1)]] \equiv \mathfrak{s}[\text{cond}(\text{eq}(a(a(a(1))),1),0,a(a(a(a(1)))))] = 0$$

but,

$$\mathfrak{s}'[a(a(a(a(1))))] = 1$$

Looking at the situation from the perspective of Floyd's method, we have the following situation: If we are in state $\mathfrak{s}$ before executing the assignment command

$$a(1) = 0$$

we have $\mathfrak{s}[a(a(a(a(1))))[0\backslash a(1)]{=}0] = \mathfrak{t}$. However, after execution we are in a *pc*-variant $\mathfrak{s}''$ of $\mathfrak{s}'$, and we have $\mathfrak{s}''[a(a(a(a(1)))){=}0]{=}\mathfrak{f}$. Notice that, if we allowed assignments of integer expressions to subscript variables, we could generate verification condition consequents having nested subscripts even if we continued to banish nested subscripts from inductive assertions. Let $\mathfrak{s}$ be as before. Beginning in state $\mathfrak{s}$ we execute the sequence of commands

k	**assert**	true
$k{+}1$	$a(1) = 0$	
$k{+}2$	$z = a(1)$	
$k{+}3$	$y = a(z)$	
$k{+}4$	$x = a(y)$	
$k{+}5$	**assert**	$a(x) = 0$

and we end in state $\mathfrak{s}*$, a *z-y-x-pc*-variant of $\mathfrak{s}'$. We have $\mathfrak{s}[p_k] = \mathfrak{s}[\text{true}] = \mathfrak{t}$, and the verification condition

$$\ldots,\text{true} \vdash a(a(a(a(1))))[0\backslash a(1)] = 0$$

holds, but $\mathfrak{s}*[p_{k+5}] = \mathfrak{s}*[a(x)=0]=\mathfrak{f}$. Thus, without the prohibition on nested subscripts, our version of Floyd's method would be unsound.[8]

3.5. SOME SAMPLE PROOFS

EXAMPLE 1

We are given an input file in which the first record specifies the length of the input file (i.e., *in*(1) tells us how many more records to input). The following structured FC+ program determines whether the first *in*(1) records *in*(2), . . . , *in*(*in*(1)+1) in the input file all contain 1. If they are all 1, the program prints a 1, and if they are not the program prints a 0. The program has three simple variables (*i*, *allone*, and *x*) but no subscript variables. The specification consists of the precondition

$$in(1)\geq 0 \;\&\; \forall X(2\leq X\leq in(1)+1 \rightarrow \mathrm{I}(in(X)))$$

and the postcondition

$$(\forall X(2\leq X\leq in(1)+1 \rightarrow in(X)=1) \rightarrow out(1)=1) \;\&$$
$$(\exists X(2\leq X\leq in(1)+1 \;\&\; in(X)\neq 1) \rightarrow out(1)=0)$$

1 **start** $in(1)\geq 0 \;\&\; \forall X(2\leq X\leq in(1)+1 \rightarrow \mathrm{I}(in(X)))$
2 **input** i
3 $allone = 1$
4 **assert** $(\forall X(i+2\leq X\leq in(1)+1 \rightarrow in(X)=1) \rightarrow allone=1) \;\&$
$(\exists X(i+2\leq X\leq in(1)+1 \;\&\; in(X)\neq 1) \rightarrow allone=0) \;\&$
$0\leq i\leq in(1) \;\&\; cin=2+in(1)-i \;\&\; cout=1,i$
5 **if** $(i<1 \vee allone=0)$ **goto** 11
6   **input** x
7   **if** $x=1$ **goto** 9
8         $allone = 0$
9     $i = i-1$
10   **goto** 4
11 **print** *allone*
12 **stop** $(\forall X(2\leq X\leq in(1)+1 \rightarrow in(X)=1) \rightarrow out(1)=1) \;\&$
$(\exists X(2\leq X\leq in(1)+1 \;\&\; in(X)\neq 1) \rightarrow out(1)=0)$

There are four paths in the program.

$$a = \langle 1,2,3,4\rangle \qquad c = \langle 4,5,6,7,9,10,4\rangle$$

$$b = \langle 4,5,6,7,8,9,10,4\rangle \qquad d = \langle 4,5,11,12\rangle$$

[8] As noted in footnote 4, a more general but, unfortunately, more complicated definition of substitution that allows for nested subscripts will be discussed in Example 4 of the next section.

The four verification conditions are as follows:

$$(\mathrm{VC}_a)\quad cin{=}cout{=}1,\ p_1,\ \mathrm{b}_a \vdash p_{4,a}$$
$$cin{=}cout{=}1,\ in(1)\geqslant 0\ \&\ \forall X(2\leqslant X\leqslant in(1)+1 \rightarrow \mathrm{I}(in(X))),$$
$$\text{true}$$
$$\vdash (\forall X(in(cin)+2\leqslant X\leqslant in(1)+1 \rightarrow in(X)=1) \rightarrow 1=1)\ \&$$
$$(\exists X(in(cin)+2\leqslant X\leqslant in(1)+1\ \&\ in(X)\neq 1) \rightarrow 1=0)\ \&$$
$$0\leqslant in(cin)\leqslant in(1)\ \&\ cin+1=2+in(1)-in(cin)\ \&\ cout=1$$

$$(\mathrm{VC}_b)\quad p_1,\ p_4,\ \mathrm{b}_b \vdash p_{4,b}$$
$$in(1)\geqslant 0\ \&\ \forall X(2\leqslant X\leqslant in(1)+1 \rightarrow \mathrm{I}(in(X))),$$
$$(\forall X(i+2\leqslant X\leqslant in(1)+1 \rightarrow in(X)=1) \rightarrow allone=1)\ \&$$
$$(\exists X(i+2\leqslant X\leqslant in(1)+1\ \&\ in(X)\neq 1) \rightarrow allone=0)\ \&$$
$$0\leqslant i\leqslant in(1)\ \&\ cin=2+in(1)-i\ \&\ cout=1,$$
$$\sim(i<1 \vee allone=0)\ \&\ \sim(in(cin)=1)$$
$$\vdash (\forall X(i-1+2\leqslant X\leqslant in(1)+1 \rightarrow in(X)=1) \rightarrow 0=1)\ \&$$
$$(\exists X(i-1+2\leqslant X\leqslant in(1)+1\ \&\ in(X)\neq 1) \rightarrow 0=0)\ \&$$
$$0\leqslant i-1\leqslant in(1)\ \&\ cin+1=2+in(1)-(i-1)\ \&\ cout=1$$

$$(\mathrm{VC}_c)\quad p_1,\ p_4,\ \mathrm{b}_c \vdash p_{4,c}$$
$$in(1)\geqslant 0\ \&\ \forall X(2\leqslant X\leqslant in(1)+1 \rightarrow \mathrm{I}(in(X))),$$
$$(\forall X(i+2\leqslant X\leqslant in(1)+1 \rightarrow in(X)=1) \rightarrow allone=1)\ \&$$
$$(\exists X(i+2\leqslant X\leqslant in(1)+1\ \&\ in(X)\neq 1) \rightarrow allone=0)\ \&$$
$$0\leqslant i\leqslant in(1)\ \&\ cin=2+in(1)-i\ \&\ cout=1,$$
$$\sim(i<1 \vee allone=0)\ \&\ in(cin)=1$$
$$\vdash (\forall X(i-1+2\leqslant X\leqslant in(1)+1 \rightarrow in(X)=1) \rightarrow allone=1)\ \&$$
$$(\exists X(i-1+2\leqslant X\leqslant in(1)+1\ \&\ in(X)\neq 1) \rightarrow allone=0)\ \&$$
$$0\leqslant i-1\leqslant in(1)\ \&\ cin+1=2+in(1)-(i-1)\ \&\ cout=1$$

$$(\mathrm{VC}_d)\quad p_1,\ p_4,\ \mathrm{b}_d \vdash p_{12,d}$$
$$in(1)\geqslant 0\ \&\ \forall X(2\leqslant X\leqslant in(1)+1 \rightarrow \mathrm{I}(in(X))),$$
$$(\forall X(i+2\leqslant X\leqslant in(1)+1 \rightarrow in(X)=1) \rightarrow allone=1)\ \&$$
$$(\exists X(i+2\leqslant X\leqslant in(1)+1\ \&\ in(X)\neq 1) \rightarrow allone=0)\ \&$$
$$0\leqslant i\leqslant in(1)\ \&\ cin=2+in(1)-i\ \&\ cout=1,\ i<1 \vee allone=0$$
$$\vdash (\forall X(2\leqslant X\leqslant in(1)+1 \rightarrow in(X)=1) \rightarrow$$
$$\mathrm{cond}(\mathrm{eq}(1,cout),allone,out(1))=1)\ \&$$
$$(\exists X(2\leqslant X\leqslant in(1)+1\ \&\ in(X)\neq 1) \rightarrow$$
$$\mathrm{cond}(\mathrm{eq}(1,cout),allone,out(1))=0)$$

The only well-foundedness condition is for loop cutpoint 4, as follows:

$$(\mathrm{WC}_4)\quad p_1,\ p_4 \vdash E_4 \succcurlyeq 0$$
$$in(1)\geqslant 0\ \&\ \forall X(2\leqslant X\leqslant in(1)+1 \rightarrow \mathrm{I}(in(X))),$$
$$(\forall X(i+2\leqslant X\leqslant in(1)+1 \rightarrow in(X)=1) \rightarrow allone=1)\ \&$$
$$(\exists X(i+2\leqslant X\leqslant in(1)+1\ \&\ in(X)\neq 1) \rightarrow allone=0)\ \&$$

$0 \leq i \leq in(1)$ & $cin=2+in(1)-i$ & $cout=1$
$\vdash \quad i \geq 0$

And the two termination conditions are for paths b and c, as follows:

(TC$_b$) $\quad p_1, p_4, \mathrm{b}_b \vdash E_4 > E_{4,b}$
$in(1) \geq 0$ & $\forall X(2 \leq X \leq in(1)+1 \rightarrow \mathrm{I}(in(X)))$,
$(\forall X(i+2 \leq X \leq in(1)+1 \rightarrow in(X)=1) \rightarrow allone=1)$ &
$(\exists X(i+2 \leq X \leq in(1)+1$ & $in(X) \neq 1) \rightarrow allone=0)$ &
$0 \leq i \leq in(1)$ & $cin=2+in(1)-i$ & $cout=1$,
$\sim(i<1 \vee allone=0)$ & $\sim(in(cin)=1)$
$\vdash \quad i > i-1$

(TC$_c$) $\quad p_1, p_4, \mathrm{b}_c \vdash E_4 > E_{4,c}$
$in(1) \geq 0$ & $\forall X(2 \leq X \leq in(1)+1 \rightarrow \mathrm{I}(in(X)))$,
$(\forall X(i+2 \leq X \leq in(1)+1 \rightarrow in(X)=1) \rightarrow allone=1)$ &
$(\exists X(i+2 \leq X \leq in(1)+1$ & $in(X) \neq 1) \rightarrow allone=0)$ &
$0 \leq i \leq in(1)$ & $cin=2+in(1)-1$ & $cout=1$,
$\sim(i<1 \vee allone=0)$ & $in(cin)=1$
$\vdash \quad i > i-1$

EXAMPLE 2

We are given an input file with 0 or more records containing some nonzero numbers. The end of the input is marked by a *sentinel record,* which contains the number 0. We are given the task of determining whether the records in the input file (up to but not including the sentinel record) constitute a palindrome (i.e., whether it reads the same from front to back as from back to front).

To help state the specification formally, we introduce the definition schema (one for each unary operation symbol f) for the μ-operator.

(D.μ_f) $\quad \mu_f(X,W)=Y \leftrightarrow$
$(1 \leq X \leq Z \& f(Z)=W \& \forall U(X \leq U < Z \rightarrow f(U) \neq W) \rightarrow Y=Z)$
$\& (X \geq 1 \& \forall U(U \geq X \rightarrow f(U) \neq W) \rightarrow Y=0)$ &
$(X \leq 0 \rightarrow Y=0)$

(read: "$\mu_f(X,W)$ is the smallest natural number U such that $U \geq X \geq 1$ and $f(U)=W$"). In our specification, the precondition states that there is a sentinel record

$$\exists X(X \geq 1 \& in(X)=0) \ \& \ \forall X(1 \leq X < \mu_{in}(1,0) \rightarrow \mathrm{I}(in(X))$$

and the postcondition is

$$(\forall X(1 \leqslant X < \mu_{in}(1,0) \rightarrow a(X) = a(\mu_{in}(1,0) - X)) \rightarrow out(1) = 1)\ \&$$
$$(\exists X(1 \leqslant X < \mu_{in}(1,0)\ \&\ a(X) \neq a(\mu_{in}(1,0) - X)) \rightarrow out(1) = 0)$$

```
 1  start   ∃X(X≥1&in(X)=0)&∀X(1≤X<μ_in(1,0)→I(in(X))
 2  j = 1
 3  input a(1)
 4  assert  ∀X(1≤X≤j→a(X)=in(X))&
            ∀X(1≤X<j→in(X)≠0) & 1≤j≤μ_in(1,0)&
            j=cin−1&cout=1, μ_in(1,0)−j
 5  if a(j)=0 goto 9
 6        j = j+1
 7        input a(j)
 8  goto 4
 9  p = 1
10  n = (j−1)/2
11  i = 1
12  assert  ∀X(1≤X≤μ_in(1,0)→a(X)=in(X)) &
            j=cin−1=μ_in(1,0)&cout=1&n=(j−1)/2&
            1≤i≤n+1 & (∀X(1≤X<i→a(X)=a(j−X))→p=1)
            & (∃X(1≤X<i&a(X)≠a(j−X))→p=0), n+1−i
13  if (p=0 ∨ i>n) goto 18
14        if a(i)=a(j−i) goto 16
15          p = 0
16        i = i+1
17  goto 12
18  print p
19  stop    (∀X(1≤X<μ_in(1,0)→a(X)=a(μ_in(1,0)−X))→out(1)=1)
            & (∃X(1≤X<μ_in(1,0)&
            a(X)≠a(μ_in(1,0)−X))→out(1)=0)
```

One of the more interesting verification conditions is for path f=⟨12,13,18,19⟩. Consider the following:

(VC$_f$)

$$p_1, p_{12}, b_f \vdash p_{19,f}$$
$$\exists X(X \geqslant 1\ \&\ in(X) = 0)\ \&\ \forall X(1 \leqslant X < \mu_{in}(1,0) \rightarrow I(in(X)),$$
$$\forall X(1 \leqslant X \leqslant \mu_{in}(1,0) \rightarrow a(X) = in(X))\ \&$$
$$j = cin - 1 = \mu_{in}(1,0)\ \&\ cout = 1\ \&$$
$$n = (j-1)/2\ \&\ 1 \leqslant i \leqslant n+1\ \&$$
$$(\forall X(1 \leqslant X < i \rightarrow a(X) = a(j-X)) \rightarrow p = 1)\ \&$$
$$(\exists X(1 \leqslant X < i\ \&\ a(X) \neq a(j-X)) \rightarrow p = 0),\ p = 0 \lor i > n$$
$$\vdash$$

$$(\forall X(1 \leqslant X < \mu_{in}(1,0) \rightarrow a(X) = a(\mu_{in}(1,0) - X)) \rightarrow \text{cond}(\text{eq}(1,cout),p,out(1)) = 1) \ \&$$
$$(\exists X(1 \leqslant X < \mu_{in}(1,0) \& a(X) \neq a(\mu_{in}(1,0) - X)) \rightarrow \text{cond}(\text{eq}(1,cout),p,out(1)) = 0)$$

EXAMPLE 3

We have the task of printing out the input file, sorted into ascending order. As in Example 1, the first record in the input file $in(1)$ specifies the length of the input file. We will use the exchange sort algorithm.

Expressing the specification for the program in (first-order) arithmetic presents some technical difficulties. For the moment, we will ignore these difficulties and postpone discussing them until the next section. Informally, the sort has been performed properly if the output file (from record 1 to record $in(1)$) is (1) ordered (in ascending order), and (2) a permutation of the input file (from record 2 to $in(1)+1$). Expressing (1) presents no problem. Let $[X..Y] = \{m\colon m \text{ is an integer } \& X \leqslant m \leqslant Y\}$ be the set of integers between X and Y. In the theory of integers, we introduce the following definition schema (i.e., one such definition for each unary operation symbol f),

$$\textbf{(D.ordered}_f\textbf{)} \qquad \text{ordered}_f(X,Y) \leftrightarrow \forall Z(X \leqslant Z < Y \rightarrow f(Z) \leqslant f(Z+1))$$

which expresses what it means for f to be ordered (monotonically increasing) over $[X\ .\ .\ Y]$. To say that f' over $[X'\ .\ .\ X'+Y-1]$ is a permutation of f over $[X\ .\ .\ X+Y-1]$ means that there exists a one–one function g from the integers over $[0\ .\ .\ Y-1]$ onto $[0\ .\ .\ Y-1]$ such that

$$\forall Z(0 \leqslant Z < Y \rightarrow f'(X'+Z) = f(X+g(Z)))$$

which, for the moment, we assume can be expressed with the predicate $\text{perm}_{f,f'}(X,X',Y)$. So, our specification consists of the precondition

$$in(1) \geqslant 0 \ \& \ \forall X(2 \leqslant X \leqslant in(1)+1 \rightarrow \text{I}(in(X)))$$

and the postcondition

$$\text{ordered}_{out}(1,in(1)) \ \& \ \text{perm}_{in,out}(2,1,in(1))$$

In our program, the subscript variables are j, k, and n, and the only simple variable is t.

```
1  start     in(1)≥0 & ∀X(2≤X≤in(1)+1 → I(in(X)))
2  input n
3  j=1
4  assert    ∀X(1≤X<j → a(X)=in(X+1)) & 1≤j≤n+1 & n=in(1)
             & cin=1+j & cout=1, ⟨n+1−j, 0⟩
```

```
5    if j>n goto 9
6        input a(j)
7        j=j+1
8    goto 4
9    j=n
10   assert    ordered_a(j,n) & perm_{in,a}(2,1,n) &
               ∀X(j<X≤n → ∀Y(1≤Y≤j → a(Y)≤a(X)) &
               1≤j≤n=in(1) & cout=1, ⟨j,n⟩
11   if j<2 goto 23
12       k=j−1
13       assert    p_10 & ∀X(k<X≤j → a(X)≤a(j)) &
                   0≤k≤j−1, ⟨j,k⟩
14       if k<1 goto 21
15           if a(k)≤a(j) goto 19
16               t=a(j)
17               a(j)=a(k)
18               a(k)=t
19           k=k−1
20       goto 13
21       j=j−1
22   goto 10
23   j=1
24   assert    ordered_a(1,n) & perm_{in,a}(2,1,n) &
               ∀X(1≤X<j → out(X)=a(X)) & 1≤j=cout≤n+1 &
               n=in(1), ⟨n+1−j, 0⟩
25   if j>n goto 29
26       print a(j)
27       j=j+1
28   goto 24
29   stop      ordered_out(1,in(1)) & perm_{in,out}(2,1,in(1))
```

There are 10 paths in the program. We give the verification and termination conditions for path f=⟨13,14,15,16,17,18,19,20,13⟩.

$$
\begin{array}{ll}
(\mathrm{VC}_f) & p_1, p_{13}, \mathrm{b}_f \vdash p_{13,f} \\
& in(1)\geq 0 \;\&\; \forall X(2\leq X\leq in(1)+1 \rightarrow \mathrm{I}(in(X))),\ \mathrm{ordered}_a(j,n) \;\& \\
& \mathrm{perm}_{in,a}(2,1,n) \;\&\; \forall X(j<X\leq n \rightarrow \forall Y(1\leq Y\leq j \rightarrow a(Y)\leq a(X)) \;\& \\
& 1\leq j\leq n=in(1) \;\&\; cout=1 \;\&\; \forall X(k<X\leq j \rightarrow a(X)\leq a(j)) \;\& \\
& 0\leq k\leq j-1,\ \sim(k<1) \;\&\; \sim(a(k)\leq a(j)) \\
& \vdash \\
& \forall Z(j\leq Z<n \rightarrow \mathrm{cond}(\mathrm{eq}(Z,k),a(j),\mathrm{cond}(\mathrm{eq}(Z,j),a(k),a(Z))) \\
& \quad \leq \mathrm{cond}(\mathrm{eq}(Z+1,k),a(j),\mathrm{cond}(\mathrm{eq}(Z+1,j),a(k),a(Z+1)))) \;\& \\
& \mathrm{perm}_{in,a}(2,1,n)[k-1\backslash k][t\backslash a(k)][a(k)\backslash a(j)][a(j)\backslash t] \;\& \\
& \forall X(j<X\leq n \rightarrow \forall Y(1\leq Y\leq j \rightarrow \\
& \quad\quad \mathrm{cond}(\mathrm{eq}(Y,k),a(j),\mathrm{cond}(\mathrm{eq}(Y,j),a(k),a(Y))) \leq \\
& \quad\quad\quad \mathrm{cond}(\mathrm{eq}(X,k),a(j),\mathrm{cond}(\mathrm{eq}(X,j),a(k),a(X)))) \;\&
\end{array}
$$

$$1 \leqslant j \leqslant n = in(1) \ \&\ cout = 1 \ \&\ \forall X(k-1 < X \leqslant j \rightarrow \\ \quad \text{cond}(\text{eq}(X,k), a(j), \text{cond}(\text{eq}(X,j), a(k), a(X))) \leqslant \\ \quad\quad \text{cond}(\text{eq}(j,k), a(j), \text{cond}(\text{eq}(j,j), a(k), a(j)))) \ \& \\ 0 \leqslant k-1 \leqslant j-1$$

$$(\text{TC}_f) \quad p_1, p_{13}, \text{b}_f \vdash E_{13} > E_{13,f} \\ in(1) \geqslant 0 \ \&\ \forall X(2 \leqslant X \leqslant in(1)+1 \rightarrow \text{I}(in(X))),\ \text{ordered}_a(j,n) \ \& \\ \text{perm}_{in,a}(2,1,n) \ \&\ \forall X(j < X \leqslant n \rightarrow \forall Y(1 \leqslant Y \leqslant j \rightarrow a(Y) \leqslant a(X)) \ \& \\ 1 \leqslant j \leqslant n = in(1) \ \&\ cout = 1 \ \&\ \forall X(k < X \leqslant j \rightarrow a(X) \leqslant a(j)) \ \& \\ 0 \leqslant k \leqslant j-1,\ \sim(k<1) \ \&\ \sim(a(k) \leqslant a(j)) \\ \vdash \ \langle j,k \rangle > \langle j,k-1 \rangle$$

Notice that, for example, in the verification condition consequent of (VC_f), we have

$$\text{ordered}_a(j,n)[k-1 \backslash k][t \backslash a(k)][a(k) \backslash a(j)][a(j) \backslash t] \equiv \\ \forall Z(j \leqslant Z < n \rightarrow \text{cond}(\text{eq}(Z,k), a(j), \text{cond}(\text{eq}(Z,j), a(k), a(Z))) \\ \leqslant \text{cond}(\text{eq}(Z+1,k), a(j), \text{cond}(\text{eq}(Z+1,j), a(k), \\ a(Z+1))))$$

and we have written out the substitution accordingly, although

$$p_1, p_{13}, \text{b}_f \vdash \text{ordered}_a(j,n) \leftrightarrow \\ \text{ordered}_a(j,n)[k-1 \backslash k][t \backslash a(k)][a(k) \backslash a(j)][a(j) \backslash t]$$

because substitution is a purely syntactic (non-proof theoretic) operation. However, because we have not provided an explicit definition of a permutation, we have not written out the substitution

$$\text{perm}_{in,a}(2,1,n)[k-1 \backslash k][t \backslash a(k)][a(k) \backslash a(j)][a(j) \backslash t]$$

The verification condition (VC_f) is, to say the least, overwhelming. We have not been writing out all of the verification (and well-foundedness and termination) conditions because of their complexity. To this end, struck by the difficulty of understanding verification conditions for all but the simplest of programs, computer scientists have been developing programming tools to assist the human user in comprehending and proving verification conditions.

EXAMPLE 4

We are again given the task of printing out the input file, sorted into ascending order. The specification is exactly as in Example 3, and the algorithm is much the same except that we use the index array b to perform an "in place" sort, we work in the sort from the smallest to the largest integer (reverse order from that used in Example 3), and we print the "next smallest" integer as soon as we find it. We use this example to illustrate how nested array subscripts might be handled.

One way of handling nested subscripts is to introduce a class of index arrays **Tarray.** The additions to our abstract syntax are as follows:

Tarray: *ia*, . . .
Tvar: *h*, . . .
$h ::= ia(se)$
Texp: *te*, . . .
$te ::= m \mid h \mid j \mid \text{succ}(te) \mid \ldots \mid te{+}te' \mid \ldots$

and we add clauses to the definitions of **Ivar, Iexp, Avar,** and **Icom** so that $a(te)$ (as opposed to the more restricted $a(se)$ used previously) counts as an integer variable, h (i.e., $ia(se)$) is an integer expression and an assertion variable, and the assignment $h{=}te$ counts as an intermediate command. The operational semantics of the intermediate commands **(IC)** is modified in the obvious manner.

For this approach, we do not have to modify our definition of substitution, and the proof of the Coincidence Lemma when $v \equiv h$ and $v \equiv a(te)$ is entirely similar to the proof in Section 3.4. Because of the simplicity of this approach, we have adopted it in the example that follows.

A second, more general, approach is to allow nested subscripts without restriction. In other word, the classes **Svar** and **Sexp** are abolished, and the abstract syntax of **Ivar** becomes simply

$$i ::= x \mid a(e)$$

The definition of substitution becomes more complicated as one defines

$$a(t)[t' \backslash a(t'')] \equiv \text{cond}(\text{eq}(t[t' \backslash a(t'')], t''), t', a(t[t' \backslash a(t'')])$$

The proof of the Coincidence Lemma is more difficult, but soundness does hold.[9]

To formulate our inductive assertions, we introduce the identity operation symbol with the equational definition

$$\textbf{(D.id)} \qquad \text{id}(X) = X$$

and the composition operation symbol with the equational definition schema

$$(\textbf{D.comp}_{f,f'}) \qquad \text{comp}_{f,f'}(X) = f(f'(X))$$

[9] A soundness proof can be extracted from de Bakker's text.

The array b is an index array.

```
 1  start      in(1)≥0 & ∀X(2≤X≤in(1)+1 → I(in(X)))
 2  input n
 3  j = 1
 4   assert       ∀X(1≤X<j → b(X)=X) & 1≤j≤n+1 & n=in(1) &
                  cin=2 & cout=1, ⟨n+1−j, 0⟩
 5  if j>n goto 9
 6          b(j) = j
 7          j = j+1
 8   goto 4
 9   j = 1
10  assert      ∀X(1≤X≤n → b(X)=X) & ∀X(1≤X<j →
                  a(X)=in(X+1)) & 1≤j≤n+1 & n=in(1) &
                cin=1+j & cout=1, ⟨n+1−j, 0⟩
11   if j>n goto 15
12          input a(j)
13          j = j+1
14   goto 10
15   j = 1
16   assert     ∀X(1≤X<j → out(X)=a(b(X))) &
                ∀X(1≤X≤n → a(X)=in(X+1)) &
                ordered_comp_{a,b}(1,j) & perm_{b,id}(1,1,n) &
                ∀X(1≤X<j → ∀Y(j≤Y≤n → a(b(X))≤a(b(Y))) &
                1≤j=cout≤n=in(1), ⟨n+1−j,n⟩
17   if j>n−1 goto 30
18          k = j+1
19          assert   p16 & ∀X(j≤X<k → a(b(j))≤a(b(X))) &
                     j+1≤k≤n+1, ⟨n+1−j,n+1−k⟩
20          if k>n goto 27
21                if a(b(k))≥a(b(j)) goto 25
22                     t = b(j)
23                     b(j) = b(k)
24                     b(k) = t
25                k = k+1
26          goto 19
27          print a(b(j))
28          j = j+1
29  goto 16
30  if n=0 goto 32
31          print a(b(n))
32  stop        ordered_out(1,in(1)) & perm_{in,out}(2,1,in(1))
```

In p_{16} (and p_{19}), instead of the two conjuncts

$$\forall X(1 \leq X \leq n \rightarrow a(X)=in(X+1)) \;\&\; \mathrm{perm}_{b,\mathrm{id}}(1,1,n)$$

we could have used

$$\text{perm}_{in,\text{comp}_{a,b}}(2,1,n)$$

making the p_{16}'s of Examples 3 and 4 more similar. In the next section we will discuss our reason for formulating the p_{16} of Example 4 as we did.

The verification condition for path $h=\langle 19,20,21,22,23,24,25,26,19\rangle$ is as follows:

$$
\begin{array}{ll}
(\text{VC}_h) & p_1, p_{19}, \text{b}_h \vdash p_{19,h} \\
& in(1)\geq 0 \;\&\; \forall X(2\leq X\leq in(1)+1 \rightarrow \text{I}(in(X))), \\
& \forall X(1\leq X<j \rightarrow out(X)=a(b(X))) \;\&\; \\
& \forall X(1\leq X\leq n \rightarrow a(X)=in(X+1)) \;\&\; \\
& \text{ordered}_{\text{comp}_{a,b}}(1,j) \;\&\; \text{perm}_{b,id}(1,1,n) \;\&\; \\
& \forall X(1\leq X<j \rightarrow \forall Y(j\leq Y\leq n \rightarrow a(b(X))\leq a(b(Y))) \;\&\; \\
& 1\leq j=cout\leq n=in(1) \;\&\; \forall X(j\leq X<k \rightarrow a(b(j))\leq a(b(X))) \;\&\; \\
& j+1\leq k\leq n+1, \sim(k>n) \;\&\; \sim(a(b(k))\geq a(b(j))) \\
& \vdash \\
& \forall X(1\leq X<j \rightarrow \\
& \quad out(X)=a(\text{cond}(\text{eq}(X,k),b(j),\text{cond}(\text{eq}(X,j),b(k),b(X)))) \;\&\; \\
& \forall X(1\leq X\leq n \rightarrow a(X)=in(X+1)) \;\&\; \\
& \forall Z(1\leq Z<j \rightarrow \\
& \quad a(\text{cond}(\text{eq}(Z,k),b(j),\text{cond}(\text{eq}(Z,j),b(k),b(Z)))) \leq \\
& \quad\quad a(\text{cond}(\text{eq}(Z+1,k),b(j),\text{cond}(\text{eq}(Z+1,j),b(k),b(Z+1))))) \\
& \text{perm}_{b,id}(1,1,n)[k+1\backslash k][t\backslash b(k)][b(k)\backslash b(j)][b(j)\backslash t] \;\&\; \\
& \forall X(1\leq X<j \rightarrow \forall Y(j\leq Y\leq n \rightarrow \\
& \quad a(\text{cond}(\text{eq}(X,k),b(j),\text{cond}(\text{eq}(X,j),b(k),b(X)))) \leq \\
& \quad\quad a(\text{cond}(\text{eq}(Y,k),b(j),\text{cond}(\text{eq}(Y,j),b(k),b(Y))))) \;\&\; \\
& 1\leq j=cout\leq n=in(1) \;\&\; \forall X(j\leq X<k+1 \rightarrow \\
& \quad a(\text{cond}(\text{eq}(j,k),b(j),\text{cond}(\text{eq}(j,j),b(k),b(j)))) \leq \\
& \quad\quad a(\text{cond}(\text{eq}(X,k),b(j),\text{cond}(\text{eq}(X,j),b(k),b(X))))) \;\&\; \\
& j+1\leq k+1\leq n+1
\end{array}
$$

EXAMPLE 5

For the purposes of this example, we extend the syntax in the natural manner to accommodate two-dimensional arrays.

Before we can state the specification for our program, we must introduce some graph theoretic concepts. An *adjacency matrix* a is an $m\times m$ array and, viewed formally, is the characteristic function for a finite relation R_a—that is,

$$
\begin{array}{l}
1\leq X\leq m \& 1\leq Y\leq m \rightarrow (a(X,Y)=0 \vee a(X,Y)=1) \;\&\; \\
\qquad\qquad\qquad\qquad\qquad (R_a(X,Y)\leftrightarrow a(X,Y)=1)
\end{array}
$$

The *transitive closure* TC(R) of a relation R is the smallest transitive relation that includes R—that is, $R \subset \mathrm{TC}(R)$, $\mathrm{TC}(R)$ is transitive, and, for any transitive relation S such that $R \subset S$, $\mathrm{TC}(R) \subset S$. The characteristic function for $\mathrm{TC}(R_a)$ is represented by the $m \times m$ array *path* called the *path matrix*.

Our task is to compute, given an adjacency matrix, the path matrix. The first record in the input file is $in(1)=m$, and the adjacency matrix is stored row-wise in the input records from 2 to $m*m+1$. We are to print the path matrix row-wise. In other words, the precondition is

$$in(1) \geqslant 1 \; \& \; \forall X(2 \leqslant X \leqslant in(1) ** 2+1 \rightarrow (in(X)=0 \vee in(X)=1))$$

and the postcondition (p_{43}, which we attempt to express in the text that follows) states that the first $in(1)*in(1)$ records of the output file contain the path matrix stored row-wise.

To compute the transitive closure, we use the Roy–Warshall Algorithm.[10] The idea behind the algorithm is as follows: A path from node i to node j can pass through zero or more nodes distinct from i and j. We wish to define a 3-ary operation symbol p in a manner so that $\mathrm{p}(k,i,j) = 1$ $(0 \leqslant k \leqslant m)$ if there is a path from i to j that passes through nodes in some subset of the set of nodes $[1 \,.\,.\, k]$, and we want $\mathrm{p}(k,i,j) = 0$ otherwise. Note that if $a(i,j) = 1$, then $\mathrm{p}(k,i,j) = 1$ for every k from 0 to m. Because the adjacency matrix is stored row-wise on the input file and $m = in(1)$, we take

$$a(i,j) = in((i-1)*in(1)+j+1)$$

As we know of no explicit definition, the definition of $\mathrm{p}(k,i,j)$ proceeds inductively. We have, for $k \geqslant 0$

$$\begin{aligned} \mathrm{p}(0,I,J) &= in((I-1)*in(1)+J+1) \\ \mathrm{p}(\mathrm{succ}(K),I,J) &= \mathrm{cond}(\mathrm{eq}(\mathrm{p}(K,I,J),1),\, 1, \\ &\qquad \mathrm{p}(K,I,\mathrm{succ}(K))*\mathrm{p}(K,\mathrm{succ}(K),J)) \end{aligned}$$

The key insight incorporated into the Roy–Warshall Algorithm is that $path(i,j) = 1$ iff $\mathrm{p}(m,i,j) = 1$. Assuming that the input file (adjacency matrix) has been read into the path matrix, the inductive definition is captured by the **for** program:

```
for k:=1 to m do
   for i:=1 to m do
      if path(i,k)=1 then
        for j:=1 to m do
           if path(i,j)=0 then
              path(i,j):=path(k,j)
```

[10] For further discussion of the Roy–Warshall Algorithm, see Berztiss or Tenenbaum and Augenstein (who refer to the algorithm as "the Warshall Algorithm").

which is translated into lines 14 to 31 of the following FC+ program:

```
1  start        in(1)≥1 &
                ∀X(2≤X≤in(1)**2+1→(in(X)=0∨in(X)=1))
2  input m
3  i = 1
4  assert       p4, ⟨m+1−i,m+1, 0⟩
5  if i>m goto 14
6     j = 1
7     assert       p7, ⟨m+1−i,m+1−j, 0⟩
8     if j>m goto 12
9       input path(i,j)
10      j = j+1
11    goto 7
12    i = i+1
13 goto 4
14 k = 1
15 assert       p15, ⟨m+1−k,m+1,m+1⟩
16 if k>m goto 32
17    i = 1
18    assert       p18, ⟨m+1−k,m+1−i,m+1⟩
19    if i>m goto 30
20      if path(i,k)≠1 goto 30
21        j = 1
22        assert     p22, ⟨m+1−k,m+1−i,m+1−j⟩
23        if j>m goto 28
24          if path(i,j)≠0 goto 26
25            path(i,j) = path(k,j)
26          j = j+1
27        goto 22
28      i = i+1
29    goto 18
30    k = k+1
31 goto 15
32 i = 1
33 assert       p33, ⟨m+1−i,m+1, 0⟩
34 if i>m goto 43
35    j = 1
36    assert       p36, ⟨m+1−i,m+1−j, 0⟩
37    if j>m goto 41
38      print path(i,j)
39      j = j+1
40    goto 36
41    i = i+1
42 goto 33
43 stop         p43
```

Expressing most of the inductive assertions presents no difficulty. For example, we take p_4 to be

$$\forall X,Y(1\leqslant X<i \& 1\leqslant Y\leqslant m \rightarrow path(X,Y)=in((X-1)*m+Y+1) \& 1\leqslant i\leqslant m+1 \& m=in(1) \& cin=(\mathrm{i}-1)*m+2 \& cout=1$$

and p_7 can be expressed in a similar manner (exercise). Next, we exhibit p_{15}

$$\forall X,Y(1\leqslant X\leqslant m \& 1\leqslant Y\leqslant m \rightarrow path(X,Y)=\mathrm{p}(k-1,X,Y) \& 1\leqslant k\leqslant m+1 \& m=in(1) \& cout=1$$

leaving statements of p_{18} and p_{22} as an exercise. It might seem that the postcondition p_{43} could be expressed as follows:

$$\forall X,Y(1\leqslant X\leqslant in(1) \& 1\leqslant Y\leqslant in(1) \rightarrow out((X-1)*in(1)+Y+1)=\mathrm{p}(in(1),X,Y))$$

However, expressing the postcondition presents technical difficulties that we will discuss briefly in the next section.

Except for the verification condition for the path ending with the **stop** command ($\langle 33,34,43\rangle$), writing out the verification, well-foundedness, and termination conditions do not present technical problems. For example, the verification condition for path $a=\langle 1,2,3,4\rangle$ is as follows:

$$(\mathrm{VC}_a)\quad cin=cout=1,\ p_1,\ \mathrm{b}_a \vdash p_{4,a}$$
$$cin=cout=1,\ in(1)\geqslant 1 \& \forall X(2\leqslant X\leqslant in(1)**2+1 \rightarrow (in(X)=0 \vee in(X)=1)), \mathrm{true}$$
$$\vdash \forall X,Y(1\leqslant X<1 \& 1\leqslant Y\leqslant in(cin) \rightarrow path(X,Y)=in((X-1)*in(cin)+Y+1) \& in(cin)=in(1) \& cin+1=(1-1)*in(cin)+2 \& cout=1$$

3.6. COMPARISON OF FIRST-ORDER AND SECOND-ORDER SPECIFICATIONS

The purpose of this section is to discuss briefly an issue raised in Examples 3 through 5 of the preceding section. Specifically, some difficulties arose in expressing the concepts of a permutation and of the transitive closure. We now address the issue of whether the language of first-order arithmetic, which we have been using, is sufficiently expressive for stating program specifications. Perhaps the expressive power of second-order arithmetic, which we discussed briefly in Section 0.4, is more appropriate, and second-order logic is the proper underlying logic for a program specification language.

Recall that, in Example 3 of the preceding section, the postcondition for the sort algorithm states that the output file (from record 1 to record $in(1)$) should (1) be ordered in ascending order, and (2) be a permutation of the input file (from record 2 to $in(1)+1$). We saw that expressing (1) is straightforward. A problem arises, however, in expressing (2) when there is a possibility of repetitions in the input file (i.e., when there is a possibility that $in(Z)=in(Z')$ for some distinct Z and Z' between 2 and $in(1)+1$). We noted that, to say that f' over $[X' \,.\,.\, X'+Y-1]$ is a permutation of f over $[X \,.\,.\, X+Y-1]$ means that there exists a bijection g such that

$$\forall Z(0\leqslant Z<Y\rightarrow f'(X'+Z)=f(X+g(Z)))$$

We do not know an explicit definition of the concept of a permutation in first-order arithmetic. However, in second-order arithmetic, if we have function variables as well as predicate variables, we can define the concept of a permutation as follows:

(D.pmut) $$\begin{aligned}&\mathrm{pmut}(f',X',f,X,Y)\leftrightarrow\exists g(\forall U,V(g(U)=g(V)\rightarrow U=V)\ \&\\ &\forall V\exists U(g(U)=V)\ \&\\ &\forall Z(0\leqslant Z<Y\rightarrow f'(X'+Z)=f(X+g(Z)))\end{aligned}$$

If repetitions in the input data were prohibited, we could readily express the concept of a permutation in first-order arithmetic. We can, however, introduce the predicate 'norep' into the theory of integers with the explicit definition schema (one definition for each f)

(D.norep$_f$) $$\mathrm{norep}_f(X,Y)\leftrightarrow\forall Z,Z'(X\leqslant Z<Z'\leqslant Y\rightarrow f(Z)\neq f(Z'))$$

expressing that, in the interval between X and Y, there are no repetitions in f. We then introduce the predicate 'idrange' with the explicit definition schema (one for each pair of unary operation symbols f and f')

(D.idrange$_{f,f'}$) $$\begin{aligned}&\mathrm{idrange}_{f,f'}(X,X',Y)\leftrightarrow\\ &\forall Z(X\leqslant Z<X+Y\rightarrow\exists Z'(X'\leqslant Z'<X'+Y\ \&\\ &\qquad f(Z)=f'(Z')))\end{aligned}$$

that expresses that f over $[X \,.\,.\, X+Y-1]$ and f' over $[X' \,.\,.\, X'+Y-1]$ have the same range. Now, in second-order arithmetic we have

$$\models \mathrm{norep}_f(X,X+Y-1)\&\mathrm{idrange}_{f,f'}(X,X',Y)\rightarrow\mathrm{pmut}(f',X',f,X,Y)$$

which assures us that, in a first-order specification, if $\mathrm{norep}_{in}(2,in(1)+1)$ is a conjunct in the precondition, then $\mathrm{idrange}_{in,out}(2,1,in(1))$ will do in lieu of $\mathrm{pmut}(in,2,out,1,in(1))$ as a conjunct in the postcondition. However, prohibiting the input file from containing repetitions is normally not a reasonable restriction. The expressive power of second-order arithmetic seems to be needed.

In Example 4, we used the index array b, and had as two conjuncts in p_{16} and p_{19},

$$\forall X(1 \leqslant X \leqslant n \rightarrow a(X) = in(X+1)) \ \& \ \mathrm{perm}_{b,\mathrm{id}}(1,1,n)$$

Now, replacing the conjunct $\mathrm{perm}_{b,\mathrm{id}}(1,1,n)$ (which we do not know how to express in first-order arithmetic) with the conjunct $\mathrm{idrange}_{b,\mathrm{id}}(1,1,n)$ (which we can express), we have in second-order arithmetic

$$p_{16} \models \mathrm{pmut}(\mathrm{comp}_{a,b}, 1, in, 2, n)$$

and

$$p_{19} \models \mathrm{pmut}(\mathrm{comp}_{a,b}, 1, in, 2, n)$$

because

$$\forall X(1 \leqslant X \leqslant n \rightarrow a(X) = in(X+1)) \ \& \ \mathrm{idrange}_{b,\mathrm{id}}(1,1,n)$$
$$\models \mathrm{pmut}(\mathrm{comp}_{a,b}, 1, in, 2, n)$$

The index array b exhibits the function g that is required to exist by definition **(D.pmut).** In principle, the same idea could be incorporated into the statement of the postcondition. That is, we could incorporate into the postcondition a conjunct exhibiting b that permutes the input file into the output file. However, it would seem that the index array b should be irrelevant to the specification because it would rule out programs that do not use an index array, such as the program in Example 3.

Let us turn to Example 5. A problem exists in our statement of the postcondition p_{43}. It is known that the concept of the transitive closure is not first-order definable. Roughly, this means that there are nonstandard models of p_{43} in which the relation represented by the output file is not the transitive closure of the relation represented by the input file. In second-order arithmetic, the postcondition (that the output file represents the transitive closure of the relation represented by the input file) could be expressed.[11]

[11] Note that in the following PROLOG program for computing *path*, the transitive closure of *adjacent*, the logical reading of the clauses

path(*X*,*Y*) if *adjacent*(*X*,*Y*)
path(*X*,*Y*) if *adjacent*(*X*,*Z*) and *path*(*Z*,*Y*)

yields only that *adjacent* $\subset$ *path*, not that *path* is transitive (suppose *path*(*a*,*b*), *path*(*b*,*c*), but neither *adjacent*(*a*,*b*) nor *path*(*a*,*c*)), and much less that *path* is the transitive closure of *adjacent*. (Suppose *path* is the universal relation, which happens to be transitive and includes *adjacent*.)

These examples suggest that first-order logic, the customary underlying logic in the program verification literature, should be replaced by second-order logic. However, many logicians have argued against adopting second-order logic, and we will repeat their reasons here. First, Gödel showed that in first-order arithmetic all of the computable functions are representable. This means that the concepts of a permutation and of the transitive closure are representable in arithmetic because we can write programs to compute them.[12] Second, second-order logic lacks some desirable properties that first-order logic has, such as completeness and compactness. Other things being equal, first-order logic is to be preferred. Third, second-order logic is not really a logic, but rather a part of mathematics proper because it incorporates set theory. Fourth, much of the expressive power of second-order logic can be captured in, for example, (1) first-order set theory, (2) a language in between first- and second-order logic permitting infinite conjunctions, or (3) first-order logic supplemented with a device for expressing the transitive closure, and so forth. As a result, there is really no need to go to the extremes of second-order logic.

The question of whether first-order logic is the proper logic for program specification and verification (or for all of computer science, for that matter) is a fundamental research problem, and we will not attempt to solve it here. Instead, we will take the customary approach and stick with first-order arithmetic, despite its obvious disadvantages. We would like to point out, however, that routine formal program verification of real-world programs is not feasible until the issue of which logic is proper has been resolved. If we cannot express a specification formally, we cannot even begin the task of formal program verification.[13]

[12] Strictly speaking, these considerations imply only that the concepts of the permutation of a *finite* function and the transitive closure of a *finite* relation are representable in first-order arithmetic. In any case, the shortest assertion that represents, for instance, the (finite) transitive closure might be very long indeed. The problem is that the only known means to represent many primitive recursive functions involves the complicated encoding scheme of Gödel's Beta Function Lemma. For details on this Lemma, see Boolos and Jeffrey or Loeckx and Sieber.

Note that the concept of finiteness is not expressible in first-order logic, as the following considerations show. Suppose Finite were a set of assertions expressing that the domain of discourse is finite. Let $\{x_i: i \geq 0\}$ be an infinite set of variables foreign to Finite, $S_i = \{\sim x_j = x_k: x_j \not\equiv x_k \ \& \ 0 \leq j \leq i \ \& \ 0 \leq k \leq i\}$, and

$$S = \bigcup_{i \geq 0} S_i$$

As explained in Boolos and Jeffrey, the Compactness Theorem (which holds in first-order logic) states that a set of assertions is satisfiable iff each of its finite subsets is. Clearly, every finite subset of $S \cup$ Finite is satisfiable. Hence, by the Compactness Theorem, $S \cup$ Finite is satisfiable. But this is impossible because there are infinitely many distinct objects in the domain (because there are infinitely many x_i's and $\sim x_i = x_j$ if $x_i \not\equiv x_j$). Hence, the concept of finiteness cannot be expressed in first-order logic.

[13] For further discussion of first-order versus second-order logic and references to the literature, see Shapiro. The related discussion and references in Gurevitch are also valuable, as they are directed towards computer science applications. Gurevitch contains a proof that the concept of the transitive closure is not expressible in first-order logic.

EXERCISES

Proving Programs Correct

1. The other paths in the exchange sort program in Example 3, Section 3.5, are as follows:

$$a = \langle 1,2,3,4 \rangle \qquad g = \langle 13,14,15,19,20,13 \rangle$$
$$b = \langle 4,5,6,7,8 \rangle \qquad h = \langle 13,14,21,22,10 \rangle$$
$$c = \langle 4,5,9,10 \rangle \qquad i = \langle 24,25,26,27,28,24 \rangle$$
$$d = \langle 10,11,12,13 \rangle \qquad j = \langle 24,25,29 \rangle$$
$$e = \langle 10,11,23,24 \rangle$$

   Write out the verification, well-foundedness, and termination conditions.

2. Write an FC+ program to echo print the input file. The length of the input file is given by the first input record $in(1)$. Using the combined Floyd method, prove that your program is totally correct. The precondition is

$$in(1) \geqslant 0 \;\&\; \forall X(2 \leqslant X \leqslant in(1) + 1 \rightarrow \mathrm{I}(X))$$

   To facilitate expression of the postcondition, we introduce the definition schema

$$\textbf{(D.idseq}_{f,f'}\textbf{)} \qquad \mathrm{idseq}_{f,f'}(X,X',Y) \leftrightarrow \forall Y(0 \leqslant X < Y \rightarrow f(X+Z) = f'(X'+Z))$$

   which expresses that the two subsequences f (beginning at the X-th slot) and f' (beginning at the X'-th slot) of length Y are identical. Then, the postcondition is simply

$$\mathrm{idseq}_{in,out}(2,1,in(1))$$

3. Write an FC+ program to convert a natural number n into a number representing n in binary notation. For example, if 13 is the number to be converted, the number representing n would be 1101 (printed by one **print** command). The precondition is

$$in(1) \geqslant 0$$

   (a) State the postcondition (formally).
   (b) Prove that your program is totally correct.

4. Write an FC+ program to reverse the conversion of the preceding exercise. For example, if 1101 is the binary representation to be converted to decimal form, 13 would be the output of the conversion (printed by one **print** command). The precondition is $in(1) \geqslant 0$.
   (a) State the postcondition.
   (b) Prove that your program is totally correct.
5. (a) Write an FC+ program to insert a number into a sequence of numbers that are arranged in ascending order. There are no repetitions in the input data. If the number to be inserted already occurs in the input file, the program merely echo prints the input file. The first input record $in(1)$ contains the number to be inserted, and the second input record $in(2)$ gives the length of the input file. Prove that your program is totally correct. The precondition is

$$\mathrm{I}(in(1)) \ \&\ in(2) \geqslant 0 \ \&\ \mathrm{norep}_{in}(3,in(1)+2) \ \&$$
$$\mathrm{ordered}_{in}(3,in(1)+2),$$

The postcondition can be expressed as

$$(\exists X(3 \leqslant X \leqslant in(1)+2 \& in(X)=in(1)) \rightarrow \mathrm{idseq}_{in,out}(3,1,in(1))) \ \&$$
$$(\forall X(3 \leqslant X \leqslant in(1)+2 \rightarrow in(X) \neq in(1)) \rightarrow \mathrm{ordered}_{out}(1,in(1)+1) \ \&$$
$$\exists X(1 \leqslant X \leqslant in(1)+1 \& out(X)=in(1) \ \&\ \mathrm{idseq}_{in,out}(3,1,X-1) \ \&$$
$$\mathrm{idseq}_{in,out}(3+X,X+1,in(1)-X))$$

   (b) Simplify the statement of the postcondition in part (a) by introducing one or more helpful predicate or operation symbols. For example, you might introduce a definition schema (**D.concat**$_{f,f'}$) to "concatenate" two sequences (operations).
6. Write an FC+ program to delete a number from a sequence of numbers that are arranged in ascending order. There are no repetitions in the input data. If the number to be deleted does not occur in the input file, the program merely echo prints the input file. The first input record $in(1)$ contains the number to be inserted, and the second input record $in(2)$ provides the length of the input file. The precondition is

$$\mathrm{I}(in(1)) \ \&\ in(2) \geqslant 0 \ \&\ \mathrm{norep}_{in}(3,in(1)+2) \ \&$$
$$\mathrm{ordered}_{in}(3,in(1)+2).$$

   (a) State the postcondition.
   (b) Prove that your program is totally correct.
7. Write a linear search program to determine if the integer on record $in(1)$ occurs on one of the records $in(3), \ldots, in(2+in(2))$. If it does occur,

print the number of the first record on which it occurs. If it does not occur, print a 0. The length of the input file is given by $in(2)$. Do not use any arrays.

Prove that your program is totally correct. The specification consists of the precondition

$$\mathrm{I}(in(1)) \;\&\; in(2) \geqslant 0 \;\&\; \forall X(3 \leqslant X \leqslant 2+in(2) \rightarrow \mathrm{I}(X))$$

and the postcondition

$$(\exists X(3 \leqslant X \leqslant 2+in(2) \& in(X)=in(1)) \rightarrow out(1)=\mu_{in}(3,in(1))) \;\&$$
$$(\forall X(3 \leqslant X \leqslant 2+in(2) \rightarrow in(X) \neq in(1)) \rightarrow out(1)=0)$$

8. (a) Follow the instructions for Exercise 7 with the following modifications: you are not given the length of the input file and you are to prove only that your program is partially correct. (Why can't you prove total correctness?) The specification consists of the precondition

$$\forall X(1 \leqslant X \rightarrow \mathrm{I}(X))$$

and the postcondition

$$out(1) = \mu_{in}(2,in(1))$$

(b) Would it help if the precondition were strengthened to read as follows?

$$\exists X(2 \leqslant X \;\&\; in(1)=in(X)) \;\&\; \forall X(2 \leqslant X \rightarrow \mathrm{I}(X))$$

For Exercises 9 through 11, the following conditions hold: We understand that a set of positive integers is represented by a sequence of numbers (with no repetitions) arranged in ascending order. Two sets are contained on the input file, and the end of each of the two sets is marked by a sentinel record containing the number 0. The precondition is

$$\begin{aligned}&\mathrm{ordered}_{in}(1,\mu_{in}(1,0)) \;\&\; \mathrm{ordered}_{in}(\mu_{in}(1,0)+1,\\ &\qquad\qquad \mu_{in}(\mu_{in}(1,0)+1,0)-\mu_{in}(1,0)-1) \;\&\\ &\mathrm{norep}_{in}(1,\mu_{in}(1,0)) \;\&\; \mathrm{norep}_{in}(\mu_{in}(1,0)+1,\\ &\qquad\qquad \mu_{in}(\mu_{in}(1,0)+1,0)-\mu_{in}(1,0)-1)\end{aligned}$$

---

9. Write an FC+ program to compute the intersection of two sets. The postcondition is

$$\begin{aligned}
&\text{ordered}_{out}(1,cout-1) \;\&\; \text{norep}_{out}(1,cout-1) \;\&\\
&\forall X(1 \leq X < cout \rightarrow \exists Y(1 \leq Y < \mu_{in}(1,0) \;\&\; out(X)=in(Y)) \;\&\\
&\quad \exists Z(\mu_{in}(1,0)+1 \leq Z < \mu_{in}(\mu_{in}(1,0)+1,0) \;\&\; out(X)=in(Z))) \;\&\\
&(\forall X(\exists Y(1 \leq Y < \mu_{in}(1,0) \;\&\; in(Y)=X) \;\&\\
&\quad \exists Z(\mu_{in}(1,0)+1 \leq Z < \mu_{in}(\mu_{in}(1,0)+1,0) \;\&\; in(Z)=X)) \rightarrow\\
&\exists W(1 \leq W < cout \;\&\; out(W)=X))
\end{aligned}$$

Prove that your program is totally correct.

10. Write an FC+ program to compute the union of two sets.

(a) State the postcondition.

(b) Prove that your program is totally correct.

11. Write an FC+ program to compute the (set) difference between two sets (i.e., the set of all and only those positive integers that belong to the first set but not to the second set).

(a) State the postcondition.

(b) Prove that your program is totally correct.

Exercises 12 through 16 involve two-dimensional square arrays. The syntax, and so on, is as in Example 5, Section 3.5, and the arrays are stored row-wise on the input file. In Exercises 12 through 15, we understand the array a to be the characteristic function for a binary relation R_a as in Example 5. The precondition is

$$in(1) \geq 1 \;\&\; \forall X(2 \leq X \leq in(1)**2+1 \rightarrow (in(X)=0 \vee in(X)=1))$$

---

12. Prove that the Roy–Warshall Algorithm of Example 5, Section 3.5, terminates. That is, prove the FC+ program in Example 5 totally correct wrt the precondition just given and the postcondition true.

13. Write an FC+ program to determine if the binary relation represented on the input file is reflexive. The postcondition is

$$\begin{aligned}
&\forall X(1 \leq X \leq in(1) \rightarrow in((X-1)*in(1)+X+1)=1) \rightarrow out(1)=1)) \;\&\\
&\exists X(1 \leq X \leq in(1) \;\&\; in((X-1)*in(1)+X+1)=0) \rightarrow out(1)=0))
\end{aligned}$$

Prove that your program is totally correct.

14. Write an FC+ program to determine if the binary relation represented on the input file is symmetric.

(a) State the postcondition.

(b) Prove that your program is totally correct.

15. Write an FC+ program to determine if the binary relation represented on the input file is transitive.

(a) State the postcondition.

(b) Prove that your program is totally correct.

16. Write an FC+ program to perform matrix multiplication. (Remember that the product matrix of two $n \times n$ matrices a and b is the $n \times n$ matrix c, such that $c(i,j)=a(i,1)*b(1,j)+ . . . +a(i,n)*b(n,j)$ for every i and j from 1 to n.) In the input file we have $in(1)=n$, records 2 to $n*n+1$ contain the matrix a, and records $n*n+2$ to $2*n*n+1$ contain the matrix b. The output file is to contain the matrix c stored row-wise on records 1 to $n*n$. In other words, the precondition is

$$in(1)\geqslant 1 \ \& \ \forall X(2\leqslant X\leqslant 2*in(1)*in(1)+1 \rightarrow \mathrm{I}(X))$$

The output file is to contain the matrix c stored row-wise in records 1 to $n*n$.

(a) State the postcondition.

(b) Prove that your program is totally correct.

17. Write an FC+ program implementing the bubble-sort algorithm. The specification is the same as for Example 3, Section 3.5, except that a sentinel record marks the end of the input file, as in Example 2.

(a) State the specification.

(b) Prove that your program is totally correct.

18. The following FC+ program, a version of the sieve of Eratosthenes algorithm, prints all of the primes from 2 to $n = in(1)$. The precondition is $in(1)\geqslant 2$.

(a) State the postcondition.

(b) Prove that your program is totally correct (inserting **assert** commands and renumbering commands as needed).

```
1    start      in(1)≥2
2    input      n
3    i = 2
4    if i>n goto 8
5    sieve(i) = 1
6    i = i+1
7    goto 4
8    i = 2
9    j = i*i
10   if j>n goto 17
11   if sieve(i)=0 goto 15
12   sieve(j) = 0
13   j = j+i
```

```
14      if j≤n goto 12
15      i = i+1
16      goto 9
17      i = 2
18      if i>n goto 23
19      if sieve(i)=0 goto 21
20      print i
21      i = i+1
22      goto 18
23      stop        postcondition
```

19. The following program reads in the number $n = in(1)$ of records in a catalog, then reads the catalog from the records $in(2), \ldots, in(1+in(1))$, and finally performs a binary search to determine if the integer on the last record $in(2+in(1))$ occurs in the catalog. If it does occur, it prints the number of the first record on which it occurs; it prints 0 otherwise. Prove that the program is totally correct. The specification consists of the precondition

$$p \equiv in(1) \geq 0 \;\&\; \forall X(2 \leq X \leq 2+in(1) \rightarrow \mathrm{I}(X))$$

and the postcondition

$$q \equiv (\exists X(2 \leq X \leq 1+in(1) \& in(X)=in(2+in(1))) \rightarrow out(1)=\mu_{in}(2, in(1))) \;\&\; (\forall X(2 \leq X \leq 1+in(1) \rightarrow in(X) \neq in(2+in(1))) \rightarrow \mathrm{out}(1)=0)$$

```
 1      start       in(1)≥0 & ∀X(2≤X≤2+in(1) → I(X))
 2      input       hi
 3      hi = hi+1
 4      i = 2
 5      if i>hi goto 9
 6          input a(i)
 7          i = i+1
 8      goto 5
 9      input key
10      lo = 1
11      found = 0
12      if (low>hi ∨ found=1) goto 22
13          mid = (lo+hi)/2
14          if key≠a(mid) goto 17
15              found = 1
16          goto 21
17              if key≥a(mid) goto 20
18                  hi = mid−1
```

```
19              goto 21
20                   lo = mid+1
21      goto 12
22      if found=0 goto 25
23           print mid
24      goto 26
25           print found
26      stop      q
```

20. The following FC+ program computes Ackermann's Function. Prove that the program is totally correct wrt the specification written on the **start** and **stop** commands.

```
1       start      m≥0&n≥0
2       if m≠0 goto 5
3       a=n+1
4       goto 23
5       v(1)=1
6       p(1)=0
7       v(1)=v(1)+1
8       p(1)=p(1)+1
9       i=1
10      if p(i)≠1 goto16
11      v(i+1)=v(1)
12      p(i+1)=0
13      if i≠m goto 7
14      if p(m+1)=n goto 22
15      goto 7
16      if p(i)≠v(i+1) goto 7
17      v(i+1)=v(1)
18      p(i+1)=p(i+1)+1
19      if i=m goto 14
20      i=i+1
21      goto 10
22      a=v(1)
23      stop       a=ack(m,n)
```

Semantics

21. We wish to extend the syntax and semantics to allow *bounded array assignments.* That is, if a and b are arrays, we wish to allow, for instance, assignments of the form

$$a(j{:}j'') = b(j'{:}j'')$$

meaning roughly the same thing as the j'' assignments

$$a(j) = b(j')$$
$$\vdots \qquad \vdots$$
$$a(j{+}j'') = b(j'{+}j'')$$

(a) Redesign the syntax and operational semantics of this chapter to accommodate useful forms of bounded assignments.
(b) Modify the VCG algorithm of Section 3.3 as required by part (a) to preserve soundness.

22. In Example 1, Section 3.5, the postcondition does not prohibit writing garbage on the output records from 2 on. Should we add $cout{=}2$ as a conjunct to the postcondition? Similarly, in Examples 2 through 5, our specifications are incomplete because we do not restrict what is written at the end of the output file. Do we ever need to state in a specification that only finitely many output records should be printed? Discuss the issue of the *completeness* of a specification regarding the output file. In other words, should we require that specifications be spelled out so that the contents of the input file uniquely determine the values of *cin* and *cout,* as well as the contents of the output file, on termination?

23. This exercise explores the possibility of making **assert** commands executable. Let n be the location of the **stop** command. Outline the design of an **assert** subroutine that transfers control to location $n{+}1$, where a

$n{+}1$ **goto** $n{+}1$

command has been placed, if the inductive assertion on the **assert** command does not hold or its Floydian expression is less than $\langle 0 \rangle$. Execution of the **assert** command causes a '**goto** $s[pc]{+}1$' to be stored in location $n{+}2$, its (encoded) inductive assertion to be stored in integer variable %ia, a 1 to be stored in integer variable %*fep* if it has a Floydian expression (and, if it does not, a 0 to be stored in integer variable %*fep*), its (encoded) Floydian expression (if it has one) to be stored in integer variable %*fe*, and program control to be transferred to location $n{+}3$. Assume that you can rewind the input and output files, read the output file, and save and restore *cin* and *cout*. What plausible restrictions might you place on the form of the inductive assertions to make the problem more tractable?

24. Consider the alternative, more general definition of substitution described in Example 4, Section 3.5. Prove the Coincidence Lemma.

Programming Projects

25. Write an interpreter for the class of FC+ programs. The input for your program consists of an FC+ program and the contents of the input file *in*. Your output should show a trace of program execution.

26. Write a program to (a) find all paths in an FC+ program and (b) find all paths that require a termination condition. The input for your program is an FC+ program. Label paths in the format illustrated in the text.
27. Write a program that, when given an FC+ program as input, generates all verification, well-foundedness, and termination conditions. Be sure to label these conditions and the paths in the format illustrated in the text so that, for example, each verification condition can be readily associated with the path it covers.

CHAPTER 4

The Translation of **while** Programs with Arrays, Input and Output, and a Stack into Flowchart Programs

In this chapter, we augment the class of **while** programs presented in Chapter 1 with arrays, input and output, and a stack. We call this extended class of programs the **while+** *programs.* Our principal aim is to study what is sometimes called the "translational semantics" of **while+** programs.[1] In the

[1] The terminology "translational semantics" came into vogue because, since the beginning of computer science as a discipline, much research has centered around language translators. Some early researchers believed that the best way to understand the meaning of, for instance,

course of our study, we will develop a Hoare Logic of total correctness for **while+** programs. We will then compare the Hoare Axiomatization of **while+** programs with the Floyd method for proving the correctness of FC+ programs.

We extend a familiar translation to a translation of **while+** programs into FC+ programs, noting that key semantic properties are preserved under the translation and its inverse (preimage). To make the translation more interesting, we supplement the **while+** programs with a stack, so that our source language **while+** programs have both a more abstract data type (the stack) and higher-level control structures (the conditional and **while** statements) than our target language FC+ programs. Although a Hoare Axiomatization of total correctness might be derived from the translation, a direct approach appears to yield a simpler axiomatization.

The translation $\mathfrak{T}$ does not preserve the adequacy of Floydian expressions in the following sense: We may have Floydian expressions that are adequate for a Hoare proof of the total correctness of an asserted **while+** program AP, but the translations of these Floydian expressions may not be adequate for a Floyd proof of the total correctness of the FC+ program $\mathfrak{T}[AP]$. In failing to preserve adequacy, the translation reveals a significant manner in which the Floyd and Hoare methods differ. In the Hoare method for **while+** programs, the proof of an asserted program can proceed independently of its context, whereas, in the Floyd method for FC+ programs, context cannot be disregarded.

In Section 4.1, we present the syntax, operational semantics, and total correctness axiomatization for the class of **while+** programs. In Section 4.2, we define the translation mapping **while+** programs into FC+ programs, and, in Section 4.3, we prove the correctness of the translation and the soundness of the total correctness axiomatization. Finally, in Section 4.4, we present a few sample proofs using our axiomatization and compare the Floyd and Hoare methods.

Since Chapter 2, we have been studying total correctness, as opposed to the more limited notion of partial correctness, and we shall continue to do so. *Throughout the remainder of this text, we understand the symbols* $\vdash$ *and* $\models$,

---

while+ programs was either in terms of FC+ programs or the meaning of FC+ programs. However, the "translational semantics" terminology is a bit misleading for three reasons. First, FC+ programs are syntactic objects. Second, the semantics of FC+ programs are at least as complicated as the semantics of **while+** programs. Third, the terminology conflicts with that in mathematics and logic. In particular, the FC+ programs are an unsuitable paradigm for judging the correctness of all possible implementations of the **while+** programs, which might also be realized (indirectly) by other translators mapping the **while+** programs into different low-level virtual machines and (directly) by interpreters.

In logic, one speaks of a theory as being interpreted in another theory (e.g., the theory of strings is interpretable in Peano Arithmetic); so here, by analogy, we will sometimes speak of **while+** programs being interpreted in FC+ programs.

when used in the context of asserted programs, to denote the provability and validity relations in the Hoare logic of total correctness.

4.1. SYNTAX, OPERATIONAL SEMANTICS, AND TOTAL CORRECTNESS AXIOMATIZATION

To accommodate subscripted variables, modifications to the syntax of **while** programs (Chapter 1), resulting in the syntax of **while+** programs, proceeds in much the same manner as the development of the syntax of FC+ programs, described in the preceding chapter. In addition, to handle the stack, we introduce **push** and **pop** statements and variables giving the *depth* of the stack, the top of the stack, and an indication of whether or not the stack is empty (1=empty, 0=nonempty). From a logical point of view, stack is a unary operation symbol and *depth,* top, and empty are 0-ary operation symbols. Further, *stack* and *depth* are introduced first into arithmetic, unaccompanied by axioms, whereas top and empty are introduced subsequently with equational definitions. These logical differences are reflected in the language user's point of view. To the programmer, the variables top and empty are "visible" in the sense that they can be explicitly referenced in programs (although they cannot be assigned a value with assignment or input statements). On the other hand, the variable *depth* and the elements of the *stack* (other than top) are "hidden" and cannot be referenced in programs, although they can be referenced in assertions.

As in the preceding chapter (aside from the alternative syntax described in Example 4, Section 3.5), the set of *subscript variables* is **Svar,** the set of array *subscript expressions* is **Sexp,** the set of *simple variables* is **Simp,** the set of *array variables* is **Array,** the set of *integer variables* is **Ivar,** the set of integer expressions is **Iexp,** and the set of boolean expressions is **Bexp.** We have added the set of (visible) *stack variables,* **Stvar,** consisting of top and empty, and we have added the stack variables to the class of integer expressions. The abstract syntax is as follows:

Svar: $j, \ldots$
Sexp: $se, \ldots$
$\quad se ::= m \mid j \mid \mathrm{succ}(se) \mid \ldots \mid se{+}se' \mid \ldots$
Simp: $x, \ldots$
Array: $a, \ldots$
Ivar: $i, \ldots$
$\quad i ::= x \mid a(se)$
Stvar: $k, \ldots$
$\quad k ::= \mathrm{top} \mid \mathrm{empty}$
Iexp: $e, \ldots$
$\quad e ::= m \mid k \mid j \mid i \mid \mathrm{succ}(e) \mid \ldots \mid e{+}e' \mid \ldots$
Bexp: $b, \ldots$
$\quad b ::= e{=}e' \mid \ldots \mid {\sim}b \mid b \& b' \mid \ldots$

The *input file* (*in*), the *current input record number* (*cin*), the *output file* (*out*), and the *current output record number* (*cout*) are to be understood as in the preceding chapter. Because program execution can alter the *stack*, the elements of the *stack* (the $stack_m$ for each numeral m), the stack variables, and the stack depth are added to the class of assertion variables. Otherwise, the syntax of the *assertion variables* **(Avar)**, the *assertion expressions* **(Aexp)**, and the *assertions* **(Assn)** is as in the preceding chapter. The abstract syntax is as follows:

Avar: $v, \ldots$
$v ::= k \mid depth \mid stack_{se} \mid j \mid i \mid cin \mid cout \mid out(e)$
Aexp: $t, \ldots$
$t ::= m \mid v \mid in(t) \mid \mathrm{succ}(t) \mid \ldots \mid t{+}t' \mid \ldots$
Assn: $p, \ldots$
$p ::= t{=}t' \mid \ldots \mid {\sim}p \mid p\&p' \mid \ldots \mid \forall Xp \mid \exists Xp$

The conventions regarding the form of assertions occurring in the programming and arithmetic parts of our proofs are entirely similar to those in the preceding chapter. Similarly, the syntactic notion of *substitution* is defined as in the preceding chapter with the addition of the clause

$$stack_{qse}[e\backslash stack_{se}] \equiv \mathrm{cond}(\mathrm{eq}(qse,se),e,stack_{qse})$$

The syntax of *statements* **(Stat)** is much as in Chapter 1, except that modifications along the lines of those in the preceding chapter are needed to accommodate arrays and input-output, and additional statements (**push** and **pop**) are required to manipulate the stack. The abstract syntax is as follows:

Stat: $S, \ldots$
$S ::=$ **d** | $j{:=}se$ | $i{:=}\ e$ | **push**(e) | **pop** |
read(j) | **read**(i) | **write**(e) |
$S;S'$ | **if** b **then** S **else** S' | **while** b **do** S

As in Chapter 1, an *annotated statement* is like a statement except that each **while** statement must be preceded by an assertion. Similarly, an *asserted program* is as defined in Chapter 1, *except in the case when* $AP \equiv \{p\}S\{q\}$ *and* S *is the full program. In this case, we understand that the precondition implicitly contains the conjunct* $depth{=}0\ \&\ cin{=}cout{=}1$. Consequently, the precondition is really

$$p\ \&\ depth{=}0\ \&\ cin{=}cout{=}1$$

Recall our requirement for FC+ programs that all **assert** commands used as loop cutpoints contain a Floydian expression E. Since we have added the class of assertion expressions, an n-tuple $E{\equiv}\langle t_1, \ldots, t_n\rangle$ of assertion expressions will serve as a Floydian expression in this chapter. Analogously, as we develop a logic of total correctness for **while+** programs, we impose the following *requirement on each assertion p serving as the intermediate assertion of an annotated* **while** *statement: the assertion p must be a conjunction of the form* $r\&E\geqslant 0$. To eliminate ambiguity, we require that r be bracketed by parentheses when r is a conjunction of the form $r'\&t\geqslant 0$.

We now illustrate the syntax of **while+** programs. Our **while+** program is similar to the FC+ program of Section 3.1, and that FC+ program is almost (but not quite) the image of our **while+** program under the translation to be described in the next section. Recall that the first record in the input file $in(1)$ gives the length of the input file. Our **while+** program reads in the next $in(1)$ records $in(2), \ldots, in(in(1)+1)$ and then writes them out in reverse order (i.e., in the order $in(in(1)+1), \ldots, in(2)$). Instead of using an array for intermediate storage, as in Chapter 3, we now use the stack. The only stack variable occurring in the program is top, the only integer variable is x, and, again as in Chapter 3, the only subscript variables are j and n.

$\{in(1) \geqslant 0 \;\&\; \forall X(2 \leqslant X \leqslant in(1)+1 \rightarrow \mathrm{I}(in(X)))\}$
read(n);
$\{\forall X(1 \leqslant X < j \rightarrow stack_X = in(X+1)) \;\&\; 1 \leqslant j \leqslant n+1 \;\&\; n = in(1) \;\&$
$j = cin-1 = depth+1 \;\&\; cout = 1 \;\&\; n+1-j \geqslant 0\}$
for $j:=1$ **to** n **do**
    begin
    read(x);
    push(x)
    end;
$\{\forall X(1 \leqslant X \leqslant n \rightarrow stack_X = in(X+1)) \;\&$
$\forall X(depth < X \leqslant n \rightarrow in(X+1) = out(n+1-X)) \;\&\; 0 \leqslant depth \leqslant n = in(1) \;\&$
$cout = n+1-depth \;\&\; depth \geqslant 0\}$
while empty $\neq 1$ **do**
    begin
    write(top);
    pop
    end
$\{\forall X(1 \leqslant X \leqslant in(1) \rightarrow in(X+1) = out(in(1)+1-X))\}$

As for the *semantics*, the semantics of assertion expressions is as before, except that now an *unextended state* assigns an integer to *depth* and to each stack element $stack_m$. Handling the stack elements in much the same manner as arrays, we set $\mathfrak{s}[stack_{se}] = \mathfrak{s}[stack_{\mathfrak{s}[se]}]$, and we define a *v-variant* in the case when $v \equiv stack_{se}$ as follows:

The state $\mathfrak{s}'$ is a $stack_{se}$-variant of $\mathfrak{s}$ provided that

(a) For every integer m such that $m \neq \mathfrak{s}[se]$, $\mathfrak{s}'[stack_m] = \mathfrak{s}[stack_m]$
(b) $\mathfrak{s}'[depth] = \mathfrak{s}[depth]$, $\mathfrak{s}'[cin] = \mathfrak{s}[cin]$, and $\mathfrak{s}'[cout] = \mathfrak{s}[cout]$
(c) For every subscript variable j, $\mathfrak{s}'[j] = \mathfrak{s}[j]$

(d) For every simple variable x, $\mathfrak{s}'[x] = \mathfrak{s}[x]$

(e) For every array variable a and for every integer m, $\mathfrak{s}'[a(m)] = \mathfrak{s}[a(m)]$

(f) For every integer m, $\mathfrak{s}'[in(m)] = \mathfrak{s}[in(m)]$

(g) For every integer m, $\mathfrak{s}'[out(m)] = \mathfrak{s}[out(m)]$

To suit the other cases, the definition of a v-variant in Chapter 3 is adapted in the obvious manner.

The *operational semantics* of the dummy, composition, conditional, and **while** statements are the same as in Chapter 1, as are the semantics of assignments restricted to subscript variables. The semantics of assignment statements in general (including assignments to subscripted variables) and the semantics of the **read** and **write** statements are entirely similar to the semantics of the FC+ intermediate commands **input** and **print** given in Chapter 3. For example, we have

$$\mathfrak{s}[\mathbf{write}(e)] = \mathfrak{s}\{\mathfrak{s}[e], \mathfrak{s}[cout]+1 \backslash out(\mathfrak{s}[cout]), cout\}$$

The principal additions to the operational semantics are the clauses for the **push** and **pop** statements. We have

$$\mathfrak{s}[\mathbf{push}(e)] = \mathfrak{s}\{\mathfrak{s}[e], \mathfrak{s}[depth]+1 \backslash stack_{\mathfrak{s}[depth]+1}, depth\}$$

$$\mathfrak{s}[\mathbf{pop}] = \mathfrak{s}\{\mathfrak{s}[depth]-1 \backslash depth\}$$

The semantics of statements is summarized in Figure 4.1.

$$
\begin{aligned}
\mathfrak{s}[\mathbf{d}] &= \mathfrak{s} \\
\mathfrak{s}[j{=}se] &= \mathfrak{s}\{\mathfrak{s}[se] \backslash j\} \\
\mathfrak{s}[x{=}e] &= \mathfrak{s}\{\mathfrak{s}[e] \backslash x\} \\
\mathfrak{s}[a(se){=}e] &= \mathfrak{s}\{\mathfrak{s}[e] \backslash a(\mathfrak{s}[se])\} \\
\mathfrak{s}[\mathbf{push}(e)] &= \mathfrak{s}[\mathfrak{s}[e], \mathfrak{s}[depth]+1 \backslash stack_{\mathfrak{s}[depth]+1}, depth\} \\
\mathfrak{s}[\mathbf{pop}] &= \mathfrak{s}\{\mathfrak{s}[depth]-1 \backslash depth\} \\
\mathfrak{s}[\mathbf{read}\ j] &= \mathfrak{s}\{\mathfrak{s}[in(\mathfrak{s}[cin])], \mathfrak{s}[cin]+1 \backslash j, cin\} \\
\mathfrak{s}[\mathbf{read}\ x] &= \mathfrak{s}\{\mathfrak{s}[in(\mathfrak{s}[cin])], \mathfrak{s}[cin]+1 \backslash x, cin\} \\
\mathfrak{s}[\mathbf{read}\ a(se)] &= \mathfrak{s}\{\mathfrak{s}[in(\mathfrak{s}[cin])], \mathfrak{s}[cin]+1 \backslash a(\mathfrak{s}[se]), cin\} \\
\mathfrak{s}[\mathbf{write}(e)] &= \mathfrak{s}\{\mathfrak{s}[e], \mathfrak{s}[cout]+1 \backslash out(\mathfrak{s}[cout]), cout\} \\
\mathfrak{s}[S';S''] &= \mathfrak{s}[S'][S''] \\
\mathfrak{s}[\mathbf{if}\ b\ \mathbf{then}\ S'\ \mathbf{else}\ S''] &= \mathfrak{s}[S']\ \mathbf{if}\ \mathfrak{s}[b]{=}\mathrm{t} \\
&= \mathfrak{s}[S'']\ \text{otherwise} \\
\mathfrak{s}[\mathbf{while}\ b\ \mathbf{do}\ S'] &= \mathfrak{s}*\ \text{if there is a finite sequence of states} \\
&\quad \langle \mathfrak{s}_0, \mathfrak{s}_1, \ldots, \mathfrak{s}_m \rangle (m \geq 0) \text{ such that } \mathfrak{s}{=}\mathfrak{s}_0,\ \mathfrak{s}*{=}\mathfrak{s}_m, \\
&\quad \mathfrak{s}_m[b]{=}\mathrm{f}, \text{ and, for each } i \text{ such that } 0 \leq i \leq m-1, \\
&\quad \mathfrak{s}_i[b]{=}\mathrm{t} \text{ and } \mathfrak{s}_{i+1}{=}\mathfrak{s}_i[S'].
\end{aligned}
$$

FIGURE 4.1. The operational semantics of **while+** statements.

The addition of the stack and of the input and output files means that we must modify the definition of an initial state along the lines of the definition in Chapter 3. We say that a state $\mathfrak{s}$ for a **while+** program S (having precondition p) is *initial* if $\mathfrak{s}[p] = \mathrm{t}$, $\mathfrak{s}[depth] = 0$, and $\mathfrak{s}[cin] = \mathfrak{s}[cout] = 1$. The definitions of *partial* and *total* correctness are as in Chapter 1. And as we deal with the Hoare Logic of total correctness from now on, we understand $AP \equiv \{p\}S\{q\}$ to be *valid,* written $\models\{p\}S\{q\}$, if S is totally correct wrt the specification $\langle p,q \rangle$.

Similarly, in the Hoare Axiomatization, from this point on we will take '$\vdash$' to be *the provability relation* in the Hoare logic of total correctness. The Dummy and Assignment Axioms, and the Composition, Conditional, and Consequence Rules are to be understood as in Chapter 1. The **While** Rule, however, must be strengthened because we are developing a logic of total correctness. We must demonstrate that a **while** statement terminates (for a given precondition). Let $E = \langle t_1, \ldots t_k \rangle$, $p \equiv r \& E \succcurlyeq \langle 0 \rangle$, $y_1, \ldots, y_k$ ($k \geq 1$) be simple variables foreign to the assertion p and to the statement **while** b **do** S, $Y = \langle y_1, \ldots, y_k \rangle$, and $Y = E \equiv y_1 = t_1 \& \ldots \& y_k = t_k$. Our new version of the ***While Rule*** is now as follows:

$$\frac{\{p \& b \& Y = E\} S \{p \& Y \succ E\}}{\{p\} \textbf{while } b \textbf{ do } S \{p \& {\sim} b\}}$$

Intuitively, E is a Floydian expression, the conjunct $E \succcurlyeq \langle 0 \rangle$ in the assertion p is the well-foundedness condition, and the conjunct $Y \succ E$ in the postcondition of the premise of the **While** Rule is the termination condition. The y_i's are required to be *new* (i.e., foreign to p and **while** b **do** S) for two reasons: first, $\{p \& b\} \cup \{Y = E\}$ must be satisfiable if $p \& b$ is, and second, the body S of the **while** statement must preserve the value of Y, the old value of E (before executing S), to compare against the new value of E (after executing S).

We require axioms for the **read** and **write** statements.

THE READ AXIOMS[2]

$\{p[cin+1 \backslash cin][in(cin) \backslash j]\}$
    read(j)
$\{p\}$

$\{p[cin+1 \backslash cin][in(cin) \backslash i]\}$
    read(i)
$\{p\}$

[2] We have two different read axioms because i and j are in different syntactic classes.

THE WRITE AXIOM

$$\{p[cout{+}1\backslash cout][e\backslash out(cout)]\}$$
$$\textbf{write}(e)$$
$$\{p\}$$

Axioms are also required for the **push** and **pop** statements. They are read-off from the clauses giving the operational semantics of the **push** and **pop** statements. The **Push** Axiom is much like the **Write** Axiom: The stack *depth* is incremented, and the integer expression *e* is put on the top of the stack (at $stack_{depth+1}$).

THE PUSH AXIOM

$$\{p[e\backslash stack_{depth+1}][depth{+}1\backslash depth]\}$$
$$\textbf{push}(e)$$
$$\{p\}$$

THE POP AXIOM

$$\{p[depth{-}1\backslash depth]\}$$
$$\textbf{pop}$$
$$\{p\}$$

To supplement the **Push** and **Pop** Axioms, we must also add axioms for top and empty. The Top and Empty Axioms have the syntactic form of the axioms of arithmetic rather than Hoare axioms, as they are not asserted programs. In fact, the Top and Empty Axioms are equational definitions introducing the symbols 'top' and 'empty' into arithmetic.

THE TOP AXIOM

$$\mathrm{top} = stack_{depth}$$

THE EMPTY AXIOM

$$\mathrm{empty} = \mathrm{eq}(depth,0)$$

The complete Hoare Total Correctness Axiomatization is given in Figure 4.2.

In Section 4.3, we will sketch a soundness proof for the Hoare Axiomatization in the style given in preceding chapters. In the general case, we cannot derive the soundness of the Hoare Axiomatization in a simple manner from the **While+** Interpretation Theorem, which states that the translation of the class of asserted **while+** programs into the class of FC+ programs is correct.

A. Axioms and Rules of Inference for Asserted Programs

1. The Dummy Axiom

$$\{p\}\mathbf{d}\{p\}$$

2. The Assignment Axioms

$$\{p[se\backslash j]\}j := se\{p\}$$

$$\{p[e\backslash i]\}i := e\{p\}$$

3. The Push Axiom

$$\{p[e\backslash stack_{depth+1}][depth+1\backslash depth]\}\ \mathbf{push}(e)\ \{p\}$$

4. The Pop Axiom

$$\{p[depth-1\backslash depth]\}\ \mathbf{pop}\ \{p\}$$

5. The Read Axioms

$$\{p[cin+1\backslash cin][in(cin)\backslash j]\}\ \mathbf{read}(j)\ \{p\}$$

$$\{p[cin+1\backslash cin][in(cin)\backslash i]\}\ \mathbf{read}(i)\ \{p\}$$

6. The Write Axiom

$$\{p[cout+1\backslash cout][e\backslash out(cout)]\}\ \mathbf{write}(e)\ \{p\}$$

7. The Composition Rule

$$\frac{\{p\}S\{q\},\quad \{q\}S'\{r\}}{\{p\}S;S'\{r\}}$$

FIGURE 4.2. The Hoare total correctness axiomatization of **while+** programs.

8. The Conditional Rule

$$\frac{\{p\&b\}S\{q\},\quad \{p\&\sim b\}S'\{q\}}{\{p\}\ \textbf{if}\ b\ \textbf{then}\ S\ \textbf{else}\ S'\{q\}}$$

9. The **While** Rule

$$\frac{\{p\&b\&Y=E\}S\{p\&Y\succ E\}}{\{p\}\textbf{while}\ b\ \textbf{do}\ S\{p\&\sim b\}}$$

where $E=\langle t_1, \ldots, t_k\rangle$

$p\equiv r\&E\succcurlyeq\langle 0\rangle$

$y_1, \ldots, y_k (k\geqslant 1)$ are simple variables foreign to the assertion p and to the statement **while** b **do** S

$Y=\langle y_1, \ldots, y_k\rangle$

$Y=E\equiv y_1=t_1\ \&\ \ldots\ \&\ y_k=t_k$

10. The Consequence Rule

$$\frac{p\rightarrow p',\quad \{p'\}S\{q'\},\quad q'\rightarrow q}{\{p\}S\{q\}}$$

B. Axioms of Arithmetic

1. The Top Axiom

$$\text{top} = stack_{depth}$$

2. The Empty Axiom

$$\text{empty} = \text{eq}(depth,0)$$

FIGURE 4.2. *(Continued)*

4.2. THE TRANSLATION

Introductory texts for inherently unstructured languages such as BASIC, FORTRAN, and assembly language teach structured programming techniques. Typically, the introductory BASIC text uses a device such as structured pseudocode to introduce the class of **while** programs and then describes a translation of algorithms expressed in pseudocode into BASIC. The only significant differences between our **while+** programs and pseudocode are that we use assertions and we have the stack primitives **push, pop,** top, and empty "built-in" (as part of our virtual machine). The only significant differences between our structured FC+ programs and the structured BASIC programs of an introductory text are that we require that a **start** command be placed at the beginning of a full program, that a **stop** command be placed at the end of a full program, that the translation of a **while+** statement begin with an **assert** command, and that the commands be numbered (labeled) sequentially. The following table depicts **Tr**, an informal version of our translation restricted to **while** programs, in the style of an introductory BASIC text:

while statement S	FC commands **Tr**[S]
d	$x = x$
$x := e$	$x = e$
$S;S'$	**Tr**[S] **Tr**[S']
if b **then** S **else** S'	**if** $\sim b$ **goto** m **Tr**[S] **goto** m' m **Tr**[S'] m' . . .
{. . . . .} **while** b **do** S	m **assert** ______, ___ **if** $\sim b$ **goto** m' **Tr**[S] **goto** m m' . . .

Our translation $\mathfrak{T}$ of **while+** programs is a formalized version of the informal translation **Tr**. Except when applied to a **while+** annotated statement, the translation $\mathfrak{T}$ has one argument—the syntactic object in the language of **while+** programs to be translated. When applied to a **while+** annotated statement, the translation $\mathfrak{T}$ has two arguments—the first being the annotated statement and the second giving the location at which the translation is to begin. First, we define the translation of the assertion variables. Let AP be the full asserted program to be translated, dep be a subscript variable foreign to *AP*, and *st* be an array variable foreign to *AP*. We have

$$\begin{aligned}
\mathfrak{T}[depth] &= dep \\
\mathfrak{T}[\text{top}] &= st(dep) \\
\mathfrak{T}[\text{empty}] &= \text{eq}(dep,0) \\
\mathfrak{T}[stack_{se}] &= st(se) \\
\mathfrak{T}[v] &= v \text{ for any assertion variable } v \text{ distinct from} \\
&\qquad depth, \text{ top, empty, and } stack_{se}
\end{aligned}$$

Similarly, for a quantified variable *X*, we set

$$\mathfrak{T}[X] = X$$

The translation $\mathfrak{T}$ of the assertion variables induces the translation of assertion expressions

$$\begin{aligned}
\mathfrak{T}[m] &= m \\
\mathfrak{T}[in(t)] &= in(\mathfrak{T}[t]) \\
\mathfrak{T}[\text{succ}(t)] &= \text{succ}(\mathfrak{T}[t]) \\
&\vdots
\end{aligned}$$

and the translation of assertions

$$\begin{aligned}
\mathfrak{T}[t{=}t'] &= \mathfrak{T}[t]{=}\mathfrak{T}[t'] \\
&\vdots \\
\mathfrak{T}[\sim p] &= \sim\mathfrak{T}[p] \\
&\vdots \\
\mathfrak{T}[\exists X p] &= \exists X \mathfrak{T}[p]
\end{aligned}$$

Before we can define the translation of an annotated statement *A*, we must define the *length* $\mathfrak{l}[A]$ of the translation of *A*. Intuitively, $\mathfrak{l}[A]$ gives the number of FC+ locations required to hold the image of *A* under the translation $\mathfrak{T}$, as can be read off from the definition of $\mathfrak{T}[A,n]$, which follows:

$$\begin{aligned}
\mathfrak{l}[\mathbf{d}] &= 0 \\
\mathfrak{l}[j{:=}se] &= 1 \\
\mathfrak{l}[i{:=}e] &= 1 \\
\mathfrak{l}[\mathbf{push}(e)] &= 2 \\
\mathfrak{l}[\mathbf{pop}] &= 1 \\
\mathfrak{l}[\mathbf{read}(j)] &= 1 \\
\mathfrak{l}[\mathbf{read}(i)] &= 1 \\
\mathfrak{l}[\mathbf{write}(e)] &= 1 \\
\mathfrak{l}[A;A'] &= \mathfrak{l}[A]+\mathfrak{l}[A'] \\
\mathfrak{l}[\mathbf{if}\ b\ \mathbf{then}\ A\ \mathbf{else}\ A'] &= \mathfrak{l}[A]+\mathfrak{l}[A']+2 \\
\mathfrak{l}[\{p\}\mathbf{while}\ b\ \mathbf{do}\ A] &= \mathfrak{l}[A]+3
\end{aligned}$$

Now we can define the translation $\mathfrak{T}[A,n]$ of an annotated statement A[3]

$$
\begin{array}{rll}
\mathfrak{T}[\mathbf{d},n] = & & \circledcirc \\
\mathfrak{T}[j{:=}se,n] = & n & j{=}se \\
\mathfrak{T}[i{:=}e,n] = & n & i{=}e \\
\mathfrak{T}[\mathbf{push}(e),n] = & n & dep{=}dep{+}1 \\
 & n{+}1 & st(dep){=}e \\
\mathfrak{T}[\mathbf{pop},n] = & n & dep{=}dep{-}1 \\
\mathfrak{T}[\mathbf{read}(j),n] = & n & \mathbf{input} \quad j \\
\mathfrak{T}[\mathbf{read}(i),n] = & n & \mathbf{input} \quad i \\
\mathfrak{T}[\mathbf{write}(e),n] = & n & \mathbf{print}\ e \\
\mathfrak{T}[A;A',n] = & & \mathfrak{T}[A,n] \\
 & & \mathfrak{T}[A',n{+}\mathfrak{l}[A]]
\end{array}
$$

$$
\begin{array}{ll}
\multicolumn{2}{l}{\mathfrak{T}[\mathbf{if}\ b\ \mathbf{then}\ A\ \mathbf{else}\ A',n] =} \\
n & \mathbf{if}\ {\sim}\mathfrak{T}[b]\ \mathbf{goto}\ k \\
 & \quad \mathfrak{T}[A,n{+}1] \\
k{-}1 & \mathbf{goto}\ k' \\
 & \quad \mathfrak{T}[A',k] \\
 & \text{where } k{=}n{+}\mathfrak{l}[A]{+}2 \text{ and } k'{=}k{+}\mathfrak{l}[A']
\end{array}
$$

$$
\begin{array}{ll}
\multicolumn{2}{l}{\mathfrak{T}[\{p\&E{\cdot}\succcurlyeq\langle 0\rangle\}\mathbf{while}\ b\ \mathbf{do}\ A,n] =} \\
n & \mathbf{assert} \quad \mathfrak{T}[p\&E{\cdot}\succcurlyeq\langle 0\rangle],\ \mathfrak{T}[E] \\
n{+}1 & \mathbf{if}\ {\sim}\mathfrak{T}[b]\ \mathbf{goto}\ k \\
 & \quad \mathfrak{T}[A,n{+}2] \\
k{-}1 & \mathbf{goto}\ n \\
 & \quad \text{where } k{=}n{+}\mathfrak{l}[A]{+}3
\end{array}
$$

Note that each FC+ command in the target program is assigned a label.

In the case of asserted programs, we need only define the translation for a full asserted program $AP \equiv \{p\}S\{q\}$. We have

$$
\begin{array}{lll}
\multicolumn{3}{l}{\mathfrak{T}[\{p\}A\{q\}] =} \\
1 & \mathbf{start} & \mathfrak{T}[p] \\
2 & dep = 0 & \\
 & \mathfrak{T}[A,3] & \\
k & \mathbf{stop} & \mathfrak{T}[q] \\
 & \text{where } k{=}3{+}\mathfrak{l}[A] &
\end{array}
$$

Note that, in the translation of the full asserted program AP, we ignore the conjuncts $depth = 0$ & $cin = cout = 1$ implicit in the precondition.

[3] In Section 4.4, Example 2, we will show that the translation $\mathfrak{T}$ of $\{p\&E{\cdot}\succcurlyeq\langle 0\rangle\}$**while** b **do** A does not preserve the adequacy of the Floydian expression E. The **While+** Interpretation Theorem (Section 4.3) establishes that $\mathfrak{T}$ *does* preserve the adequacy of loop invariants as needed in partial correctness proofs.

The translation is summarized in Figure 4.3. To illustrate the translation, we display the FC+ program that is the image under the translation $\mathfrak{T}$ of the **while+** program presented Section 4.1.

```
1    start    in(1)≥0 & ∀X(2≤X≤in(1)+1 → I(in(X)))
2    dep = 0
3    input n
4    j = 1
5    assert    ∀X(1≤X<j → st(X)=in(X+1)) & 1≤j≤n+1 &
          n=in(1) & j=cin−1=dep+1 & cout=1 & n+1−j≥0, n+1−j
6    if j>n goto 12
7         input x
8         dep = dep+1
9         st(dep) = x
10        j = j+1
11   goto 5
12   assert    ∀X(1≤X≤n → st(X)=in(X+1)) &
     ∀X(dep<X≤n → in(X+1)=out(n+1−X)) & 0≤dep≤n=in(1) &
     cout=n+1−dep & dep≥0, dep
13   if eq(dep,0)=1 goto 17
14        print st(dep)
15        dep = dep−1
16   goto 12
17   stop     ∀X(1≤X≤in(1) → in(X+1)=out(in(1)+1−X))
```

4.3. CORRECTNESS OF THE TRANSLATION

In this section, we show that the translation $\mathfrak{T}$ is correct in the sense that, for any full asserted program $AP \equiv \{p\}A\{q\}$, the annotated **while+** program A is totally correct wrt the specification $\langle p,q\rangle$ iff its translation, the FC+ program $\mathfrak{T}[A]$, is totally correct wrt the specification $\langle \mathfrak{T}[p],\mathfrak{T}[q]\rangle$. Many of the proofs either use the Coincidence Lemma (with arrays and input/output) of Chapter 3 or follow the lines of its proof. Some of the proofs are rather long, and so we will only sketch parts of them. The reader might find it useful to fill in details as an exercise.

Before presenting the major results of this section, we need two minor lemmas. The first is a restatement of a result presented in Chapter 1.

SETTING LEMMA (WITH ARRAYS, INPUT/OUTPUT, AND STACK): For any states $\mathfrak{s}$ and $\mathfrak{s}'$, any statement S such that $\mathfrak{s}' = \mathfrak{s}[S]$, and any simple integer variable x, if no assignment to x occurs in S, then $\mathfrak{s}'[x] = \mathfrak{s}[x]$.

Proof: As in Chapter 1. □

A. The Translation of Assertion Variables

Let *AP* be the full asserted program to be translated, *dep* be a subscript variable foreign to *AP*, and *st* be an array variable foreign to *AP*.

$$\mathfrak{T}[depth] = dep$$
$$\mathfrak{T}[\mathrm{top}] = st(dep)$$
$$\mathfrak{T}[\mathrm{empty}] = \mathrm{eq}(dep,0)$$
$$\mathfrak{T}[stack_{se}] = st(se)$$
$$\mathfrak{T}[v] = v \text{ for any assertion variable } v \text{ distinct from } depth, \text{ top, empty, and } stack_{se}$$

B. The Translation of Quantified Variables

$$\mathfrak{T}[X] = X$$

C. The Translation of Assertion Expressions

$$\mathfrak{T}[m] = m$$
$$\mathfrak{T}[in(t)] = in(\mathfrak{T}[t])$$
$$\mathfrak{T}[\mathrm{succ}(t)] = \mathrm{succ}(\mathfrak{T}[t])$$
$$\vdots$$
$$\mathfrak{T}[t+t'] = \mathfrak{T}[t] + \mathfrak{T}[t']$$
$$\vdots$$

D. The Translation of Assertions

$$\mathfrak{T}[t=t'] = \mathfrak{T}[t]=\mathfrak{T}[t']$$
$$\vdots$$
$$\mathfrak{T}[\sim p] = \sim\mathfrak{T}[p]$$
$$\mathfrak{T}[p\&p'] = \mathfrak{T}[p]\&\mathfrak{T}[p']$$
$$\vdots$$
$$\mathfrak{T}[\forall Xp] = \forall X\mathfrak{T}[p]$$
$$\mathfrak{T}[\exists Xp] = \exists X\mathfrak{T}[p]$$

E. The Lengths of The Translations of Annotated Statements

$$\mathfrak{l}[\mathbf{d}] = 0$$
$$\mathfrak{l}[j{:=}se] = 1$$
$$\mathfrak{l}[i{:=}e] = 1$$
$$\mathfrak{l}[\mathbf{push}(e)] = 2$$
$$\mathfrak{l}[\mathbf{pop}] = 1$$

FIGURE 4.3. The translation $\mathfrak{T}$ of **while+** programs into FC+ programs.

$$\begin{aligned}
\mathfrak{l}[\mathbf{read}(j)] &= 1\\
\mathfrak{l}[\mathbf{read}(i)] &= 1\\
\mathfrak{l}[\mathbf{write}(e)] &= 1\\
\mathfrak{l}[A;A'] &= \mathfrak{l}[A]+\mathfrak{l}[A']\\
\mathfrak{l}[\mathbf{if}\ b\ \mathbf{then}\ A\ \mathbf{else}\ A'] &= \mathfrak{l}[A]+\mathfrak{l}[A']+2\\
\mathfrak{l}[\{p\}\mathbf{while}\ b\ \mathbf{do}\ A] &= \mathfrak{l}[A]+3
\end{aligned}$$

F. The Translation of Annotated Statements

$$\begin{array}{rll}
\mathfrak{T}[\mathbf{d},n] = & & \circledcirc\\
\mathfrak{T}[j{:=}se,n] = & n & j{=}se\\
\mathfrak{T}[i{:=}e,n] = & n & i{=}e\\
\mathfrak{T}[\mathbf{push}(e),n] = & n & dep{=}dep{+}1\\
 & n{+}1 & st(dep){=}e\\
\mathfrak{T}[\mathbf{pop},n] = & n & dep{=}dep{-}1\\
\mathfrak{T}[\mathbf{read}(j),n] = & n & \mathbf{input}\ j\\
\mathfrak{T}[\mathbf{read}(i),n] = & n & \mathbf{input}\ i\\
\mathfrak{T}[\mathbf{write}(e),n] = & n & \mathbf{print}\ e\\
\mathfrak{T}[A;A',n] = & & \mathfrak{T}[A,n]\\
 & & \mathfrak{T}[A',n{+}\mathfrak{l}[A]]\\
\mathfrak{T}[\mathbf{if}\ b\ \mathbf{then}\ A\ \mathbf{else}\ A',n] = & & \\
 & n & \mathbf{if}\ {\sim}\mathfrak{T}[b]\ \mathbf{goto}\ k\\
 & & \quad\mathfrak{T}[A,n{+}1]\\
 & k{-}1 & \mathbf{goto}\ k'\\
 & & \quad\mathfrak{T}[A',k]\\
 & & \text{where } k = n+\mathfrak{l}[A]+2 \text{ and } k' = k+\mathfrak{l}[A']\\
\mathfrak{T}[\{p\&E \succcurlyeq \langle 0\rangle\}\mathbf{while}\ b\ \mathbf{do}\ A,n] = & & \\
 & n & \mathbf{assert}\ \mathfrak{T}[p\&E \succcurlyeq \langle 0\rangle],\mathfrak{T}[E]\\
 & n{+}1 & \mathbf{if}\ {\sim}\mathfrak{T}[b]\ \mathbf{goto}\ k\\
 & & \quad\mathfrak{T}[A,n{+}2]\\
 & k{-}1 & \mathbf{goto}\ n\\
 & & \text{where } k = n+\mathfrak{l}[A]+3
\end{array}$$

G. The Translation of Full Asserted Programs

$$\begin{array}{rll}
\mathfrak{T}[\{p\}A\{q\}] = & 1 & \mathbf{start}\ \mathfrak{T}[p]\\
 & 2 & dep = 0\\
 & & \mathfrak{T}[A,3]\\
 & k & \mathbf{stop}\ \mathfrak{T}[q]\\
 & & \text{where } k = 3+\mathfrak{l}[A]
\end{array}$$

Note: In the translation of the full asserted program *AP*, we ignore the conjuncts $depth = 0$ & $cin = cout = 1$ implicit in the precondition.

FIGURE 4.3. *(Continued)*

VARIANT PRESERVATION LEMMA: Let $y_i(1 \leq i \leq n)$ be a simple integer variable foreign to S, and $\mathfrak{s}'$ be a y_1- . . . -y_n-variant of $\mathfrak{s}$. Then $\mathfrak{s}'[S]$ is a y_1- . . . -y_n-variant of $\mathfrak{s}[S]$,

Proof: By induction on the complexity of S. □

To distinguish the states of FC+ programs from the states of **while**+ programs in this section, we will use the small letters $\mathfrak{c}, \mathfrak{c}'$, . . . for FC+ states and continue to use $\mathfrak{s}, \mathfrak{s}'$, . . . for **while**+ states. We say that an FC+ state $\mathfrak{c}$ *realizes* a **while**+ state $\mathfrak{s}$ if $\mathfrak{c}[\mathfrak{T}[v]] = \mathfrak{s}[v]$ for every **while**+ assertion variable v. Because $\mathfrak{T}[v] \neq pc$ for any **while**+ assertion variable v, each **while**+ state is realized by infinitely many FC+ states.

REALIZATION LEMMA: For any **while**+ state $\mathfrak{s}$ and any FC+ state $\mathfrak{c}$ such that $\mathfrak{c}$ realizes $\mathfrak{s}$

(a) $\mathfrak{c}[\mathfrak{T}[t]] = \mathfrak{s}[t]$ for every **while**+ assertion expression t, and
(b) $\mathfrak{c}[\mathfrak{T}[p]] = \mathfrak{s}[p]$ for every **while**+ assertion p.

Proof: The proofs are much like the proof of the Coincidence Lemma in Chapter 0, proceeding by induction on the complexity of t (p), except that the proof of the basis in part (a) follows immediately from the fact that the FC+ state $\mathfrak{c}$ realizes the **while**+ state $\mathfrak{s}$. □

Let $AP \equiv \{p\}A\{q\}$ be full, and S be the statement of A. The following lemma expresses the fact that the diagram

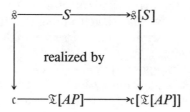

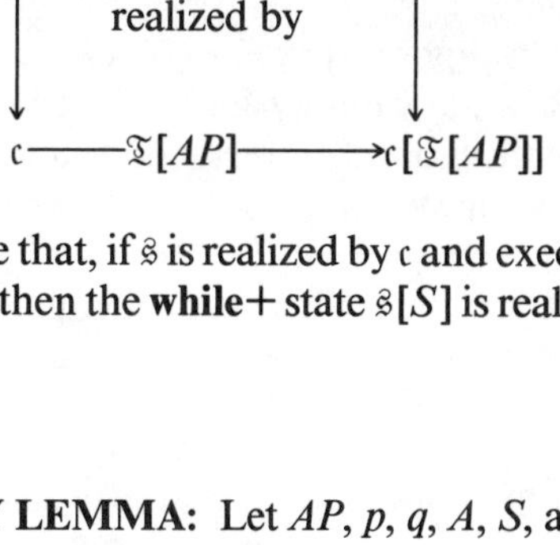

commutes in the sense that, if $\mathfrak{s}$ is realized by $\mathfrak{c}$ and execution of S ($\mathfrak{T}[AP]$) is initiated in state $\mathfrak{s}$ ($\mathfrak{c}$), then the **while**+ state $\mathfrak{s}[S]$ is realized by the FC+ state $\mathfrak{c}[\mathfrak{T}[AP]]$.

COMMUTATIVITY LEMMA: Let AP, p, q, A, S, and n be as previously described, $\mathfrak{c}$ be an FC+ state such that $\mathfrak{c}[pc]=1$, and $\mathfrak{s}$ be a **while**+ state such that (1) the precondition p (and all conjuncts implicit in p) are true in $\mathfrak{s}$, and (2) $\mathfrak{c}\{0\backslash dep\}$ realizes $\mathfrak{s}$. Then $\mathfrak{c}[\mathfrak{T}[AP]]$ realizes $\mathfrak{s}[S]$.

Proof: Because $\mathfrak{s}[p] = \mathrm{t}$, and p contains the implicit conjunct $depth{=}0$, $\mathfrak{s}[depth] = 0 = \mathfrak{c}[\textbf{start} \; . \; . \; .][dep{=}0][dep]$. So, by the Setting Lemma, $\mathfrak{c}[\mathfrak{T}[AP]]$ realizes $\mathfrak{s}[S]$ iff $\mathfrak{c}\{0\backslash dep\}[\mathfrak{T}[A,3]]$ realizes $\mathfrak{s}[S]$. Proof that $\mathfrak{c}\{0\backslash dep\}[\mathfrak{T}[A,3]]$ realizes $\mathfrak{s}[S]$ proceeds by induction on the complexity of the annotated statement A. □

The major results of this section are given in the two theorems that follow. The first, the **While+** Interpretation Theorem, states that the translation $\mathfrak{T}$ is correct in the sense that a **while+** program is correct iff its translation is correct. The second, the **While+** Total Correctness Soundness Theorem, is, in the Hoare Logic of total correctness, the counterpart of the **While** Partial Correctness Soundness Theorem of Chapter 1. The proof of this second theorem must be direct, as we cannot appeal to the **While+** Interpretation Theorem because the adequacy of Floydian expressions is not preserved under the translation $\mathfrak{T}$. We will illustrate this fact in Example 2 of the next section.

WHILE+ INTERPRETATION THEOREM: $\models\{p\}A\{q\}$ iff the FC+ program $\mathfrak{T}[\{p\}A\{q\}]$ is totally correct wrt the specification $\langle \mathfrak{T}[p], \mathfrak{T}[q] \rangle$.

Proof: Immediate from the Realization and Commutativity Lemmas. □

WHILE+ TOTAL CORRECTNESS SOUNDNESS THEOREM: If $\vdash AP$, then $\models AP$.

Proof: The proof is long and tedious, and so we will not give a detailed proof. The top and empty axioms are valid because they are equational definitions, and so are fixtures of our virtual machine. Proof of the validity of the **Push, Pop, Read,** and **Write** Axioms proceeds much as the proof of the Assignment Axiom in Chapter 1. So, we shall sketch a proof that the (total correctness) **While** Rule is validity-preserving in the sense that, if the antecedent is valid, then so is the consequent.

Let $p \equiv r \& E \not> \langle 0 \rangle$. Suppose $\models\{r \& E \not> \langle 0 \rangle \& b \& Y{=}E\}S\{p \& Y > E\}$. We wish to show that $\models\{p\}$**while** b **do** $S\{p \& {\sim} b\}$. By essentially the same argument as in the proof of the (partial correctness) **While** Validity-Preservation Lemma in Chapter 1, we have $\models\{r \& E \not> \langle 0 \rangle\}$**while** b **do** $S\{p \& {\sim} b\}$ if **while** b **do** S terminates.

Now we apply the Coincidence Lemma and argue much as in the Floyd Method Soundness Theorem. Let $\mathfrak{s}$ be any state such that $\mathfrak{s}[p \& b] = \mathrm{t}$ and $\mathfrak{s}+$ be a y_1- . . . -y_n-variant of $\mathfrak{s}$ such that $\mathfrak{s}+[y_i] = \mathfrak{s}[e_i]$ for each i from 1 to n. By the definition of $\mathfrak{s}+$, $\mathfrak{s}+[Y{=}E] = \mathrm{t}$, and, by the Coincidence Lemma, part (b), $\mathfrak{s}+[p \& b] = \mathrm{t}$. If we are in state $\mathfrak{s}'$ at the beginning of the body S of the **while** loop, then we are in state $\mathfrak{s}+' = \mathfrak{s}+[S]$ after executing S. Because the variables in Y are new, we have $\mathfrak{s}+[Y] = \mathfrak{s}+'[Y]$ by the Setting Lemma, and so $\mathfrak{s}+[E] > \mathfrak{s}+'[E]$ because $\mathfrak{s}+[Y] = \mathfrak{s}+[E]$ and $\mathfrak{s}+'[Y] > \mathfrak{s}+'[E]$.

Hence, $\mathfrak{s}[E] > \mathfrak{s}[S][E]$ by the Variant Preservation and Coincidence Lemmas. In any state $\mathfrak{s}$ in which we may be in at the beginning of S, we have $\mathfrak{s}[E] \succcurlyeq \langle 0 \rangle$ preserved by S (a conjunct in the precondition and postcondition of the antecedent of the **While** Rule). Consequently, the set of n-tuples of integers $\mathfrak{s}[E]$ is well-founded. Hence, because each execution of S decreases the value of $\mathfrak{s}[E]$, S can be executed only finitely many times. Hence, the **while** statement must terminate.

The proof continues as in the proof of the **While** Partial Correctness Soundness Theorem in Chapter 1. □

4.4. COMPARISON OF THE HOARE AXIOMATIZATION AND THE FLOYD METHOD

Our main objective in this section is to compare the relative merits of the Floyd and Hoare methods. To examine this issue, we will study two examples showing how proofs typically proceed using the Hoare Total Correctness Axiomatization. The second example reveals the significant manner in which the Floyd and Hoare methods differ. The proofs correspond to proofs of FC and FC+ programs using the Floyd method discussed in the two preceding chapters, and the reader is asked to compare the Hoare proofs with the Floyd proofs.

EXAMPLE 1

We illustrate part of the proof of the asserted **while+** program presented in Section 4.1.[4] Recall that this program writes the input in reverse order. There are no conceptual difficulties in the proof, and so we will prove only the initial fragment, illustrating the role of the implicit conjuncts $depth = 0$ & $cin{=}cout{=}1$ in the precondition of the full asserted program, and the final fragment consisting of the **while** loop in which the elements of the stack are popped and written out.

Regarding the initial fragment, an application of the assignment and Read Axioms together with the Composition Rule yields

(1) $\{\forall X(1 \leq X < 1 \rightarrow stack_X = in(X+1))$ & $1 \leq 1 \leq in(cin)+1$ & $in(cin) = in(1)$ & $1 = cin+1-1 = depth+1$ & $cout = 1$ & $in(cin)+1-1 \geq 0\}$
read(n);
$j{:=}1$
$\{\forall X(1 \leq X < j \rightarrow stack_X = in(X+1))$ & $1 \leq j \leq n+1$ & $n = in(1)$ & $j = cin-1 = depth+1$ & $cout = 1$ & $n+1-j \geq 0\}$

[4] Review the example in Section 3.3. Specifically, examine the verification condition (VC_d), the termination condition (TC_d), and the well-foundedness condition (WC_{10}).

Due to the fact that

$$\vdash in(1) \geqslant 0 \ \&\ \forall X(2 \leqslant X \leqslant in(1)+1 \rightarrow \mathrm{I}(in(X)))\ \&\ depth=0\ \&\ cin=cout=1 \\ \rightarrow \forall X(1 \leqslant X < 1 \rightarrow stack_X = in(X+1))\ \&\ 1 \leqslant 1 \leqslant in(cin)+1\ \& \\ in(cin)=in(1)\ \&\ 1=cin+1-1=depth+1\ \&\ cout=1\ \& \\ in(cin)+1-1 \geqslant 0$$

we can apply the Consequence Rule to (1) to obtain:

(2) $\{in(1) \geqslant 0\ \&\ \forall X(2 \leqslant X \leqslant in(1)+1 \rightarrow \mathrm{I}(in(X)))\ \&\ depth=0\ \&\ cin=cout=1\}$
read(n);
$j:=1$
$\{\forall X(1 \leqslant X < j \rightarrow stack_X = in(X+1))\ \&\ 1 \leqslant j \leqslant n+1\ \&\ n=in(1)\ \&\ j=cin-1=depth+1\ \&\ cout=1\ \&\ n+1-j \geqslant 0\}$

We have written out the implicit conjuncts in the precondition of (2), although we do not when writing out the precondition of the full program. Regarding the final fragment, we wish to show the following:

(3) $\{\forall X(1 \leqslant X \leqslant n \rightarrow stack_X = in(X+1))\ \&\ \forall X(depth < X \leqslant n \rightarrow in(X+1)=out(n+1-X))\ \&\ 0 \leqslant depth \leqslant in(1)\ \&\ cout=n+1-depth\ \&\ depth \geqslant 0\}$

```
while empty≠1 do
    begin
    write(top);
    pop
    end
```

$\{\forall X(1 \leqslant X \leqslant in(1) \rightarrow in(X+1)=out(in(1)+1-X))\}$

To do so, we first invoke the **Pop** Axiom to obtain

(4) $\{\forall X(1 \leqslant X \leqslant n \rightarrow stack_X = in(X+1))\ \&\ \forall X(depth-1 < X \leqslant n \rightarrow in(X+1)=out(n+1-X))\ \&\ 0 \leqslant depth-1 \leqslant in(1)\ \&\ cout=n+1-(depth-1)\ \&\ depth-1 \geqslant 0\ \&\ y > depth-1\}$
pop
$\{\forall X(1 \leqslant X \leqslant n \rightarrow stack_X = in(X+1))\ \&\ \forall X(depth < X \leqslant n \rightarrow in(X+1)=out(n+1-X))\ \&\ 0 \leqslant depth \leqslant in(1)\ \&\ cout=n+1-depth\ \&\ depth \geqslant 0\ \&\ y > depth\}$

Then, applying the **Write** Axiom and the Composition Rule, we obtain

(5) $\{\forall X(1\leq X\leq n \rightarrow stack_X=in(X+1))\ \&$
$\forall X(depth-1<X\leq n \rightarrow$
$in(X+1)=cond(eq(n+1-X,cout),top,$
$out(n+1-X)))\ \&$
$0\leq depth-1\leq in(1)\ \&\ cout+1=n+1-(depth-1)\ \&\ depth-1\geq 0\ \&$
$y>depth-1\}$

write(top);

pop

$\{\forall X(1\leq X\leq n \rightarrow stack_X=in(X+1))\ \&$
$\forall X(depth<X\leq n \rightarrow in(X+1)=out(n+1-X))\ \&\ 0\leq depth\leq in(1)\ \&$
$cout=n+1-depth\ \&\ depth\geq 0\ \&\ y>depth\}$

Therefore, because (using the Top and Empty Axioms) we can show

$\vdash \forall X(1\leq X\leq n \rightarrow stack_X=in(X+1))\ \&$
$\forall X(depth<X\leq n \rightarrow in(X+1)=out(n+1-X))\ \&\ 0\leq depth\leq in(1)\ \&$
$cout=n+1-depth\ \&\ depth\geq 0\ \&\ empty\neq 1\ \&\ y=depth$
$\rightarrow$
$\forall X(1\leq X\leq n \rightarrow stack_X=in(X+1))\ \&$
$\forall X(depth-1<X\leq n \rightarrow$
$in(X+1)=cond(eq(n+1-X,cout),top,$
$out(n+1-X)))\ \&$
$0\leq depth-1\leq in(1)\ \&\ cout+1=n+1-(depth-1)\ \&$
$depth-1\geq 0\ \&\ y>depth-1,$

we have the following:

(6) $\{\forall X(1\leq X\leq n \rightarrow stack_X=in(X+1))\ \&$
$\forall X(depth<X\leq n \rightarrow in(X+1)=out(n+1-X))\ \&\ 0\leq depth\leq in(1)\ \&$
$cout=n+1-depth\ \&\ depth\geq 0\ \&\ empty\neq 1\ \&\ y=depth\}$

write(top);

pop

$\{\forall X(1\leq X\leq n \rightarrow stack_X=in(X+1))\ \&$
$\forall X(depth<X\leq n \rightarrow in(X+1)=out(n+1-X))\ \&\ 0\leq depth\leq in(1)\ \&$
$cout=n+1-depth\ \&\ depth\geq 0\ \&\ y>depth\}$

by the Consequence Rule applied to (5). Therefore, (3) by the **While** Rule applied to (6).

EXAMPLE 2

In this example we tackle the gcd algorithm, and seek to show its total correctness.[5] Since we already proved it to be partially correct in Example 5

[5] Compare Example 5 in Section 2.5, Example 5 in Section 1.5., and Exercise 15 in Chapter 2.

of Section 1.5, here it will be sufficient to show that the algorithm terminates. So, we take true to be the postcondition (instead of $out(1) = gcd(in(1), in(2))$), and we introduce the predicate $P(X, Y)$ (read "X and Y are positive integers") with the explicit definition

$$\textbf{(D.P)} \qquad P(X,Y) \leftrightarrow 1 \leqslant X \leqslant in(1) \;\&\; 1 \leqslant Y \leqslant in(2) \;\&\; X+Y \geqslant 0$$

The Floydian expression for all three **while** loops is to be $x+y$. The idea is that either x will decrease or y will, so $x+y$ is sure to decrease. We have the asserted **while+** program

```
{1≤in(1) & 1≤in(2)}
read(x);
read(y);
{P(x,y)}
while x≠y do
   begin
     {P(x,y)}
     while x>y do x:=x−y;
     {P(x,y)}
     while y>x do y:=y−x
   end;
write(x)
{true}
```

It is sufficient to demonstrate

```
(1) {P(x,y)}
    while x≠y do
       begin
         {P(x,y)}
         while x>y do x:=x−y;
         {P(x,y)}
         while y>x do y:=y−x
       end
     {P(x,y) & ~x≠y}
```

We now sketch the proof of (1). By the Assignment Axiom, we have

(2) $\{P(x-y,y) \;\&\; (x-y>y \rightarrow t>2*y) \;\&\; (x-y=y \rightarrow t>x-y+y) \;\&$
$(y>x-y \rightarrow t>2*(x-y)) \;\&\; t'>x-y+y\}$
$x{:=}x-y$
$\{P(x,y) \;\&\; (x>y \rightarrow t>2*y) \;\&\; (x=y \rightarrow t>x+y) \;\&\; (y>x \rightarrow t>2*x \;\&$
$t'>x+y\}$

Because $\vdash P(x,y) \,\&\, x \neq y \,\&\, t=x+y \,\&\, x>y \,\&\, t'=x+y \rightarrow$
$P(x-y,y) \,\&\, (x-y>y \rightarrow t>2*y) \,\&$
$(x-y=y \rightarrow t>x-y+y) \,\&\, (y>x-y \rightarrow t>2*(x-y)) \,\&$
$t'>x-y+y$

we have

(3) $\{P(x,y) \,\&\, x \neq y \,\&\, t=x+y\}$
while $x>y$ **do** $x:=x-y$
$\{P(x,y) \,\&\, (x>y \rightarrow t>2*y) \,\&\, (x=y \rightarrow t>x+y) \,\&\, (y>x \rightarrow t>2*x) \,\&$
$\sim x>y\}$

by the Consequence and **While** Rules applied to (2). Applying the Consequence Rule again, we have from (3)

(4) $\{P(x,y) \,\&\, x \neq y \,\&\, t=x+y\}$
while $x>y$ **do** $x:=x-y$
$\{P(x,y) \,\&\, (x \geq y \rightarrow t>x+y) \,\&\, (y>x \rightarrow t>2*x)\}$

because

$\vdash P(x,y) \,\&\, (x>y \rightarrow t>2*y) \,\&\, (x=y \rightarrow t>x+y) \,\&\, (y>x \rightarrow t>2*x) \,\&$
$\sim x>y \rightarrow P(x,y) \,\&\, (x \geq y \rightarrow t>x+y) \,\&\, (y>x \rightarrow t>2*x)$

Similarly, we have from the Assignment Axiom

(5) $\{P(x,y-x) \,\&\, (x \geq y-x \rightarrow t>x+y-x) \,\&\, (y-x>x \rightarrow t>2*x) \,\&$
$t''>x+y-x\}$
$y:=y-x$
$\{P(x,y) \,\&\, (x \geq y \rightarrow t>x+y) \,\&\, (y>x \rightarrow t>2*x) \,\&\, t''>x+y\}$

Due to the fact that

$\vdash P(x,y) \,\&\, (x \geq y \rightarrow t>x+y) \,\&\, (y>x \rightarrow t>2*x) \,\&\, y>x \,\&$
$t''=x+y \rightarrow$
$P(x,y-x) \,\&\, (x \geq y-x \rightarrow t>x+y-x) \,\&\, (y-x>x \rightarrow t>2*x) \,\&$
$t''>x+y-x$

we have

(6) $\{P(x,y) \,\&\, (x \geq y \rightarrow t>x+y) \,\&\, (y>x \rightarrow t>2*x)\}$
while $y>x$ **do** $y:=y-x$
$\{P(x,y) \,\&\, (x \geq y \rightarrow t>x+y) \,\&\, (y>x \rightarrow t>2*x) \,\&\, \sim y>x\}$

by the Consequence and **While** Rules applied to (5). Applying the Consequence Rule again, we have

(7) $\{P(x,y) \,\&\, (x \geq y \rightarrow t>x+y) \,\&\, (y>x \rightarrow t>2*x)\}$
while $y>x$ **do** $y:=y-x$
$\{P(x,y) \,\&\, t>x+y\}$

because

$\vdash$P(x,y) & ($x \geqslant y \rightarrow t > x+y$) & ($y > x \rightarrow t > 2*x$) & $\sim y > x \rightarrow$
P(x,y) & $t > x+y$

Applying the Composition Rule to (4) and (7), we have, finally,

(8) {P(x,y) & $x \neq y$ & $t = x+y$}
while $x > y$ **do** $x := x - y$;
while $y > x$ **do** $y := y - x$
{P(x,y) & $t > x+y$}
Hence, (1) by the **While** Rule applied to (8).

The reader might find it useful to compare the translation of the gcd algorithm with the FC program in Example 5, Section 2.5, in which a cutpoint was inserted at the beginning of each loop. The Floydian expressions one obtains from the translation are not adequate for proving termination using the Floyd method, as the reader can readily verify. The translation $\mathfrak{T}$ does not preserve the adequacy of Floydian expressions.

The Hoare proof just given is no more complex than the Floyd proof required for Exercise 15, Chapter 2. In fact, the Hoare proof is considerably simpler than the Floyd proof one faces if, in the Floyd method, one can only insert cutpoints at the beginning of (the translation of) **while** loops.[6] The Floyd method was designed for proving the correctness of arbitrary flowchart programs in which loops need not be nested, and so one must show that the Floydian expression in a loop becomes smaller as execution proceeds from one loop cutpoint to the next. In the Hoare method, however, when one is dealing with the nested loops of **while+** programs, one need show only that the Floydian expression in a loop becomes smaller after execution has traversed the entire loop body. The Hoare proof of a complex **while+** program proceeds by proving its immediate constituents. That is, if there are nested loops, one tackles the proof of the innermost loops first, working outwards to the outermost loop. The Floyd method requires ingenuity in placing cutpoints, whereas the Hoare method does not. There appears to be no simple mechanical translation of Hoare proofs into Floyd proofs (or Floyd proofs into Hoare proofs) that "preserves simplicity".

EXERCISES

Proving Programs Correct

1. (a) Write a **while+** program to compute x/y using only the operation symbols 'abs', 'pred', and 'succ'. The precondition is $p \equiv$ I(x) & I(y), and the postcondition is $r \equiv z = x/y$.

[6] See the FC program in Example 5, Section 2.5.

(b) Using the Hoare (Total Correctness) Axiomatization, prove that your asserted program is totally correct.

2. (a) Write a **while+** program to determine if an integer x is prime. The precondition is $p \equiv \mathrm{I}(x)$, and the postcondition is $r \equiv$

$$(\mathrm{prime}(x) \rightarrow xprime{=}1) \ \&\ ({\sim}\mathrm{prime}(x) \rightarrow xprime{=}0)$$

(b) Using the Hoare Axiomatization, prove that your asserted program is totally correct.

3. (a) Write a **while+** program to find the n-th prime number. Let nthprime(X) = X-th prime number. The precondition is $p \equiv n \geqslant 1$ and the postcondition is $r \equiv nthprimen = \mathrm{nthprime}(n)$.

(b) Using the Hoare Axiomatization, prove that your asserted program is totally correct.

4. (a) Write a **while+** program to determine if an integer x is a perfect number. Let perfect(X) hold provided X is a perfect number. The precondition is $p \equiv x \geqslant 1$, and the postcondition is $r \equiv$

$$(\mathrm{perfect}(x) \rightarrow xperfect{=}1) \ \&\ ({\sim}\mathrm{perfect}(x) \rightarrow xperfect{=}0)$$

(b) Using the Hoare Axiomatization, prove that your asserted program is totally correct.

5. Consider the **while** program of Chapter 1, Exercise 11, which computes $g = \mathrm{gcd}(x,y)$. Using the Hoare Axiomatization, prove that this program terminates. The precondition is $x \geqslant 1 \ \&\ y \geqslant 1$, and the postcondition is true.

6. Consider the **while** program of Chapter 1, Exercise 12, which computes $g = \mathrm{gcd}(x,y)$. Using the Hoare Axiomatization, prove that this program terminates. The precondition is $\mathrm{I}(x) \ \&\ \mathrm{I}(y)$, and the postcondition is true.

7. Consider the **while** program of Chapter 1, Exercise 13, which computes $sqrtx = \mathrm{sqrt}(x)$, the integer square root of x. Using the Hoare Axiomatization, prove that this program terminates. The precondition is $\mathrm{I}(x)$, and the postcondition is true.

8. Consider the **while** program of Chapter 1, Exercise 14, which computes $z = x{**}y$. Using the Hoare Axiomatization, prove that this program terminates. The precondition is $\mathrm{I}(x) \& \mathrm{I}(y)$, and the postcondition is true.

9. Write a **while+** program to compute the intersection of two sets. We understand that a set of positive integers is represented by a sequence of numbers, with no repetitions, arranged in ascending order. Two sets are contained on the input file, and the end of each of the sets is marked by a

sentinel record containing the number 0. The precondition is

$$\text{ordered}_{in}(1,\mu_{in}(1,0))\ \&\ \text{ordered}_{in}(\mu_{in}(1,0)+1,\ \mu_{in}(\mu_{in}(1,0)+1,0)-\mu_{in}(1,0)-1)\ \&$$
$$\text{norep}_{in}(1,\mu_{in}(1,0))\ \&\ \text{norep}_{in}(\mu_{in}(1,0)+1,\ \mu_{in}(\mu_{in}(1,0)+1,0)-\mu_{in}(1,0)-1)$$

and the postcondition is

$$\begin{aligned}&\text{ordered}_{out}(1,cout-1)\ \&\ \text{norep}_{out}(1,cout-1)\ \&\\ &\forall X(1\leqslant X<cout \rightarrow \exists Y(1\leqslant Y<\mu_{in}(1,0)\ \&\ out(X)=in(Y))\ \&\\ &\quad \exists Z(\mu_{in}(1,0)+1\leqslant Z<\mu_{in}(\mu_{in}(1,0)+1,0)\ \&\ out(X)=in(Z)))\ \&\\ &(\forall X(\exists Y(1\leqslant Y<\mu_{in}(1,0)\ \&\ in(Y)=X)\ \&\\ &\quad\ \exists Z(\mu_{in}(1,0)+1\leqslant Z<\mu_{in}(\mu_{in}(1,0)+1,0)\ \&\ in(Z)=X))\rightarrow\\ &\ \exists W(1\leqslant W<cout\ \&\ out(W)=X)).\end{aligned}$$

Using the Hoare Axiomatization, prove that your program is totally correct.

10. Write a **while+** program to implement the quicksort algorithm. Using the Hoare Axiomatization, prove that your program is totally correct wrt the precondition

$$in(1)\geqslant 0\ \&\ \forall X(2\leqslant X\leqslant in(1)+1\rightarrow \text{I}(in(X)))$$

and the postcondition

$$\text{ordered}_{out}(1,in(1))\ \&\ \text{perm}_{in,out}(2,1,in(1))$$

11. Consider the FC+ program of Chapter 3, Exercise 18, which implements the Eratosthenes Algorithm, writing out all of the primes from 2 to $n = in(1)$. Convert the algorithm into a **while+** program and, using the Hoare Axiomatization, prove that your program terminates. The precondition is $in(1) \geqslant 2$, and the postcondition is true.

12. The following **while+** program uses a stack to compute Ackermann's Function. Using the Hoare Axiomatization, prove that the algorithm is totally correct wrt the precondition $in(1)\geqslant 0\ \&\ in(2)\geqslant 0$ and the postcondition $out(1)=\text{ack}(in(1),in(2))$

```
{in(1)≥0 & in(2)≥0}
read m;
read n;
while m≠0 ∨ empty=0 do
      if m=0 then
```

```
                begin
                a:=n+1;
                m:=top;
                pop;
                n:=a
                end
        else
                if n=0 then
                        begin
                        m:=m-1;
                        n:=1
                        end
                else
                        begin
                        push(m-1);
                        n:=n-1
                        end;
a:=n+1;
write(a)
end
{out(1)=ack(in(1),in(2))}
```

Semantics

13. Modify the syntax, operation semantics, and Hoare Axiomatization of this chapter to permit the use of more than one stack. You might, for instance, let top(*se*) be the top of the *se*-th stack.

14. Give counterexamples showing that the **While** Rule is unsound (i.e., does not preserve validity) if the y_i's (the new simple variables) are no longer required to be foreign to both the assertion p and the statement **while** b **do** S, but are only required to be foreign to

(a) The assertion p and the boolean expression b,

(b) The assertion p and the statement S, or

(b) The statement **while** b **do** S.

15. State a useful proof rule for the **repeat-until** statement. Prove that your rule is validity-preserving.

16. Prove that the following rules of inference are validity-preserving in the Hoare logic of total correctness.

(a) *Incremental Proof Rule*

$$\frac{\{p\}S\{q\},\quad \{p\}S\{q'\}}{\{p\}S\{q\&q'\}}$$

(b) *Proof by Cases Rule*

$$\frac{\{p\}S\{q\},\quad \{p'\}S\{q\}}{\{p\vee p'\}S\{q\}}$$

17. Prove or disprove: A sound axiomatization can be obtained by dropping the Top and Empty Axioms, changing the operational semantics of the **push** and **pop** statements to read as follows:

$$\mathcal{S}[\mathbf{push}(e)] = \mathcal{S}\{\mathcal{S}[e],\mathcal{S}[e],\mathcal{S}[\mathrm{eq}(depth+1,0)],\mathcal{S}[depth]+1 \setminus \mathrm{top}, stack_{\mathcal{S}[depth]+1}, \mathrm{empty}, depth\}$$

$$\mathcal{S}[\mathbf{pop}] = \mathcal{S}\{\mathcal{S}[stack_{\mathcal{S}[depth]-1}],\mathcal{S}[\mathrm{eq}(depth-1,0)],\mathcal{S}[depth]-1 \setminus \mathrm{top},\mathrm{empty}, depth\}$$

and modifying the **Push** and **Pop** Axioms to read as follows:

$$\{p[e\setminus \mathrm{top}][e\setminus stack_{depth+1}][\mathrm{eq}(depth+1,0)\setminus \mathrm{empty}][depth+1\setminus depth]\}\ \mathbf{push}(e)\ \{p\}$$

and

$$\{p[stack_{depth-1}\setminus \mathrm{top}][\mathrm{eq}(depth-1,0)\setminus \mathrm{empty}][depth-1\setminus depth]\}\ \mathbf{pop}\ \{p\}$$

18. Prove or disprove: The translation $\mathfrak{T}$ preserves the adequacy of Floydian expressions when there are no nested loops.

19. In this exercise we consider security features as required in **read** and **write** protection.

(a) Suppose a program should not read any records from n on. Incorporate this requirement as a conjunct in the postcondition.

(b) Suppose a program should not write any record from n on. Incorporate this requirement as a conjunct in the postcondition.

(c) Suppose a variable is not to be read by a user. Can you define the concept of reading a variable semantically? Syntactically? Can you think of some way to incorporate read protection for a variable into the specification?

(d) Suppose a variable is not to be written by a user. Can you define the concept of setting a variable semantically? Syntactically? Can you think of some way to incorporate write protection for a variable into the specification?

(e) Suppose a variable is not to be used (read or written) by a user. Can you define the concept of using a variable semantically? Syntactically? Can you think of some way to incorporate use protection for a variable into the specification?

20. Restrict the translation in Section 4.2 to the syntax of **while** programs given in Chapter 1, so that the translation maps the **while** programs into the FC programs of Chapter 2 without the Floydian expressions. Define the restricted translation in the style of Section 4.2. What details can be dropped from the proof of correctness in Section 4.3?

21. Modify the translation $\mathfrak{T}$ so that the adequacy of Floydian expressions is preserved. Prove that your translation does, in fact, preserve adequacy. When you begin, be sure to prove a version of the **While** Interpretation Theorem for your translation.

22. Give an example of the following:

(a) A **while+** program that can be proven to be totally correct.

(b) A totally correct **while+** program that cannot be proven totally correct.

(c) A partially but not totally correct **while+** program that can be proven to be partially correct.

(d) A partially but not totally correct **while+** program that cannot be proven to be partially correct.

(e) A **while+** program that is not partially correct.

Programming Projects

23. In your favorite programming language, implement the translation you developed in Exercise 20.

24. Implement the translation described in Section 4.2 in your favorite programming language.

25. In your favorite programming language, write an interpreter for the **while+** programs.

26. Write a proof-checker for the Hoare Axiomatization presented in this chapter.

CHAPTER 5

The Total Correctness of **while** Programs with Functions and Procedures

In this chapter, we extend the syntax and semantics of **while** programs to function and procedure declarations and calls. We call our new class of programs *SP programs*. We will study two parameter-passing mechanisms, which are frequently referred to as the "call by reference" (also known as the "call by location") and the "call by value."[1] As promised in earlier chapters,

[1] More technically, the operational semantics of SP programs realizes the call by constant-value using the call by value. The call by constant-value can also be implemented using a call by reference. The semantics of the two implementations are different. This difference is explored in Exercise 14.

we also develop a more adequate formalism for dealing with nonterminating function calls and other execution-time errors.

In Section 5.0, we develop free arithmetic, a natural formalism for representing errors. In free arithmetic, an erroneous integer expression, such as 5/0, denotes an error object that is not an integer. The quantifiers range over integers but not over error objects, so that assertion that 5/0 does not exist

$$\forall X(X \neq 5/0)$$

is true in free arithmetic (whereas it is false in the "standard" arithmetic of Chapter 0). The advantage of using free arithmetic as the underlying arithmetic of Hoare logic, yielding what we will call "free Hoare logic", can be seen by considering the following asserted program (?). In the Hoare logic of total correctness presented in the preceding chapter, the erroneous asserted **while** program

(?) $\{\text{true}\}y{:=}5/0\{\mathrm{I}(y)\}$

is provable in the Hoare Axiomatization and valid in the semantics. The asserted **while** program (?) is neither provable nor valid in the free Hoare logic of total correctness introduced in this chapter. To handle errors, we modify the natural deduction system, Peano Axiomatization, and semantics presented in Chapter 0 to suit the free case. In the semantics, we introduce "error assignments" that assign truth-values in an arbitrary manner to assertions containing erroneous integer expressions. By using the device of error assignments, we can retain a classical two-valued logic (a considerable advantage, in our opinion) and, at the same time, block the validity of intuitively invalid assertions.

In Section 5.1, we extend the syntax of Chapter 1 to handle user-defined functions and procedures. We distinguish the function variables of our programs from the operation symbols of free arithmetic: Function variables receive their meanings from user-defined functions in our programs. To present a simple deductive system (Section 5.3), we banish occurrences of global integer variables in our subprograms. Our syntax is designed to permit calls by reference (to procedures) and by value (to functions) while, at the same time, blocking recursive calls and aliasing. Recursion will be the principal topic of Chapter 6.

In Section 5.2, we supplement states, the only kind of semantic mapping dealt with in previous chapters, with "environments." Previously, we had what is sometimes known as a "direct" semantics, in that a state was a total function that mapped an integer variable directly to an integer. The introduction of functions and procedures, accompanied by the concept of the scope of a variable, requires a more subtle semantics. In this chapter, an environment maps an integer variable, for example, to a location, and a state is (intuitively) a partial function mapping a location to an integer. We also provide for an environment to interpret a function or procedure variable.

Furthermore, we modify the operational semantics of the assignment, conditional, and **while** statements to enable our operational semantics of SP programs to mesh with the semantics of free arithmetic and so enable the proper treatment of execution-time errors. Because we do not permit recursion, we use (for simplicity) a static storage scheme.

In Section 5.3, we present our Hoare Axiomatization for proving total correctness. The concept of a proof is somewhat more complicated than in Chapter 1 because of scoping issues arising from the introduction of user-defined functions and procedures. The idea behind our approach is to prove the subprograms of a program correct before proving the program itself, as we supplement the program's virtual machine with the "operations" provided by its subprograms. We outline the modifications to Section 1.4 needed for proving soundness in Section 5.4, and, in Section 5.5, we sketch a few sample proofs.

5.0. FREE ARITHMETIC: NATURAL DEDUCTION, AXIOMATIZATION, AND SEMANTICS

In this section, we develop free arithmetic, which will be used throughout the remainder of this text to express facts about execution-time errors. The syntax, the natural deduction system, the Peano Axiomatization, and the semantics of Chapter 0 require some modification to suit the free case. The modifications to the syntax are minimal: To the list of integer expressions in Section 0.1, we add the error constant $\perp$ (pronounced "bottom"). This is necessary because the error constant is current in much of the related computer science literature. It does not, however, play a critical role in the theory presented in this chapter.

The rules for the propositional connectives are the same in the natural deduction system. The introduction and elimination rules for the two quantifiers require modification, as shown in the following schematics:

THE UNIVERSAL QUANTIFIER INTRODUCTION RULE (∀I) AND THE UNIVERSAL QUANTIFIER ELIMINATION RULE (∀E)

∀I

1	p_1	
2	p_2	
.	.	
m	p_m	
.	.	
a	$\exists X(X=x)$	
.	.	
b	$q[x\backslash X]$	
$b+1$	$\forall Xq$	(**∀I**,$a-b$)

∀E

1	p_1	
2	p_2	
.	.	
m	p_m	
.	.	
a	$\forall Xq$	
.	.	
b	$\forall X(X=e)$	
.	.	
n	$q[e\backslash X]$	(**∀E**,a,b)

As in Chapter 0, in the schematization of the two rules for the universal quantifier, we understand that X may be any quantified variable, e any integer expression, and x any integer variable subject to the following restriction:

Restriction: *In the Rule* **∀I**, *x must be foreign to $\forall Xq$ and each p_i ($1 \leq i \leq m$).*

Notice the modifications to the rules for the universal quantifier as presented in Chapter 0. In the Introduction Rule, we can assume that x exists (line a) in proving that $q[x \backslash X]$ (line b) because x is a new integer variable and so is arbitrarily chosen. The assumption that x exists was not needed in Chapter 0 because the existence of any integer variable is a presupposition of standard logic, and the existence of x could be proven using the Existential Quantifier Introduction Rule of Chapter 0. In fact, "free logic" received its name because it is free of the "existential presuppositions" of standard logic deplored by Bertrand Russell.

Roughly, the justification for line a is as follows: If x cannot exist, then nothing can because x is new. If nothing exists, then each universal quantification, in particular $\forall Xq$, is vacuously true. In the Universal Quantifier Elimination Rule, we need to establish the existence of e (line b) before we can instantiate the universal quantification (line a).

THE EXISTENTIAL QUANTIFIER INTRODUCTION RULE (∃I) AND THE EXISTENTIAL QUANTIFIER ELIMINATION RULE (∃E)

∃I

1	p_1	
2	p_2	
•	•	
m	p_m	
•	•	
a	$q[e \backslash X]$	
•	•	
b	$\exists X(X=e)$	
•	•	
n	$\exists Xq$	($\exists$I,a,b)

∃E

1	p_1	
2	p_2	
•	•	
m	p_m	
•	•	
a	$\exists Xq$	
•	•	
b	$q[x \backslash X] \& \exists X(X=x)$	
•	•	
c	r	
$c+1$	r	($\exists$E,a,$b-c$)

Restriction: *In the Rule* **∃E**, *x must be foreign to $\exists Xq$, r, and each p_i ($1 \leq i \leq m$).*

Notice that the Existential Quantifier Introduction Rule requires proof that e exists (line b), and the Elimination Rule allows us to assume that x exists as well as that $q[x \backslash X]$ (line b).

The complete set of natural deduction rules for free logic are summarized in Figure 5.1.

THE REITERATION RULE (R)

R

1	p_1	
2	p_2	
.	.	
m	p_m	
.	.	
n	p_i	(**R**,i) $(1 \leq i \leq m)$

THE CONDITIONAL INTRODUCTION RULE (→I) AND THE CONDITIONAL ELIMINATION RULE (→E)

→I

1	p_1	
2	p_2	
.	.	
m	p_m	
.	.	
a	q	
.	.	
b	r	
$b+1$	$q \rightarrow r$	(→**I**,$a-b$)

→E

1	p_1	
2	p_2	
.	.	
m	p_m	
.	.	
a	$q \rightarrow r$	
.	.	
b	q	
.	.	
n	r	(→**E**,a,b)

THE NEGATION INTRODUCTION RULE (~I) AND THE NEGATION ELIMINATION RULE (~E)

~I

1	p_1	
2	p_2	
.	.	
m	p_m	
.	.	
a	q	
.	.	
b	r	
.	.	
c	$\sim r$	
$c+1$	$\sim q$	(~**I**,$a-c$)

~E

1	p_1	
2	p_2	
.	.	
m	p_m	
.	.	
a	$\sim\sim q$	
.	.	
n	q	(~**E**,a)

FIGURE 5.1. The free logic natural deduction rules.

THE CONJUNCTION INTRODUCTION RULE (&I) AND THE CONJUNCTION ELIMINATION RULE (&E)

&I

1	p_1	
2	p_2	
.	.	
m	p_m	
.	.	
a	q_1	
.	.	
b	q_2	
.	.	
n	$q_1 \& q_2$	$(\&\mathbf{I}, a, b)$

&E

1	p_1	
2	p_2	
.	.	
m	p_m	
.	.	
a	$q_1 \& q_2$	
.	.	
n	q_i	$(\&\mathbf{E}, a)$ $(i=1$ or $2)$

THE DISJUNCTION INTRODUCTION RULE (∨I) AND THE DISJUNCTION ELIMINATION RULE (∨E)

∨I

1	p_1	
2	p_2	
.	.	
m	p_m	
.	.	
a	q_i	$(i=1$ or $2)$
.	.	
n	$q_1 \vee q_2$	$(\vee\mathbf{I}, a)$

∨E

1	p_1	
2	p_2	
.	.	
m	p_m	
.	.	
a	$q_1 \vee q_2$	
.	.	
b	│ q_1	
.	│ .	
c	│ r	
d	│ q_2	
.	│ .	
e	│ r	
$e+1$	r	$(\vee\mathbf{E}, a, b-c, d-e)$

THE BICONDITIONAL INTRODUCTION RULE (↔I) AND THE BICONDITIONAL ELIMINATION RULE (↔E)

↔I

1	p_1	
2	p_2	
.	.	
m	p_m	
.	.	
a	│ q	
.	│ .	
b	│ r	
c	│ r	
.	│ .	
d	│ q	
$d+1$	$q \leftrightarrow r$	$(\leftrightarrow\mathbf{I}, a-b, c-d)$

↔E

1	p_1	
2	p_2	
.	.	
m	p_m	
.	.	
a	$q \leftrightarrow r$ (or $r \leftrightarrow q$)	
.	.	
b	q	
.	.	
n	r	$(\leftrightarrow\mathbf{E}, a, b)$

FIGURE 5.1. *(Continued)*

THE UNIVERSAL QUANTIFIER INTRODUCTION RULE (∀I) AND THE UNIVERSAL QUANTIFIER ELIMINATION RULE (∀E)

∀I

1	p_1
2	p_2
·	·
m	p_m
·	·
a	$\exists X(X=x)$
·	·
b	$q[x\backslash X]$
$b+1$	$\forall Xq$ (**∀I**,$a-b$)

∀E

1	p_1
2	p_2
·	·
m	p_m
·	·
a	$\forall Xq$
·	·
b	$\exists X(X=e)$
·	·
n	$q[e\backslash X]$ (**∀E**,a,b)

Restriction: In the Rule **∀I**, x must be foreign to $\forall Xq$ and each $p_i\,(1\leqslant i\leqslant m)$.

THE EXISTENTIAL QUANTIFIER INTRODUCTION RULE (∃I) AND THE EXISTENTIAL QUANTIFIER ELIMINATION RULE (∃E)

∃I

1	p_1
2	p_2
·	·
m	p_m
·	·
a	$q[e\backslash X]$
·	·
b	$\exists X(X=e)$
·	·
n	$\exists Xq$ (**∃I**,a,b)

∃E

1	p_1
2	p_2
·	·
m	p_m
·	·
a	$\exists Xq$
·	·
b	$q[x\backslash X]\&\exists X(X=x)$
·	·
c	r
$c+1$	r (**∃E**,a,$b-c$)

X may be any quantified variable, e any integer expression, and x any integer variable subject to the following restriction:

Restriction: In the Rule **∃E**, x must be foreign to $\exists Xq$, r, and each p_i $(1\leqslant i\leqslant m)$.

FIGURE 5.1. *(Continued)*

THE EQUALITY INTRODUCTION RULE (=I), THE EQUALITY REPLACEMENT RULE (=R), AND THE EQUALITY SYMMETRY RULE (=.sym)

=I

$$
\begin{array}{l|l l}
1 & p_1 & \\
2 & p_2 & \\
\cdot & \cdot & \\
m & \underline{p_m} & \\
\cdot & \cdot & \\
n & e=e & (=\mathbf{I})
\end{array}
$$

=R

$$
\begin{array}{l|l l}
1 & p_1 & \\
2 & p_2 & \\
\cdot & \cdot & \\
m & \underline{p_m} & \\
\cdot & \cdot & \\
a & e_1=e_2 & \\
\cdot & \cdot & \\
b & q & \\
\cdot & \cdot & \\
n & q[e_2\backslash\backslash e_1] & (=\mathbf{R},a,b)
\end{array}
$$

=.sym

$$
\begin{array}{l|l l}
1 & p_1 & \\
2 & p_2 & \\
\cdot & \cdot & \\
m & \underline{p_m} & \\
\cdot & \cdot & \\
a & e_1=e_2 & \\
\cdot & \cdot & \\
n & e_2=e_1 & (=\mathbf{.sym},a)
\end{array}
$$

e, e_1, and e_2 may be any integer expressions.

FIGURE 5.1. *(Continued)*

We illustrate our free natural deduction system with proofs of the following laws:

Law of Existence:	$\forall Y \exists X(X=Y)$
Distribution Law:	$\forall X(p \rightarrow q) \rightarrow (\forall Xp \rightarrow \forall Xq)$
Specification Law:	$\forall Xp \rightarrow (\exists X(X=e) \rightarrow p[e\backslash X])$
Law of Nonexistence:	$\forall X(\sim X=e) \rightarrow (\exists X(X=e') \rightarrow \sim e'=e)$

The laws of existence and distribution are sometimes used as axioms in axiomatizations of free logic.

Proof of the Law of Existence

$$
\begin{array}{l l l}
1 & \quad | \ \underline{\exists X(X=y)} & \\
2 & \quad | \ \exists X(X=y) & (\mathbf{R},1) \\
3 & \forall Y \exists X(X=Y) & (\forall\mathbf{I},1-2)
\end{array}
$$

Proof of the Distribution Law

1	$\forall X(p\rightarrow q)$	
2	$\forall Xp$	
3	$\exists Y(Y=x)$	
4	$\exists Y(Y=x)$	(**R**,3)
5	$\forall Xp$	(**R**,2)
6	$p[x\backslash x]$	($\forall$**E**,4,5)
7	$\forall X(p\rightarrow q)$	(**R**,1)
8	$p[x\backslash X]\rightarrow q[x\backslash X]$	($\forall$**E**,4,7)
9	$q[x\backslash X]$	($\rightarrow$**E**,6,8)
10	$\forall Xq$	($\forall$**I**,3–9)
11	$\forall Xp\rightarrow\forall Xq$	($\rightarrow$**I**,2–10)
12	$\forall X(p\rightarrow q)\rightarrow(\forall Xp\rightarrow\forall Xq)$	($\rightarrow$**I**,1–11)

Proof of the Specification Law

1	$\forall Xp$	
2	$\exists X(X=e)$	
3	$\exists X(X=e)$	(**R**,2)
4	$\forall Xp$	(**R**,1)
5	$p[e\backslash X]$	($\forall$**E**,3,4)
6	$\exists X(X=e)\rightarrow p[e\backslash X]$	($\rightarrow$**I**,2–5)
7	$\forall Xp\rightarrow(\exists(X=e)\rightarrow p[e\backslash X])$	($\rightarrow$**I**,1–6)

Proof of the Law of Nonexistence:

1	$\forall X(\sim X=e)$	
2	$\exists X(X=e')$	
3	$\exists X(X=e')$	(**R**,2)
4	$\forall X(\sim X=e)$	(**R**,1)
5	$\sim e'=e$	($\forall$**E**,3,4)
6	$\exists X(X=e')\rightarrow\sim e'=e$	($\rightarrow$**I**,2–5)
7	$\forall X(\sim X=e)\rightarrow(\exists X(X=e')\rightarrow\sim e'=e)$	($\rightarrow$**I**,1–6)

Turning to the axiomatization of Section 0.3, the axioms for the primitive symbols must be supplemented in free arithmetic with axioms assuring the existence of the integers and the nonexistence of the error object $\perp$. We require axioms stating that 0 is an integer, that the successor operation is total, that $\perp$ is not an integer, that $\perp$ is the only error object, and that each of our primitive operations is "strict." The strictness axioms guarantee the propagation of errors in free arithmetic so that, for example, we have

$$\vdash\sim X=\mathrm{succ}(5/0)$$

because

$$\vdash\sim X=5/0$$

(0.E)	$\exists X(X=0)$
(succ.E)	$\exists Y(Y=\mathrm{succ}(X))$
(⊥.~E)	$\sim X=\bot$
(⊥.un)	$\sim X=e \rightarrow e=\bot$[2]
(succ.st)	$\exists X(X=\mathrm{succ}(e)) \rightarrow \exists X(X=e)$
(+.st)	$\exists X(X=e+e') \rightarrow \exists X(X=e) \& \exists X(X=e')$
(*.st)	$\exists X(X=e*e') \rightarrow \exists X(X=e) \& \exists X(X=e')$
(.st)**	$\exists X(X=e**e') \rightarrow \exists X(X=e) \& \exists X(X=e')$

Notice that the last five axioms are actually axiom schemas because e can be any integer expression.

We must modify the terminology on definitions introduced in Chapter 0 to suit the free case. Let **(D.p)** $\equiv \forall X_1 \ldots \forall X_n q(X_1, \ldots, X_n)$ be an explicit definition of the n-ary predicate p. An axiom (schema) **(DF.p)** introducing p is said to be a *full explicit definition* if **(DF.p)** $\equiv q(e_1, \ldots, e_n)$. The new axioms (D.I) and (D.cond), which we will discuss below, illustrate the need for full explicit definitions. We call a predicate symbol introduced with a full explicit definition a *full* predicate, and one that is introduced (or could be in principle) with an explicit definition (but not a full explicit definition) a *nonfull* predicate. An axiom **(CD.p)** introducing p is a *conditional definition* if

$$\textbf{(CD.p)} \equiv \forall X_1 \ldots \forall X_n(r(X_1, \ldots X_n) \rightarrow q(X_1, \ldots X_n))$$

for some assertion $\forall X_1 \ldots \forall X_n r(X_1, \ldots X_n)$. An entirely similar terminology is used in the case of n-ary operation symbols. Exercise 14 illustrates the use of conditional equational definitions. If need be, a conditional definition can be converted into an explicit definition, and an explicit definition can be converted into a full explicit definition. Full explicit definitions can be regarded as "abbreviations" in the sense discussed in Chapter 0.

The division operation symbol '/' must now be regarded as primitive because it is an intuitively partial operation. (If we retained the explicit definition in Chapter 0, it would be total.) To shorten the division axiom **(/.~=0)**, we also take the operation symbol 'abs' to be primitive. We have

(abs)	$\mathrm{abs}(X) = Y \leftrightarrow (X \geqslant 0 \rightarrow Y=X) \& (\sim X \geqslant 0 \rightarrow Y+X=0)$
(/.0)	$\sim X/0 = Y$

[2] If we were distinguishing run-time detectable errors, such as the evaluation of '5/0', from errors due to nonterminating (diverging) evaluations of integer expressions, **(⊥.un)** would not hold. See Exercise 11 in this chapter and the next. Of course, the distinction between the two sorts or errors is not absolute because, for example, division by 0 on some older calculators often did not terminate. These machines did not check for a 0 divisor and performed division by the method of successive subtractions, much as in the algorithm presented in Example 2 of Chapter 1.

(/.~=0) $\sim Y=0 \rightarrow (X/Y=Z \leftrightarrow$
$(\text{abs}(Y*Z) \leqslant \text{abs}(X) < \text{abs}(Y)*\text{succ}(\text{abs}(Z)))\ \&$
$(Z\geqslant 0 \leftrightarrow Y*X\geqslant 0))$

Otherwise, the order in which we introduced new symbols in Chapter 0 is preserved. In particular, the axiom **(D.mod)**, which introduces the operation symbol 'mod', does not have to be modified.

Our axioms for '/' can be shown to be "noncreative" in the sense discussed in Chapter 0. Strictly speaking, before any new operation symbol is introduced into free arithmetic, a proof (in free arithmetic) of its uniqueness condition (with the concept of "uniqueness condition" as presented in Chapter 0 modified to suit the free case) should be given. For example, the uniqueness condition for the binary operation '—' is as follows:

$$z+y=x\ \&\ z'+y=x \rightarrow z=z'$$

The proof proceeds by cases, depending on if x, y, z, and z' exist. Proof of the corresponding existence condition is required only in the case of intuitively total operations such as the binary operation '—'. As in Chapter 0, we will omit the usually tedious proofs of existence and uniqueness conditions.

We also require axioms expressing the strictness of 'abs', '/', and each new operation symbol.

(abs.st) $\exists X(X=\text{abs}(e)) \rightarrow \exists X(X=e)$
(/.st) $\exists X(X=e/e') \rightarrow \exists X(X=e)\&\exists X(X=e')$
(−.st) $\exists X(X=e-e') \rightarrow \exists X(X=e)\&\exists X(X=e')$
(pred.st) $\exists X(X=\text{pred}(e)) \rightarrow \exists X(X=e)$
(n.st) $\exists X(X=-e) \rightarrow \exists X(X=e)$
(mod.st) $\exists X(X=e \bmod e') \rightarrow \exists X(X=e)\&\exists X(X=e')$

Except when explicitly stated otherwise, we will understand that an axiom of strictness accompanies each new operation symbol introduced, whether by an equational or explicit definition, or by noncreative axioms.

To facilitate comparison with the axioms of (standard) arithmetic in Figure 0.1 of Chapter 0, Figure 5.2 displays the corresponding axioms of free arithmetic. As before, the dashed line separates the axioms for the primitive symbols of arithmetic from the axioms for the defined symbols.

In general, our definitions of new predicates will be the same as in the preceding chapters, as will be our definitions of strict and (intuitively) total operations. For example, the definitions of the predicate '$\leqslant$' and of the operation symbol 'max' are as in preceding chapters. We do not alter definition

(D.$\leqslant$) $X \leqslant Y \leftrightarrow Y \geqslant X$

(Ind)	$p(0)\ \&\ \forall X(X \geqslant 0 \rightarrow (p(X) \rightarrow p(\mathrm{succ}(X))))$ $\ \&\ \forall X(0 \geqslant \mathrm{succ}(X) \rightarrow (p(\mathrm{succ}(X)) \rightarrow p(X))) \rightarrow \forall Y p(Y)$
(≥.tr)	$X \geqslant Y\ \&\ Y \geqslant Z \rightarrow X \geqslant Z$
(≥.as)	$X \geqslant Y\ \&\ Y \geqslant X \rightarrow X = Y$
(≥.di)	$X \geqslant Y \vee Y \geqslant X$
(succ.≥)	$\mathrm{succ}(X) \geqslant X$
(succ.=)	$\mathrm{succ}(X) = \mathrm{succ}(Y) \rightarrow X = Y$
(succ.≠)	$X \geqslant 0 \rightarrow \sim(\mathrm{succ}(X) = 0)$
(+.0)	$X + 0 = X$
(+.succ)	$X + \mathrm{succ}(Y) = \mathrm{succ}(X + Y)$
(*.0)	$X * 0 = 0$
(*.succ)	$X * \mathrm{succ}(Y) = X * Y + X$
(.0)**	$X ** 0 = \mathrm{succ}(0)$
(.+)**	$Y \geqslant 0 \rightarrow X ** \mathrm{succ}(Y) = (X ** Y) * X$
(.−)**	$0 \geqslant \mathrm{succ}(Y) \rightarrow X ** Y = 0$
(abs)	$\mathrm{abs}(X) = Y \leftrightarrow (X \geqslant 0 \rightarrow Y = X)\ \&\ (\sim X \geqslant 0 \rightarrow Y + X = 0)$
(/.0)	$\sim X/0 = Y$
(/.~=0)	$\sim Y = 0 \rightarrow (X/Y = Z \leftrightarrow$ $(\mathrm{abs}(Y * Z) \leqslant \mathrm{abs}(X) < \mathrm{abs}(Y) * \mathrm{succ}(\mathrm{abs}(Z)))\ \&$ $(Z \geqslant 0 \leftrightarrow Y * X \geqslant 0))$
(0.E)	$\exists X(X = 0)$
(succ.E)	$\exists Y(Y = \mathrm{succ}(X))$
(⊥.~E)	$\sim X = \perp$
(⊥.un)	$\sim X = e \rightarrow e = \perp$
(succ.st)	$\exists X(X = \mathrm{succ}(e)) \rightarrow \exists X(X = e)$
(+.st)	$\exists X(X = e + e') \rightarrow \exists X(X = e) \& \exists X(X = e')$
(*.st)	$\exists X(X = e * e') \rightarrow \exists X(X = e) \& \exists X(X = e')$
(.st)**	$\exists X(X = e ** e') \rightarrow \exists X(X = e) \& \exists X(X = e')$
(abs.st)	$\exists X(X = \mathrm{abs}(e)) \rightarrow \exists X(X = e)$
(/.st)	$\exists X(X = e/e') \rightarrow \exists X(X = e) \& \exists X(X = e')$

(D.≠)	$X \neq Y \leftrightarrow \sim(X = Y)$
(D.≤)	$X \leqslant Y \leftrightarrow Y \geqslant X$
(D.>)	$X > Y \leftrightarrow \sim(X \leqslant Y)$
(D.<)	$X < Y \leftrightarrow Y > X$
(D.−)	$X - Y = Z \leftrightarrow Z + Y = X$
(D.pred)	$\mathrm{pred}(X) = X - \mathrm{succ}(0)$
(D.n)	$-X = 0 - X$
(D.mod)	$X \bmod Y = X - (X/Y) * Y$
(−.st)	$\exists X(X = e - e') \rightarrow \exists X(X = e) \& \exists X(X = e')$
(pred.st)	$\exists X(X = \mathrm{pred}(e)) \rightarrow \exists X(X = e)$
(n.st)	$\exists X(X = -e) \rightarrow \exists X(X = e)$
(mod.st)	$\exists X(X = e \bmod e') \rightarrow \exists X(X = e) \& \exists X(X = e')$
⋮	⋮
(D.−1)	$-1 = \mathrm{pred}(0)$
(D.1)	$1 = \mathrm{succ}(0)$
(D.−2)	$-2 = \mathrm{pred}(-1)$
(D.2)	$2 = \mathrm{succ}(1)$
⋮	⋮

FIGURE 5.2. The axioms of free arithmetic.

because we do not wish to fix the truth-value of, for example, the assertion $\perp \leq \perp$, as neither it nor its negation is intuitively valid. There are some exceptions to the rule. The axiom introducing the unary "integer" predicate 'I' (sometimes called the "existence predicate" in the free logic literature) is the full explicit definition

$$\textbf{(DF.I)} \qquad \mathrm{I}(e) \leftrightarrow \exists X(X=e)$$

We use a full explicit definition because $\mathrm{I}(\perp)$ is (intuitively) false. We also have to modify the axioms introducing the 3-ary operation symbol 'cond' so that 'cond' conforms more closely to the usual conventions in the computer science literature. The operation 'cond' is strict only in its first argument, so an axiom of strictness

$$\mathrm{I}(\mathrm{cond}(e,e',e'')) \rightarrow \mathrm{I}(e)\&\mathrm{I}(e')\&\mathrm{I}(e'')$$

does *not* accompany its introduction. Instead, to illustrate the form of a *full* equational definition, we introduce the operation symbol 'cond' with[3]

$$\textbf{(DF.cond)} \quad \mathrm{cond}(e,e',e'') = e{+} \leftrightarrow (e{=}1 \rightarrow e{+}{=}e')\ \& \\ (e=0 \rightarrow e{+}{=}e'')\ \&\ ({\sim}(e{=}0 \vee e{=}1) \rightarrow e{+}{=}\perp)$$

Much as in the case of the division operator, we have to modify the axioms introducing the operation symbol 'gcd' because gcd(0,0) is (intuitively) undefined.

$$\textbf{(gcd.=0,0)} \quad {\sim}X{=}\mathrm{gcd}(0,0)$$

$$\textbf{(gcd.}{\sim}\textbf{=0,0)}$$
$$\begin{aligned}
&{\sim}(X{=}0\ \&\ Y{=}0) \rightarrow \\
&\quad (\mathrm{gcd}(X,Y){=}Z \leftrightarrow (X{=}0\ \&\ {\sim}Y{=}0 \rightarrow Z{=}Y)\ \& \\
&\qquad ({\sim}X{=}0\ \&\ Y{=}0 \rightarrow Z{=}X)\ \& \\
&\qquad ({\sim}X{=}0\ \&\ {\sim}Y{=}0 \rightarrow \\
&\qquad\quad ((X \bmod Z){=}0\ \&\ (Y \bmod Z){=}0\ \& \\
&\qquad\quad \forall Z'((X \bmod Z'){=}0\ \&\ (Y \bmod Z'){=}0 \rightarrow Z' \leq Z) \\
&\qquad\quad)))
\end{aligned}$$

As usual, an axiom of strictness accompanies the introduction of the operation symbol 'gcd', so the axioms for 'gcd' could be readily converted into a full explicit definition. Similarly, full explicit definitions can be given for '/' and 'mod'. The axioms introducing most of the other intuitively partial operations are to be expressed in forms entirely similar to those just illustrated for the binary operation symbols '/', 'mod', and 'gcd'.

As we introduce user-defined functions in this chapter, we will sometimes write a user-defined function instead of explicitly defining a new operation symbol in free arithmetic. The user-defined function f becomes the value of

[3] Intuitively, e is the characteristic function for a boolean expression b_e. We have $e = 1$ when b_e is true, and $e = 0$ when b_e is false.

the function variable 'f' in the context of the program in which it is defined, and supplements the program's virtual machine. For a user-defined function, we will derive an assertion of free arithmetic and use it, in certain contexts, as an axiom in an extension of free arithmetic. It is important to contrast the approach in this chapter with that of preceding chapters: An axiom governing a user-defined function is valid only within the scope of the function definition within the program. Moreover, the axioms for user-defined functions, unlike the explicit definitions of free arithmetic, must be proven correct using our Hoare Axiomatization.

The definitions of proof, provable, theorem, and other proof theoretic concepts are understood in a manner entirely similar to that explained in Chapter 0, and we now use the single turnstile $\vdash$ to denote the provability relation in free arithmetic. Additionally, many of Chapter 0's proofs can be easily edited to suit the free case once existence conditions, as presupposed in Chapter 0, have been established. For example, the reader should compare the proof of $\text{pred}(\text{succ}(X))=X$ in (standard) arithmetic (Theorem 1, Section 0.2), with its proof in free arithmetic (Theorem 4, which follows).

Theorem 1 states that addition is a total operation, and its proof relies critically on **(succ.E)** (line 24) and **(succ.st)** (line 47), which state that the successor operation is total and strict. Theorem 4 depends on Theorem 3, which states that subtraction is total. Theorem 3, in turn, hinges on Theorem 2, which is the "existence condition" for the binary operator '—'. Proofs that the other (intuitively) total operations are, in fact, total proceed in manners similar to those illustrated in the proofs of Theorems 1 and 3.

THEOREM 1: $\exists Z(Z=X+Y)$

Proof

1	$\exists Z(Z=x)$	
2	$\forall Z(Z=x)$	(**R**,1)
3	$X+0=X$	**(+.0)**
4	$x+0=x$	(**∀E**,2,3)
5	$x=x+0$	**(=.sym,4)**
6	$\exists Z(Z=x+0)$	(=**R**,2,5)
7	$\exists Z(Z=X+0)$	(**∀I**,1–6)
8	$\exists X(X=x)$	
9	$\exists Y(Y=y)$	
10	$y\geqslant 0$	
11	$\exists Z(Z=x+y)$	
12	$\exists Z(Z=x+y)$	(**R**,11)
13	$z=x+y\&\exists Z(Z=z)$	
14	$\exists X(X=x)$	(**R**,8)
15	$\exists Y(Y=y)$	(**R**,9)
16	$z=x+y\&\exists Z(Z=z)$	(**R**,13)
17	$X+\text{succ}(Y)=\text{succ}(X+Y)$	**(+.succ)**

18	$x+\mathrm{succ}(y)=\mathrm{succ}(x+y)$	$(\forall\mathbf{E},14,15,17)$
19	$z=x+y$	$(\&\mathbf{E},16)$
20	$x+y=z$	$(=.\mathbf{sym},19)$
21	$x+\mathrm{succ}(y)=\mathrm{succ}(z)$	$(=\mathbf{R},18,20)$
22	$\mathrm{succ}(z)=x+\mathrm{succ}(y)$	$(=.\mathbf{sym},21)$
23	$\exists Z(Z=z)$	$(\&\mathbf{E},16)$
24	$\exists Z(Z=\mathrm{succ}(X))$	$(\mathbf{succ.E})$
25	$\exists Z(Z=\mathrm{succ}(z))$	$(\forall\mathbf{E},23,24)$
26	$\exists Z(Z=x+\mathrm{succ}(y))$	$(=\mathbf{R},22,25)$
27	$\exists Z(Z=x+\mathrm{succ}(y))$	$(\exists\mathbf{E},12-26)$
28	$\exists Z(Z=x+y)\rightarrow\exists Z(Z=x+\mathrm{succ}(y))$	$(\rightarrow\mathbf{I},11-27)$
29	$y\geqslant 0\rightarrow(\exists Z(Z=x+y)\rightarrow\exists Z(Z=x+\mathrm{succ}(y)))$	$(\rightarrow\mathbf{I},10-28)$
30	$Y\geqslant 0\rightarrow(\exists Z(Z=X+Y)\rightarrow\exists Z(Z=X+\mathrm{succ}(Y)))$	$(\forall\mathbf{I},8-29)$
31	$\exists X(X=x)$	
32	$\exists Y(Y=y)$	
33	$0\geqslant\mathrm{succ}(y)$	
34	$\exists Z(Z=x+\mathrm{succ}(y))$	
35	$\exists Z(Z=x+\mathrm{succ}(y))$	$(\mathbf{R},34)$
36	$z=x+\mathrm{succ}(y)\&\exists Z(Z=z)$	
37	$\exists X(X=x)$	$(\mathbf{R},31)$
38	$\exists Y(Y=y)$	$(\mathbf{R},32)$
39	$z=x+\mathrm{succ}(y)\&\exists Z(Z=z)$	$(\mathbf{R},36)$
40	$X+\mathrm{succ}(Y)=\mathrm{succ}(X+Y)$	$(\mathbf{+.succ})$
41	$x+\mathrm{succ}(y)=\mathrm{succ}(x+y)$	$(\forall\mathbf{E},37,38,40)$
42	$z=x+\mathrm{succ}(y)$	$(\&\mathbf{E},39)$
43	$x+\mathrm{succ}(y)=z$	$(=.\mathbf{sym},42)$
44	$z=\mathrm{succ}(x+y)$	$(=\mathbf{R},41,43)$
45	$\exists Z(Z=z)$	$(\&\mathbf{E},39)$
46	$\exists Z(Z=\mathrm{succ}(x+y))$	$(=\mathbf{R},44,45)$
47	$\exists Z(Z=\mathrm{succ}(x+y))\rightarrow\exists Z(Z=x+y)$	$(\mathbf{succ.st})$
48	$\exists Z(Z=x+y)$	$(\rightarrow\mathbf{E},46,47)$
49	$\exists Z(Z=x+y)$	$(\exists\mathbf{E},35-48)$
50	$\exists Z(Z=x+\mathrm{succ}(y))\rightarrow\exists Z(Z=x+y)$	$(\rightarrow\mathbf{I},34-49)$
51	$0\geqslant\mathrm{succ}(y)\rightarrow(\exists Z(Z=x+\mathrm{succ}(y))\rightarrow \exists Z(Z=x+y))$	$(\rightarrow\mathbf{I},33-50)$
52	$0\geqslant\mathrm{succ}(Y)\rightarrow(\exists Z(Z=X+\mathrm{succ}(Y))\rightarrow \exists Z(Z=X+Y))$	$(\forall\mathbf{I},31-51)$
53	$\forall X\exists Z(Z=X+0)\ \&\ \forall X(Y\geqslant 0\rightarrow(\exists Z(Z=X+Y)\rightarrow \exists Z(Z=X+\mathrm{succ}(Y))))\ \&\ \forall X(0\geqslant\mathrm{succ}(Y)\rightarrow (\exists Z(Z=X+\mathrm{succ}(Y))\rightarrow\exists Z(Z=X+Y)))$	$(\&\mathbf{I},7,30,52)$
54	$\forall X\exists Z(Z=X+0)\ \&\ \forall X(Y\geqslant 0\rightarrow(\exists Z(Z=X+Y)\rightarrow \exists Z(Z=X+\mathrm{succ}(Y))))\ \&\ \forall X(0\geqslant\mathrm{succ}(Y)\rightarrow (\exists Z(Z=X+\mathrm{succ}(Y))\rightarrow\exists Z(Z=X+Y)))\rightarrow \forall X\exists Z(Z=X+Y)$	$(\mathbf{Ind})$
55	$\exists Z(Z=X+Y)$	$(\rightarrow\mathbf{E},53,54)$

□

THEOREM 2: $\exists Z(Z+Y=X)$

Proof: Theorem 2 expresses the existence condition (see Section 0.3) for the subtraction operator '−', showing that it is total. Note that in free arithmetic we do not have to postpone introducing the subtraction operator until after we have proved its existence condition. The proof proceeds by induction on y and is left as an exercise. □

THEOREM 3: $\exists Z(Z=X-Y)$

Proof

1	$\exists X(X=x)$	
2	$\exists Y(Y=y)$	
3	$\exists X(X=x)$	**(R**,1)
4	$\exists Y(Y=y)$	**(R**,2)
5	$\exists Z(Z+Y=X)$	**(Theorem 2)**
6	$\exists Z(Z+y=x)$	**(∀E**,3–5)
7	$z+y=x\&\exists Z(Z=z)$	
8	$\exists X(X=x)$	**(R**,1)
9	$\exists Y(Y=y)$	**(R**,2)
10	$z+y=x\&\exists Z(Z=z)$	**(R**,7)
11	$z+y=x$	**(&E**,10)
12	$\exists Z(Z=z)$	**(&E**,10)
13	$X-Y=Z \leftrightarrow Z+Y=X$	**(D.−)**
14	$x-y=z \leftrightarrow z+y=x$	**(∀E**,8,9,12,13)
15	$x-y=z$	**(↔E**,11,14)
16	$z=x-y$	**(=.sym**,15)
17	$\exists Z(Z=x-y)$	**(∃I**,12,16)
18	$\exists Z(Z=x-y)$	**(∃E**,6–17)
19	$\exists Z(Z=X-Y)$	**(∀I**,1–18)

□

THEOREM 4: $\text{pred}(\text{succ}(X))=X$

Proof

1	$\exists X(X=x)$	
2	$\exists X(X=x)$	**(R**,1)
3	$\text{pred}(X)=X-\text{succ}(0)$	**(D.pred)**
4	$\exists Y(Y=\text{succ}(X))$	**(succ.E)**
5	$\exists Y(Y=\text{succ}(x))$	**(∀E**,2,4)
6	$\exists X(X=0)$	**(0.E)**
7	$\exists Y(Y=\text{succ}(0))$	**(∀E**,4,6)
8	$\text{pred}(\text{succ}(x))=\text{succ}(x)-\text{succ}(0)$	**(∀E**,3,5)

9	succ(x)−succ(0)=pred(succ(x))	**(=.sym**,8)
10	$\exists Z(Z=X-Y)$	**(Theorem 3)**
11	$\exists Z$(Z=succ(x)−succ(0))	(**∀E**,5,7,10)
12	$\exists Z$(Z=pred(succ(x)))	(**=R**,9,11)
13	$X-Y=Z \leftrightarrow Z+Y=X$	**(D.−)**
14	succ(x)−succ(0)=pred(succ(x)) ↔ pred(succ(x))+succ(0)=succ(x)	(**∀E**,5,7,12,13)
15	pred(succ(x))+succ(0)=succ(x)	(**↔E**,9,14)
16	X+succ(Y) = succ($X+Y$)	**(+.succ)**
17	pred(succ(x))+succ(0) = succ(pred(succ(x))+0)	(**∀E**,6,12,16)
18	$X+0=X$	**(+.0)**
19	pred(succ(x))+0 = pred(succ(x))	(**∀E**,12,18)
20	pred(succ(x))+succ(0) = succ(pred(succ(x)))	(**=R**,17,19)
21	succ(pred(succ(x))) = succ(x)	(**=R**,15,20)
22	succ(X)=succ(Y) → $X=Y$	**(succ.=)**
23	succ(pred(succ(x)))=succ(x) → pred(succ(x))=x	(**∀E**,2,12,22)
24	pred(succ(x))=x	(**→E**,21,23)
25	pred(succ(X))=X	(**∀I**,1–24)

□

We turn now to the intended semantics of free arithmetic. We use a meaning function $\mathfrak{M}$ instead of a state as a primitive meaning function in this section, as $\mathfrak{M}$ maps the integer variables to the integers plus the error object ⊥. The states of this chapter are (intuitively) partial functions mapping the set of locations into the set of integers, and must be supplemented with "environments". In Section 5.2, we will see that our meaning functions are to be analyzed, in part, as the composition of an environment with a state.

We supplement the domain of discourse $\mathfrak{Z}$ (the integers) with the error object ⊥, taking the domain of discourse in the present chapter to be $\mathfrak{Z}+=\mathfrak{Z}\cup\{\bot\}$. (In the free logic literature, the integers are sometimes said to belong to the "inner" domain of existing individuals, whereas ⊥ is said to belong to the "outer" domain of nonexistants.) Let $\mathfrak{c}$ be any total function mapping the integer variables into $\mathfrak{Z}+$. As before, the domain of truth-values is $\mathfrak{Tv}=\{\mathfrak{t},\mathfrak{f}\}$. An *error assignment* $\mathfrak{N}$ is a function mapping, for each nonfull monadic predicate p, $p(\bot)$ into $\mathfrak{Tv}$, and, for each nonfull binary predicate q and each numeral m, $q(\bot,m)$, $q(m,\bot)$, and $q(\bot,\bot)$ into $\mathfrak{Tv}$. Possibly using $\mathfrak{N}$, $\mathfrak{M}$ extends $\mathfrak{c}\in$**Ivar**→$\mathfrak{Z}+$ to the other integer expressions, taking, for each integer expression e, $\mathfrak{M}[e]$ to be a member of $\mathfrak{Z}+$.[4] Using the error assignment $\mathfrak{N}$, $\mathfrak{M}$ is extended to the assertions, taking, for each assertion p, $\mathfrak{M}[p]$ to be a member of $\mathfrak{Tv}$.

[4] We place no restriction on the error assignment $\mathfrak{N}$. Equations (1)–(7) and every equation that we will introduce later, do not use $\mathfrak{N}$. However, we do not prohibit $\mathfrak{N}$'s use.

The free semantics of integer expressions and assertions is given in Figure 5.3. Notice that $\mathfrak{M}[\bot=\bot] = \mathfrak{t}$ in our semantics, thus preserving the law of identity in free arithmetic, but we might have either $\mathfrak{M}[\bot\geqslant\bot)] = \mathfrak{t}$ or $\mathfrak{M}[\bot\geqslant\bot)] = \mathfrak{f}$. We also have $\mathfrak{M}[\mathrm{I}(\bot)] = \mathfrak{M}[\exists X(X=\bot)] = \mathfrak{f}$ because there is no numeral m such that $\mathfrak{M}[m]=\bot$. We have not provided semantic equations for most of the nonprimitive symbols of arithmetic as these semantic equations can be readily constructed by analogy from the semantic equations (1) to (13).

(0) $\mathfrak{M}[x] = \mathfrak{c}[x]$

(1) $\mathfrak{M}[\bot] = \bot$

(2) $\mathfrak{M}[m] = m$

(3) $\mathfrak{M}[\mathrm{succ}(e)] = \mathrm{succ}(\mathfrak{M}[e])$ if $\mathfrak{M}[e]\in\mathfrak{Z}$
$\quad = \bot$ otherwise

(4) $\mathfrak{M}[e+e'] = \mathfrak{M}[e]+\mathfrak{M}[e']$ if $\mathfrak{M}[e],\mathfrak{M}[e']\in\mathfrak{Z}$
$\quad = \bot$ otherwise

⋮

(5) $\mathfrak{M}[e/e'] = \mathfrak{M}[e]/\mathfrak{M}[e']$ if $\sim\mathfrak{M}[e'] = 0$ and $\mathfrak{M}[e],\mathfrak{M}[e']\in\mathfrak{Z}$
$\quad = \bot$ otherwise

(6) $\mathfrak{M}[e \bmod e'] = \mathfrak{M}[e] \bmod \mathfrak{M}[e']$ if $\sim\mathfrak{M}[e'] = 0$ and $\mathfrak{M}[e],\mathfrak{M}[e']\in\mathfrak{Z}$
$\quad = \bot$ otherwise

(7) $\mathfrak{M}[\mathrm{cond}(e,e',e'')] = \mathfrak{M}[e']$ if $\mathfrak{M}[e] = 1$
$\quad = \mathfrak{M}[e'']$ if $\mathfrak{M}[e] = 0$
$\quad = \bot$ otherwise

⋮

(8) $\mathfrak{M}[e=e'] = \mathfrak{M}[e]=\mathfrak{M}[e']$

(9) $\mathfrak{M}[e\neq e'] = \mathfrak{M}[e] \neq \mathfrak{M}[e']$ if $\mathfrak{M}[e],\mathfrak{M}[e']\in\mathfrak{Z}$
$\quad = \mathfrak{N}[\bot\neq m]$ if $\mathfrak{M}[e] = \bot$ and $\mathfrak{M}[e'] = m$
$\quad = \mathfrak{N}[m\neq\bot]$ if $\mathfrak{M}[e] = m$ and $\mathfrak{M}[e'] = \bot$
$\quad = \mathfrak{N}[\bot\neq\bot]$ otherwise

(10) $\mathfrak{M}[e\geqslant e'] = \mathfrak{M}[e] \geqslant \mathfrak{M}[e']$ if $\mathfrak{M}[e],\mathfrak{M}[e']\in\mathfrak{Z}$
$\quad = \mathfrak{N}[\bot\geqslant m]$ if $\mathfrak{M}[e] = \bot$ and $\mathfrak{M}[e'] = m$
$\quad = \mathfrak{N}[m\geqslant\bot]$ if $\mathfrak{M}[e] = m$ and $\mathfrak{M}[e'] = \bot$
$\quad = \mathfrak{N}[\bot\geqslant\bot]$ otherwise

⋮

(11) $\mathfrak{M}[\sim p] = \sim\mathfrak{M}[p]$

(12) $\mathfrak{M}[p\&p'] = \mathfrak{M}[p]\ \&\ \mathfrak{M}[p']$

⋮

(13) $\mathfrak{M}[\forall Xp] =$ For each numeral m, $\mathfrak{M}[p[m\backslash X]]$

⋮

FIGURE 5.3. The free semantics of integer expressions and assertions.

The definitions of satisfiable, unsatisfiable, entails, valid, and other semantic concepts are as in Chapter 0. Appropriating the double turnstile $\models$ for the semantic consequence relation in free arithmetic, we have the following theorem:

SOUNDNESS OF FREE ARITHMETIC THEOREM: Let A be a set of assertions and p be an assertion. Then

$$\text{if } A \vdash p, \text{ then } A \models p$$

The proof is similar to that sketched for the Soundness of Arithmetic Theorem (the "standard" case) in Section 0.6. As a corollary, we have the following:

THEOREM ON EXTENSIONS BY FULL EXPLICIT DEFINITIONS: A theory T is satisfiable if T is an extension by full explicit definitions of free arithmetic.

5.1. SYNTAX

In this section, we develop the syntax of SP programs by incorporating function and procedure declarations and calls into the syntax of Chapter 1. We develop limited parameter-passing mechanisms allowing parameters to be passed by value to functions and by location to procedures. We do not permit recursion or "aliasing," as will be explained shortly.

The abstract syntax of integer expressions and assertions is much as in Chapter 0. We extend the syntax of integer expressions by adding the error constant $\bot$ to the list of integer expressions and by introducing the class of (integer) n-ary ($n \geq 0$) function variables **Fvar** with typical numbers f, ... (Normally, the error constant $\bot$ will occur rarely in assertions and never in the boolean or integer expressions of executable statements.)

The class of procedure variables **Pvar** has typical members pr, ... We understand the class of subprogram variables **Spvar** to be **Fvar** $\cup$ **Pvar** with typical members sp, . . . , and the class of variables **Var** to be **Ivar** $\cup$ **Spvar** with typical members v, ... Finally, we introduce the class of program variables **Pgva** with typical members pg, ... The abstract syntax is as follows:

Ivar: x, . . .
Fvar: f, . . .
Pvar: pr, . . .
Spvar: sp, . . .
$sp ::= f \mid pr$

Var: $v, \ldots$
$v ::= x \mid sp$
Pgva: $pg, \ldots$
Iexp: $e, \ldots$
$e ::= \bot \mid m \mid x \mid \mathrm{succ}(e) \mid \ldots \mid e{+}e' \mid \ldots \mid f(e_1, \ldots, e_n)$

We say that the integer expression $f(e_1, \ldots, e_n)$ is a *function call* and that the integer expressions $e_1, \ldots, e_n$ are *actual parameters*. We understand that a *degree* $\mathfrak{d}_f \geqslant 0$ is associated with each function variable f so that, for example, if $\mathfrak{d}_f = 2$, $f(e)$ and $f(e_1,e_2,e_3)$ are not well-formed integer expressions. Similarly, each procedure variable has a degree.

The abstract syntax of the set of assertions **Assn** and the set of boolean expressions **Bexp** is as in Chapter 1.

Assn: $p, q, r, \ldots$
$p ::= e{=}e' \mid \ldots \mid {\sim}p \mid p\&q \mid \ldots \mid \forall Xp \mid \exists Xp$
Bexp: $b, b', \ldots$
$b ::= e{=}e' \mid \ldots \mid {\sim}b \mid b\&b' \mid \ldots$

Turning to the syntax of SP programs, we supplement the syntax of the sets of statements **Stat** and annotated statements **Asta** with a Pascal-like syntax $pr(x_1, \ldots, x_n)$ for *procedure calls.*

Stat: $S, S', \ldots$
$S ::=$ **d** $\mid x{:=}e \mid S;S' \mid$ **if** b **then** S **else** $S' \mid$
while b **do** $S \mid pr(x_1, \ldots, x_n)$
Asta: $A, A', \ldots$
$A ::=$ **d** $\mid x{:=}e \mid$ **if** b **then** A **else** $A' \mid$
$\{p\}$ **while** b **do** $A \mid pr(x_1, \ldots, x_n)$

As one step towards blocking aliasing, we require that the *actual parameters* $x_1, \ldots, x_n$ be distinct in a procedure call $pr(x_1, \ldots, x_n)$.

The syntax of asserted statements (called asserted programs in Chapter 1) **Aprg** is as before.

Aprg: $AP, \ldots$
$AP ::= \{p\}A\{q\}$

As in Chapter 1, we will frequently ignore any intermediate assertions occurring in an asserted statement AP. The definitions of the *statement* of AP and a *specification* for AP are also as before.

Because declarations can occur in SP programs, a program is no longer simply a statement, as it was in Chapter 1. We introduce the block **Block,** function **Func,** procedure **Proc,** and program **Prog** declarations with a syntax designed (for simplicity) to eliminate nested subprogram declarations. A routine declaration **Rout** is either a function, procedure, or program declaration.

Block: $B, \ldots$
  B ::= **var** $y_1, \ldots, y_n$; **begin** AP **end**
Func: $Fu, \ldots$
  Fu ::= **function** $f(x_1, \ldots, x_n);B$
Proc: $Pr, \ldots$
  Pr ::= **procedure** $pr(x_1, \ldots, x_n);B$
Prog: $P, \ldots$
  P ::= **program** $pg;Fu_1; \ldots ;Fu_j;Pr_1; \ldots ;Pr_k;B$
Rout: $R, \ldots$
  R ::= $Fu \mid Pr \mid P$

Regarding blocks, the variables $y_1, \ldots, y_n$ must be (pairwise) distinct. The asserted statement AP is called the *body* of the block, and the statement of AP is called the *statement body* of the block.

In a function declaration, the part

function $f(x_1, \ldots, x_n)$

is said to be the *function heading declaring* the function *named* f in the program, and the integer variables $x_1, \ldots, x_n$ occurring in parentheses are called *formal parameters.* The variables y_i declared in a function are called *local variables.* The formal parameters must be distinct and disjoint from the local variables. The formal parameters and the local variables are said to be *declared in* the function. Entirely similar terminology and conventions are used in the case of a procedure declaration.

In a program declaration, the part

program pg

is called the *program heading,* and pg the *name* of the program. The variables (i.e., the function variables, the procedure variables, and the integer variables $y_1, \ldots, y_n$) declared within a program declaration are called *global variables.* We say that the global variables are *declared* in the program. The global (function, procedure) variables must be distinct. Abusing our terminology slightly, we call a routine's declaration minus its heading the *block* of the routine.

The *specification* of a program (a function, a procedure) is the specification bracketing its statement body. The *program statement* is the program stripped of its specification. The set of *input variables* of a program with specification $\langle p,q \rangle$ is $\mathfrak{ivar}[p]$, and the set of *output variables* is $\mathfrak{ivar}[q] - \mathfrak{ivar}[p]$. Much as in Chapter 1, we seek to prohibit changes to the values of input variables in the program block. We say that an integer variable x in a block is *syntactically vulnerable* if there is an assignment to x in that block or x is passed as the i-th actual parameter to a procedure pr and the i-th formal parameter of pr is syntactically vulnerable in pr's block. We prohibit programs in which the input variables in the program block are syntactically vulnerable.

Our scope rules, which we will explain more fully in the next paragraph, are a modified version of those found in Pascal. We prohibit occurrences of global integer variables within a subprogram, and we do not allow a subprogram to call itself or contain forward subprogram references. The first restriction blocks aliasing and the second prevents recursion. A variable occurring in the body of the program block must be declared (a global variable). The only variables that can occur in a function f's statement body are f's local variables and formal parameters, function variables previously defined in the program declaration, and f itself. When f occurs in the statement body of function f, f is understood to be governed by the syntax of integer variables (as opposed to the syntax of function variables), so that, for example, it can occur in the statement

$$f:=f+1$$

The only variables that can occur in the statement body of a procedure are its local variables and formal parameters, and previously defined subprogram variables.[5] In a subprogram call, because each subprogram variable has a definite degree, there are sure to be the same number of actual parameters as there are formal parameters in the heading of the invoked subprogram.

We distinguish between the "apparent scope" and the "scope" of a variable. The "apparent scope" rules are more similar to the scope rules in Pascal and will play a key role in some of the exercises at the end of this chapter. The *apparent scope* of an integer variable declared in the **var** declaration of a block is to be understood in a somewhat different manner than the apparent scope of a function or procedure variable. If x is a global integer variable and x is declared in a subprogram block, the subprogram is said to have *redeclared x*. The *apparent scope* of a global integer variable x consists of the program block and each subprogram block in which x is not redeclared. The *apparent scope* of a variable declared in a subprogram block consists of that block alone. The *scope* of an integer variable declared in a routine's block consists of that block alone. In other words, subprograms that do not redeclare a global integer variable x are in the apparent scope of x but not in x's scope because references to global integer variables in subprograms are prohibited. On the other hand, the *apparent scope* of a global subprogram variable sp consists of all subprogram blocks and the program block, whereas

[5] By "subprogram variables", we mean, of course, variables that are used to "name" subprograms. We do not consider the operation and predicate symbols previously defined in free arithmetic (i.e., prior to a program's declaration) to be variables.

the *scope* consists of all subprogram blocks that are declared after *sp* and the program block. In other words, the apparent scope of a variable is a Pascal-like extension of its scope.[6]

To simplify our semantics and deductive system, we impose some additional restrictions on function and procedure declarations, and, accordingly, introduce some new terminology. We say that an integer variable x is *new in* a subprogram block if x is neither a global integer variable nor an integer variable declared in that subprogram block. An integer expression e (assertion p) is said to be *in* a set of integer variables Iv if $\mathfrak{ivar}[e] \subset Iv$ ($\mathfrak{ivar}[p] \subset Iv$).

Turning to the restrictions on functions, first we prohibit global side effects in the body of a function f and preserve the initial values of the formal parameters at the time f is called by restricting assignments to local variables and the function variable f itself. Prohibiting assignments to the formal parameters has much the same advantage of prohibiting the setting of the program's input variables.[7] Second, we stipulate that the precondition of a function f's body be of the form

$$\mathrm{I}(x_1)\& \ . \ . \ . \ \&\mathrm{I}(x_n) \ \& \ p$$

where the x_i's are f's formal parameters, and p is an assertion in the set of formal parameters $\{x_i\}$. Third, the postcondition of a function f's body must be of the form

$$f = e(x_1, \ . \ . \ . \ ,x_n)$$

where the integer expression $e(x_1, \ . \ . \ . \ ,x_n)$ is in the set of formal parameters $\{x_i\}$.

Regarding procedures, first we mandate that a procedure's precondition be of the form

$$x_1 = z_1 \ \& \ . \ . \ . \ \& \ x_n = z_n \ \& \ q$$

where the x_i's are the formal parameters, the z_i's are distinct and new in the procedure block, and q is an assertion in the set of formal parameters $\{x_i\}$. Intuitively, the z_i's are the initial values of the x_i's and are called *history*

[6] If the scope of an integer variable was extended so as to be coextensive with its apparent scope, the Hoare Axiomatization (Section 5.3) would be unsound because of aliasing. This extension of the concept of scope for integer variables would require no modifications in the operational semantics presented in Section 5.2. In the case of subprogram variables, however, this extension would require major changes in the operational semantics, as the static storage management scheme presented in the next section could not handle recursion.

[7] Due to the prohibition against assignments to formal parameters in function bodies, this parameter passing mechanism is sometimes referred to as "call by constant-value". See Footnote 1 in this chapter.

variables. Second, we stipulate that the postcondition be of the form

$$x_1 = e_1(z_1, \ldots, z_n) \,\&\, \ldots \,\&\, x_n = e_n(z_1, \ldots, z_n)$$

where the $e_i(z_1, \ldots, z_n)$'s are integer expressions in $\{z_i\}$.

We close this section with an example. **Program** *illustration* sets *b* (*s*) to the larger (smaller) of *u* ** *v* and *w* ** *z* using the programmer-defined **function** *ex* and the **procedure** *swap*. The function *ex* computes *ex*(*x*,*y*) = *x* ** *y* using the method of successive multiplications, and the **procedure** *swap* exchanges its parameters.

```
program illustration;
function ex(x,y);
      var t;
      begin
      {I(x) & I(y) & y≥0}
      ex := 1;
      {I(t) & I(1) & I(x) & I(y) & ex=x**(y−t) & 0≤t≤y}
      for t:=y downto 1 do
          ex := ex*x
      {ex=x**y}
      end;
procedure swap(x,y);
      var t;
      begin
      {x=zx & y=zy & I(x) & I(y)}
      t := x;
      x := y;
      y := t
      {x=zy & y=zx}
      end;
var b,s,u,v,w,z;
begin
{I(u) & I(v) & v≥0 & I(w) & I(z) & z≥0}
b := ex(u,v);
s := ex(w,z);
if s>b then swap(b,s)
{b=max(u**v,w**z) & s=min(u**v,w**z)}
end.
```

The following diagram depicts the apparent scope (*a*) and the scope (*s*) of each variable declared in **program** *illustration* and its subprograms. For example, the apparent scope of the function variable *ex* (declared in **program** *illustration*) consists of **function** *ex*'s block, **procedure** *swap*'s block, and

program *illustration*'s block, whereas its scope consists only of *swap*'s and *illustration*'s blocks.

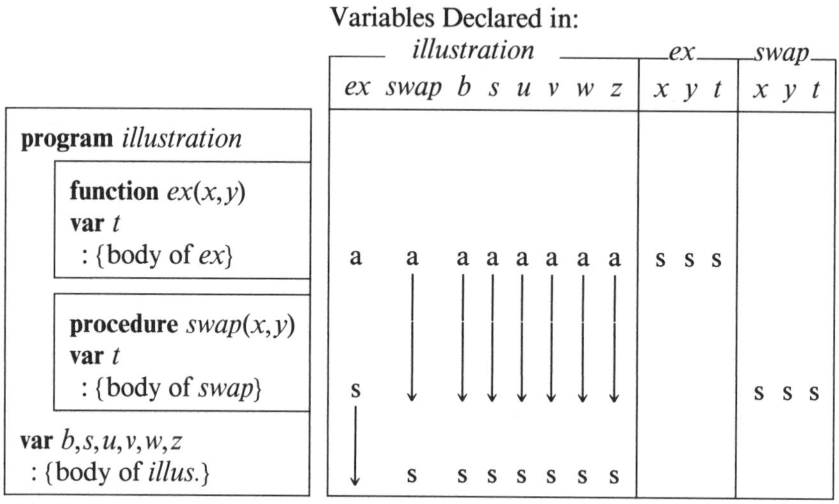
Variables Declared in:
illustration
ex
swap
ex swap b s u v w z
x y t
x y t
program illustration
function ex(x,y)
var t
: {body of ex}
procedure swap(x,y)
var t
: {body of swap}
var b,s,u,v,w,z
: {body of illus.}
a a a a a a a a
s s s
s
s s s
s s s s s s s

5.2. OPERATIONAL SEMANTICS: STATES AND ENVIRONMENTS

In this section, we supplement the states of Chapter 1 with subprogram stores and, most importantly, environments. We also refine the meaning function $\mathfrak{M}$, which we introduced in Section 5.0, understanding it to be a product function consisting of an error assignment, an environment, a function and a procedure store, and a state. As in Pascal, variables are statically or lexically scoped. Because we do not permit recursion, we use a static storage management scheme. That is, no run-time allocation of storage is required.

In developing the semantics, we need some additional terminology and notation. Let $f \in A \rightarrow C$ be a function mapping A into C and $B \subset A$. We write $\mathfrak{domain}[f]$ for the *domain* of f, A, and $\mathfrak{image}[f]$ for the *image* of f, $\{f(x): x \in A\}$. We also write $f \upharpoonright B$ for the *restriction of* f to B, $\{\langle x, f(x)\rangle : x \in B\}$.

An *environment* maps a variable to an *address* (sometimes called a *location*).[8] Intuitively, an address is given by a positive integer, and it can contain a function or procedure declaration or an integer variable. More formally, the set of *addresses* **Addr** is the set of positive integers with typical members *ad*, ... A *function store* $\mathfrak{fs}$ *(procedure store* $\mathfrak{ps}$, *state* $\mathfrak{s}$*)* is a partial function mapping the set of addresses to the set of function declarations (the set of procedure declarations, $\mathfrak{Z}$+).

[8] Some researchers prefer the term *location* to that of *address* because of the perceived connotation of the latter term. Both terms are in common usage in the literature.

$$\mathfrak{en} \in \textbf{Env} = \textbf{Var} \to \textbf{Addr}$$

$$\mathfrak{fs} \in \textbf{Fstore} = \textbf{Addr} \to \textbf{Func}$$

$$\mathfrak{ps} \in \textbf{Pstore} = \textbf{Addr} \to \textbf{Proc}$$

$$\mathfrak{s} \in \textbf{States} = \textbf{Addr} \to \mathfrak{Z}+$$

We say that a function store $\mathfrak{fs}$ is $\mathfrak{en}$-$\mathfrak{ps}$-*closed* if $\mathfrak{domain}[\mathfrak{en} \upharpoonright \textbf{Fvar}]$ is a superset of the set of function variables occurring in

$$\{A_{\mathfrak{fs}[\mathfrak{en}[f]]}: f \in \mathfrak{domain}[\mathfrak{en} \upharpoonright \textbf{Fvar}]\} \cup \{A_{\mathfrak{ps}[\mathfrak{en}[pr]]}: pr \in \mathfrak{domain}[\mathfrak{en} \upharpoonright \textbf{Pvar}]\}$$

where

$$A_{\mathfrak{fs}[\mathfrak{en}[f]]} \; (A_{\mathfrak{ps}[\mathfrak{en}[pr]]})$$

is the body of the function (procedure) declaration stored at address $\mathfrak{fs}[\mathfrak{en}[f]]$ ($\mathfrak{ps}[\mathfrak{en}[pr]]$). Similarly, a procedure store $\mathfrak{ps}$ is $\mathfrak{en}$-*closed* if $\mathfrak{domain}[\mathfrak{en} \upharpoonright \textbf{Pvar}]$ is a superset of the set of procedure variables occurring in

$$\{A_{\mathfrak{ps}[\mathfrak{en}[pr]]}: pr \in \mathfrak{domain}[\mathfrak{en} \upharpoonright \textbf{Pvar}]\}$$

We define the environment of a block by cases, depending on whether it is the (main) program block, a function block, or a procedure block. If the block is the program block in the declaration

program *pg*;
  Fu_1; . . . ; Fu_j; Pr_1; . . . ; Pr_k; **var** x_1, . . . ,x_m; **begin** *S* **end**

the (*static* and *run-time*) *program (block) environment*, also known as the *global environment*, is $\mathfrak{en}_g$. The global environment $\mathfrak{en}_g$ has the j functions declared stored in locations 1 to j, the k procedures declared stored in locations $j+1$ to $j+k$, and the m locations from $j+k+1$ to $j+k+m$ set aside for storing the m global integer variables.[9]

$$\mathfrak{en}_g = \{\langle f_i, i\rangle: 1 \leq i \leq j\} \cup \{\langle \mathfrak{pr}_i, j+i\rangle: 1 \leq i \leq k\} \cup \\ \{\langle x_i, j+k+i\rangle: 1 \leq i \leq m\}$$

The description of the environment of a function block is a bit more involved. Let f be the a-th function declared in the program block with the

[9] Environments, states, and stores are functions. In the following definitions, we represent these functions by their graphs (sets of ordered pairs) so that new functions can be defined using the familiar set operations.

heading $f(x_1, \ldots, x_n)$ and body

var $w_1, \ldots, w_b$; **begin** S **end**

Let SV be the set of subprogram variables declared in the program block, and Y be the set of global integer variables that are not redeclared in function f. Let h be the number of variables declared in the program block and in every function $f_1, \ldots, f_{a-1}$ declared before function f *plus* $a-1$ (the number of locations required to store the values returned by the first $a-1$ functions). In the storage allocated for function f, space must be allocated for formal parameters (because parameters are passed to functions by value), for local variables, and for the function name f itself (because f is treated as if it were a local variable through which the function returns its value). The formal parameters are stored first, the local variables next, followed by the integer variable f (which we denote by f_{ivar} when the need arises to distinguish it from the corresponding function variable f). So, the contribution to function f's environment from its formal parameters is as follows:

$$E_X = \{\langle x_i, h+i\rangle : 1 \leq i \leq n\}$$

The contribution to its environment from its local variables is

$$E_W = \{\langle w_i, h+n+i\rangle : 1 \leq i \leq b\}$$

and the contribution from its own name is

$$E_f = \{\langle f, h+n+b+1\rangle\}$$

Then, the (*static* and *run-time*) *environment* en_f *of (the function block of)* f is[10]

$$\mathrm{en}_f = \mathrm{en}_g \restriction (SV \cup Y) \cup E_X \cup E_W \cup E_f$$

The environment for a procedure block is somewhat similar to that of a function block except that the call by reference mechanism requires that the contribution of a procedure's parameters to its environment be determined at run time. Moreover, in the storage allocated for a procedure, space is provided for storing the initial values of the formal parameters but not the formal parameters themselves (because parameters are passed to procedures by reference). Likewise, no space is set aside for the procedure name because a procedure name, unlike a function name, cannot be assigned—or be used to return—an integer value.

[10] We could define en_f so that its domain would consist of the variables whose scope includes f's body. Defining en_f as in the text enables the reader to tackle Exercises 12 and 17 at the end of this chapter without redefining en_f. Similar remarks apply to the definition of en_{pr}, which follows.

Let *pr* be the *a*-th procedure block with heading $pr(x_1, \ldots, x_n)$ and body

$$\textbf{var } w_1, \ldots, w_b; \textbf{ begin } AP \textbf{ end}$$

where the precondition of $AP \equiv x_1 = z_1 \,\&\, \ldots \,\&\, x_n = z_n \,\&\, q$. Let SV be as before, and Y be the set of global variables that are not redeclared in procedure *pr*. Let h be the number of variables declared in the program block, in every function block, and in every procedure declared before procedure *pr* *plus* the number of function declarations. The storage required for *pr*'s environment is for the initial values of its formal parameters and its local variables.

$$E_Z = \{\langle z_i, h+i\rangle: \quad 1 \leqslant i \leqslant n\}$$

$$E_W = \{\langle w_i, h+n+i\rangle: \quad 1 \leqslant i \leqslant b\}$$

The *static environment* $\mathfrak{en}_{pr}$ of *(the procedure block of) pr* is as follows:

$$\mathfrak{en}_{pr} = \mathfrak{en}_{\mathbf{g}} \restriction (SV \cup Y) \cup E_Z \cup E_W$$

A subprogram store assigns a subprogram declaration to an address. If there are j function declarations in the program declaration, the function store $\mathfrak{fs}$ assigns 1 the first function declaration $Fu_1, \ldots,$ and j the j-th function declaration Fu_j.

$$\mathfrak{fs} = \{\langle i, Fu_i\rangle: \quad 1 \leqslant i \leqslant j\}$$

Similarly, if there are k procedure declarations $Pr_1, \ldots, Pr_k$, the procedure store $\mathfrak{ps}$ assigns the k locations following those set aside for the function declarations to the procedure declarations.

$$\mathfrak{ps} = \{\langle j+i, Pr_i\rangle: \quad 1 \leqslant i \leqslant k\}$$

We turn next to refining the meaning function $\mathfrak{M}$ described in Section 5.0. We now understand $\mathfrak{M}$ to be a 5-tuple consisting of an error assignment, an environment, a function store, a procedure store, and a state.

$$\mathfrak{M} = \langle \mathfrak{N}, \mathfrak{en}, \mathfrak{fs}, \mathfrak{ps}, \mathfrak{s}\rangle$$

We require that the domains of $\mathfrak{image}[\mathfrak{en} \restriction \mathbf{Ivar}]$, $\mathfrak{image}[\mathfrak{en} \restriction \mathbf{Fvar}]$, and $\mathfrak{image}[\mathfrak{en} \restriction \mathbf{Pvar}]$ be (pairwise) disjoint, $\mathfrak{fs}$ be $\mathfrak{en}$-$\mathfrak{ps}$-closed, $\mathfrak{ps}$ be $\mathfrak{en}$-closed, and $\mathfrak{image}[\mathfrak{en} \restriction \mathbf{Fvar}] = \mathfrak{domain}[\mathfrak{fs}]$, and $\mathfrak{image}[\mathfrak{en} \restriction \mathbf{Pvar}] = \mathfrak{domain}[\mathfrak{ps}]$. We say that we are *refining* the meaning of the meaning function, as opposed to *redefining* it because, when applied to an integer variable x, a meaning function $\mathfrak{M}$ is simply the composition of a state $\mathfrak{s}$ with an environment $\mathfrak{en}$.

$$\mathfrak{M}[x] = \mathfrak{s}[\mathfrak{en}[x]]$$

understanding that, if $\mathrm{en}[x]$ is not in the domain of state $\mathfrak{s}$, $\mathfrak{M}[x] = \perp$.[11] The introduction of an environment, a function store, and a state enables us to handle the meaning of user-defined functions. Let $\mathfrak{M}$ be as above, f be a user-defined function, and

$$S_{\mathfrak{fs}[\mathrm{en}[f]]}$$

be the statement body of the function declaration $\mathfrak{fs}[\mathrm{en}[f]]$ stored in address $\mathrm{en}[f]$. The meaning of the function call $f(e_1, \ldots, e_n)$ (an integer expression) is as follows:

$$\begin{aligned}\mathfrak{M}[f(e_1, \ldots, e_n)] &= \mathfrak{M}''[f] \text{ if } \mathfrak{M}[e_i] \in Z \text{ for each } i \text{ from 1 to } n \\ &\qquad \text{and } \mathfrak{M}'[S_{\mathfrak{fs}[\mathrm{en}[f]]}] \text{ is defined,} \\ &= \perp \text{ otherwise}\end{aligned}$$

where $\mathfrak{M}$ is as before,

$\mathfrak{M}'' = \langle \mathfrak{N}, \mathrm{en}_f, \mathfrak{fs}, \mathfrak{ps}, \mathfrak{M}'[S_{\mathfrak{fs}[\mathrm{en}[f]]}] \rangle$

$\mathfrak{M}' = \langle \mathfrak{N}, \mathrm{en}_f, \mathfrak{fs}, \mathfrak{ps}, \mathfrak{s}' \rangle$,

$\mathfrak{M}'[S_{\mathfrak{fs}[\mathrm{en}[f]]}]$ is as defined in Figure 5.5 (see text, which follows), and

$\mathfrak{s}' = \mathfrak{s}\{\mathfrak{M}[e_1], \ldots, \mathfrak{M}[e_n] \backslash \mathrm{en}_f[x_1], \ldots, \mathrm{en}_f[x_n]\}$

Intuitively, the state $\mathfrak{s}'$ is the first state entered after function f is called, and is like the calling state $\mathfrak{s}$ except that the actual parameters have been plugged in for the formal parameters. $\mathfrak{M}'$ is the meaning function inside f when f is first entered, $\mathfrak{M}'[S_{\mathfrak{fs}[\mathrm{en}[f]]}]$ is the state inside f just before f exits, and $\mathfrak{M}''$ is the meaning function inside f just before f exits. A user-defined function f is strict because each actual parameter e_i is passed by value to f (i.e., each e_i is evaluated whenever f is called).

$\mathfrak{M}$ is extended to the integer expressions by supplementing clauses (3) to (7) in Figure 5.3 with the clause for function calls, seen previously, and is extended to the boolean expressions and assertions exactly as in Figure 5.3. The refined semantics of integer expressions and assertions are summarized in Figure 5.4.

Before turning to the operational semantics of statements, we introduce some additional notation. The set of *outermost integer expressions* $\mathfrak{E}[p]$ in an assertion p is defined inductively as follows:

$$\begin{aligned}&\mathfrak{E}[e{=}e'] = \{e, e'\} \\ &\vdots \\ &\mathfrak{E}[\sim q] = \mathfrak{E}[q] \\ &\mathfrak{E}[q \& r] = \mathfrak{E}[q] \cup \mathfrak{E}[r] \\ &\vdots \\ &\mathfrak{E}[\forall X p] = \cup_{m \in \mathfrak{Z}} \mathfrak{E}[p[m \backslash X]] \\ &\vdots\end{aligned}$$

[11] If x has not been declared in the program block, then $\mathrm{en}_g[x] \notin \mathfrak{domain}[\mathfrak{s}]$. Similarly, in subprogram sp, if x is not a global variable and has not been declared in sp, then $\mathrm{en}_{sp}[x] \notin \mathfrak{domain}[\mathfrak{s}]$.

(0) $\mathfrak{M}[x] = \mathfrak{s}[\mathrm{en}[x]]$

(1) $\mathfrak{M}[\bot] = \bot$

(2) $\mathfrak{M}[m] = m$

(3) $\mathfrak{M}[\mathrm{succ}(e)] = \mathrm{succ}(\mathfrak{M}[e])$ if $\mathfrak{M}[e] \in \mathfrak{Z}$
$= \bot$ otherwise

(4) $\mathfrak{M}[e+e'] = \mathfrak{M}[e]+\mathfrak{M}[e']$ if $\mathfrak{M}[e], \mathfrak{M}[e'] \in \mathfrak{Z}$
$= \bot$ otherwise

⋮

(5) $\mathfrak{M}[e/e'] = \mathfrak{M}[e]/\mathfrak{M}[e']$ if $\sim\mathfrak{M}[e'] = 0$ and $\mathfrak{M}[e], \mathfrak{M}[e'] \in \mathfrak{Z}$
$= \bot$ otherwise

(6) $\mathfrak{M}[e \bmod e'] = \mathfrak{M}[e] \bmod \mathfrak{M}[e']$ if $\sim\mathfrak{M}[e'] = 0$ and $\mathfrak{M}[e], \mathfrak{M}[e'] \in \mathfrak{Z}$
$= \bot$ otherwise

(7) $\mathfrak{M}[\mathrm{cond}(e,e',e'')] = \mathfrak{M}[e']$ if $\mathfrak{M}[e] = 1$
$= \mathfrak{M}[e'']$ if $\mathfrak{M}[e] = 0$
$= \bot$ otherwise

⋮

(8) $\mathfrak{M}[f(e_1, \ldots, e_n)] = \mathfrak{M}''[f]$ if $\mathfrak{M}[e_i] \in \mathfrak{Z}$ for each i from 1 to n
and $\mathfrak{M}'[S_{\mathfrak{fs}[\mathrm{en}[f]]}]$ is defined
$= \bot$ otherwise

where $\mathfrak{M}'' = \langle \mathfrak{N}, \mathrm{en}_f, \mathfrak{fs}, \mathfrak{ps}, \mathfrak{M}'[S_{\mathfrak{fs}[\mathrm{en}[f]]}] \rangle$
$\mathfrak{M}' = \langle \mathfrak{N}, \mathrm{en}_f, \mathfrak{fs}, \mathfrak{ps}, \mathfrak{s}' \rangle$
$\mathfrak{s}' = \mathfrak{s}\{\mathfrak{M}[e_1], \ldots, \mathfrak{M}[e_n] \backslash \mathrm{en}_f[x_1], \ldots, \mathrm{en}_f[x_n]\}$
$S_{\mathfrak{fs}[\mathrm{en}[f]]}$ is the statement body of f's declaration

⋮

(9) $\mathfrak{M}[e{=}e'] = \mathfrak{M}[e] = \mathfrak{M}[e']$

(10) $\mathfrak{M}[e \neq e'] = \mathfrak{M}[e] \neq \mathfrak{M}[e']$ if $\mathfrak{M}[e], \mathfrak{M}[e'] \in \mathfrak{Z}$
$= \mathfrak{N}[\bot \neq m]$ if $\mathfrak{M}[e] = \bot$ and $\mathfrak{M}[e'] = m$
$= \mathfrak{N}[m \neq \bot]$ if $\mathfrak{M}[e] = m$ and $\mathfrak{M}[e'] = \bot$
$= \mathfrak{N}[\bot \neq \bot]$ otherwise

(11) $\mathfrak{M}[e \geqslant e'] = \mathfrak{M}[e] \geqslant \mathfrak{M}[e']$ if $\mathfrak{M}[e], \mathfrak{M}[e'] \in \mathfrak{Z}$
$= \mathfrak{N}[\bot \geqslant m]$ if $\mathfrak{M}[e] = \bot$ and $\mathfrak{M}[e'] = m$
$= \mathfrak{N}[m \geqslant \bot]$ if $\mathfrak{M}[e] = m$ and $\mathfrak{M}[e'] = \bot$
$= \mathfrak{N}[\bot \geqslant \bot]$ otherwise

⋮

(12) $\mathfrak{M}[\sim p] = \sim\mathfrak{M}[p]$

(13) $\mathfrak{M}[p \& p'] = \mathfrak{M}[p] \& \mathfrak{M}[p']$

⋮

(14) $\mathfrak{M}[\forall X p] =$ for each numeral m, $\mathfrak{M}[p[m \backslash X]]$

⋮

FIGURE 5.4. The refined free semantics of integer expressions and assertions.

$\mathfrak{M}[\mathbf{d}] = \mathfrak{s}$
$\mathfrak{M}[x{:=}e] = \mathfrak{s}\{\mathfrak{M}[e]\backslash \mathrm{en}[x]\}$ if $\mathfrak{M}[e] \in \mathfrak{Z}$
$\mathfrak{M}[S;S'] = \mathfrak{M}'[S']$, where $\mathfrak{M}' = \langle \mathfrak{N}, \mathrm{en}, \mathfrak{fs}, \mathfrak{ps}, \mathfrak{M}[S]\rangle$
$\mathfrak{M}[\textbf{if } b \textbf{ then } S \textbf{ else } S'] = \mathfrak{M}[S]$ if $\mathfrak{M}[\mathfrak{E}[b]] \subset \mathfrak{Z}$ and $\mathfrak{M}[b] = \mathrm{t}$
$= \mathfrak{M}[S']$ if $\mathfrak{M}[\mathfrak{E}[b]] \subset \mathfrak{Z}$ and $\mathfrak{M}[b] = \mathrm{f}$
$\mathfrak{M}[\textbf{while } b \textbf{ do } S] = \mathfrak{s}*$ if there is a finite sequence of states $\langle \mathfrak{s}_0, \ldots, \mathfrak{s}_m\rangle$ $(m \geq 0)$ such that $\mathfrak{s} = \mathfrak{s}_0$, $\mathfrak{s}* = \mathfrak{s}_m$, $\mathfrak{M}_i = \langle \mathfrak{N}, \mathrm{en}, \mathfrak{fs}, \mathfrak{ps}, \mathfrak{s}_i\rangle$ and $\mathfrak{M}_i[\mathfrak{E}[b]] \subset \mathfrak{Z}$ for each i from 1 to m, $\mathfrak{M}_m[b] = \mathrm{f}$, and $\mathfrak{M}_i[b] = \mathrm{t}$, and $\mathfrak{s}_{i+1} = \mathfrak{M}_i[S]$ for each i from 0 to $m-1$.
$\mathfrak{M}[pr(x'_1, \ldots, x'_n)] = \mathfrak{M}'[S_{\mathfrak{ps}[\mathrm{en}[pr]]}] \upharpoonright \mathrm{image}*[\mathrm{en}]$
where $\mathfrak{M}' = \langle \mathfrak{N}, \mathrm{en}+_{pr}, \mathfrak{fs}, \mathfrak{ps}, \mathfrak{s}'\rangle$
$\mathrm{en}+_{pr} = \mathrm{en}_{pr} \cup \{\langle x_i, \mathrm{en}[x'_i]\rangle : x_i\ (1 \leq i \leq n)$ a formal parameter of $pr\}$,
$\mathfrak{s}' = \mathfrak{s}\{\mathfrak{M}[x'_1], \ldots, \mathfrak{M}[x'_n]\backslash \mathrm{en}+_{pr}[z_1], \ldots, \mathrm{en}+_{pr}[z_n]\}$,
the z_i's are the new integer variables,
$S_{\mathfrak{ps}[\mathrm{en}[pr]]}$ is the statement body of pr's declaration, and
$\mathrm{image}*[\mathrm{en}]$ is as described in the text.

FIGURE 5.5. The operational semantics of SP statements.

If $\mathfrak{E}$ is a set of integer expressions, we understand $\mathfrak{M}[\mathfrak{E}]$ to be $\{\mathfrak{M}[e]: e \in \mathfrak{E}\}$. The purpose of introducing the concept of outermost integer expressions is to "expose" those integer expressions within a boolean expression or an assertion that might evaluate to $\perp$.

Figure 5.5 supplies the operational semantics of statements. This semantics is somewhat more involved than that of Chapter 1 because we must handle not only procedure calls, but also allow for execution-time errors arising from referencing undefined integer variables and attempting to compute undefined integer and boolean expressions.[12] The clause for procedure calls is the most complex.

Let k be the number of procedures declared in the main program and $\mathrm{image}*[\mathrm{en}_{\mathbf{g}}] = \mathrm{image}[\mathrm{en}_{\mathbf{g}}]$. Understand

$$\mathrm{image}*[\mathrm{en}_{pr_k}] = \mathrm{image}[\mathrm{en}_{pr_k}] \cup \mathrm{image}[\mathrm{en}_{\mathbf{g}}]$$

And, for each i such that $k-1 \geq i \geq 1$,

$$\mathrm{image}*[\mathrm{en}_{pr_i}] = \mathrm{image}[\mathrm{en}_{pr_i}] \cup \mathrm{image}*[\mathrm{en}_{pr_{i+1}}]$$

If **procedure** pr_i calls **procedure** $pr_{i'}$, $(1 \leq i' < i)$, the addresses in $\mathrm{image}*[\mathrm{en}_{pr_i}]$ should retain their values after **procedure** $pr_{i'}$, returns control to **procedure**

[12] As noted in Chapter 1, the dummy statement **d** cannot be defined in terms of the assignment statement $x{:=}x$ because, if $\mathfrak{M}[x] = \perp$, we have $\mathfrak{M}[\mathbf{d}] = \mathfrak{s}$ but $\mathfrak{M}[x{:=}x]$ is undefined.

pr_i. We have the following:

$$\mathfrak{M}[pr(x'_1, \ldots, x'_n)] = \mathfrak{M}'[S_{\mathfrak{ps}[\mathrm{en}[pr]]}] \restriction \mathrm{image}*[\mathrm{en}]$$

where $\mathfrak{M}' = \langle \mathfrak{N}, \mathrm{en}+_{pr}, \mathfrak{fs}, \mathfrak{ps}, \mathfrak{s}' \rangle$

$\mathrm{en}+_{pr} = \mathrm{en}_{pr} \cup$

$\{\langle x_i, \mathrm{en}[x'_i]\rangle : x_i (1 \leq i \leq n)$ a formal parameter of $pr\}$,

$\mathfrak{s}' = \mathfrak{s}\{\mathfrak{M}[x'_1], \ldots, \mathfrak{M}[x'_n] \backslash \mathrm{en}+_{pr}[z_1], \ldots, \mathrm{en}+_{pr}[z_n]\}$

the z_i's are the new integer variables, and

$S_{\mathfrak{ps}[\mathrm{en}[pr]]}$ is the statement body of *pr*'s declaration.

Intuitively, $\mathfrak{M}$ is the meaning function in the calling program at the time *pr* is called, $\mathfrak{M}'$ is the meaning function inside *pr* when it is first entered, $\mathrm{en}+_{pr}$ is the environment of *pr* when the actual parameters (the x'_i's) are plugged in for the formal parameters (the x_i's), and $\mathfrak{s}'$ is the state in *pr* when it is first entered after initializing the history variables (the z_i's) to the current values of the actual parameters.

In the clause for $\mathfrak{M}[pr(x'_1, \ldots, x'_n)]$, we restrict the state resulting from the call of *pr* to image*[en] so that local variables of *pr* will be undefined if *pr* is called again. If we did not restrict the resulting state, our local variables would have the problematic semantics of ALGOL60 **OWN** variables, which do not have initial values but do retain their values from one call to the next.

The environment $\mathrm{en}+_{pr}$ is called the *run-time environment* of *pr* when called by $pr(x'_1, \ldots, x'_n)$ in environment en. Note that a procedure may have any number of run-time environments, whereas a program or a function (in a program) has at most *one* run-time environment. For example, in **program** *illustration,* the static and run-time environment en_{g} in the main program has the following values:

$\mathrm{en}_{\mathrm{g}}[ex] = 1$	$\mathrm{en}_{\mathrm{g}}[swap] = 2$	$\mathrm{en}_{\mathrm{g}}[b] = 3$	$\mathrm{en}_{\mathrm{g}}[s] = 4$
$\mathrm{en}_{\mathrm{g}}[u] = 5$	$\mathrm{en}_{\mathrm{g}}[v] = 6$	$\mathrm{en}_{\mathrm{g}}[w] = 7$	$\mathrm{en}_{\mathrm{g}}[z] = 8$

Because neither subprogram redeclares a variable declared in the program block, the environments of the subprograms are extensions of the global environment en_{g}. The static and run-time environment en_{ex} in the **function** *ex* extends en_{g} so that

$\mathrm{en}_{ex}[x] = 9$	$\mathrm{en}_{ex}[y] = 10$	$\mathrm{en}_{ex}[t] = 11$	$\mathrm{en}_{ex}[ex_{\mathrm{ivar}}] = 12$

The first time function *ex* is called (with *u* and *v* as the actual parameters), the state $\mathfrak{s}$—immediately upon entering *ex*—has $\mathfrak{s}[9] = \mathfrak{s}[5]$ and $\mathfrak{s}[10] = \mathfrak{s}[6]$. For example, if at the beginning of **program** illustration's execution the variable *u* (*v*, *w*, *z*) had the value 5 (3, 2, 7) and all other variables were undefined, the following diagram depicts the environments, the stores, and the state $\mathfrak{s}$ immediately on entering *ex* the first time that it is called:

		Named by in Environment		
Address	Contents	$\mathfrak{en}_g$	$\mathfrak{en}_{ex}$	$\mathfrak{en}_{swap}$ (static)
1	$\mathfrak{fs}[1]$=**function** *ex*	*ex*	*ex*	*ex*
2	$\mathfrak{ps}[2]$=**procedure** *swap*	*swap*	*swap*	*swap*
3	$\mathfrak{s}[3]=\perp$	*b*	*b*	*b*
4	$\mathfrak{s}[4]=\perp$	*s*	*s*	*s*
5	$\mathfrak{s}[5]=5$	*u*	*u*	*u*
6	$\mathfrak{s}[6]=3$	*v*	*v*	*v*
7	$\mathfrak{s}[7]=2$	*w*	*w*	*w*
8	$\mathfrak{s}[8]=7$	*z*	*z*	*z*
9	$\mathfrak{s}[9]=5$		*x*	
10	$\mathfrak{s}[10]=3$		*y*	
11	$\mathfrak{s}[11]=\perp$		*t*	
12	$\mathfrak{s}[12]=\perp$		$ex_{\mathfrak{ivar}}$	
13	$\mathfrak{s}[13]=\perp$			*t*

The second time that *ex* is called (with *w* and *z* the actual parameters), the initial state $\mathfrak{s}$ has $\mathfrak{s}[9] = \mathfrak{s}[7] = 2$, and $\mathfrak{s}[10] = \mathfrak{s}[8] = 7$. The static environment $\mathfrak{en}_{swap}$ in the **procedure** *swap* extends $\mathfrak{en}_g$ so that $\mathfrak{en}_{swap}[t] = 13$. When *swap* is called (with *b* and *s* the actual parameters), the run-time environment $\mathfrak{en}+_{swap}$ extends $\mathfrak{en}_{swap}$ so that $\mathfrak{en}+_{swap}[x] = 3$, and $\mathfrak{en}+_{swap}[y] = 4$. The following diagram depicts the environments, the stores, and the state $\mathfrak{s}$ immediately on entering **procedure** *swap*:

		Named by in Environment		
Address	Contents	$\mathfrak{en}_g$	$\mathfrak{en}_{ex}$	$\mathfrak{en}+_{swap}$ (run-time)
1	$\mathfrak{fs}[1]$=**function** *ex*	*ex*	*ex*	*ex*
2	$\mathfrak{ps}[2]$=**procedure** *swap*	*swap*	*swap*	*swap*
3	$\mathfrak{s}[3]=125$	*b*	*b*	*b*, *x*
4	$\mathfrak{s}[4]=128$	*s*	*s*	*s*, *y*
5	$\mathfrak{s}[5]=5$	*u*	*u*	*u*
6	$\mathfrak{s}[6]=3$	*v*	*v*	*v*
7	$\mathfrak{s}[7]=2$	*w*	*w*	*w*
8	$\mathfrak{s}[8]=7$	*z*	*z*	*z*
9	$\mathfrak{s}[9]=\perp$		*x*	
10	$\mathfrak{s}[10]=\perp$		*y*	
11	$\mathfrak{s}[11]=\perp$		*t*	
12	$\mathfrak{s}[12]=\perp$		$ex_{\mathfrak{ivar}}$	
13	$\mathfrak{s}[13]=\perp$			*t*

A variable v is said to be an *alias* for a variable v' in an environment *en* if v' and v are distinct and $\mathfrak{en}[v] = \mathfrak{en}[v']$. An environment is *alias-free wrt* a routine R if no variable occurring in R is an alias for another. That is, $\mathfrak{en}$ is alias-free wrt R if $\mathfrak{en}$ restricted to the variables occurring in R is one–one. Notice that the run-time environment $\mathfrak{en}+_{swap}$, which we just illustrated, is alias-free wrt **procedure** *swap* because *swap* does not use the global variables b and s. Since (1) distinct locations are assigned to global variables, subprogram local variables, the formal parameters of functions, the local variables used by functions to return their values, and the new variables in procedures, (2) the actual parameters in a procedure call must be distinct, and (3) no reference to a global integer variable is permitted in a subprogram, we have

ALIAS-FREE ENVIRONMENT PROPOSITION: Each routine R in a program has an environment that is alias-free wrt R.

The Alias-Free Environment Proposition will be used to justify a version of the Coincidence Lemma in Section 5.4.

The definitions of validity for assertions and asserted statements are relativized to an environment and to function and procedure stores. Let $\mathfrak{M}$ be as before, and $\mathfrak{en}* \subset \mathfrak{en}$ be sure that $\mathfrak{en}* \upharpoonright \mathbf{Fvar} = \mathfrak{en} \upharpoonright \mathbf{Fvar}$ and $\mathfrak{en}* \upharpoonright \mathbf{Pvar} = \mathfrak{en} \upharpoonright \mathbf{Pvar}$. (Intuitively, $\mathfrak{en}*$ is the static environment.) Let $\mathfrak{var}[p]$ ($\mathfrak{var}[A]$) be the set of variables occurring in the assertion p (the set of assertions A). An assertion p is an $\mathfrak{en}*$-$\mathfrak{fs}$-*consequence* of a set of assertions A, written $A \models_{\mathfrak{en}*\text{-}\mathfrak{fs}} p$, if $\mathfrak{var}[p] \cup \mathfrak{var}[A] \subset \mathfrak{domain}[\mathfrak{en}*]$ and $\mathfrak{M}[p] = \mathfrak{t}$ for every error assignment $\mathfrak{N}$, every environment $\mathfrak{en} \supset \mathfrak{en}*$, every procedure store $\mathfrak{ps}$, and every state $\mathfrak{s}$ such that $\mathfrak{M}[q] = \mathfrak{t}$ for every $q \in A$. An assertion p is $\mathfrak{en}*$-$\mathfrak{fs}$-*valid,* written $\models_{\mathfrak{en}*\text{-}\mathfrak{fs}} p$, if $\{\} \models_{\mathfrak{en}*\text{-}\mathfrak{fs}} p$. It is easily shown that, if A and p are free of function variables, then A entails p (in the sense of Section 5.0) iff $A \models_{\mathfrak{en}*\text{-}\mathfrak{fs}} p$ for any environment $\mathfrak{en}*$ and any function store $\mathfrak{fs}$ such that $\mathfrak{var}[p] \cup \mathfrak{var}[A] \subset \mathfrak{domain}[\mathfrak{en}*]$. We leave the definition of entailment, designed to cover the case when A and p can contain function variables, as an exercise.

Let $AP \equiv \{p\}S\{q\}$, and $\mathfrak{M}$ be as before with $\mathfrak{en}$ such that $v \in \mathfrak{domain}[\mathfrak{en}]$ for every variable $v \in \mathfrak{var}[AP]$. In our logic of total correctness, the truth-value assigned the asserted statement AP is as follows:

$$\begin{aligned} \mathfrak{M}[AP] &= \mathfrak{t} \text{ provided } \mathfrak{M}[S] \text{ is defined and } \mathfrak{M}[S][q] = \mathfrak{t} \text{ if } \mathfrak{M}[p] = \mathfrak{t} \\ &= \mathfrak{f} \text{ otherwise} \end{aligned}$$

AP is $\mathfrak{en}*$-$\mathfrak{fs}$-$\mathfrak{ps}$-*valid,* written $\models_{\mathfrak{en}*\text{-}\mathfrak{fs}\text{-}\mathfrak{ps}} AP$, if $\mathfrak{M}[AP] = \mathfrak{t}$ for every error assignment $\mathfrak{N}$, every $\mathfrak{en} \supset \mathfrak{en}*$, and every state $\mathfrak{s}$ such that $\mathfrak{var}[AP] \subset \mathfrak{domain}[\mathfrak{en}]$, $\mathfrak{image}[\mathfrak{en} \upharpoonright F\mathfrak{var}] = \mathfrak{domain}[\mathfrak{fs}]$, and $\mathfrak{image}[\mathfrak{en} \upharpoonright \mathbf{Pvar}] = \mathfrak{domain}[\mathfrak{ps}]$. A routine is $\mathfrak{en}*$-$\mathfrak{fs}$-$\mathfrak{ps}$-*valid* if its body is.

Let $P \equiv$
program pg; Fu_1; . . . ; Fu_j; Pr_1; . . . ; Pr_k; **var** x_1, . . . ,x_n;
begin AP **end**

and PS be the program statement of P. Let $AP \equiv \{p\}S\{q\}$ be the body of the program block, $\mathfrak{en}'$ its environment, $\mathfrak{fs}'$ its function store, $\mathfrak{ps}'$ its procedure store, $\mathfrak{M}$ be as before, and $\mathfrak{M}' = \langle \mathfrak{N}, \mathfrak{en}', \mathfrak{fs}', \mathfrak{ps}', \mathfrak{s} \rangle$. The meaning assigned PS by the meaning function $\mathfrak{M}$ is given by the equation

$$\mathfrak{M}[PS] = \mathfrak{M}'[S]$$

The truth-conditions for a program are given by the equation $\mathfrak{M}[P] = \mathfrak{M}'[AP]$, and we understand P to be *valid* provided $\mathfrak{M}[P] = \mathrm{t}$ for every meaning function $\mathfrak{M}$.

PROPOSITION ON PROGRAM VALIDITY: Program P is valid iff it is $\mathfrak{en}'$-$\mathfrak{fs}'$-$\mathfrak{ps}'$-valid.

5.3. PROVING TOTAL CORRECTNESS

In this section, we develop an axiomatization for a free Hoare logic of total correctness with run-time errors arising from nondenoting integer expressions as well as from nonterminating **while** statements. From this point on, we understand '$\vdash$' to be the provability relation in the free Hoare logic of total correctness as well as in appropriate extensions of free arithmetic. The Dummy Axiom and the Composition Rule are to be understood as in Chapter 1. The Assignment Axiom and the Conditional Rule from Chapter 1, however, must be strengthened because an undefined integer expression might be referenced. The **While** Rule must also be strengthened for this reason, but we will modify the version from Chapter 4 (instead of Chapter 1). The reasoning behind this is simple; in Chapter 4 we developed a logic of total correctness (but with execution time-errors arising solely from the nontermination of **while** statements). We also require axioms for functions and procedure calls. The Function-Call Axioms are interesting in that they extend free arithmetic in proofs in the scope of functions that have been proven correct wrt their specifications.

We first exhibit the syntactic form of the Function-Call Axioms, delaying an explanation of where they can be used in proofs until after we have presented the free Hoare Axiomatization. Let P be an SP program, f be a function variable declared in P's program block, $x_1, \ldots, x_n$ be the formal parameters of **function** f, and the body of f be $AP \equiv$

$$\{\mathrm{I}(x_1) \& \ldots \& \mathrm{I}(x_n) \& p\}$$
$$S$$
$$\{f = e(x_1, \ldots, x_n)\}$$

In other words, the user-defined function f has been introduced into the program block with the declaration

function $f(x_1, \ldots, x_n)$; **var** $y_1, \ldots, y_m$; AP

THE FUNCTION-CALL AXIOM (SCHEMA): For function *f*, this axiom is as follows:

$$\textbf{(FC.f)} \quad (p[X_1, \ldots, X_n \backslash x_1, \ldots, x_n] \rightarrow f(X_1, \ldots, X_n) = e(X_1, \ldots, X_n)) \;\&\; (\mathrm{I}(f(e_1, \ldots, e_n)) \rightarrow \mathrm{I}(e_1) \& \ldots \& \mathrm{I}(e_n))$$

The first conjunct in **(FC.f)** expresses the main content of the axiom (a "specification" of a sort for *f*), whereas the second conjunct expresses the strictness of *f*.

We will call an extension of free arithmetic obtained by adding the assertions in the set of Function-Call Axioms FCA (with no two distinct function-call axiom schemas for the same function variable) to free arithmetic *the FCA-extension of free arithmetic,* written Ax_{FCA}. If an assertion *p* is provable in Ax_{FCA}, we write $\vdash_{FCA} p$, and, if $FCA = \{\}$, simply $\vdash p$ as before. The Function-Call Axiom **(FC.f)** extends free arithmetic by introducing the function variable *f*, and our machine must call the user-defined (software program) function *f* to apply *f* to its arguments. In contrast, an operation symbol '*o*' (or predicate symbol '*p*') of free arithmetic is "built-into the hardware (or firmware)" in the sense that a machine embodying the operational semantics of the preceding section can apply *o* to its arguments without calling any user-defined function (or procedure). No function-call axioms are required for reasoning about operations built into the hardware.

As in Chapter 1, our rules of inference are of the form if $\vdash p_1, \ldots, \vdash p_m$ and $\vdash AP_1, \ldots, \vdash AP_n$, then $\vdash AP$ written more graphically as

$$\frac{p_1, \ldots, p_m, AP_1, \ldots, AP_n}{AP}$$

The p_i are proved using an appropriate extension of free arithmetic (to be explained in the text that follows) whereas the AP_j are proved using our free Hoare Axiomatization.

The *basic free Hoare Axiomatization* **Hax** has two axioms and four rules of inference. The Dummy Axiom is as in Chapter 1, but the Assignment Axiom must be strengthened because, in the assignment statement $x{:=}e$, the precondition must insure that no run-time errors occur during the evaluation of the integer expression *e*.

THE ASSIGNMENT AXIOM

$$\{\mathrm{I}(e) \& p[e \backslash x]\} x{:=}e \{p\}$$

Intuitively, the conjunct I(*e*) is added to the precondition of the Assignment Axiom because, if *e* is defined, then so is the assignment statement $x{:=}e$.

The Composition Rule is as in Chapter 1. Before presenting the Conditional and **While** Rules, we must introduce some additional notation. Let p be an assertion and $\mathfrak{C}[p]=\{e_1, \ldots, e_n\}$. Understand $I(p)$ to be $I(e_1)\&\ldots\&I(e_n)$. The Conditional **(While)** Rule mandates that $I(b)$ be established because the integer expression b occurring in the conditional statement **if** b **then** S **else** S' (the **while** statement **while** b **do** S) must contain outermost integer expressions that are defined.

THE CONDITIONAL RULE

$$\frac{\{I(b)\&p\&b\}S\{q\},\quad \{I(b)\&p\&{\sim}b\}S'\{q\}}{\{I(b)\&p\}\textbf{if } b \textbf{ then } S \textbf{ else } S'\{q\}}$$

THE WHILE RULE

Let $y_1, \ldots, y_k$ $(k \geqslant 1)$ be integer variables foreign to the assertion p and the statement **while** b **do** S, $Y=\langle y_1, \ldots, y_k\rangle$, $E=\langle e_1, \ldots, e_k\rangle$, $I(E)\equiv I(e_1)\&\ldots\&I(e_k)$, $p\equiv I(b)\&r\&I(E)\&E \cdot\!\!\geqslant \langle 0\rangle$, and $Y=E\equiv y_1=e_1 \& \ldots \& y_k=e_k$. Our free version of the **While** *Rule* is as follows:

$$\frac{\{p\&b\&Y{=}E\}S\{p\&Y\succ E\}}{\{p\}\textbf{while } b \textbf{ do } S\{p\&{\sim}b\}}$$

In the **While** Rule, the intuitions behind the introduction of Y and E are as in the preceding chapter: E is a Floydian expression, the conjunct r in assertion p is, roughly, the loop invariant of Chapter 1, the conjunct $E \cdot\!\!\geqslant \langle 0\rangle$ in the assertion p is the well-foundedness condition, and the conjunct $Y\succ E$ in the postcondition of the premise of the **While** Rule is the termination condition. Notice that we require that $I(b)$ and $I(E)$ be conjuncts in p. This was unnecessary in Chapter 4's **While** Rule because every integer expression was defined in standard arithmetic.

In the Consequence Rule, the proofs of $p\rightarrow p'$ and $q'\rightarrow q$ must be carried out in free arithmetic (unextended with function-call axioms). Otherwise, the Consequence Rule is as in Chapter 1.

THE CONSEQUENCE RULE

$$\frac{p\rightarrow p',\quad \{p'\}S\{q'\},\quad q'\rightarrow q}{\{p\}S\{q\}}$$

A *proof* is to be understood as in Chapter 1. This concludes the presentation of the basic free Hoare Axiomatization.

The Procedure-Call Axioms bear some similarity to the Function-Call Axioms, except that the former are asserted statements. Let the formal parameters of procedure pr be $x_1, \ldots, x_n, z_1, \ldots, z_n$ be the new integer variables, and the body of *pr* be $AP \equiv$

$$\begin{array}{l}\{x_1=z_1\&\ldots\&x_n=z_n\&q\}\\ \quad S\\ \{x_1=e_1(z_1,\ldots,z_n)\&\ldots\&x_n=e_n(z_1,\ldots,z_n)\}\end{array}$$

That is, *pr* is a procedure variable introduced in the program block with the declaration

$$\textbf{procedure}\ pr(x_1,\ldots,x_n);\ \textbf{var}\ y_1,\ldots,y_m;\ AP$$

Let *pr* be called with the following statement:

$$pr(x'_1,\ldots,x'_n)$$

THE PROCEDURE-CALL AXIOM (SCHEMA): For procedure *pr*, this axiom is as follows:

$$\begin{array}{l}\{p[e_1(x'_1,\ldots,x'_n),\ldots,e_n(x'_1,\ldots,x'_n)\backslash x'_1,\ldots,x'_n]\\ \quad \&\ q[x'_1,\ldots,x'_n\backslash x_1,\ldots,x_n]\}\\ \qquad pr(x'_1,\ldots,x'_n)\\ \{p\}\end{array}$$

Notice the similarity between the form of a Procedure-Call Axiom and the form of the Assignment Axiom. We shall explore this similarity in detail in the next chapter, when we discuss the concept of the "weakest precondition" of a statement and a postcondition.

We will now define the concept of an extended free Hoare Axiomatization, which uses the axioms and rules of inference listed in Figure 5.6. Let *FCA* be a set of function-call axioms, and *PCA* be a set of procedure-call axioms. An *extended free Hoare Axiomatization* $\mathbf{Hax}_{FCA,PCA}$ with respect to the set of function-call axioms *FCA* and the set of procedure-call axioms *PCA*, is an axiomatization consisting of the basic free Hoare Axiomatization plus the procedure-call axioms in *PCA*, with *the designated extension* of free arithmetic for $\mathbf{Hax}_{FCA,PCA}$ (referred to in the Consequence Rule) being the *FCA*-extension of free arithmetic. A *proof* of an asserted statement *AP* in the extended free Hoare Axiomatization $\mathbf{Hax}_{FCA,PCA}$, written $\vdash_{FCA,PCA} AP$, is a finite sequence of assertions and asserted programs $\langle a_1,\ldots,a_n\rangle$ such that $AP \equiv a_n$ and, for each i from 1 to n, a_i is one of the following:

(1) A theorem of the *FCA*-extension of free arithmetic.
(2) An axiom of the basic free Hoare Axiomatization **Hax.**
(3) A procedure-call axiom belonging to *PCA*.
(4) Obtained from one or more preceding lines by an application of one of the rules of inference (3) through (6).

A. Arithmetic Part (for Assertions)

The following axiom supplements the axioms of free arithmetic shown in Figure 5.2:

The Function-Call Axiom (Schema)

$$\textbf{(FC.f)} \quad (p[X_1, \ldots, X_n \backslash x_1, \ldots, x_n] \rightarrow f(X_1, \ldots, X_n) = e(X_1, \ldots, X_n)) \;\&\; (\mathrm{I}(f(e_1, \ldots, e_n)) \rightarrow \mathrm{I}(e_1) \;\&\; \ldots \;\&\; \mathrm{I}(e_n))$$

where f is declared with the declaration

$$\textbf{function} f(x_1, \ldots, x_n); \textbf{ var } y_1, \ldots, y_m; AP;$$

$$AP \equiv \{\mathrm{I}(x_1) \;\&\; \ldots \;\&\; \mathrm{I}(x_n) \& p\} \; S \; \{f = e(x_1, \ldots, x_n)\}$$

and f is called by the integer expression

$$f(e_1, \ldots, e_n)$$

Restriction: Use of an **(FC.f)** axiom in an FCA-extension of free arithmetic proof is permitted only if **(FC.f)**$\in$FCA (see text).

B. Program Part (for Asserted Statements)

1. **The Dummy Axiom**

   $\{p\}\mathbf{d}\{p\}$

2. **The Assignment Axiom**

   $\{\mathrm{I}(e) \& p[e \backslash x]\} x := e \{p\}$

3. **The Composition Rule**

   $$\frac{\{p\}S\{q\}, \quad \{q\}S'\{r\}}{\{p\}S;S'\{r\}}$$

4. **The Conditional Rule**

   $$\frac{\{\mathrm{I}(b)\&p\&b\}S\{q\}, \quad \{\mathrm{I}(b)\&p\&\sim b\}S'\{q\}}{\{\mathrm{I}(b)\&p\}\textbf{if } b \textbf{ then } S \textbf{ else } S'\{q\}}$$

5. **The While Rule**

   $$\frac{\{p\&b\&Y=E\}S\{p\&Y \succ E\}}{\{p\}\textbf{while } b \textbf{ do } S\{p\&\sim b\}}$$

FIGURE 5.6. The axioms and rules of inference used in extended free Hoare total correctness axiomatizations for SP programs.

where $y_1, \ldots, y_k (k \geqslant 1)$ are integer variables foreign to the assertion p and the statement **while** b **do** S,

$$Y = \langle y_1, \ldots, y_k \rangle$$
$$E = \langle e_1, \ldots, e_k \rangle$$
$$\mathrm{I}(E) \equiv \mathrm{I}(e_1) \,\&\, \ldots \,\&\, \mathrm{I}(e_k)$$
$$p \equiv \mathrm{I}(b) \& r \& \mathrm{I}(E) \& E \succcurlyeq \langle 0 \rangle$$
$$Y = E \equiv y_1 = e_1 \,\&\, \ldots \,\&\, y_k = e_k$$

6. **The Consequence Rule**

$$\frac{p \rightarrow p', \quad \{p'\}S\{q'\}, \quad q' \rightarrow q}{\{p\}S\{q\}}$$

Restriction: The proofs of $p \rightarrow p'$ and $q' \rightarrow q$ must be carried out in the designated FCA extension of free arithmetic (see part A, and the text).

7. **The Procedure-Call Axiom (Schema)**

$$\{p[e_1(x'_1, \ldots, x'_n), \ldots, e_n(x'_1, \ldots, x'_n) \backslash x'_1, \ldots, x'_n]$$
$$\& \; q[x'_1, \ldots, x'_n \backslash x_1, \ldots, x_n]\}$$
$$pr(x'_1, \ldots, x'_n)$$
$$\{p\}$$

where pr is declared with the declaration

procedure $pr(x_1, \ldots, x_n)$; **var** $y_1, \ldots, y_m; AP$;,

$AP \equiv$

$$\{x_1 = z_1 \,\&\, \ldots \,\&\, x_n = z_n \& q\}$$
$$S$$
$$\{x_1 = e_1(z_1, \ldots, z_n) \,\&\, \ldots \,\& x_n = e_n(z_1, \ldots, z_n)\}$$

$z_1, \ldots, z_n$ are new integer variables, and pr is called with the statement $pr(x'_1, \ldots, x'_n)$.

Restriction: Use of one of **procedure** pr's procedure-call axioms is permitted in an extended free Hoare Axiomatization $\mathbf{Hax}_{FCA,PCA}$ proof only if that axiom belongs to PCA (see text).

FIGURE 5.6. *(Continued)*

Note that, by the preceding definitions, the extended free Hoare Axiomatization $\mathbf{Hax}_{\{\},\{\}}$ is the same as the basic free Hoare Axiomatization **Hax**, and we write $\vdash AP$ if $\vdash_{\{\},\{\}} AP$.

Whether an extended free Hoare axiomatization $\mathbf{Hax}_{FCA,PCA}$ is "appropriate" for program and subprogram proving depends on the scope of subprogram variables. Let P be an SP program and f_i be the i-th function declared in the program P. $\mathbf{Hax}_{FCA,PCA}$ is *appropriate* for proving the function f_1 (in program P) if $FCA = PCA = \{\}$, and a *proof* of f_1 is a proof of the body AP of

f_1 in **Hax**. $\mathbf{Hax}_{FCA,PCA}$ is *appropriate* for proving the function f_i ($i \geqslant 2$) if

(1) $PCA = \{\}$,
(2) $FCA \subset \{(\mathbf{FC.f}_j)\text{: } 1 \leqslant j < i\}$, and
(3) for each function call axiom ($\mathbf{FC.f}_j$) belonging to *FCA*, there is a proof of f_j in an extended free Hoare Axiomatization appropriate for f_j,

and a *proof* of f_i is a proof of the body of f_i in an extended free Hoare Axiomatization $\mathbf{Hax}_{FCA,PCA}$ appropriate for f_i.

Let pr_i be the i-th procedure declared in program *P*. $\mathbf{Hax}_{FCA,PCA}$ is *appropriate* for proving the **procedure** pr_1 if

(1) $FCA \subset \{(\mathbf{FC.f}_j)$: **function** f_j is declared in **program** $P\}$,
(2) for each function *f* such that a Function-Call Axiom (**FC.f**) belongs to *FCA*, there is a proof of *f* in an extended free Hoare Axiomatization appropriate for *f*, and
(3) $PCA = \{\}$,

and a *proof* of pr_1 is a proof of the body of pr_1 in an extended free Hoare Axiomatization $\mathbf{Hax}_{FCA,\{\}}$ appropriate for pr_1.

$\mathbf{Hax}_{FCA,PCA}$ is *appropriate* for proving the **procedure** pr_i ($i \geqslant 2$) if

(1) *FCA* is a subset of $\{(\mathbf{FC.f}_j)$: **function** f_j is declared in **program** $P\}$;
(2) for each **function** *f* such that Function-Call Axiom (**FC.f**) belongs to *FCA*, there is a proof of *f* in an extended free Hoare Axiomatization appropriate for *f*;
(3) *PCA* is a subset of the Procedure-Call Axioms for $pr_1, \ldots, pr_{i-1}$;
(4) for each **procedure** *pr* such that a Procedure-Call Axiom for *pr* belongs to *PCA*, there is a proof of *pr* in an extended free Hoare Axiomatization appropriate for *pr*,

and a *proof* of pr_i is a proof of the body of pr_i in an extended free Hoare Axiomatization $\mathbf{Hax}_{FCA,PCA}$ appropriate for pr_i.

$\mathbf{Hax}_{FCA,PCA}$ is *appropriate* for proving the **program** *P* if

(1) *FCA* is a subset of $\{(\mathbf{FC.f}_j)$: **function** f_j is declared in **program** $P\}$;
(2) for each **function** *f* such that a Function-Call Axiom (**FC.f**) belongs to *FCA*, there is a proof of *f* in an extended free Hoare Axiomatization appropriate for *f*;
(3) *PCA* is a subset of the Procedure-Call Axioms for the procedures declared in *P*; and

(4) for each **procedure** *pr* such that a Procedure-Call Axiom for *pr* belongs to *PCA*, there is a proof of *pr* in an extended free Hoare Axiomatization appropriate for *pr*,

and a *proof* of *P* is a proof of the body of *P* in an extended free Hoare Axiomatization $\mathbf{Hax}_{FCA,PCA}$ appropriate for *P*.

We illustrate the use of our free Hoare Axiomatization with a proof of the total correctness of **program** *illustration,* which as we recall from Section 5.1, sets *b* (*s*) to the larger (smaller) of $u ** v$ and $w ** z$ using the programmer-defined **function** *ex* and **procedure** *swap.*

```
program illustration;
function ex(x,y);
        :
procedure swap(x,y);
        :
var b,s,u,v,w,z;
begin
{I(u) & I(v) & v≥0 & I(w) & I(z) & z≥0}
b := ex(u,v);
s :=ex(w,z);
if s>b then swap(b,s)
        else d
{b=max(u**v,w**z) & s=min(u**v,w**z)}
end
```

To prove this correct with respect to the the precondition

$$I(u) \ \& \ I(v) \ \& \ v \geq 0 \ \& \ I(w) \ \& \ I(z) \ \& \ z \geq 0$$

and postcondition

$$\{b = \max(u**v, w**z) \ \& \ s = \min(u**v, w**z)\}$$

we must prove the asserted statement

```
{I(u) & I(v) & v≥0 & I(w) & I(z) & z≥0}
        b := ex(u,v);
        s := ex(w,z);
        if s>b then swap(b,s)
                else d
{b=max(u**v,w**z) & s=min(u**v,w**z)}
```

that constitutes the body of the program block in the appropriate extended free Hoare Axiomatization $\mathbf{Hax}_{\{(\mathbf{FC.ex})\},\{(\mathbf{PC.swap})\}}$, where **(FC.ex)** and **(PC.swap)** are the Function- and Procedure-Call Axioms.

(FC.ex) $(Y \geq 0 \rightarrow ex(X,Y)=X{**}Y))$ & $(\mathrm{I}(ex(e,e')) \rightarrow \mathrm{I}(e) \& \mathrm{I}(e'))$

and

(PC.swap) $\{\mathrm{I}(b)$ & $\mathrm{I}(s)$ & $s=\max(u{**}v,w{**}z)$ & $b=\min(u{**}v,w{**}z)\}$
swap(b,s)
$\{\mathrm{I}(s)$ & $\mathrm{I}(b)$ & $b=\max(u{**}v,w{**}z)$ & $s=\min(u{**}v,w{**}z)\}$

Continuing with the proof of the program, we show

(1) $\{\mathrm{I}(s)$ & $\mathrm{I}(b)$ & $b=u{**}v$ & $s=w{**}z\}$
if $s>b$ **then** *swap*(b,s) **else d**
$\{\mathrm{I}(s)$ & $\mathrm{I}(b)$ & $b=\max(u{**}v,w{**}z)$ & $s=\min(u{**}v,w{**}z)\}$

by applying the Conditional Rule to

(2) $\{\mathrm{I}(s)$ & $\mathrm{I}(b)$ & $b=u{**}v$ & $s=w{**}z$ & $s>b\}$
swap(b,s)
$\{\mathrm{I}(s)$ & $\mathrm{I}(b)$ & $b=\max(u{**}v,w{**}z)$ & $s=\min(u{**}v,w{**}z)\}$

and

(3) $\{\mathrm{I}(s)$ & $\mathrm{I}(b)$ & $b=u{**}v$ & $s=w{**}z$ & $\sim s>b\}$
d
$\{\mathrm{I}(s)$ & $\mathrm{I}(b)$ & $b=\max(u{**}v,w{**}z)$ & $s=\min(u{**}v,w{**}z)\}$

We obtain (2) by applying the Consequence Rule to **(PC.swap),** and (3) by applying the Consequence Rule to the following:

(4) $\{\mathrm{I}(s)$ & $\mathrm{I}(b)$ & $b=\max(u{**}v,w{**}z)$ & $s=\min(u{**}v,w{**}z)\}$
d
$\{\mathrm{I}(s)$ & $\mathrm{I}(b)$ & $b=\max(u{**}v,w{**}z)$ & $s=\min(u{**}v,w{**}z)\}$

which is an instance of the Dummy Axiom. Applying the Assignment Axiom twice and the Composition Rule once, we obtain

(5) $\{\mathrm{I}(ex(u,v))$ & $\mathrm{I}(ex(w,z))$ & $ex(u,v)=u{**}v$ & $ex(w,z)=w{**}z\}$
$b:=ex(u,v);\ s:=ex(w,z)$
$\{\mathrm{I}(s)$ & $\mathrm{I}(b)$ & $b=u{**}v$ & $s=w{**}z\}$

The proof of the **program** *illustration* is completed by applying the Composition Rule to (1) and (5), and then applying the Consequence Rule. In the application of the Consequence Rule, **(FC.ex)** and the fact that, in free arithmetic, the exponentiation operator '**' can be proven total, insure the following:

$$\vdash I(u)\ \&\ I(v)\ \&\ v\geq 0\ \&\ I(w)\ \&\ I(z)\ \&\ z\geq 0\ \&\ \text{true} \rightarrow$$
$$I(ex(w,z))\ \&\ I(ex(u,v))\ \&\ ex(u,v)=u{*}{*}v\ \&\ ex(w,z)=w{*}{*}z$$

Turning to the justification of **(FC.ex)**, we must prove the function *ex* by using the basic free Hoare Axiomatization **Hax** to prove the asserted statement constituting its body.

```
{I(x) & I(y) & y≥0}
ex := 1;
t := y;
{I(t) & I(1) & I(x) & I(y) & ex=x**(y−t) & t≥0}
while t≥1 do
    begin
    ex := ex*x;
    t := t−1
    end
{ex=x**y}
```

The correspondence between the variables in our program and those in the schematized Function-Call Axiom **(FC.f)** is clear: The integer variables x and y are the formal parameters x_1 and x_2, $y \geq 0$ is the assertion p in the precondition, *ex* is the function variable *f*, and $x ** y$ is the integer expression $e(x_1,x_2)$. The proof of this asserted statement is entirely similar to the proof in Section 1.3.

Turning to the justification of the Procedure-Call Axiom **(PC.swap)**, we must prove the correctness of the **procedure** *swap* by proving its body in the extended free Hoare Axiomatization $\textbf{Hax}_{\{(FC.ex)\},\{\}}$. Because **procedure** *swap* does not call **function** *ex*, it suffices to use the basic free Hoare Axiomatization **Hax** in proving *swap*'s body.

```
{x=zx & y=zy & I(x) & I(y)}
t := x;
x := y;
y := t
{x=zy & y=zx}
```

The correspondence between the variables in our program and those in the Procedure-Call Axiom **(PC.swap)** is as follows: x and y are the formal parameters x_1 and x_2, b and s are the actual parameters x_1' and x_2', zx and zy are the new variables z_1 and z_2 as well as the integer expressions $e_2(z_1,z_2)$ and $e_1(z_1,z_2)$, and true (which we have omitted for the sake of brevity) is the assertion q. This asserted statement is easily demonstrated using the Assignment Axiom (three times) and the Composition and Consequence Rules.

5.4. SOUNDNESS

In this section, we sketch the soundness of extended free Hoare Axiomatizations for proving the total correctness of functions, procedures, and programs. We begin with the restatement of two key lemmas.

ENVIRONMENTAL COINCIDENCE LEMMA: Let R be a routine, x (e and e', p) be an integer variable (integer expressions, an assertion) occurring in R, en be a run-time environment of R, and $\mathrm{en}[e]$ ($\mathrm{en}[p]$) be $\mathrm{image}[\mathrm{en} \upharpoonright \mathrm{ivar}[e]]$ ($\mathrm{image}[\mathrm{en} \upharpoonright \mathrm{ivar}[p]]$). Let $\mathfrak{M} = \langle \mathfrak{N},\mathrm{en},\mathfrak{fs},\mathfrak{ps},\mathfrak{s}\rangle$, $\mathfrak{s}' = \mathfrak{s}\{\mathfrak{M}[e']\backslash \mathrm{en}[x]\}$, and $\mathfrak{M}' = \langle \mathfrak{N},\mathrm{en},\mathfrak{fs},\mathfrak{ps},\mathfrak{s}'\rangle$.

(a) If $\mathrm{en}[x] \notin \mathrm{en}[e]$, then $\mathfrak{M}'[e] = \mathfrak{M}[e]$.
(b) If $\mathrm{en}[x] \notin \mathrm{en}[p]$, then $\mathfrak{M}'[p] = \mathfrak{M}[p]$.
(c) $\mathfrak{M}'[e] = \mathfrak{M}[e[e'\backslash x]]$.
(d) $\mathfrak{M}'[p] = \mathfrak{M}[p[e'\backslash x]]$.

Proof: The proof is similar to the proof of the Coincidence Lemma in Chapter 0. For illustration, we give the proof in the basis of (c) when $e \equiv y$. Suppose $x \equiv y$. Due to the fact that $e' \equiv x[e'\backslash x]$, we have $\mathfrak{M}'[e] = \mathfrak{M}[x[e'\backslash x]]$ by the definition of $\mathfrak{M}'$. On the other hand, suppose x and y are distinct. Because en is alias-free wrt R by the Alias-Free Environment Proposition, we have $\mathrm{en}[x] \neq \mathrm{en}[y]$, and so $\mathfrak{M}'[y] = \mathfrak{M}[y]$. Hence, $\mathfrak{M}'[y] = \mathfrak{M}[y[e'\backslash x]]$ because x and y are distinct. □

If aliasing were allowed (i.e., if the antecedent were dropped from (c)), neither (c) nor (d) would hold. Consider the following counterexample to a version of (c) permitting aliasing, with $e \equiv y$ and $e' \equiv 1$. Suppose x and y are distinct but y is an alias for x, so $\mathrm{en}[x] = \mathrm{en}[y]$. Let $\mathfrak{s}[\mathrm{en}[x]] = \mathfrak{s}[\mathrm{en}[y]] = 0$, and $\mathfrak{s}' = \mathfrak{s}\{1\backslash \mathrm{en}[x]\} = \mathfrak{s}\{1\backslash \mathrm{en}[y]\}$. Now $\mathfrak{M}'[y] = \mathfrak{s}'[\mathrm{en}[y]] = 1$, but $\mathfrak{M}[y[1\backslash x]] = \mathfrak{s}[\mathrm{en}[y]] = 0$.

ENVIRONMENTAL SETTING LEMMA: Let $\mathfrak{M}$ be as in the previous lemma, R be a routine with statement S, $\mathfrak{s}' = \mathfrak{M}[S]$, and $\mathfrak{M}' = \langle \mathfrak{N},\mathrm{en},\mathfrak{fs},\mathfrak{ps},\mathfrak{s}'\rangle$.

(a) For any integer variable x, if x is not syntactically vulnerable in routine R, then $\mathfrak{M}[x] = \mathfrak{M}'[x]$.
(b) For any integer expression e, if no integer variable occurring in e is syntactically vulnerable in routine R, then $\mathfrak{M}[e] = \mathfrak{M}'[e]$.

Proof: (a) By induction on the complexity of S. (b) By induction on the complexity of e, using part (a) in the basis. □

Let R, $\mathfrak{M}$, and $\mathrm{en}* \subset \mathrm{en}$ be as before. We next proceed to show that the axioms of the basic free Hoare Axiomatization are en*-$\mathfrak{fs}$-$\mathfrak{ps}$-valid and that its rules of inference are en*-$\mathfrak{fs}$-$\mathfrak{ps}$-validity preserving for any $\mathrm{en}* \subset \mathrm{en}$, any **function store** $\mathfrak{fs}$, and any **procedure store** $\mathfrak{ps}$.

DUMMY VALIDITY LEMMA: $\models_{\mathrm{en}*\text{-}\mathfrak{fs}\text{-}\mathfrak{ps}}\{p\}\mathbf{d}\{p\}$

Proof: Much as in Chapter 1. □

ASSIGNMENT VALIDITY LEMMA: $\models_{\mathrm{en}*\text{-}\mathfrak{fs}\text{-}\mathfrak{ps}}\{\mathrm{I}(e)\&p[e\backslash x]\}x{:=}e\{p\}$

Proof: Let $\mathfrak{M}$ be as before. Suppose $\mathfrak{M}[\mathrm{I}(e)\&p[e\backslash x]] = \mathrm{t}$. Because $\mathfrak{M}[\mathrm{I}(e)] = \mathrm{t}$, $\mathfrak{M}[e]{\in}Z$, and so $\mathfrak{s}' = \mathfrak{M}[x{:=}e] = \mathfrak{s}\{\mathfrak{M}[e]\backslash\mathrm{en}[x]\}$ is defined by the operational semantics. Let $\mathfrak{M}' = \langle \mathfrak{N},\mathrm{en},\mathfrak{fs},\mathfrak{ps},\mathfrak{s}' \rangle$. Since en is alias-free wrt R, we have $\mathfrak{M}'[p] = \mathfrak{M}[p[e\backslash x]] = \mathrm{t}$ by the assumption and the Environmental Coincidence Lemma, part (d). □

From the counterexample to the Coincidence Lemma, part (c), when aliasing is allowed we can see that the Assignment Axiom is en*-$\mathfrak{fs}$-$\mathfrak{ps}$-invalid in the presence of unrestricted aliasing. To see this, consider the asserted statement

$$\{x{=}0\}y{=}1\{x{=}0\}$$

which is false in any meaning function with environment en and state $\mathfrak{s}$ in which y is an alias for x (i.e., $\mathrm{en}[y] = \mathrm{en}[x]$) and $\mathfrak{s}[x] = 0$. A similar situation arises in the case of procedure calls with nondistinct actual parameters, resulting in aliasing within the procedure body. Consider the following correct **procedure:**

procedure *one*(x,y);
begin
$\{x{=}zx \;\&\; y{=}zy \;\&\; \mathrm{true}\}$
$y{:=}1$
$\{x{=}zx \;\&\; y{=}1 \;\&\; \mathrm{true}\}$
end

From **procedure** *one*'s Call Axiom we could derive the invalid asserted statement

$$\{x{=}0\}one(x,x)\{x{=}0\}$$

if we did not mandate the distinctness of actual parameters.

THE COMPOSITION RULE en*-$\mathfrak{fs}$-$\mathfrak{ps}$-VALIDITY-PRESERVATION LEMMA

$\{p\}S\{q\}, \quad \{q\}S'\{r\}$
$\{p\}S;S'\{r\}$

Proof: Much as in Chapter 1. □

THE CONDITIONAL RULE en*-$\mathfrak{fs}$-$\mathfrak{ps}$-VALIDITY-PRESERVATION LEMMA

$\{\mathrm{I}(b)\&p\&b\}S\{q\}, \quad \{\mathrm{I}(b)\&p\&{\sim}b\}S'\{q\}$
$\{\mathrm{I}(b)\&p\}$ **if** b **then** S **else** $S'\{q\}$

Proof: Assume the en*-$\mathfrak{fs}$-$\mathfrak{ps}$-validity of the antecedent of the Conditional Rule. Let $\mathfrak{M}$ be as defined previously, $\mathfrak{M}[\mathrm{I}(b)\&p] = \mathrm{t}$, $\mathfrak{M}' = \langle \mathfrak{N}, \mathrm{en}, \mathfrak{fs}, \mathfrak{ps}, \mathfrak{M}[S] \rangle$ if $\mathfrak{M}[S]$ is defined, and $\mathfrak{M}'' = \langle \mathfrak{N}, \mathrm{en}, \mathfrak{fs}, \mathfrak{ps}, \mathfrak{M}[S'] \rangle$ if $\mathfrak{M}[S']$ is defined. First, suppose $\mathfrak{M}[b] = \mathrm{t}$. Then, by the assumptions, $\mathfrak{M}[S]$ is defined and $\mathfrak{M}'[q] = \mathrm{t}$. Similarly, if $\mathfrak{M}[b] = \mathfrak{f}$, then $\mathfrak{M}[S']$ is defined and $\mathfrak{M}''[q] = \mathrm{t}$. Hence, $\mathfrak{M}''' = \langle \mathfrak{N}, \mathrm{en}, \mathfrak{fs}, \mathfrak{ps}, \mathfrak{M}[$**if** b **then** S **else** $S']\rangle$ is defined by the operational semantics since $\mathfrak{M}[\mathfrak{E}[b]] \subset \mathfrak{Z}$ because $\mathfrak{M}[\mathrm{I}(b)] = \mathrm{t}$. And, because either $\mathfrak{M}''' = \mathfrak{M}'$ or $\mathfrak{M}''' = \mathfrak{M}''$, $\mathfrak{M}'''[q] = \mathrm{t}$. □

THE WHILE RULE en*-$\mathfrak{fs}$-$\mathfrak{ps}$-VALIDITY-PRESERVATION LEMMA

Let $y_1, \ldots, y_k$ $(k \geq 1)$ be new integer variables, $Y = \langle y_1, \ldots, y_k \rangle$, $E = \langle e_1, \ldots, e_k \rangle$, $\mathrm{I}(E) \equiv \mathrm{I}(e_1)\& \ldots \&\mathrm{I}(e_k)$, $p \equiv \mathrm{I}(b)\&r\&\mathrm{I}(E)\&E \not\succcurlyeq \langle 0 \rangle$, and $Y = E \equiv y_1 = e_1 \& \ldots \& y_k = e_k$. Then

$\{p\&b\&Y{=}E\}S\{p\&Y \succ E\}$
$\{p\}$**while** b **do** $S\{p\&{\sim}b\}$

Proof: Left as an exercise. □

THE CONSEQUENCE RULE en∗-f𝔰-p𝔰-VALIDITY-PRESERVATION LEMMA

$p \to p'$, $\{p'\}S\{q'\}$, $q' \to q$
$\{p\}S\{q\}$

Proof: Similar to the proof in Chapter 1. □

SOUNDNESS OF THE BASIC FREE HOARE AXIOMATIZATION THEOREM

If $\vdash AP$, then $\models_{en*\text{-}f\mathfrak{s}\text{-}p\mathfrak{s}} AP$.

Proof: Similar to the proof in Chapter 1, but appealing to the Soundness of Free Arithmetic Theorem. □

Let 𝔐 and en∗ be as before, *FCA* be a set of Function-Call Axioms (with no two distinct axiom schemas introducing the same function symbol into free arithmetic), and $\mathbf{Ax}_{FCA}$ be the *FCA*-extension of free arithmetic. In the following definitions, we say "in **function** *f*" as short for "in **function** *f* declared within program *P*". Similarly, we use the phrase "in **procedure** *pr*" for brevity. We understand $\mathbf{Ax}_{FCA}$ to be en∗-f𝔰-*sound in* a program *P* (**function** *f*, **procedure** *pr*) with static environment en∗ and function store *fs* provided that the extended free Hoare Axiomatization $\mathbf{Hax}_{FCA,()}$ is appropriate for proving *P* (*f*, *pr*) and $\models_{en*\text{-}f\mathfrak{s}} p$ if $\vdash_{FCA} p$. An extended free Hoare Axiomatization $\mathbf{Hax}_{FCA,PCA}$ is en∗-f𝔰-p𝔰-*sound* in a **program** *P* (**function** *f*, **procedure** *pr*) with static environment en∗, function store f𝔰, and procedure store p𝔰 provided that $\mathbf{Hax}_{FCA,PCA}$ is appropriate for proving *P* (*f*, *pr*) and $\models_{en*\text{-}f\mathfrak{s}\text{-}p\mathfrak{s}} AP$ if $\vdash_{FCA,PCA} AP$. For short, we say that $\mathbf{Ax}_{FCA}$ ($\mathbf{Hax}_{FCA,PCA}$) is *sound in P* if it is en∗-f𝔰-sound (en∗-f𝔰-p𝔰-sound) in *P*.

To establish the en∗-f𝔰-p𝔰-soundness of extended free Hoare Axiomatizations, we first establish the en∗-f𝔰-soundness of *FCA*-extensions of free arithmetic. Second, we show that in any extended free Hoare Axiomatization $\mathbf{Hax}_{FCA,PCA}$ appropriate for proving a **program** *P* (**function** *f*, **procedure** *pr*), each Function-Call Axiom belonging to *FCA* is en∗-f𝔰-valid. Finally, we sketch a proof showing that in any extended free Hoare Axiomatization $\mathbf{Hax}_{FCA,PCA}$ appropriate for proving a **program** *P* (**procedure** *pr*), each Procedure-Call Axiom belonging to *PCA* is en∗-f𝔰-p𝔰-valid. The en∗-f𝔰-p𝔰-soundness of extended free Hoare Axiomatizations follows by an argument entirely similar to that in the proof of Soundness of the Basic Hoare Axiomatization Theorem.

THE SOUNDNESS OF FCA-EXTENSIONS OF FREE ARITHMETIC LEMMA

(a) An *FCA*-extension of free arithmetic is satisfiable.
(b) If $FCA \vdash p$ and $\models_{\mathrm{en*\text{-}f}\mathfrak{s}} q$ for each $q \in FCA$, then $\models_{\mathrm{en*\text{-}f}\mathfrak{s}} p$.

Proof: (a) By the Theorem on Extensions by Full Explicit Definitions. (b) By the Soundness of Free Arithmetic Theorem. □

THE FUNCTION-CALL AXIOM en*-f𝔰-VALIDITY LEMMA

Let f be a function variable declared in the program block, $x_1, \ldots, x_n$ be the formal parameters of **function** f, and the body of f be $AP \equiv$

$$\{\mathrm{I}(x_1)\& \ldots \&\mathrm{I}(x_n)\&p\}$$
$$S$$
$$\{f=e(x_1, \ldots, x_n)\}$$

Let f be called in another routine R with the integer expression $f(e_1, \ldots, e_n)$, let $\mathfrak{M} = \langle \mathfrak{N}, \mathrm{en}, \mathfrak{fs}, \mathfrak{ps}, \mathfrak{s} \rangle$ be the meaning function in the calling routine at the time f is invoked, and let en* be as previously defined. Suppose $\vdash_{FCA,\{\}} AP$ in an extended free Hoare Axiomatization $\mathbf{Hax}_{FCA,\{\}}$ appropriate for proving f. Then, **(FC.f)** is en*-f𝔰-valid, that is

$$\models_{\mathrm{en*\text{-}f}\mathfrak{s}} (p[X_1, \ldots, X_n \backslash x_1, \ldots, x_n] \rightarrow$$
$$f(X_1, \ldots, X_n) = e(X_1, \ldots, X_n)) \;\&$$
$$(\mathrm{I}(f(e_1, \ldots, e_n)) \rightarrow \mathrm{I}(e_1)\& \ldots \&\mathrm{I}(e_n))$$

Furthermore, for any extended free Hoare Axiomatization $\mathbf{Hax}_{FCA',\{\}}$ such that $\mathbf{(FC.f)} \in FCA'$, if $\mathbf{Hax}_{FCA',\{\}}$ is appropriate for proving a routine R with static environment en*, function store f𝔰, and procedure store p𝔰, then $\mathbf{Hax}_{FCA',\{\}}$ is en*-f𝔰-p𝔰-sound.

Proof: We show that, if a function f is provable in an extended free Hoare Axiomatization $\mathbf{Hax}_{FCA,\{\}}$ appropriate for it, then for every routine R and for every axiomatization $\mathbf{Hax}_{FCA',\{\}}$ such that $\mathbf{(FC.f)} \in FCA'$ and $\mathbf{Hax}_{FCA',\{\}}$ is appropriate for proving R, (1) the axiom **(FC.f)** is en*-f𝔰-valid and (2) $\mathbf{Hax}_{FCA',\{\}}$ is en*-f𝔰-p𝔰-sound. Let j be the number of function declarations, $1 \leqslant l \leqslant j$, f_l be the l-th function declared in the program, and $FCA_l = \{(\mathbf{DC}.f_i)$: $1 \leqslant i < l$, $(\mathbf{DC}.f_i) \in FCA''$ and $\mathbf{Hax}_{FCA'',\{\}}$ is appropriate for proving $f_l\}$. It suffices to show that $\mathbf{Hax}_{FCA_l,\{\}}$ is en*-f𝔰-p𝔰-sound for every l such that $1 \leqslant l \leqslant j$. The proof is by induction on $l \geqslant 1$. In the basis, we have $l=1$, no function calls occur within the body of function $f_1 \equiv f$, $FCA_l = \{\}$, and $\vdash AP$. For each i from 1 to n, suppose $\mathfrak{M}[e_i] \in \mathfrak{Z}$, and let m_i be any integer such that $\mathfrak{M}[e_i] =$

m_i. Suppose $\mathfrak{M}[p[m_1, \ldots, m_n \backslash x_1, \ldots, x_n]] = \mathrm{t}$. Let $\mathfrak{M}' = \langle \mathfrak{N}, \mathfrak{en}_f, \mathfrak{fs}, \mathfrak{ps}, \mathfrak{s}' \rangle$ be the meaning function immediately after f is entered with the actual parameters plugged in for the formal parameters. Because $\vdash AP$, we have $\models_{\mathfrak{en}_f*\text{-}\mathfrak{fs}\text{-}\mathfrak{ps}} AP$ by the Soundness of the Basic Free Hoare Axiomatization Lemma. Since $\mathfrak{M}[e_i]=m_i$ for each i from 1 to n, and $\mathfrak{M}[p[m_1, \ldots, m_n \backslash x_1, \ldots x_n]] = \mathrm{t}$, $\mathfrak{M}'[\mathrm{I}(x_1)\& \ldots \&\mathrm{I}(x_n)\&p] = \mathrm{t}$. Hence, because $\models_{\mathfrak{en}_f*\text{-}\mathfrak{fs}\text{-}\mathfrak{ps}} AP$, we have $\mathfrak{s}''=\mathfrak{M}'[S]$ is defined and, understanding $\mathfrak{M}''=\langle \mathfrak{N}, \mathfrak{en}_f, \mathfrak{fs}, \mathfrak{ps}, \mathfrak{s}'' \rangle$, we have $\mathfrak{M}''[f=e]=\mathrm{t}$. By the Environmental Setting Lemma, $\mathfrak{M}''[x_i] = \mathfrak{M}'[x_i] = \mathfrak{M}[e_i] = m_i$ for each i from 1 to n. We have the following:

$$
\begin{aligned}
&\mathfrak{M}[f(e_1, \ldots, e_n)] \\
&\quad = \mathfrak{M}''[f] \text{ by the operational semantics} \\
&\quad = \mathfrak{M}''[e(x_1, \ldots, x_n)] \text{ because } \models AP \\
&\quad = \mathfrak{M}''[e(m_1, \ldots, m_n)] \text{ by the Environmental Coincidence} \\
&\qquad\qquad \text{Lemma, part (a), because } m_i = \mathfrak{M}''[x_i] \\
&\quad = \mathfrak{M}[e(m_1, \ldots, m_n)] \text{ because } e(m_1, \ldots, m_n) \text{ is in } \{\} \\
&\quad = \mathfrak{M}[e(e_1, \ldots, e_n)] \text{ because } m_i = \mathfrak{M}[e_i]
\end{aligned}
$$

Hence, for any integers $m_1, \ldots, m_n$ such that $m_i = \mathfrak{M}[e_i]$ for each i from 1 to n, if $\mathfrak{M}[p[e_1, \ldots e_n \backslash x_1, \ldots, x_n]] = \mathrm{t}$, then $\mathfrak{M}[f(e_1, \ldots, e_n)] = \mathfrak{M}[e(e_1, \ldots, e_n)]$. Hence,

$$
\mathfrak{M}[p[X_1, \ldots, X_n \backslash x_1, \ldots, x_n] \rightarrow f(X_1, \ldots, X_n) = e(X_1, \ldots, X_n)] = \mathrm{t}.
$$

So, the first (or specification) conjunct of **(FC.f)**,

$$
p[X_1, \ldots, X_n \backslash x_1, \ldots, x_n] \rightarrow f(X_1, \ldots, X_n) = e(X_1, \ldots, X_n)
$$

is $\mathfrak{en}*$-$\mathfrak{fs}$-valid. The $\mathfrak{en}*$-$\mathfrak{fs}$-validity of the second (or strictness) conjunct

$$
\mathrm{I}(f(e_1, \ldots, e_n)) \rightarrow \mathrm{I}(e_1)\& \ldots \&\mathrm{I}(e_n)
$$

in **(FC.f)** follows immediately from the operational semantics. By the Soundness of *FCA*-Extensions of Free Arithmetic Lemma, the {**(FC.f)**}-extension of free arithmetic is $\mathfrak{en}*$-$\mathfrak{fs}$-sound. Hence, by essentially the same argument as in the proof of the Soundness of the Basic Free Hoare Axiomatization Lemma, $\mathbf{Hax}_{\{(\mathbf{FC.f})\},\{\}}$ is $\mathfrak{en}*$-$\mathfrak{fs}$-$\mathfrak{ps}$-sound. The induction step when $l \geq 2$ proceeds in a similar manner. Whereas in the basis, the $\mathfrak{en}*$-$\mathfrak{fs}$-$\mathfrak{ps}$-soundness of the basic free Hoare Axiomatization insures that the **function** f's body AP is $\mathfrak{en}_{f_1}*$-$\mathfrak{fs}$-$\mathfrak{ps}$-valid, the induction hypothesis (that the axiomatization $\mathbf{Hax}_{FCA_{l-1},\{\}}$ is $\mathfrak{en}*$-$\mathfrak{fs}$-$\mathfrak{ps}$-sound) insures that a similar proposition is in the induction step. □

THE PROCEDURE CALL AXIOM en*-fs-ps VALIDITY LEMMA

Let the formal parameters of procedure *pr* be $x_1, \ldots, x_n, z_1, \ldots, z_n$ be the new integer variables, and the body of *pr* be $AP \equiv$

$$\{x_1 = z_1 \& \ldots \& x_n = z_n \& q\}$$
$$S$$
$$\{x_1 = e_1(z_1, \ldots, z_n) \& \ldots \& x_n = e_n(z_1, \ldots, z_n)\}$$

Let *pr* be called in another routine R with the statement $pr(x'_1, \ldots, x'_n)$, and let $\mathfrak{M} = \langle \mathfrak{N}, en, fs, ps, s \rangle$ be the meaning function in R at the time *pr* is invoked. Suppose $\vdash_{FCA,PCA} AP$ in an extended free Hoare Axiomatization $\mathbf{Hax}_{FCA,PCA}$ appropriate for proving *pr*. Then, the Procedure-Call Axiom **(PC.pr)** for **procedure** *pr* is en*-fs-ps-valid. That is,

$$\models_{en*\text{-}fs\text{-}ps} \{p[e_1(x'_1, \ldots, x'_n), \ldots, e_n(x'_1, \ldots, x'_n) \backslash x'_1, \ldots, x'_n]$$
$$\& \; q[x'_1, \ldots, x'_n \backslash x_1, \ldots, x_n]\}$$
$$pr(x'_1, \ldots, x'_n)$$
$$\{p\}$$

Furthermore, for any extended free Hoare Axiomatization $\mathbf{Hax}_{FCA',PCA'}$ such that **(PC.pr)**$\in PCA'$, if $\mathbf{Hax}_{FCA',PCA'}$ is appropriate for proving a routine R with static environment en*, function store fs, and procedure store ps, then $\mathbf{Hax}_{FCA',PCA'}$ is en*-fs-ps-sound.

Proof: We sketch the proof, leaving out some of the more messy details. We begin by supposing that

$$\vdash_{FCA,PCA} \{x_1 = z_1 \& \ldots \& x_n = z_n \& q\}$$
$$S$$
$$\{x_1 = e_1(z_1, \ldots, z_n) \& \ldots \& x_n = e_n(z_1, \ldots, z_n)\}$$

Let $\mathfrak{M}$, the meaning function in the calling routine at the time *pr* is invoked, en* be as before, and

$$\mathfrak{M}[p[e_1(x'_1, \ldots, x'_n), \ldots, e_n(x'_1, \ldots, x'_n) \backslash x'_1, \ldots, x'_n]$$
$$\& \; q[x'_1, \ldots, x'_n \backslash x_1, \ldots, x_n]] = \mathrm{t}$$

Let $\mathfrak{M}'$ be the meaning function in **procedure** *pr* immediately after *pr* is entered, and $\mathfrak{M}''$ be the meaning function in procedure *pr* immediately after *pr*'s statement body S is executed. We must show that $\mathfrak{M}[pr(x'_1, \ldots, x'_n)][p] = \mathrm{t}$. Let l be the l-th procedure. The proof proceeds much as in the proof of the Function-Call Axiom en*-fs-Validity Lemma. In the basis, we have $l=1$ and, for each j from 1 to n

$\mathfrak{M}[e_j(x_1', \ldots, x_n')]$
$= \mathfrak{M}'[e_j(x_1, \ldots, x_n)]$ by the operational semantics and the Environmental Coincidence Lemma, part (a), because $e_j(x_1, \ldots, x_n)$ is in the $\{x_i\}$
$= \mathfrak{M}'[e_j(z_1, \ldots, z_n)]$ by the operational semantics
$= \mathfrak{M}''[e_j(z_1, \ldots, z_n)]$ by the Environmental Setting Lemma due to the fact that the z_k's are new in pr
$= \mathfrak{M}''[x_j]$ by the assumption $\vdash_{FCA,()} AP$ and the Function-Call Axiom $\mathfrak{en}*$-$\mathfrak{fs}$-Validity Lemma
$= \mathfrak{M}[pr(x_1', \ldots, x_n')][x_j']$ by the operational semantics

Now, by the Environmental Setting Lemma, $\mathfrak{M}[pr(x_1', \ldots, x_n')]$ is an $\mathfrak{en}[x_1']$- . . . -$\mathfrak{en}[x_n']$-variant of $\mathfrak{s}$. Because $\mathfrak{en}$ is alias-free wrt R, we have the following:

$\mathfrak{M}[pr(x_1', \ldots, x_n')][p]$
$= \mathfrak{M}[p[e_1(x_1', \ldots, x_n'), \ldots, e_n(x_1', \ldots, x_n')\backslash x_1', \ldots, x_n']]$
$= \mathfrak{t}$ by the Environmental Coincidence Lemma, part (d)

In the induction step, we use the induction hypothesis instead of the Function-Call Axiom $\mathfrak{en}*$-$\mathfrak{fs}$-Validity Lemma. □

Using the two preceding lemmas to extend the argument used in establishing the Soundness of the Basic Free Hoare Axiomatization Theorem, we have

THE $\mathfrak{en}*$-$\mathfrak{fs}$-$\mathfrak{ps}$-SOUNDNESS OF EXTENDED FREE HOARE AXIOMATIZATIONS THEOREM: If $\mathbf{Hax}_{FCA,PCA}$ is appropriate for proving a **program** P (a **function** f, a **procedure** pr) with static environment $\mathfrak{en}*$, function store $\mathfrak{fs}$, and procedure store $\mathfrak{ps}$, then $\mathbf{Hax}_{FCA,PCA}$ is $\mathfrak{en}*$-$\mathfrak{fs}$-$\mathfrak{ps}$-sound.

5.5. SOME SAMPLE PROOFS

The sample proofs of SP programs presented in this section illustrate some of the more subtle features of extended free Hoare Axiomatizations. The basic techniques for program proving are similar to those illustrated in Chapters 1 and 4.

EXAMPLE 1

Our first **program** *ex1* is valid and provable in the appropriate extended free Hoare Axiomatization $\mathbf{Hax}_{(),((\mathbf{PC.swap}),(\mathbf{PC.sort2}))}$, where **(PC.swap)** and

(PC.sort2) are the Procedure-Call Axioms for **procedure**'s *swap* and *sort2*. **Procedure** *sort2*, which arranges two integer variables into ascending order, is $\mathfrak{en}*$-$\mathfrak{fs}$-$\mathfrak{ps}$-valid and provable in the appropriate extended free Hoare Axiomatization $\mathbf{Hax}_{\{\},\{(\mathbf{PC.swap})\}}$. We have already discussed **procedure** *swap* in the context of **program** *illustration*.

```
program ex1;
procedure swap(x,y);
      var t;
      begin
      {x=zx & y=zy & I(x) & I(y)}
      t := x;
      x := y;
      y := t;
      {x=zy & y=zx}
      end;
procedure sort2(x,y);
      begin
      {x=zx1 & y=zy1 & I(x) & I(y)}
      if x>y then swap(x,y)
      {x=min(zx1,zy1) & y=max(zx1,zy1)}
      end;
var x1,x2,x3,y1,y2,y3;
begin
{I(x1) & I(x2) & I(x3)}
y1 := x1;
y2 := x2;
y3 := x3;
sort2(y1,y2);
sort2(y2,y3);
sort2(y1,y2)
{y1=min(x1,min(x2,x3)) &
 y2=max(min(x1,x2),min(max(x1,x2),x3)) &
 y3=max(max(x1,x2),x3)}
end
```

The Procedure-Call Axioms for **procedures** *swap* and *sort2* are as follows:

(PC.swap) $\{p[y',x'\backslash x',y'] \;\&\; \mathrm{I}(x') \;\&\; \mathrm{I}(y')\}$
$\quad swap(x',y')$
$\{p\}$

(PC.sort2) $\{p[\min(x',y'),\max'(x',y')\backslash x',y'] \;\&\; \mathrm{I}(x') \;\&\; \mathrm{I}(y')\}$
$\quad sort2(x',y')$
$\{p\}$

The proof of **procedure** *sort2* in the appropriate extended free Hoare Axiomatization $\mathbf{Hax}_{\{\},\{(\mathbf{PC.swap})\}}$ proceeds by invoking the Procedure-Call Axiom for **procedure** swap, then the Dummy Axiom, and finally applying the Consequence Rule twice. The proof of **program** *ex1* in the appropriate extended free Hoare Axiomatization $\mathbf{Hax}_{\{\},\{(\mathbf{PC.sort2}),(\mathbf{PC,swap})\}}$ ($\mathbf{Hax}_{\{\},\{(\mathbf{PC.sort2})\}}$ would do) proceeds by applying the Procedure-Call Axiom for **procedure** *sort2* (three times), the Assignment Axiom (three times), the Composition Rule (five times), and finally the Consequence Rule (once). For example, working backwards, after the first application of **(PC.sort2)**, we have

$$
\begin{array}{l}
\{\min(y1,y2) = \min(x1,\min(x2,x3))\ \&\ \max(y1,y2) = \\
\quad \max(\min(x1,x2),\min(\max(x1,x2),x3))\ \&\ y3 = \max(\max(x1,x2)x3)\} \\
\qquad sort2(y1,y2) \\
\{y1 = \min(x1,\min(x2,x3))\ \& \\
\quad y2 = \max(\min(x1,x2),\min(\max(x1,x2),x3))\ \& \\
\quad y3 = \max(\max(x1,x2)x3)\}
\end{array}
$$

The Consequence Rule can be applied to complete the proof of **program** *ex*1 because

$$
\begin{array}{l}
\vdash \mathrm{I}(x1)\ \&\ \mathrm{I}(x2)\ \&\ \mathrm{I}(x3) \rightarrow \\
\qquad \min(\min(x1,x2),\min(\max(x1,x2),x3)) = \min(x1,\min(x2,x3))\ \& \\
\qquad \max(\min(x1,x2),\min(\max(x1,x2),x3)) = \\
\qquad\qquad \max(\min(x1,x2),\min(\max(x1,x2),x3))\ \& \\
\qquad \max(\max(x1,x2),x3) = \max(\max(x1,x2),x3)
\end{array}
$$

EXAMPLE 2

Our second **program** *ex*2 is valid and provable in the appropriate extended free Hoare Axiomatization $\mathbf{Hax}_{\{\},\{(\mathbf{PC.pr2})\}}$, even though its one **function** *f*2 is neither $\mathfrak{en}_{f2}$*-$\mathfrak{fs}$-$\mathfrak{ps}$-valid nor provable in the basic free Hoare axiomatization.

```
program ex2;
function f2();
    begin
    {true}
    while true do d
    {f2=0}
    end;
procedure pr2();
    begin
    {true}
    d
    {true}
    end;
```

```
var x;
begin
{true}
if true then
      pr2()
else
      x := f2()
{true}
end
```

Notice that **function** $f2$ is never called. The proof of **program** $ex2$ proceeds as follows. Although the body of $f2$ cannot be proven, the body of $pr2$ can be in the basic free Hoare Axiomatization (by invoking the Dummy Axiom and then applying the Consequence Rule). In $\mathbf{Hax}_{\{\},\{(\mathbf{PC.pr2})\}}$, by the Procedure-Call Axiom for **procedure** $pr2$ and the Consequence Rule, we have

(1) {I(true)&true&true} $pr2()$ {true}
By the Assignment Axiom, we have
(2) {I($f2()$)&true} x:=$f2()$ {true}
And by applying the Consequence Rule to part 2, we have
(3) {I(true)&true&~true} x:=$f2()$ {true}

The proof of the body of **program** $ex2$ is completed by applying the Conditional Rule to (1) and (3).

The key point to bear in mind is that we are able to derive (2) and complete the proof even though **function** $f2$ is incorrect. The call of **function** $f2$ is embedded in an assignment statement in the main program, and the Assignment Axiom's form makes it unnecessary to include any information about $f2$ in $\mathbf{Hax}_{\{\},\{(\mathbf{PC.pr2})\}}$.

EXAMPLE 3

Program $ex3$ is much like **program** $ex2$ in Example 2, but this time it is the **procedure** $pr3$ and not the **function** $f3$ that is incorrect.

```
program ex3;
function f3();
      begin
      {true}
      f3 := 0
      {f3=0}
      end;
procedure pr3();
      begin
      {true}
```

```
        while true do d
        {true}
        end;
var x;
begin
{true}
if true then
        x := f3()
else
        pr3()
{true}
end
```

Program *ex*3 is valid, but it is not provable in $\mathbf{Hax}_{\{(\mathbf{FC.f3})\},\{\}}$. This problem arises since we cannot derive

(2) {I(true)&true&~true} *pr*3() {true}

because we cannot prove **procedure** *pr*3 in $\mathbf{Hax}_{\{(\mathbf{FC.f3})\},\{\}}$. Unlike the call of **function** *f*2 in the preceding example, the call of **procedure** *pr*3 is not embedded in a statement for which there is an axiom (as opposed to a rule). The call of *pr*3 is "too exposed." Of course, **program** *ex*3 can be made provable in $\mathbf{Hax}_{\{(\mathbf{FC.f3})\},\{(\mathbf{PC.pr3})\}}$ by changing **procedure** *pr*3's precondition to false.

EXERCISES

Free Arithmetic

1. Using the natural deduction system for free logic, show that

(a) $\vdash \sim\exists X(p\&\sim p)$

(b) $\vdash \forall X(p \vee \sim p)$

(c) $\vdash \forall X(p\rightarrow q) \rightarrow (\forall Xp\rightarrow \forall Xq)$

(d) $\vdash \forall X(p\&q) \leftrightarrow \forall Xp\&\forall Xq$

(e) $\vdash \exists Xp \vee \forall X(p\rightarrow q)$

(f) $\vdash \exists X(p\&q)\&\forall X(q\rightarrow r) \rightarrow \exists X(p\&r)$

(g) $\vdash \forall X(p(X)\vee q(x)) \leftrightarrow \forall Xp(X)\vee q(x)$

(h) $\exists X(p\vee q) \vdash \exists Xp \vee \exists Xq$

(i) $\sim\exists X\sim p \vdash \forall Xp$

(j) $\sim\forall X\sim p \vdash \exists Xp$

(k) $\exists X\forall Yp(X,Y) \vdash \forall Y\exists Xp(X,Y)$

(l) $\forall X\forall Y(p(X)\&q(Y)\rightarrow r(X,Y)),\ \exists X\exists Y(p(X)\&\sim p(Y)\&\sim r(X,Y))$
$\vdash \exists X(\sim p(X)\&\sim q(X))$

2. Using the axiomatization of free arithmetic, show that
   (a) $\vdash \sim X<X$
   (b) $\vdash X\neq 0 \rightarrow X>0 \vee X<0$
   (c) $\vdash X\neq Y \rightarrow X>Y \vee X<Y$
   (d) $\vdash \text{succ}(X)>X$
   (e) $\vdash \text{pred}(X)<X$
   (f) $\vdash \sim(X<Y<X+\text{succ}(X))$
   (g) $\vdash (X+Y)+Z=X+(Y+Z)$
   (h) $\vdash X*1=X$
   (i) $\vdash 0*X=0$
   (j) $\vdash X*Y=Y*X$
   (k) $\vdash X\neq 0 \rightarrow 0**X=0$
   (l) $\vdash \exists Y((X\geqslant 0 \rightarrow Y=X) \;\&\; (X<0 \rightarrow Y=-X))$
   (m) $\vdash (X\geqslant 0 \rightarrow Y=X) \;\&\; (X<0 \rightarrow Y=-X) \;\&\; (X\geqslant 0 \rightarrow Y'=X) \;\&$
   $(X<0 \rightarrow Y'=-X) \rightarrow Y=Y'$
   (n) $\vdash \text{abs}(\text{abs}(X))=\text{abs}(X)$
   (o) $\vdash 1\neq 2$
3. Using the axiomatization of free arithmetic, show that
   (a) $\vdash X*(Y+Z)=X*Y+X*Z$
   (b) $\vdash X+(-X)=0$
   (c) $\vdash X-Y=X+(-Y)$
   (d) $\vdash X\geqslant Y \;\&\; X'\geqslant Y' \rightarrow X+X'\geqslant Y+Y'$
   (e) $\vdash X\geqslant Y \;\&\; X'\leqslant Y' \rightarrow X-X'\geqslant Y-Y'$
   (f) $\vdash X\geqslant 0 \;\&\; Y\geqslant Y' \rightarrow X*Y\geqslant X*Y'$
   (g) $\vdash X>0 \;\&\; X*Y\geqslant X*Y' \rightarrow Y\geqslant Y'$
   (h) $\vdash \text{abs}(X*Y)=\text{abs}(X)*\text{abs}(Y)$
   (i) $\vdash \text{abs}(X**2)=X**2$
   (j) $\vdash X \bmod 0=\perp$
   (k) $\vdash Y>0 \rightarrow X=(X/Y)*Y+(X \bmod Y)$
   (l) $\vdash X\geqslant 0 \& Y>0 \rightarrow \exists Q\exists R(0\leqslant R<Y \;\&\; X=Y*Q+R)$
4. Demonstrate that the Principle of Strong Mathematical Induction is a theorem of free arithmetic. That is, show that

$$\vdash p(0) \;\&\; \forall X(X>0 \rightarrow (\forall Y(0\leqslant Y \& Y<X \rightarrow p(Y)) \rightarrow p(X)))$$
$$\& \;\forall X(X<0 \rightarrow (\forall Y(X<Y \& Y\leqslant 0 \rightarrow p(Y)) \rightarrow p(X))) \rightarrow p(Z)$$

Proving Programs Correct

In each of the exercises in this section, your first task is to write an *SP*(main) program and the user-defined function described in the exercise. Second, prove your function correct in the basic free Hoare Axiomatization. Third, prove the program correct in an appropriate extended free Hoare Axiomatization. Finally, repeat these three steps using a **procedure** instead of a **function.** For illustration, see Exercise 5, where we exhibit the (main) programs you should use.

5. Write a **function** *fadd*(*x*,*y*) to compute $x+y$ using only the unary operation symbols 'abs', 'pred', and 'succ'. **Function** *fadd* has the parameters *x* and *y*, and the statement body of *fadd* should be a **for** statement. Write **function** *fadd* efficiently by using the smaller of abs(x) and abs(y) as the final expression in your **for** statement. The precondition of **function** *fadd* is I(x)&I(y), and the postcondition is $fadd = x + y$. The program calling **function** *fadd* is as follows:

```
program exercise1f;
function fadd(x,y);
      :
    begin
    {I(x)&I(y)}
      :
    {fadd = x+y}
    end;
var u,v,res;
begin
{I(u)&I(v)}
res := fadd(u,v)
{res=u+v}
end
```

   The program-calling procedure *pradd* is as follows:

```
program exercise1pr;
procedure pradd(x,y,w);
      :
    begin
    {x=zx & y=zy & w=zw & I(x) & I(y)}
      :
    {x=zx & y=zy & w = zx+zy}
    end;
var u,v,res;
begin
{I(u)&I(v)}
pradd(u,v,res)
{res=u+v}
end
```

6. Write a **function** *fdiv*(x,y) to compute x/y using only the operation symbols 'abs', 'pred', and 'succ'. The precondition of *fdiv* is $\mathrm{I}(x)\&\mathrm{I}(y)\&y\geqslant 1$, and its postcondition is $fdiv = x/y$.
7. Write a **function** *fprime*(x) to determine if an integer x is prime. The precondition of fprime is $\mathrm{I}(x)$, and its postcondition is $fprime =$ chprime(x), where chprime (the characteristic operation for the predicate *prime*) is introduced with the explicit definition

   (D.chprime) $\quad \mathrm{chprime}(X) = Y \leftrightarrow$
   $(\mathrm{prime}(X) \rightarrow Y = 1)\ \&\ ({\sim}\mathrm{prime}(X) \rightarrow Y = 0))$

   (Do not use either the predicate prime or its characteristic operation chprime in *fprime*'s statement body.)
8. Write a **function** *fxthprime*(x) that finds the x-th ($x\geqslant 1$) prime number. The precondition of *fxthprime* is $\mathrm{I}(x)$ and its postcondition is *fxthprime*=xthprime(x), where xthprime is a unary operation symbol introduced into free arithmetic with xthprime$(X) = X$-th prime number.
9. Write a **function** *fchperfect*(x,y) that determines if an integer x is a perfect number. The precondition of *fchperfect* is $\mathrm{I}(x)\ \&\ x\geqslant 1$, and its postcondition is $fperfect =$ chperfect(x), where chperfect (the characteristic operation for the predicate perfect) is introduced with the explicit definition

   (D.chperfect) $\quad \mathrm{chperfect}(X)=Y \leftrightarrow$
   $(\mathrm{perfect}(X) \rightarrow Y=1)\ \&\ ({\sim}\mathrm{perfect}(X) \rightarrow Y=0))$

10. Write a **function** *fgcd*(x,y) to compute the greatest common divisor of x and y. The precondition of *fgcd* is $\mathrm{I}(x)\&\mathrm{I}(y)\&(x\neq 0 \vee y\neq 0)$, and its postcondition is $fgcd = \mathrm{gcd}(x,y)$.

Semantics

11. Develop the semantics of Sections 5.0 and 5.2 without introducing either the error constant $\perp$ into the syntax or the unique error object $\perp$ into the semantics. Begin by dropping the axioms **($\perp$.~E)** and **($\perp$.un)** from free arithmetic, and continue by either
    (a) Making no further modifications to the axioms of free arithmetic, or
    (b) Introducing new axioms expressing that an error object is either an uninitialized integer variable error err_unin, or a division by 0 error err_div0, and so forth, so that, for example, 5/0=err_div0 is provable.

The solution to (b) shows one way to provide "abstract error objects" for an "abstract data type." Be warned that the solution to (b) is much more involved than that of (a).

12. Suppose procedures have been banished from our programming language. Suppose also that functions are allowed to contain occurrences of global variables but are prohibited from setting them. Reformulate the concept of extended free Hoare Axiomatizations and prove the soundness (in a suitable sense) of your system. Is your system sound if procedures are allowed?

13. This exercise deals with dynamic scoping (i.e., the most recent association rule is in SNOBOL and older dialects of LISP), as opposed to static scoping. Assume that procedures have been banned as in the preceding exercise.

(a) Redefine the meaning of $\mathfrak{M}[f(e_1, \ldots, e_n)]$ so that dynamic scoping is captured. Recall that, with dynamic scoping, if x is a global variable redeclared in function f, f calls function g, g does not redeclare x, and if g were allowed to contain x, then g would reference f's x and not the global x. (With the static scoping incorporated into the operational semantics of Section 5.2, if g were allowed to contain x, g would reference the global x.)

(b) Suppose functions could contain references to nonlocal variables but were prohibited from setting them. Reformulate the concept of an extended free Hoare Axiomatization and prove the soundness of your system. Is your system sound if procedures are allowed?

14. Modify the syntax, operational semantics, and the concept of an extended free Hoare Axiomatization so that the call by constant-value used in passing parameters to functions is realized by the call by reference mechanism (as opposed to the call by value illustrated in the text). Do not require programmer-defined functions to be strict, and the Function Call Axioms should be conditional equational definitions. Illustrate your syntax by showing how a user-defined function equivalent to cond can be implemented.

15. Modify the syntax, operational semantics, and the concept of an extended free Hoare Axiomatization so that parameters can be passed to procedures by value, by result, and by value-result, as well as by reference.

16. Modify the syntax, operational semantics, and the concept of an extended free Hoare Axiomatization so that parameters are passed to procedures by *name* (as in ALGOL60 and SIMULA67) instead of by reference.

17. Modify the syntax, operational semantics, and the concept of an extended free Hoare Axiomatization so that procedures can refer to global variables but cannot change their values. Impose appropriate syntactic restrictions on procedures and, if need be, redefine the concept of validity.

18. Modify the syntax, operational semantics, and the concept of an extended free Hoare Axiomatization so that functions can assign values to their formal parameters. In other words, functions are still called by value but the call by value mechanism no longer realizes the call by constant-value.

19. Modify the syntax, operational semantics, and the concept of an extended free Hoare Axiomatization so that function declarations can be nested within function declarations, and that function and procedure declarations can be nested within procedure declarations.

20. Modify the syntax, operational semantics, and the concept of an extended free Hoare Axiomatization so that some forward referencing is permitted but recursion is still prohibited. (In Pascal, unannounced forward-referencing is prohibited so that an efficient, one-pass compiler can be implemented. In contrast, our aim here is to block recursion and aliasing in as simple a manner as possible.)

21. Supplement extended free Hoare Axiomatizations with additional axioms or rules of inference so the **program** *ex*3 of Example 3, Section 5.5, is provable. Does your "fix" work for all similar problematic cases? Be sure to sketch a soundness proof.

22. (a) Let A be a set of assertions and p be an assertion, with A and p possibly containing function variables. Define, in free arithmetic unextended with function call axioms, $A \models p$ and $\models p$.

(b) Let AP be an asserted statement, possibly containing function and procedure variables. Define $\models AP$.

Programming Projects

23. Write an interpreter for the class of *SP* programs.

24. Write a proof-checker for the natural deduction system for free logic with equality presented in Section 5.0.

25. Write a proof-checker for extended free Hoare Axiomatizations.

CHAPTER 6

The Translation of Tail Recursive Procedures into **while** Programs

In this chapter, we introduce a class of tail recursive procedures called TR programs to motivate basic concepts of denotational semantics. Our intent is to illuminate the proof theoretic and semantic characters of **while** programs as well as of TR programs.

TR programs may have both nonrecursive and tail recursive procedures of a restricted syntactic form. We do not permit procedures with parameters, which gives TR some of the flavor of older and simpler programming languages such as BASIC and COBOL. As in Chapter 5, procedures may call other procedures that have been previously declared, but forward referencing is prohibited.

We develop the denotational semantics of TR programs and provide free Hoare Total Correctness Axiomatizations for TR and **while** programs. We also present a translation that maps TR programs into **while** programs, and prove that it is correct. When composed with the translation $\mathfrak{T}$ in Chapter 4 (with minor modifications), the class of TR programs maps into the class of FC programs of Chapter 2. As a side benefit, the translation induces a denotational semantics for the **while** programs and an operational semantics for TR programs. Finally, we show that the Hoare Axiomatization for the class of **while** programs matches up in a suitable sense with its operational semantics (and hence, with its induced denotational semantics).

In Section 6.0, we develop the mathematics necessary for our elementary denotational semantics and show that certain forms of semantic definitions, which underlie the forms to be used in Section 6.2, preserve a certain mathematical semantic structure (called a "complete partial order"). Our treatment is unencumbered by the more sophisticated mathematics required to handle the general class of recursive procedures with unrestricted (nontail as well as tail) recursive calls and forward referencing.

We present the syntax, denotational semantics, and free Hoare Total Correctness Axiomatizations for TR programs in Sections 6.1 through 6.3. Section 6.4 contains a translation of TR programs into **while** programs. Before presenting the translation, we modify the syntax, semantics, and Hoare Axiomatization for the **while** programs (from Chapter 1) to suit the free case, proceding along the lines developed in Chapter 5. Here, however, we make no provision for subprograms. To facilitate comparison with the denotational semantics of TR programs, we present the operational semantics of the **while** programs in a more formal style than in preceding chapters.

In Section 6.5, we prove that the translation is correct in the following sense: if a source TR program and its target **while** program (its image under the translation) both begin execution in the same state, they will either both fail to terminate properly, or they will both terminate in the same state. The translation induces a denotational semantics for **while** programs that is equivalent to the operational semantics in the sense that each of the two semantics assigns the same denotation to each statement.

In Section 6.6, we prove the "relative completeness" (in the sense of Cook) of the free Hoare Total Correctness Axiomatization for **while** programs. The key ingredient in the completeness proof is the concept of the "weakest precondition" of a statement and a postcondition. We note that the weakest precondition can be expressed in a form suggested by our Procedure-Call Axioms for TR programs. Relative completeness complements soundness, which carries over from the soundness theorem of Chapter 5. Together with the results of Section 6.5, relative completeness and soundness insure, in the case of **while** programs, that the Hoare Axiomatization matches up with the operational and induced denotational semantics. A similar result can be had in the case of TR programs by modifying the denotational semantics slightly.

The exercises in this chapter emphasize semantics.

6.0. COMPLETE PARTIAL ORDERS

Let $\langle A,\sqsubseteq\rangle$ be a partial order and $A'\subset A$. An element $x\in A$ is an *upper bound* of A' (wrt $\sqsubseteq$) if, for every $x'\in A'$, $x'\sqsubseteq x$. An upper bound x of A' is the *least* upper bound of A', written $\mathfrak{lub}[A']$, if each upper bound y of A' is such that $x\sqsubseteq y$. Let $x_i\in A$ $(i\geqslant 0)$ and $\langle x_i\rangle = \langle x_0, x_1, \ldots\rangle$ be an infinite sequence. The infinite sequence $\langle x_i\rangle$ is a *chain* in A if, for every $i\geqslant 0$, $x_i\sqsubseteq x_{i+1}$. If the least upper bound of (the set of elements in) $\langle x_i\rangle$ exists, we denote it by $\mathfrak{lub}[x_i]$.

Let $\langle A,\sqsubseteq\rangle$ be a partial order with a least element $\perp_A$, $A' = A-\{\perp_{A'}\}$ be nonempty, and $\sqsubseteq_{\cap A'\times A'}$ be the restriction of $\sqsubseteq$ to $A'\times A'$.[1] $\langle A', \sqsubseteq_{\cap A'\times A'}\rangle$ is a *complete partial order (cpo)* if every chain $\langle x_i\rangle$ in A' has a least upper bound. When there is no danger of ambiguity, we will denote a partial order $\langle A,\sqsubseteq\rangle$ by its underlying set, A, and we will omit subscripts on its least element ($\perp$) and its ordering relation ($\sqsubseteq$). It can be easily verified that the partial order A is also a complete partial order if A' is, and due to the presence of the least element $\perp$ in A, A is said to be *pointed*. The cpo's A and A' are *flat* (also called *discrete* in the literature) if, for every $x,x'\in A'$, $x\sqsubseteq x'$ iff $x = x'$.

We write $A\rightarrow A'$ to denote the class of functions from a nonempty set A into a nonempty set A'. The ordering of elements $\sqsubseteq'$ in a partial order $\langle A',\sqsubseteq'\rangle$ induces an ordering on $A\rightarrow A'$. Let $f,g\in A\rightarrow A'$. We understand that $f\sqsubseteq_{A\rightarrow A'} g$ if $\forall X\in A(f(X)\sqsubseteq' g(X))$.

Let A and A' be pointed cpo's. A function $f\in A\rightarrow A'$ is said to be *strict* if $f(\perp) = \perp'$. We denote the set of strict functions from A into A' by $A\rightarrow_s A'$. More generally, an n-ary function g is said to be *strict in its i-th argument* $(1\leqslant i\leqslant n)$ provided $f(x_1, \ldots, x_n) = \perp'$ if $x_i = \perp$.

In developing denotational semantics, it is convenient to use lambda notation. Let $f\in A\rightarrow A'$ be a unary function such that $f(x) = \_x\_$, where $\_x\_$ is an expression in which x may occur free. In the lambda notation, $\lambda x.\_x\_$ denotes the function f. For example, if $g(x) = x+1$, then $\lambda x.x+1$ denotes g, and, if $\lambda x.x+1$ is evaluated with the argument 3, then we have $(\lambda x.x+1)(3) = 3+1 = 4$. Let $\_x,y\_$ be an expression in which x and y may occur free. We write $\lambda xy.\_x,y\_ \in A\rightarrow(A\rightarrow A')$ as short for $\lambda x.\lambda y.\_x,y\_$, and understand $\lambda xy.\_x,y\_(x) = \lambda y.\_x,y\_\in A\rightarrow A'$. The function $\lambda\langle x,y\rangle.\_x,y\_$ is a binary function belonging to $(A\times A)\rightarrow A'$. We extend the notation in a natural manner to n-ary functions having, possibly, arguments of different types. Using the lambda notation simplifies the statement of some of the definitions that follow. For example, we understand that, if $\langle f_i\rangle$ is a chain of functions in the cpo $A\rightarrow A'$, then $\mathfrak{lub}[f_i] = \lambda x.\mathfrak{lub}[f_i(x)]$.

In conjunction with the lambda notation, it is also convenient to use a notation in function definitions similar to ALGOL60's arithmetic **if-then-**

[1] In free logic terms, A' is the inner domain and A the outer domain.

else (or LISP's **cond**). For example, instead of writing

$$\begin{aligned} e &= e' \text{ if } b \\ &= e'' \text{ otherwise} \end{aligned}$$

as has been our practice, we write with the same intended meaning

$$e = \textbf{if } b \textbf{ then } e' \textbf{ else } e''$$

and we extend this notation in a natural manner to other types. Use of the **if-then-else** notation facilitates writing the semantic definitions of Section 2, especially when it is natural to have nested **if-then-else**'s.

A member x of a partially ordered set $(A,\sqsubseteq)$ is said to be a *fixed point* of a function $f \in A \to A$ if $f(x) = x$. An element x of A is the *least* fixed point of f if (1) x is a fixed point of f and (2) $x \sqsubseteq y$ for every fixed point $y \in A$ of f. Note that if f has a least fixed point, it is unique, and we will write $\mathrm{lfp}[f]$ to denote it.

As a first and simple example of a least fixed point, consider the flat cpo $(\mathfrak{Z}+,\sqsubseteq_{\mathfrak{Z}+})$, where $\mathfrak{Z}+ = \mathfrak{Z} \cup \{\perp_{\mathfrak{Z}}\}$ is ordered by the relation $\sqsubseteq_{\mathfrak{Z}+}$, which holds between any $x,y \in \mathfrak{Z}+$ if $x = \perp$ or $x = y$. Let function $F \in (\mathfrak{Z}+ \to_s \mathfrak{Z}+) \to (\mathfrak{Z}+ \to_s \mathfrak{Z}+)$ be defined as follows:

$$\begin{aligned} F = \lambda f x.& \\ &\textbf{if } x \in \mathfrak{Z} \textbf{ then} \\ &\quad \textbf{if } x = 0 \textbf{ then} \\ &\qquad 1 \\ &\quad \textbf{else} \\ &\qquad 2 * f(x-1) \\ &\textbf{else} \\ &\quad \perp \end{aligned}$$

The powers of two function

$$\begin{aligned} \mathrm{p2} = \lambda x.& \\ &\textbf{if } x \in \mathfrak{Z} \textbf{ then} \\ &\quad \textbf{if } x \geqslant 0 \textbf{ then} \\ &\qquad 2 ** x \\ &\quad \textbf{else} \\ &\qquad 0 \\ &\textbf{else} \\ &\quad \perp \\ = \lambda x.2 ** x& \text{ by axioms } \mathbf{(**.0)}, \mathbf{(**.+)}, \mathbf{(**.-)}, \text{ and } \mathbf{(**.st)} \\ & \text{ of free arithmetic} \end{aligned}$$

is a fixed point of F because

```
F(p2) = (λfx.if x∈ℨ  then
                 if x=0 then
                   1
                 else
                   2*f(x−1)
               else
                 ⊥) (p2)
      = λx.if x∈ℨ then
                 if x=0 then
                   1
                 else
                   2*p2(x−1)
               else
                 ⊥
      = p2
```

However, neither the succ nor the totally undefined function $\perp_{\mathfrak{Z}+\to_s\mathfrak{Z}+}$ is a fixed point of F because succ(2) = 3. However,

```
F(succ)(2) = (λfx.if x∈ℨ then
                       if x=0 then
                         1
                       else
                         2*f(x−1)
                     else
                       ⊥)  (succ) (2)
           = if 2∈ℨ then
               if 2=0 then
                 1
               else
                 2*succ(2−1)
             else
               ⊥
           = 2
```

and $\perp_{\mathfrak{Z}+\to_s\mathfrak{Z}+}(0) = \perp_{\mathfrak{Z}}$, but $F(\perp_{\mathfrak{Z}+\to\mathfrak{Z}+})(0) = 1$. The least fixed point of F is $\mathrm{p2}\restriction\mathfrak{N}$, the powers of two function restricted to the natural numbers. That is,

```
p2↾𝔑 = λx.if x∈ℨ then
              if  x≥0 then
                2**x
              else
                ⊥
            else
              ⊥
```

We have $p2 \restriction \mathfrak{N} \sqsubseteq p2$ because

$$p2 \restriction \mathfrak{N}(\bot) = \bot = p2(\bot)$$
$$p2 \restriction \mathfrak{N}(x) = \bot \sqsubseteq 0 = p2(x) \text{ for every } x < 0$$
$$p2 \restriction \mathfrak{N}(x) = 2{**}x = p2(x) \text{ for every } x \geqslant 0$$

In denotational semantics, the idea is to take the denotation (meaning) of F to be $\mathfrak{lfp}[F] = p2 \restriction \mathfrak{N}$ for two important reasons. First, no function such as succ or $\bot_{\mathfrak{Z}+\to\mathfrak{Z}+}$ that is not a fixed point of F could plausibly be taken as the meaning of F. Second, as will be seen in the Tail Recursion Fixed Point Theorem discussion in Section 6.2, the least fixed point is the limit (least upper bound) of what can be achieved computationally with machines having finite resources.

As a second and more complicated example, we consider a function G (related to the **procedure** *exp* in the **program** *sample* that will be presented in Section 6.1). Let

$$G = \lambda f\langle x,y,s\rangle.$$
$$(\lambda a.H(f)(a)(x,y,s))\ (1)$$

where

$$H = \lambda fa\langle x,y,s\rangle.$$

```
if a,x,y∈ℨ then
  if a>y+1 then
    s
  else
    if a=1 then
      f(2)(x,y,1)
    else
      f(a+1)(x,y,s*x)
else
  ⊥
```

Let

$$expid = \lambda\langle x,y,s\rangle.$$
$$exp4(1)(x,y,s)$$

where

$$exp4 = \lambda a\langle x,y,s\rangle.$$

```
if a,x,y∈ℨ then
  if y≥0 then
```


$$\begin{array}{c} x{*}{*}y \\ \textbf{else} \\ s \\ \textbf{else} \\ \bot \end{array}$$

Notice that *expid* is strict in its first two arguments but not in its third. For $x = 3$ and y nonnegative, for example $y = 2$, we have the following:

$$\begin{aligned} G(expid)(3,2,s) &= H(exp4)(1)(3,2,s) \\ &= exp4(1)(3,2,s) \\ &= exp4(2)(3,2,1) \\ &= exp4(3)(3,2,3) \\ &= exp4(4)(3,2,9) \\ &= 9 \\ &= 3{*}{*}2 \end{aligned}$$

And, for y negative, for instance $y = -5$, we have the following:

$$\begin{aligned} G(expid)(x,-5,s) &= H(exp4)(1)(x,-5,s) \\ &= exp4(1)(x,-5,s) \\ &= s \end{aligned}$$

We ask the reader to compare the function *expid* with the function g3 of Example 10, Section 0.6. We have $expid(x,y,s) = \mathrm{g3}(x,y,s)$ for every $x,y,s \in \mathfrak{Z}$. In Chapter 0, we proved that

$$\begin{aligned} \mathrm{g3}(x,y,s) &= s \text{ if } y<0 \\ &= x{*}{*}y \text{ if } y \geqslant 0 \end{aligned}$$

for every $x,y,s \in \mathfrak{Z}$. That proof can be readily extended into a proof that *expid* is a fixed point of G and, in fact, $\mathfrak{lfp}[G] = expid$. In other words, *expid* is the denotation of G.

We close this section with a lemma that will be needed to justify the semantic definitions in Section 6.2.

CPO PRESERVATION LEMMA: Let $\langle A, \sqsubseteq \rangle$ and $\langle A', \sqsubseteq' \rangle$ be cpos.

(a) $A \rightarrow A'$ is a cpo.

(b) If A and A' are pointed with least elements $\bot$ and $\bot'$, then $A \rightarrow_s A'$ is a pointed cpo.

Proof: The proofs of part (a) is similar to that of part (b). We will prove part (b). Let $\langle A,\sqsubseteq\rangle$ and $\langle A',\sqsubseteq'\rangle$ be pointed cpos. We must show that $\langle A\rightarrow_s A', \sqsubseteq_{A\rightarrow_s A'}\rangle$ (1) is a partial order, (2) has a least element, and (3) is such that each of its chains has a least upper bound. To demonstrate (1) that $A\rightarrow_s A'$ is a partial order, we must show that it is reflexive, antisymmetric, and transitive. Let $f,g,h \in A\rightarrow_s A'$, $f\sqsubseteq_{A\rightarrow_s A'}g$, and $g\sqsubseteq_{A\rightarrow_s A'}h$. Because A' is a cpo, $f(x)\sqsubseteq' f(x)$ for every $x\in A$, so $f\sqsubseteq_{A\rightarrow_s A'}f$ by the definition of $\sqsubseteq_{A\rightarrow_s A'}$. Hence, $\sqsubseteq_{A\rightarrow_s A'}$ is reflexive. Similarly, we can show that (a) if $g\sqsubseteq_{A\rightarrow_s A'}f$, then $g=f$, and (b) $f\sqsubseteq_{A\rightarrow_s A'}h$. Hence, $\sqsubseteq_{A\rightarrow_s A'}$ is antisymmetric and transitive as well. As for (2), we can easily verify that $\lambda x.\bot'$ is the least element $\bot_{A\rightarrow_s A'}$ of $A\rightarrow_s A'$. Finally, concerning (3), each chain of functions $\langle f_i\rangle$ in $A\rightarrow_s A'$ has a least upper bound in $A\rightarrow_s A'$ because $\langle f_i(x)\rangle$ has a least upper bound in A' for each $x\in A$, and $\lambda x.\mathrm{lub}[f_i(x)]$ ($=\mathrm{lub}[f_i]$) is strict (because $f_i(\bot)=\bot'$ for each $i\geq 0$). □

6.1. SYNTAX

In this section we define the syntax of a class of tail recursive programs called TR programs. We limit our study to procedure subprograms without parameters and local variables. The syntax of statements is much as in Chapter 1, except that TR programs are devoid of **while** statements. Unless explicitly stated otherwise, we adopt the terminology of the preceding chapter (with possibly, the natural modifications to suit the present chapter).

The abstract syntax of integer expressions and assertions is much as in Chapter 5, as we will be working in free arithmetic. However, because we do not treat function subprograms, there is no need for function variables. As before, the class of procedure variables **Pvar** has typical members pr, . . . , and we now understand the class of variables **Var** to be **Ivar** ∪ **Pvar** with typical members v, ... The class of program variables **Pgva** has typical members pg, . . . as in Chapter 5. The abstract syntax is as follows:

Ivar: x, . . .
Pvar: pr, . . .
Var: v, . . .
$v ::= x \mid pr$
Pgva: pg, . . .
Iexp: e, . . .
$e ::= \bot \mid m \mid x \mid \mathrm{succ}(e) \mid \ldots \mid e+e' \mid \ldots$

The abstract syntax of the set of assertions **Assn** and the set of boolean expressions **Bexp** is as in Chapters 1 and 5. As for the syntax of statements, we eliminate the **while** statement from the syntax of Chapter 5 and the list of actual parameters from a procedure call.

Stat: $S, S', \ldots$
$S ::= d \mid x{:=}e \mid S;S' \mid$ **if** b **then** S **else** $S' \mid pr$

Since TR programs have no loops (**while** statements) but do permit recursion, the syntax of annotated statements must be suitably modified to incorporate "recursion invariants" while eliminating loop invariants. The syntax of annotated statements is the same as that of statements except within the context of a recursive **procedure** *pr*. In that case, we require that an assertion, called a *recursion invariant,* be suffixed to the recursive call of *pr*. Accordingly, the abstract syntax of **Asta** becomes

Asta: $A, A', \ldots$
$A ::= d \mid x{:=}e \mid A;A' \mid$ **if** b **then** A **else** $A' \mid pr \mid pr\{p\}$

The syntax of asserted statements **Aprg** is as before.

Aprg: $AP, \ldots$
$AP ::= \{p\}A\{q\}$

As before, we prohibit assignments to the input variables of a program.

The syntax of procedure **(Proc)** and program **(Prog)** declarations in Chapter 5 are modified to eliminate declarations of integer variables and formal parameters

Proc: $Pr, \ldots$
$Pr ::=$ **procedure** *pr*; **begin** *AP* **end**

Prog: $P, \ldots$
$P ::=$ **program** *pg*; Pr_1; . . . ; Pr_k; **begin** *AP* **end**

We impose two restrictions on occurrences of a procedure call *pr*. First, we prohibit forward references. So, if the procedure call statement *pr* occurs in the body of a **procedure** *pr'*, **procedure** *pr* cannot be declared after **procedure** *pr'*. Second, if **procedure** *pr* is recursive, then the annotated statement body of *pr* must be of the form

```
if b then
  begin
  S;
  pr
  {p}
  end
```

where S is free of recursive calls (i.e., calls of **procedure** *pr*). The boolean expression b is called the *guard* of **procedure** *pr*.

We associate a distinct integer variable a_{pr}, called the *activativation number* of **procedure** *pr*, with each **procedure** *pr*. (As usual, when there is no danger of ambiguity, we shall omit the subscript *pr*.) Assignments to activation numbers are prohibited. Further, we understand that the precondition of a program contains, for each (declared) **procedure** *pr*, the implicit conjunct $a_{pr} = 0$. We incorporate activation numbers into our virtual machine because they simplify the coding of many procedures and they motivate the denotational semantics.

We place restrictions on the specification of a **procedure** *pr* that are similar in spirit to those imposed in Chapter 5. We require that *pr*'s postcondition be of the form

$$z_1 = e_1(x_1, \ldots, x_n) \ \& \ \ldots \ \& \ z_n = e_n(x_1, \ldots, x_n)$$

where the precondition p is in the set of integer variables $\{x_i\}$, none of the x_i's are syntactically vulnerable in *pr*, and the $e_j(x_1, \ldots, x_n)$'s are integer expressions in $\{x_i\}$. We call the x_i's *input variables* of **procedure** *pr*, and the z_i's its *output variables.* Note that some integer variables, called variables for *pr*'s *local use,* which occur in the body of a **procedure** *pr*, may be neither input nor output variables. We prohibit occurrences of a procedure's variables for local use in the main program and in other procedures.

Finally, we impose restrictions on the syntactic form of recursion invariants. A recursion invariant for a **procedure** *pr* must be of the form

$$a \geqslant 1 \ \& \ \mathrm{I}(b) \ \& \ r \ \& \ \mathrm{I}(E) \ \& \ E \cdot\!\!\geqslant 0$$

where a is *pr*'s activation number, b is *pr*'s guard, E is a k-tuple of integer expressions, and I(b), I(E), and $E \cdot\!\!\geqslant \langle 0 \rangle$ are as in Chapter 5.

We close this section with a sample program, which the reader might wish to compare with the **program** *illustration* in Section 5.1.

```
program sample;
procedure exp;
begin
{I(x) & I(y) & y≥0}
if a≤y+1 then
  begin
  if a=1 then
    s := 1
  else
    s := x*s;
  exp
  {a≥1 & I(a) & I(y) & I(x) & y≥0 & (a≥2→s=x**(a−2)) &
```

```
    I(y+2−a) & y+2−a≥0}
    end
  {s = x**y}
  end;
  begin
  {I(u) & I(v) & v≥0 & I(w) & I(z) & z≥0}
  x := u;
  y := v;
  exp;
  t := s;
  x := w;
  y := z;
  exp;
  if t<s then
    begin
    b := s;
    s := t
    end
  else
    b := t
  {b = max(u**v, w**z) & s = min(u**v, w**z)}
  end
```

We have taken some liberties with notation to simplify **procedure** *exp*'s recursion invariant.

6.2. DENOTATIONAL SEMANTICS

In this section, we develop the denotational semantics of TR. The Tail Recursion Fixed Point Theorem, which follows, justifies the key semantic equation giving the meaning of tail recursive procedures. As in Chapter 5, we have a "procedure store." However, whereas the procedure store contained the texts of procedure bodies in Chapter 5, in this chapter the procedure store contains the meanings (denotations) of the procedures. The meaning of a procedure is of the same type as that of a statement in previous chapters—a function that, given a starting state, delivers a final state.

We understand **Ivar, Pvar, Assn,** and $\mathfrak{Tv} = \{\mathfrak{t},\mathfrak{f}\}$ to be (unpointed) flat cpos and $\mathfrak{Z}+$ to be the pointed, flat cpo described in Section 0. $\mathfrak{States}+$ is the class of (total) functions **Ivar** $\rightarrow \mathfrak{Z}+$. We understand $\mathfrak{States}+$ to be the pointed, flat cpo, with $\perp_{\mathfrak{States}}$ the state that assigns each integer variable $\perp_{\mathfrak{Z}}$ and $\sqsubseteq_{\mathfrak{States}+}$ the relation that holds between any $\mathfrak{s},\mathfrak{s}' \in \mathfrak{States}+$ (i.e., $\mathfrak{s} \sqsubseteq_{\mathfrak{States}+} \mathfrak{s}'$) iff $\mathfrak{s} = \perp_{\mathfrak{States}}$ or $\mathfrak{s} = \mathfrak{s}'$. The set of *defined* states is the flat cpo $\mathfrak{States} = \mathfrak{States}+ - \{\perp_{\mathfrak{States}}\}$.

An *error assignment* $\mathfrak{N}$ is of type $\mathfrak{EA} =$ **Assn** $\rightarrow (\mathfrak{States}+ \rightarrow \mathfrak{Tv})$ and plays much the same role as the error assignment of Chapter 5, handling nonfull predicates. The Cpo Preservation Lemma insures that $\mathfrak{Tv}$ is a cpo. We list an error assignment explicitly as an argument of each of our meaning functions, including the one for integer expressions, because an integer expression may contain a nonprimitive operation symbol.

The meaning function $\mathfrak{M}_{\mathfrak{E}}$ extends a state to the integer expressions. The role of $\mathfrak{M}_{\mathfrak{E}}$ is much the same as the meaning function in Chapter 5, restricted to the integer expressions. However, in accordance with the usual practice in denotational semantics, we make $\mathfrak{M}_{\mathfrak{E}}$ a unary function that delivers another function as its value. We have

$$\mathfrak{M}_{\mathfrak{E}} \in \mathbf{Iexp} \rightarrow ((\mathbf{Assn} \rightarrow (\mathfrak{States}+ \rightarrow \mathfrak{Tv})) \rightarrow (\mathfrak{States}+ \rightarrow_{\mathbf{s}} \mathfrak{Z}+))$$

We understand that

$$\mathfrak{M}_{\mathfrak{E}}[e][\mathfrak{R}][\bot_{\mathfrak{States}}] = \bot_{\mathfrak{Z}}$$

for any integer expression e and any error assignment $\mathfrak{R}$. Somewhat similarly, regarding the assertions, we understand that

$$\mathfrak{M}_{\mathfrak{A}}[p][\mathfrak{R}][\bot_{\mathfrak{States}}] = \mathfrak{f}$$

for any assertion p and any error assignment $\mathfrak{R}$. The free denotational semantics of integer expressions and assertions is shown in Figure 6.1.

A set of assertions A *entails* an assertion p, written $A \models p$, provided $\mathfrak{M}_{\mathfrak{A}}[p][\mathfrak{R}][\mathfrak{s}] = \mathfrak{t}$ for every error assignment $\mathfrak{R}$ and every defined state $\mathfrak{s}$ such that, for every $q \in A$, $\mathfrak{M}_{\mathfrak{A}}[q][\mathfrak{R}][\mathfrak{s}] = \mathfrak{t}$. Assertion p is valid, written $\models p$, if $\{\} \models p$.

A *state transformer* ϕ is a function that, composed with an error assignment, maps $\mathfrak{States}+$ into itself—in particular,

$$\phi \in \mathfrak{Strans}+ = \mathfrak{EA} \rightarrow (\mathfrak{States}+ \rightarrow_{\mathbf{s}} \mathfrak{States}+).$$

A. Integer Expressions

a. $\mathfrak{M}_{\mathfrak{E}}[e][\mathfrak{R}][\bot_{\mathfrak{States}}] = \bot_{\mathfrak{Z}}$

b. For any defined state $\mathfrak{s}$,

(0) $\mathfrak{M}_{\mathfrak{E}}[x][\mathfrak{R}][\mathfrak{s}] = \mathfrak{s}[x]$

(1) $\mathfrak{M}_{\mathfrak{E}}[\bot][\mathfrak{R}][\mathfrak{s}] = \bot$

(2) $\mathfrak{M}_{\mathfrak{E}}[m][\mathfrak{R}][\mathfrak{s}] = m$

(3) $\mathfrak{M}_{\mathfrak{E}}[\mathrm{succ}(e)][\mathfrak{R}][\mathfrak{s}] = \mathrm{succ}(\mathfrak{M}_{\mathfrak{E}}[e][\mathfrak{R}][\mathfrak{s}])$ if $\mathfrak{M}_{\mathfrak{E}}[e][\mathfrak{R}][\mathfrak{s}] \in \mathfrak{Z}$
$= \bot$ otherwise

FIGURE 6.1. The free denotational semantics of integer expressions and assertions.

(4) $\mathfrak{M}_{\mathfrak{E}}[e+e'][\mathfrak{N}][\mathfrak{s}] = \mathfrak{M}_{\mathfrak{E}}[e][\mathfrak{N}][\mathfrak{s}]+\mathfrak{M}_{\mathfrak{E}}[e'][\mathfrak{N}][\mathfrak{s}]$ if $\mathfrak{M}_{\mathfrak{E}}[e][\mathfrak{N}][\mathfrak{s}], \mathfrak{M}_{\mathfrak{E}}[e'][\mathfrak{N}][\mathfrak{s}] \in \mathfrak{Z}$
$= \perp$ otherwise

:

(5) $\mathfrak{M}_{\mathfrak{E}}[e/e'][\mathfrak{N}][\mathfrak{s}] = \mathfrak{M}_{\mathfrak{E}}[e][\mathfrak{N}][\mathfrak{s}]/\mathfrak{M}_{\mathfrak{E}}[e'][\mathfrak{N}][\mathfrak{s}]$ if $\mathfrak{M}_{\mathfrak{E}}[e'][\mathfrak{N}][\mathfrak{s}] \neq 0$ and $\mathfrak{M}_{\mathfrak{E}}[e][\mathfrak{N}][\mathfrak{s}], \mathfrak{M}_{\mathfrak{E}}[e'][\mathfrak{N}][\mathfrak{s}] \in \mathfrak{Z}$
$= \perp$ otherwise

(6) $\mathfrak{M}_{\mathfrak{E}}[e \bmod e'][\mathfrak{N}][\mathfrak{s}] = \mathfrak{M}_{\mathfrak{E}}[e][\mathfrak{N}][\mathfrak{s}] \bmod \mathfrak{M}_{\mathfrak{E}}[e'][\mathfrak{N}][\mathfrak{s}]$ if $\mathfrak{M}_{\mathfrak{E}}[e'][\mathfrak{N}][\mathfrak{s}] \neq 0$ and $\mathfrak{M}_{\mathfrak{E}}[e][\mathfrak{N}][\mathfrak{s}], \mathfrak{M}_{\mathfrak{E}}[e'][\mathfrak{N}][\mathfrak{s}] \in \mathfrak{Z}$
$= \perp$ otherwise

(7) $\mathfrak{M}_{\mathfrak{E}}[\text{cond}(e,e',e'')][\mathfrak{N}][\mathfrak{s}] = \mathfrak{M}_{\mathfrak{E}}[e'][\mathfrak{N}][\mathfrak{s}]$ if $\mathfrak{M}_{\mathfrak{E}}[e][\mathfrak{N}][\mathfrak{s}] = 1$
$= \mathfrak{M}_{\mathfrak{E}}[e''][\mathfrak{N}][\mathfrak{s}]$ if $\mathfrak{M}_{\mathfrak{E}}[e][\mathfrak{N}][\mathfrak{s}] = 0$
$= \perp$ otherwise

:

B. Assertions

a. $\mathfrak{M}_{\mathfrak{A}}[p][\mathfrak{N}][\perp_{\mathfrak{States}}] = \mathfrak{f}$

b. For any defined state $\mathfrak{s}$,

(1) $\mathfrak{M}_{\mathfrak{A}}[e=e'][\mathfrak{N}][\mathfrak{s}] = \mathfrak{M}_{\mathfrak{E}}[e][\mathfrak{N}][\mathfrak{s}] = \mathfrak{M}_{\mathfrak{E}}[e'][\mathfrak{N}][\mathfrak{s}]$

(2) $\mathfrak{M}_{\mathfrak{A}}[e\neq e'][\mathfrak{N}][\mathfrak{s}] = \mathfrak{M}_{\mathfrak{E}}[e][\mathfrak{N}][\mathfrak{s}] \neq \mathfrak{M}_{\mathfrak{E}}[e'][\mathfrak{N}][\mathfrak{s}]$ if $\mathfrak{M}_{\mathfrak{E}}[e][\mathfrak{N}][\mathfrak{s}], \mathfrak{M}_{\mathfrak{E}}[e'][\mathfrak{N}][\mathfrak{s}] \in \mathfrak{Z}$
$= \mathfrak{N}[\perp\neq m][\mathfrak{s}]$ if $\mathfrak{M}_{\mathfrak{E}}[e][\mathfrak{N}][\mathfrak{s}] = \perp$ and $\mathfrak{M}_{\mathfrak{E}}[e'][\mathfrak{N}][\mathfrak{s}] \in \mathfrak{Z}$
$= \mathfrak{N}[m\neq\perp][\mathfrak{s}]$ if $\mathfrak{M}_{\mathfrak{E}}[e][\mathfrak{N}][\mathfrak{s}] \in \mathfrak{Z}$ and $\mathfrak{M}_{\mathfrak{E}}[e'][\mathfrak{N}][\mathfrak{s}] = \perp$
$= \mathfrak{N}[\perp\neq\perp][\mathfrak{s}]$ otherwise

(3) $\mathfrak{M}_{\mathfrak{A}}[e\geqslant e'][\mathfrak{N}][\mathfrak{s}] = \mathfrak{M}_{\mathfrak{E}}[e][\mathfrak{N}][\mathfrak{s}] \geqslant \mathfrak{M}_{\mathfrak{E}}[e'][\mathfrak{N}][\mathfrak{s}]$ if $\mathfrak{M}_{\mathfrak{E}}[e][\mathfrak{N}][\mathfrak{s}], \mathfrak{M}_{\mathfrak{E}}[e'][\mathfrak{N}][\mathfrak{s}] \in \mathfrak{Z}$
$= \mathfrak{N}[\perp\geqslant m][\mathfrak{s}]$ if $\mathfrak{M}_{\mathfrak{E}}[e][\mathfrak{N}][\mathfrak{s}] = \perp$ and $\mathfrak{M}_{\mathfrak{E}}[e'][\mathfrak{N}][\mathfrak{s}] \in \mathfrak{Z}$
$= \mathfrak{N}[m\geqslant\perp][\mathfrak{s}]$ if $\mathfrak{M}_{\mathfrak{E}}[e][\mathfrak{N}][\mathfrak{s}] \in \mathfrak{Z}$ and $\mathfrak{M}_{\mathfrak{E}}[e'][\mathfrak{N}][\mathfrak{s}] = \perp$
$= \mathfrak{N}[\perp\geqslant\perp][\mathfrak{s}]$ otherwise

:

(4) $\mathfrak{M}_{\mathfrak{A}}[\sim p][\mathfrak{N}][\mathfrak{s}] = \sim\mathfrak{M}_{\mathfrak{A}}[p][\mathfrak{N}][\mathfrak{s}]$

(5) $\mathfrak{M}_{\mathfrak{A}}[p\&p'][\mathfrak{N}][\mathfrak{s}] = \mathfrak{M}_{\mathfrak{A}}[p][\mathfrak{N}][\mathfrak{s}]\ \&\ \mathfrak{M}_{\mathfrak{A}}[p'][\mathfrak{N}][\mathfrak{s}]$

:

(6) $\mathfrak{M}_{\mathfrak{A}}[\forall Xp][\mathfrak{N}][\mathfrak{s}] =$ For each numeral m, $\mathfrak{M}_{\mathfrak{A}}[p[m\backslash X]][\mathfrak{N}][\mathfrak{s}]$

:

FIGURE 6.1. *(Continued)*

More concretely, a state transformer is the denotational meaning of a statement (in the presence of a procedure store). By the Cpo Preservation Lemma, $\mathfrak{Strans}+$ is a cpo. $\mathfrak{Strans}+$ has as a least element $\perp_{\mathfrak{Strans}}$, which is such that $\perp_{\mathfrak{Strans}}[\mathfrak{R}] = \perp_{\mathfrak{States}+\rightarrow_s\mathfrak{States}+}$ for every error assignment $\mathfrak{R}$, where $\perp_{\mathfrak{States}+\rightarrow_s\mathfrak{States}+}[\mathfrak{s}] = \perp_{\mathfrak{States}}$ for every $\mathfrak{s} \in \mathfrak{States}+$. Extending earlier terminology, a state transformer ϕ is said to *set* an integer variable x if there is some error assignment $\mathfrak{R}$ and some state $\mathfrak{s}$ such that $\phi[\mathfrak{R}][\mathfrak{s}][x] \neq \mathfrak{s}[x]$.

Intuitively, a procedure store is much like a state in that a procedure store assigns a meaning (a state transformer) to each procedure variable just as a state assigns a meaning (an integer or $\perp$) to each integer variable. A *procedure store* $\mathfrak{ps}$, is a function mapping the set of procedure variables into the set of state transformers $\mathfrak{Strans}+$. The class of procedure stores $\mathfrak{Pstore}+$ is a pointed cpo, with least element $\perp_{\mathfrak{Pstore}}$, which assigns each procedure variable $\perp_{\mathfrak{Strans}}$. In summary, we have

$$\mathfrak{s} \in \mathfrak{States} = \mathbf{Ivar} \rightarrow \mathfrak{Z}+$$

$$\phi \in \mathfrak{Strans}+ = \mathfrak{EA} \rightarrow (\mathfrak{States}+ \rightarrow_s \mathfrak{States}+)$$

$$\mathfrak{ps} \in \mathfrak{Pstore}+ = \mathbf{Pvar} \rightarrow \mathfrak{Strans}+$$

A *state transformer functional* Φ is a function mapping the set of state transformers into itself—that is, $\Phi \in \mathfrak{Strans}+ \rightarrow \mathfrak{Strans}+$. A state transformer functional is not required to be strict. Because $\mathfrak{Strans}+$ is a cpo, by the Cpo Preservation Lemma the class of state transformer functionals $\mathfrak{Stfuns}+$ is a cpo. $\mathfrak{Stfuns}+$ is pointed with $\perp_{\mathfrak{Stfuns}}[\phi] = \perp_{\mathfrak{Strans}}$ for any $\phi \in \mathfrak{Strans}+$. Note that, if the least fixed point of a state transformer functional Φ exists, it is a state transformer—that is, $\mathfrak{lfp}[\Phi] = \phi$ for some $\phi \in \mathfrak{Strans}+$.

TAIL RECURSION FIXED POINT THEOREM: Let $a \in \mathbf{Ivar}$, $\phi' \in \mathfrak{Strans}+$ be such that ϕ' does not set the integer variable a, and Φ be the state transformer functional

$\Phi = \lambda\theta\mathfrak{R}\mathfrak{s}.$

if $\mathfrak{s} \in \mathfrak{States}$ **then**
  if $\mathfrak{s}[a] \in \mathfrak{Z}$ **and** $\mathfrak{M}_{\mathfrak{E}}[\mathfrak{E}[b]][\mathfrak{R}][\mathfrak{s}] \subset \mathfrak{Z}$ **then**
    if $\mathfrak{M}_{\mathfrak{A}}[b][\mathfrak{R}][\mathfrak{s}] = \mathrm{t}$ **then**
      $\theta[\mathfrak{R}][(\phi'[\mathfrak{R}][\mathfrak{s}])\{\mathfrak{s}[a]+1\backslash a\}]$
    else
      $\mathfrak{s}$
  else
    $\perp$
else
  $\perp$

and

$$\phi = \mathfrak{lub}[\phi_i]$$

where, for any error assignment $\mathfrak{N}$ and each $i \geqslant 0$,

$$\phi_i[\mathfrak{N}][\bot] = \bot$$

and, for any error assignment $\mathfrak{N}$ and any defined state $\mathfrak{s}$, ϕ_i is defined inductively as follows:

$$\begin{aligned}
&\phi_0[\mathfrak{N}][\mathfrak{s}] = \bot\\
&\phi_{i+1}[\mathfrak{N}][\mathfrak{s}] = \textbf{if } \mathfrak{s}[a] \in \mathfrak{Z} \textbf{ and } \mathfrak{M}_{\mathfrak{E}}[\mathfrak{E}[b]][\mathfrak{N}][\mathfrak{s}] \subset \mathfrak{Z} \textbf{ then}\\
&\qquad \textbf{if } \mathfrak{M}_{\mathfrak{A}}[b][\mathfrak{N}][\mathfrak{s}] = \mathfrak{t} \textbf{ then}\\
&\qquad\quad \phi_i[\mathfrak{N}][(\phi'[\mathfrak{N}][\mathfrak{s}])\{\mathfrak{s}[a]+1 \backslash a\}]\\
&\qquad \textbf{else}\\
&\qquad\quad \mathfrak{s}\\
&\quad \textbf{else}\\
&\qquad \bot
\end{aligned}$$

Then, Φ has a least fixed point, and $\mathfrak{lfp}[\Phi] = \phi$.

Proof: By induction on $i \geqslant 0$, each ϕ_i is a state transformer. Hence, by the definition of a cpo, so is $\phi = \mathfrak{lub}[\phi_i]$. We first show that $\mathfrak{lub}[\phi_i]$ is a fixed point of Φ. To do this, we show that, for any error assignment $\mathfrak{N}$ and any state $\mathfrak{s} \in \mathfrak{States}+$

$$\begin{aligned}
&\mathfrak{lub}[\phi_i][\mathfrak{N}][\mathfrak{s}] =\\
&\quad \textbf{if } \mathfrak{s} \in \mathfrak{States} \textbf{ then}\\
&\qquad \textbf{if } \mathfrak{s}[a] \in \mathfrak{Z} \textbf{ and } \mathfrak{M}_{\mathfrak{E}}[\mathfrak{E}[b]][\mathfrak{N}][\mathfrak{s}] \subset \mathfrak{Z} \textbf{ then}\\
&\qquad\quad \textbf{if } \mathfrak{M}_{\mathfrak{A}}[b][\mathfrak{N}][\mathfrak{s}] = \mathfrak{t} \textbf{ then}\\
&\qquad\qquad \mathfrak{lub}[\theta_i][\mathfrak{N}][(\phi'[\mathfrak{N}][\mathfrak{s}])\{\mathfrak{s}[a]+1 \backslash a\}]\\
&\qquad\quad \textbf{else}\\
&\qquad\qquad \mathfrak{s}\\
&\qquad \textbf{else}\\
&\qquad\quad \bot\\
&\quad \textbf{else}\\
&\qquad \bot\\
&\qquad = \Phi[\mathfrak{N}][[\mathfrak{lub}[\phi_i]][\mathfrak{N}][\mathfrak{s}]]
\end{aligned}$$

If $\mathfrak{s} = \bot$, $\mathfrak{s}[a] \notin \mathfrak{Z}$, or $\mathfrak{M}_{\mathfrak{E}}[\mathfrak{E}[b]][\mathfrak{N}][\mathfrak{s}] \not\subset \mathfrak{Z}$, then $\phi_i[\mathfrak{N}][\mathfrak{s}] = \bot$ for every $i \geqslant 0$, so

$$\begin{aligned}
\mathfrak{lub}[\phi_i][\mathfrak{N}][\bot] &= \mathfrak{lub}[\phi_i[\mathfrak{N}]][\bot]\\
&= \mathfrak{lub}[\phi_i[\mathfrak{N}][\bot]]\\
&= \mathfrak{lub}[\{\bot\}]
\end{aligned}$$

$$\begin{aligned}&= \bot\\ &= \Phi[\mathfrak{N}][[\mathfrak{lub}[\phi_i]][\mathfrak{N}][\bot]].\end{aligned}$$

If $\mathfrak{s}$ is a defined state, $\mathfrak{s}[a]\in\mathfrak{Z}$, $\mathfrak{M}_{\mathfrak{E}}[\mathfrak{E}[b]][\mathfrak{N}][\mathfrak{s}] \subset \mathfrak{Z}$, and $\mathfrak{M}_{\mathfrak{A}}[b][\mathfrak{N}][\mathfrak{s}] = \mathfrak{t}$, then $\phi_{i+1}[\mathfrak{N}][\mathfrak{s}] = \phi_i[\mathfrak{N}][(\phi'[\mathfrak{N}][\mathfrak{s}])\{\mathfrak{s}[a]+1\backslash a\}]$ for every $i\geqslant 0$. Consequently,

$$\begin{aligned}\mathfrak{lub}[\phi_i][\mathfrak{N}][\mathfrak{s}] &= \mathfrak{lub}[\phi_i[\mathfrak{N}][\mathfrak{s}]\\ &= \mathfrak{lub}[\phi_{i+1}[\mathfrak{N}][\mathfrak{s}]]\\ &= \mathfrak{lub}[\phi_i[\mathfrak{N}][(\phi'[\mathfrak{N}][\mathfrak{s}])\{\mathfrak{s}[a]+1\backslash a\}]]\\ &= \mathfrak{lub}[\phi_i][\mathfrak{N}][(\phi'[\mathfrak{N}][\mathfrak{s}])\{\mathfrak{s}[a]+1\backslash a\}]\\ &= \Phi[\mathfrak{N}][\mathfrak{lub}[\phi_i]][\mathfrak{N}][\mathfrak{s}].\end{aligned}$$

If $\mathfrak{s}$ is a defined state, $\mathfrak{M}_{\mathfrak{E}}[\mathfrak{E}[b]][\mathfrak{N}][\mathfrak{s}]\subset\mathfrak{Z}$, and $\mathfrak{M}_{\mathfrak{A}}[b][\mathfrak{N}][\mathfrak{s}] = \mathfrak{f}$, we have $\mathfrak{lub}[\phi_i][\mathfrak{N}][\mathfrak{s}] = \mathfrak{lub}[\phi_i[\mathfrak{N}][\mathfrak{s}]] = \mathfrak{lub}[\{\bot,\mathfrak{s}\}] = \mathfrak{s} = \Phi[\mathfrak{N}][[\mathfrak{lub}[\phi_i]][\mathfrak{N}][\mathfrak{s}]]$. Next, we demonstrate that $\mathfrak{lfp}[\Phi] = \phi$ by showing that, for any fixed point ϕ' of Φ, we have $\phi\sqsubseteq\phi'$. It suffices to show that, for each $i\geqslant 0$, $\phi_i\sqsubseteq\phi'$. We leave the proof (by simple mathematical induction) as an exercise. □

We proceed now to the semantics of statements and programs. The functional $\mathfrak{M}_{\mathfrak{S}}$ gives the semantics of statements, and we wish to have the meaning of a statement S in the presence of a procedure store $\mathfrak{ps}$, an error assignment $\mathfrak{N}$, and state $\mathfrak{s}$ be another state. That is, we want

$$\mathfrak{M}_{\mathfrak{S}}[S][\mathfrak{ps}][\mathfrak{N}][\mathfrak{s}] \in \mathfrak{States}+$$

A *pr-variant* of a procedure store $\mathfrak{ps}$ is to be understood in a similiar manner to an x-variant of a state. That is, we understand

$$\mathfrak{ps}\{\phi\backslash pr\}[pr] = \phi$$

And, if $pr \not\equiv pr'$,

$$\mathfrak{ps}\{\phi\backslash pr\}[pr'] = \mathfrak{ps}[pr']$$

In the semantic clauses shown in Figure 6.2, $\mathfrak{ps}$ is, intuitively, an initial procedure store (prior to accomodating the procedure declarations), $\mathfrak{ps}_i$ is the procedure store in the i-th procedure, and, if a program has k procedures, then $\mathfrak{ps}_{k+1}$ is its procedure store. The statement S_{pr_i} is the statement body of the i-th procedure.

Let $AP \equiv \{p\}S\{q\}$. The truth-value assigned the asserted statement AP is

$$\begin{aligned}\mathfrak{M}_{\mathfrak{A}\mathfrak{P}}[AP][\mathfrak{ps}][\mathfrak{N}][\mathfrak{s}] &= \mathfrak{t} \text{ provided}\\ &\qquad \mathfrak{M}_{\mathfrak{A}}[q][\mathfrak{N}][\mathfrak{M}_{\mathfrak{S}}[S][\mathfrak{ps}][\mathfrak{N}][\mathfrak{s}]] = \mathfrak{t}\\ &\qquad \text{if } \mathfrak{M}_{\mathfrak{A}}[p][\mathfrak{N}][\mathfrak{s}]=\mathfrak{t}\\ &= \mathfrak{f} \text{ otherwise}\end{aligned}$$

A. Procedure Stores

$\mathfrak{ps}_1 = \mathfrak{ps}$

$\mathfrak{ps}_{i+1} = \mathfrak{ps}_i\{\mathfrak{M}_{\mathfrak{S}}[S_{pr_i}][\mathfrak{ps}_i]\backslash pr_i\}$

B. Statements

a. $\mathfrak{M}_{\mathfrak{S}}[S][\mathfrak{ps}][\mathfrak{N}][\perp] = \perp$

b. For any defined state $\mathfrak{s}$,

(1) $\mathfrak{M}_{\mathfrak{S}}[\mathbf{d}][\mathfrak{ps}][\mathfrak{N}][\mathfrak{s}] = \mathfrak{s}$

(2) $\mathfrak{M}_{\mathfrak{S}}[x{:=}e][\mathfrak{ps}][\mathfrak{N}][\mathfrak{s}] = \textbf{if } \mathfrak{M}_{\mathfrak{E}}[e][\mathfrak{N}][\mathfrak{s}] \in \mathfrak{Z} \textbf{ then } \mathfrak{s}\{\mathfrak{s}[e]\backslash x\} \textbf{ else } \perp$

(3) $\mathfrak{M}_{\mathfrak{S}}[S;S'][\mathfrak{ps}][\mathfrak{N}][\mathfrak{s}] = \mathfrak{M}_{\mathfrak{S}}[S][\mathfrak{ps}][\mathfrak{N}][\mathfrak{M}_{\mathfrak{S}}[S'][\mathfrak{ps}][\mathfrak{N}][\mathfrak{s}]]$

(4) $\mathfrak{M}_{\mathfrak{S}}[\textbf{if } b \textbf{ then } S \textbf{ else } S'][\mathfrak{ps}][\mathfrak{N}][\mathfrak{s}] =$

$$
\begin{array}{l}
\textbf{if } \mathfrak{M}_{\mathfrak{E}}[\mathfrak{E}[b]][\mathfrak{N}][\mathfrak{s}] \subset \mathfrak{Z} \textbf{ then} \\
\quad \textbf{if } \mathfrak{M}_{\mathfrak{A}}[b][\mathfrak{N}][\mathfrak{s}] = \mathrm{t} \textbf{ then} \\
\quad\quad \mathfrak{M}_{\mathfrak{S}}[S][\mathfrak{ps}][\mathfrak{N}][\mathfrak{s}] \\
\quad \textbf{else} \\
\quad\quad \mathfrak{M}_{\mathfrak{S}}[S'][\mathfrak{ps}][\mathfrak{N}][\mathfrak{s}] \\
\textbf{else} \\
\quad \perp
\end{array}
$$

provided

if *b* **then** *S* **else** *S'*

either (a) does not occur in the context of a recursive **procedure** *pr* or (b) occurs in the context of a recursive **procedure** *pr* but *S* is not of the form *S''*;*pr*.

(5) $\mathfrak{M}_{\mathfrak{S}}[\textbf{if } b \textbf{ then begin } S;\ pr \textbf{ end}][\mathfrak{ps}][\mathfrak{N}][\mathfrak{s}] = \mathfrak{lfp}[\Phi]$

where $\Phi = \lambda\theta\mathfrak{N}\mathfrak{s}.$

$$
\begin{array}{l}
\textbf{if } \mathfrak{s} \in \mathfrak{States} \textbf{ then} \\
\quad \textbf{if } \mathfrak{s}[a] \in \mathfrak{Z} \textbf{ and } \mathfrak{M}_{\mathfrak{E}}[\mathfrak{E}[b]][\mathfrak{N}][\mathfrak{s}] \subset \mathfrak{Z} \textbf{ then} \\
\quad\quad \textbf{if } \mathfrak{M}_{\mathfrak{A}}[b][\mathfrak{N}][\mathfrak{s}] = \mathrm{t} \textbf{ then} \\
\quad\quad\quad \theta[\mathfrak{N}][(\mathfrak{M}_{\mathfrak{S}}[S][\mathfrak{ps}][\mathfrak{N}][\mathfrak{s}])\{\mathfrak{s}[a]+1\backslash a\}] \\
\quad\quad \textbf{else} \\
\quad\quad\quad \mathfrak{s} \\
\quad \textbf{else} \\
\quad\quad \perp \\
\textbf{else} \\
\quad \perp
\end{array}
$$

provided

if *b* **then begin** *S*; *pr* **end**

FIGURE 6.2. The denotational semantics of TR programs.

occurs in the context of recursive **procedure** *pr*.

(6) $\mathfrak{M}_{\mathfrak{S}}[pr][\mathfrak{ps}][\mathfrak{R}][\mathfrak{s}] = (\mathfrak{ps}[pr][\mathfrak{R}][\mathfrak{s}\{1\backslash a\}])\{0\backslash a\}$
provided *pr* does not occur in the context of recursive **procedure** *pr*.

C. Programs

$\mathfrak{M}_{\mathfrak{PS}}[\textbf{program}\ pg;Pr_1, \ldots ,Pr_k;S][\mathfrak{ps}][\mathfrak{R}][\mathfrak{s}] = \mathfrak{M}_{\mathfrak{S}}[S][\mathfrak{ps}_{k+1}][\mathfrak{R}][\mathfrak{s}]$

FIGURE 6.2. *(Continued)*

AP is $\mathfrak{ps}$-*valid,* written $\models_{\mathfrak{ps}} AP$, if $\mathfrak{M}_{\mathfrak{AP}}[AP][\mathfrak{ps}][\mathfrak{R}][\mathfrak{s}]=\mathrm{t}$ for every error assignment $\mathfrak{R}$ and every state $\mathfrak{s}$. A procedure or program is $\mathfrak{ps}$-*valid* if its body is.

Let $P \equiv$ **program** *pg*; Pr_1; . . . ;Pr_k; **begin** *AP* **end**

and $\mathfrak{ps}_{k+1}$ be the **program** *pg*'s procedure store. The truth-value assigned a program is given by the equation

$$\mathfrak{M}_{\mathfrak{P}}[P][\mathfrak{R}][\mathfrak{s}] = \mathfrak{M}_{\mathfrak{AP}}[AP][\mathfrak{ps}_{k+1}][\mathfrak{R}][\mathfrak{s}]$$

and we understand *P* to be *valid* provided $\mathfrak{M}_{\mathfrak{P}}[P][\mathfrak{R}][\mathfrak{s}] = \mathrm{t}$ for every error assignment $\mathfrak{R}$ and every state $\mathfrak{s}$.

We illustrate the denotational semantics of tail recursive procedures with some informal remarks about **procedure** *exp* in **program** *sample* in Section 6.1. **Procedure** *exp* sets the integer variable *s* to $x{**}y$. When *exp* is called from the main program, its activation number *a* is initialized to 1 before entry. At each recursive call, *a* is incremented, and, on return of control to the main program, is reset to 0. In our semantics, there is no bound on the number of times *exp* can be called. However, if it could not be called at all, the maximum value of *a* would be 0; if it could be called only once (and so not recursively), the maximum value of *a* would be 1; and, in general, if it could be called $n \geq 1$ times recursively, the maximum value of *a* would be $n+1$.

Consider the definition of the ϕ_i in the Tail Recursion Fixed Point Theorem. If *exp* could be called *a* times at most, ϕ_a would yield the finite fragment of the infinite $\mathfrak{lub}[\phi_i]$ that could be computed. When $a \geq 2$, ϕ_a can produce the desired result $x{**}y$ for $y = 0, \ldots, a-2$. For example, if the maximum number of times that *exp* could be activated (called) were $a=0$ or $a=1$, then *exp* could not compute a correct result ($x{**}y$) for any *y*. If the maximum number of times that *exp* could be activated was $a=4$, then *exp* would compute correct results for $y = 0,1,2$, storing $x{**}y$ in *s*, but *exp* would not compute a correct result for values of $y \geq 3$. As it is, with no bound on the number of activations, *exp* sets the integer variable *s* to $x{**}y$ if $y \geq 0$ and, if $y<0$, *s* remains unchanged.

The following diagram depicts the values assigned *s* by the ϕ_as determined by **procedure** *exp* in the case when $\mathfrak{s}[x] = 3$ and $\mathfrak{s}[y] = 2$:

a	ϕ_a **assigns** s
0	$\perp$
1	$\perp$
2	$\perp$
3	$\perp$
4	9
5	9
⋮	⋮
∞	9

The reader is asked to think of ϕ_∞ as $\mathfrak{lub}[\phi_a]$, the limit of the ϕ_a's as a approaches ∞. In other words, the meaning of a procedure call statement *exp* in the main program is

$$\lambda\mathfrak{N}\mathfrak{s}'.\textbf{if } \mathfrak{s}'\in\mathfrak{States} \textbf{ and } \mathfrak{s}'[x],\mathfrak{s}'[y]\in\mathfrak{Z} \textbf{ then}$$
$$\mathfrak{s}'\{expid(\mathfrak{s}'[x],\mathfrak{s}'[y],\mathfrak{s}'[s])\backslash s\}$$
$$\textbf{else}$$
$$\perp$$

where *expid* is the function presented in Section 6.0.

6.3. PROVING TOTAL CORRECTNESS

The *basic free Hoare Axiomatization* for TR, **Htr,** is like that for the *SP* programs of the preceding chapter minus the **While** Rule. As shown in Figure 6.3, **Htr** uses the axioms and rules numbered 1 through 5, the Dummy and Assignment Axioms, and the Composition, Conditional, and Consequence Rules. In the Consequence Rule, proofs of $p \rightarrow p'$ and $q' \rightarrow q$ are to be carried out in free arithmetic (unextended by axioms describing the behavior of subprograms, as in Chapter 5). A *proof* is to be understood as in Chapter 1.

Before presenting the concept of an extended free Hoare Axiomatization for TR, we exhibit the form of the Procedure-Call Axiom for **procedure** *pr*.

THE PROCEDURE-CALL AXIOM (SCHEMA): For procedure *pr*, this axiom is as follows:

$$\{p[e_1(x_1, \ldots, x_n), \ldots, e_n(x_1, \ldots, x_n)\backslash z_1, \ldots, z_n] \;\&\; q\}$$
$$pr$$
$$\{p\}$$

A. The Basic Free Hoare Axiomatization (Htr)

1. The Dummy Axiom

$$\{p\}\mathbf{d}\{p\}$$

2. The Assignment Axiom

$$\{(\mathrm{I}(e)\ \&\ p[e\backslash x]\}x := e\{p\}$$

3. The Composition Rule

$$\frac{\{p\}S\{q\},\quad \{q\}S'\{r\}}{\{p\}S;S'\{r\}}$$

4. The Conditional Rule

$$\frac{\{\mathrm{I}(b)\&p\&b)S\{q\},\quad \{\mathrm{I}(b)\&p\&\sim b\}S'\{q\}}{\{\mathrm{I}(b)\&p\}\textbf{if } b \textbf{ then } S \textbf{ else } S'\{q\}}$$

5. The Consequence Rule

$$\frac{p\rightarrow p',\ \{p'\}S\{q'\},\quad q'\rightarrow q}{\{p\}S\{q\}}$$

Restriction: The proofs of $p\rightarrow p'$ and $q'\rightarrow q$ must be carried out in free arithmetic.

B. Extended Free Hoare Axiomatizations ($\mathbf{Htr}_{PCA}$'s)

6. The Procedure-Call Axiom for Procedure *pr*

$$\{p[e_1(x_1, \ldots, x_n), \ldots, e_n(x_1, \ldots, x_n)\backslash z_1, \ldots, z_n]\ \&\ q\}$$
$$pr$$
$$\{p\}$$

where

$$z_1 = e_1(x_1, \ldots, x_n)\ \&\ \ldots\ \&\ z_n = e_n(x_1, \ldots, x_n)$$

is the postcondition of *pr*, q is the precondition of *pr*, q is in the set of input variables $\{x_i\}$, the z_i's are the output variables of *pr*, the $e_j(x_1, \ldots, x_n)$'s are integer expressions in $\{x_i\}$, and no integer variable occurring in p is syntactically vulnerable in **procedure** *pr* that is not an output variable for *pr*.

Restriction: Use of **procedure** *pr*'s Procedure-Call Axiom is permitted in an extended free Hoare Axiomatization Htr_{PCA} proof only if that axiom belongs to *PCA* (see text).

FIGURE 6.3. The axioms and rules of inference used in extended free Hoare total correctness axiomatizations for TR programs.

where

$$z_1 = e_1(x_1, \ . \ . \ . \ ,x_n) \ \& \ . \ . \ . \ \& z_n = e_n(x_1, \ . \ . \ . \ ,x_n)$$

is the postcondition of *pr*, *q* is the precondition of *pr*, *q* is in the set of input variables $\{x_i\}$, the z_i's are the output variables of *pr*, the $e_j(x_1, \ . \ . \ . \ ,x_n)$'s are integer expressions in $\{x_i\}$, and no integer variable occurring in *p* is syntactically vulnerable in **procedure** *pr* that is not an output variable for *pr*.

Let *PCA* be a set of Procedure-Call Axioms. An *extended free Hoare Axiomatization* for TR $\mathbf{Htr}_{PCA}$ with respect to the set of Procedure Call axioms *PCA* is an axiomatization consisting of the basic free Hoare Axiomatization for TR in addition to the Procedure-Call Axioms in *PCA*. A *proof* of an asserted statement *AP* in the extended free Hoare Axiomatization for TR $\mathbf{Htr}_{PCA}$, written $\vdash_{PCA} AP$, is a finite sequence of assertions and asserted programs $\langle a_1, \ . \ . \ . \ , a_n\rangle$ such that $AP \equiv a_n$ and, for each *i* from 1 to *n*, a_i is either

(1) A theorem of free arithmetic,
(2) An axiom of the basic free Hoare Axiomatization for TR **Htr**,
(3) A Procedure-Call Axiom belonging to *PCA*, or
(4) Obtained from one or more preceding lines by an application of one of the three rules of inference (3) through (5).

The extended free Hoare Axiomatization for TR $\mathbf{Htr}_{()}$ is the same as the basic free Hoare Axiomatization for TR **Htr**, and we write $\vdash AP$ if $\vdash_{()} AP$.

The justification of the Procedure-Call Axiom for a **procedure** *pr* depends on whether *pr* is recursive. If *pr* is not recursive, a *proof of the body of pr AP* in $\mathbf{Htr}_{PCA}$ is to be understood as a proof of *AP* in $\mathbf{Htr}_{PCA}$. That is, if *pr* is not recursive, we must demonstrate the following:

$$\{q \ \& \ a{=}1\}$$
$$S_{pr}$$
$$\{z_1{=}e_1(x_1, \ . \ . \ . \ ,x_n) \ \& \ . \ . \ . \ \& \ z_n{=}e_n(x_1, \ . \ . \ . \ , x_n)\}$$

where *q* is the precondition of *pr*, *a* is its activation number, S_{pr} is its statement body, and

$$z_1 = e_1(x_1, \ . \ . \ . \ ,x_n) \ \& \ . \ . \ . \ \& \ z_n = e_n(x_1, \ . \ . \ . \ ,x_n)$$

is its postcondition.

If *pr* is recursive, having a body of the following form:

```
{q}
if b then
  begin
```

S;
pr
$\{p\}$
end
$\{z_1{=}e_1(x_1, \ldots, x_n)\ \&\ \ldots\ \&\ z_n{=}e_n(x_1, \ldots, x_n)\}$

a *proof of the body of pr AP* in Htr_{PCA} is constituted by establishing all of the following:

(a) $\vdash q\&a{=}1 \rightarrow p$
in free arithmetic, where q is pr's precondition, a is pr's activation number, $p \equiv a{\geq}1\,\&\mathrm{I}(b)\&r\&\mathrm{I}(E)\&E \not> \langle 0 \rangle$ is pr's recursion invariant, b is pr's guard, $E = \langle e_1, \ldots, e_k \rangle$, and $\mathrm{I}(E) \equiv \mathrm{I}(e_1)\ \&\ \ldots\ \&\mathrm{I}(e_k)$.

(b) $\vdash\{p\&b\&Y{=}E\}S\{(p\&Y \succ E)[a{+}1\backslash a]\}$
in $\mathbf{Htr}_{PCA}$, where the $y_1, \ldots, y_k$ $(k{\geq}1)$ are new integer variables, $Y = \langle y_1, \ldots, y_k \rangle$, and $Y = E \equiv y_1 = e_1\ \&\ \ldots\ \&\ y_k = e_k$, and

(c) $\vdash p\ \&\ {\sim}b \rightarrow z_1 = e_1(x_1, \ldots, x_n)\ \&\ \ldots\ \&\ z_n = e_n(x_1, \ldots, x_n)$
in free arithmetic.

The ideas behind (a)–(c) are much as those underlying the **While** Rule in Chapter 5, except that in (b) we substitute $a{+}1$ for the activation number a in the postcondition, because a is incremented at the time the recursive call of pr is executed.

Whether an extended free Hoare Axiomatization for TR $\mathbf{Htr}_{PCA}$ is "appropriate" for program and procedure proving depends on the scope of procedure variables. Let P be a program and pr_i be the i-th procedure declared in the program P. $\mathbf{Htr}_{()}$ is *appropriate* for proving the procedure pr_1, and a *proof* of pr_1 is a proof of the body of pr_1 in the basic free Hoare Axiomatization for TR **Htr.** $\mathbf{Htr}_{PCA}$ is *appropriate* for proving the **procedure** pr_i $(i{\geq}2)$ if

(1) PCA is a subset of the Procedure-Call Axioms for $pr_1, \ldots, pr_{i-1}$ and,

(2) for each **procedure** pr such that a Procedure-Call Axiom for pr belongs to PCA, there is a proof of pr in an extended free Hoare Axiomatization (for TR) appropriate for pr,

and a *proof of* pr_i is a proof of the body of pr_i in an extended free Hoare Axiomatization $\mathbf{Htr}_{PCA}$ appropriate for pr_i. $\mathbf{Htr}_{PCA}$ is *appropriate* for proving the **program** P if

(1) PCA is a subset of the Procedure-Call Axioms for the procedures declared in P, and

(2) for each **procedure** *pr* such that a Procedure-Call Axiom for *pr* belongs to *PCA*, there is a proof of *pr* in an extended free Hoare Axiomatization appropriate for *pr*,

and a *proof* of *P* is a proof of the body of *P* in an extended free Hoare Axiomatization $\mathbf{Htr}_{PCA}$ appropriate for *P*.

We illustrate the use of our free Hoare Axiomatization with a sketch of the proof of the total correctness of **program** *sample*. To prove **program** *sample* in $Htr_{\{(\mathbf{PC.exp})\}}$, we must prove two things.

(1) $\{I(u)\ \&\ I(v)\ \&\ v \geq 0\ \&\ I(w)\ \&\ I(z)\ \&\ z \geq 0\}$
$x := u;$
$y := v;$
$exp;$
$t := s;$
$x := w;$
$y := z;$
$exp;$
$\{t = u{**}v\ \&\ s = w{**}z\ \&\ \mathrm{I}(u)\ \&\ \mathrm{I}(v)\ \&\ v \geq 0\ \&\ \mathrm{I}(w)\ \&\ \mathrm{I}(z)\ \&\ z \geq 0\}$

and

(2) $\{t = u{**}v\ \&\ s = w{**}z\ \&\ \mathrm{I}(u)\ \&\ \mathrm{I}(v)\ \&\ v \geq 0\ \&\ \mathrm{I}(w)\ \&\ \mathrm{I}(z)\ \&\ z \geq 0\}$
if $t<s$ **then**
  begin
  $b := s;$
  $s := t$
  end
else
  $b := t$
$\{b = \max(u{**}v, w{**}z)\ \&\ s = \min(u{**}v, w{**}z)\}$

in $\mathbf{Htr}_{\{(\mathbf{PC.exp})\}}$ and then apply the Composition Rule. The asserted statement (2) is easily proven using the Assignment Axiom and the Composition, Consequence, and Conditional Rules. On the way to demonstrating (1), we must prove

(3) $\{t = u{**}v\ \&\ x{**}y = w{**}z\ \&\ \mathrm{I}(u)\ \&\ \mathrm{I}(v)\ \&\ v \geq 0\ \&\ \mathrm{I}(w)\ \&$
$\mathrm{I}(z)\ \&\ z \geq 0\ \&\ \mathrm{I}(x)\ \&\ \mathrm{I}(y)\ \&\ y \geq 0\}$
exp
$\{t = u{**}v\ \&\ s = w{**}z\ \&\ \mathrm{I}(u)\ \&\ \mathrm{I}(v)\ \&\ v \geq 0\ \&\ \mathrm{I}(w)\ \&\ \mathrm{I}(z)\ \&\ z \geq 0\}$

in $\mathbf{Htr}_{\{(\mathbf{PC.exp})\}}$ using the Procedure-Call Axiom **(PC.exp)** for **procedure** *exp*, which is an instance of the form

(PC.exp) $\{p'[x{**}y\backslash s] \;\&\; \mathrm{I}(x) \;\&\; \mathrm{I}(y) \;\&\; y \geqslant 0\}$
$\quad exp$
$\{p'\}$

By applying the Assignment Axiom, **(PC.exp)**, and the Composition and Consequence Rules, proof of (1) in $Htr_{\{(\mathbf{PC.exp})\}}$ can be had from (3).

To justify (3), we must prove in *Htr*

(b) $\{a \geqslant 1 \;\&\; \mathrm{I}(a) \;\&\; \mathrm{I}(y) \;\&\; \mathrm{I}(x) \;\&\; y \geqslant 0 \;\&\; (a \geqslant 2 \rightarrow s = x{**}(a-2))$
$\quad \& \; \mathrm{I}(y+2-a) \;\&\; y+2-a \geqslant 0 \;\&\; a \leqslant y+1 \;\&\; y' = y+2-a\}$
if $a=1$ **then**
$\quad s := 1$
else
$\quad s := x*s;$
$\{a+1 \geqslant 1 \;\&\; \mathrm{I}(a+1) \;\&\; \mathrm{I}(y) \;\&\; \mathrm{I}(x) \;\&\; y \geqslant 0$
$\quad \& \; (a+1 \geqslant 2 \rightarrow s = x{**}(a+1-2)) \;\&\; \mathrm{I}(y+2-(a+1))$
$\quad \& \; y+2-(a+1) \geqslant 0 \;\&\; y' > y+2-(a+1)\}$

which can be readily done using the Assignment Axiom and the Conditional and Consequence Rules, and prove in free arithmetic

(a) $\mathrm{I}(x)\&\mathrm{I}(y)\&y \geqslant 0\&a=1 \rightarrow a \geqslant 1 \;\&\; \mathrm{I}(a) \;\&\; \mathrm{I}(y) \;\&\; \mathrm{I}(x) \;\&\; y \geqslant 0$
$\quad \& \; (a \geqslant 2 \rightarrow s = x{**}(a-2)) \;\&\; \mathrm{I}(y+2-a) \;\&\; y+2-a \geqslant 0$

and

(c) $a \geqslant 1 \;\&\; \mathrm{I}(a) \;\&\; \mathrm{I}(y) \;\&\; \mathrm{I}(x) \;\&\; y \geqslant 0 \;\&\; (a \geqslant 2 \rightarrow s = x{**}(a-2))$
$\quad \& \; \mathrm{I}(y+2-a) \;\&\; y+2-a \geqslant 0 \;\&\; {\sim} a \leqslant y+1 \rightarrow s = x{**}y$

6.4. THE TRANSLATION

In this section, we exhibit a translation of TR programs into **while** programs. Before presenting the translation, we modify the **while** programs of Chapter 1 to handle execution-time errors along the lines developed in Chapter 5. To facilitate the proof of the correctness of the translation, we make explicit reference to the error state in the (operational) semantic equations for **while** programs.

The syntax and semantics of integer and boolean expressions and assertions for our class of **while** programs is the same as for TR programs. The syntax of statements and annotated statements is the same also, except that the **while** programs have **while** statements instead of procedure call statements. The syntax of asserted statements (called "asserted programs" in

Chapter 1) is the same as in Chapter 5. In other words, the syntax of **while** programs is the same as in Chapter 1.

To suit the free case, the operational semantics of Chapter 1 requires modification along the lines of the operational semantics presented in Chapter 5. The operational semantics of **while** programs has the error state $\perp_{\mathfrak{States}}$, the class of defined states $\mathfrak{States}$, and the class of states $\mathfrak{States}+ = \mathfrak{States} \cup \{\perp_{\mathfrak{States}}\}$, as in the denotational semantics of TR programs. To simplify comparison of the operational semantics of **while** programs and the denotational semantics of TR programs, we present the operational semantics in terms of a functional $\mathfrak{O}$ such that, for any statement S, any error assignment $\mathfrak{R}$, and any state $\mathfrak{s}$, $\mathfrak{O}[S][\mathfrak{R}][\mathfrak{s}] \in \mathfrak{States}+$. For any statement S, we take

$$\mathfrak{O}[S][\mathfrak{R}][\perp] = \perp$$

and, for any defined state $\mathfrak{s}$, $\mathfrak{O}[S][\mathfrak{R}][\mathfrak{s}]$ is defined inductively, as shown in Figure 6.4.

The truth-value assigned an asserted statement $AP \equiv \{p\}S\{q\}$ is given by the equation

$$\begin{aligned}\mathfrak{M}_{\mathfrak{A}\mathfrak{S}}[AP][\mathfrak{R}][\mathfrak{s}] &= \mathfrak{t} \text{ provided} \\ &\qquad \mathfrak{M}_{\mathfrak{A}}[q][\mathfrak{R}][\mathfrak{O}[S][\mathfrak{R}][\mathfrak{s}]] = \mathfrak{t} \text{ if } \mathfrak{M}_{\mathfrak{A}}[p][\mathfrak{R}][\mathfrak{s}] = \mathfrak{t} \\ &= \mathfrak{f} \text{ otherwise}\end{aligned}$$

a. $\mathfrak{O}[S][\mathfrak{R}][\perp] = \perp$

b. For any defined state $\mathfrak{s}$,

(1) $\mathfrak{O}[\mathbf{d}][\mathfrak{R}][\mathfrak{s}] = \mathfrak{s}$

(2) $\mathfrak{O}[x{:=}e][\mathfrak{R}][\mathfrak{s}] = \mathfrak{s}\{\mathfrak{M}_{\mathfrak{E}}[e][\mathfrak{R}][\mathfrak{s}]\backslash x\}$ if $\mathfrak{M}_{\mathfrak{E}}[e][\mathfrak{R}][\mathfrak{s}] \in \mathfrak{Z}$
$= \perp$ otherwise

(3) $\mathfrak{O}[S;S'][\mathfrak{R}][\mathfrak{s}] = \mathfrak{O}[S'][\mathfrak{R}][\mathfrak{O}[S][\mathfrak{R}][\mathfrak{s}]]$

(4) $\mathfrak{O}[\textbf{if } b \textbf{ then } S \textbf{ else } S'][\mathfrak{R}][\mathfrak{s}]$
$= \mathfrak{O}[S][\mathfrak{R}][\mathfrak{s}]$ if $\mathfrak{M}_{\mathfrak{E}}[\mathfrak{E}[b]][\mathfrak{R}][\mathfrak{s}] \subset \mathfrak{Z}$ and $\mathfrak{M}_{\mathfrak{A}}[b][\mathfrak{R}][\mathfrak{s}] = \mathfrak{t}$
$= \mathfrak{O}[S'][\mathfrak{R}][\mathfrak{s}]$ if $\mathfrak{M}_{\mathfrak{E}}[\mathfrak{E}[b]][\mathfrak{R}][\mathfrak{s}] \subset \mathfrak{Z}$ and $\mathfrak{M}_{\mathfrak{A}}[b][\mathfrak{R}][\mathfrak{s}] = \mathfrak{f}$
$= \perp$ otherwise

(5) $\mathfrak{O}[\textbf{while } b \textbf{ do } S][\mathfrak{R}][\mathfrak{s}]$
$= \mathfrak{s}*$ if there is a finite sequence of states $\langle \mathfrak{s}_0, \ldots, \mathfrak{s}_m \rangle$ $(m \geq 0)$ such that $\mathfrak{s} = \mathfrak{s}_0$, $\mathfrak{s}* = \mathfrak{s}_m$, $\mathfrak{M}_{\mathfrak{E}}[\mathfrak{E}[b]][\mathfrak{R}][\mathfrak{s}_i] \subset \mathfrak{Z}$ for each i from 1 to m, $\mathfrak{M}_{\mathfrak{A}}[b][\mathfrak{R}][\mathfrak{s}_m] = \mathfrak{f}$, and $\mathfrak{M}_{\mathfrak{A}}[b][\mathfrak{R}][\mathfrak{s}_i] = \mathfrak{t}$ and $\mathfrak{s}_{i+1} = \mathfrak{O}_i[S][\mathfrak{R}][\mathfrak{s}]$ for each i from 0 to $m - 1$.
$= \perp$ otherwise

FIGURE 6.4. The free operational semantics of **while** statements.

and AP is *valid,* written $\models AP$, if $\mathfrak{M}_{\mathfrak{A}\mathfrak{G}}[AP][\mathfrak{N}][\mathfrak{s}] = \mathfrak{t}$ for every error assignment $\mathfrak{N}$ and every state $\mathfrak{s}$.

The *free Hoare Axiomatization for* **while** programs is the basic free Hoare Axiomatization *Hax* of Chapter 5. This concludes the presentation of our class of **while** programs.

Turning to the translation $\mathfrak{W}$ of TR programs into **while** programs, we define the translation $\mathfrak{W}_{\mathfrak{P}}$ of an *SP* program as follows:

$$\mathfrak{W}_{\mathfrak{P}}[\textbf{program } pg; Pr_1; \ldots ;Pr_k;\{p\}A\{q\}] =$$

$$\quad \{p\}$$
$$\qquad a_{pr_1} := 0;$$
$$\qquad \vdots$$
$$\qquad a_{pr_k} := 0;$$
$$\qquad \mathfrak{W}_{\mathfrak{A}}[A, 0, Pr_1; \ldots ;Pr_k]$$
$$\quad \{q\}$$

Intuitively, the initialization of the a_{pr_i} to zero realizes the conjuncts implicit in the precondition of the source TR program that require the activation number for each of the k procedures Pr_i to be zero.

The translation $\mathfrak{W}_{\mathfrak{A}}$ of an annotated statement A requires three arguments and has the following general form:

$$\mathfrak{W}_{\mathfrak{A}}[A, i, Pr_1; \ldots ;Pr_k]$$

The first argument of $\mathfrak{W}_{\mathfrak{A}}$, A, is the annotated statement itself. The second argument indicates whether A occurs within a procedure and, if so, which procedure. If the second argument is 0, then A occurs within the main **program** *pg*. If the second argument is i ($1 \leqslant i \leqslant k$), then A occurs within the body of the i-th **procedure** Pr_i. The third argument is the procedure declaration part of **program** *pg*. The second and third arguments are needed to handle the translation of procedure calls and enable recursive calls to be distinguished from nonrecursive calls. The translation $\mathfrak{W}_{\mathfrak{A}}$ for an annotated statement A is defined inductively based on the form of A as shown in Figure 6.5.

When applied to **program** *sample* in Section 6.1 (the source program), translation $\mathfrak{W}$ yields the **while** program (the target program) that follows. (For readability, we have omitted superfluous **begin–end**'s.)

$$\{I(u) \ \& \ I(v) \ \& \ v \geqslant 0 \ \& \ I(w) \ \& \ I(z) \ \& \ z \geqslant 0\}$$
$$x := u;$$
$$y := v;$$
$$a := 1;$$
$$\{a \geqslant 1 \ \& \ I(a) \ \& \ I(y) \ \& \ I(x) \ \& \ y \geqslant 0 \ \& \ (a \geqslant 2 \rightarrow s = x**(a-2)) \ \&$$
$$I(y+2-a) \ \& \ y+2-a \geqslant 0\}$$
while $a \leqslant y+1$ **do**

A. Programs

$\mathfrak{W}_{\mathfrak{P}}$[**program** $pg;Pr_1; \ldots ;Pr_k;\{p\}A\{q\}$] =

$\{p\}$
$a_{pr_1} := 0;$
$\vdots$
$a_{pr_k} := 0;$
$\mathfrak{W}_{\mathfrak{A}}[A, 0, Pr_1; \ldots ;Pr_k]$
$\{q\}$

B. Annotated Statements

(1) $\mathfrak{W}_{\mathfrak{A}}[\mathbf{d}, i, Pr_1; \ldots ;Pr_k] = \mathbf{d}$

(2) $\mathfrak{W}_{\mathfrak{A}}[x:=e, i, Pr_1; \ldots ;Pr_k] = x:=e$

(3) $\mathfrak{W}_{\mathfrak{A}}[A;A', i, Pr_1; \ldots ;Pr_k] =$
$\mathfrak{W}_{\mathfrak{A}}[A, i, Pr_1; \ldots ;Pr_k]; \mathfrak{W}_{\mathfrak{A}}[A', i, Pr_1; \ldots ;Pr_k]$

(4) $\mathfrak{W}_{\mathfrak{A}}$[**if** b **then** A **else** A', $i, Pr_1; \ldots ;Pr_k$] =

if b **then**
$\mathfrak{W}_{\mathfrak{A}}[A, i, Pr_1; \ldots ;Pr_k]$
else
$\mathfrak{W}_{\mathfrak{A}}[A', i, Pr_1; \ldots ;Pr_k]$
if $A \not\equiv A'';pr_i$

(5) $\mathfrak{W}_{\mathfrak{A}}$[**if** b **then begin** $A'';pr_i\{p\}$ **end,** $i, Pr_1; \ldots ;Pr_k$]
=

$\{p\}$
while b **do**
begin
$\mathfrak{W}_{\mathfrak{A}}[A'', i, Pr_1; \ldots ;Pr_k];$
$a_{pr_i} := a_{pr_i}+1$
end

(6) $\mathfrak{W}_{\mathfrak{A}}[pr_j, i, Pr_1; \ldots ;Pr_k] =$

begin
$a_{pr_j} := 1;$
$\mathfrak{W}_{\mathfrak{A}}[A_{pr_j}, j, Pr_1; \ldots ;Pr_k];$
$a_{pr_j} := 0;$
end

if $i \neq j$, where A_{pr_j} is the body of **procedure** Pr_j.

FIGURE 6.5. The translation $\mathfrak{W}$ of TR programs into **while** programs.

```
      begin
      if a=1 then
        s := 1
      else
        s := x*s;
      a := a+1
      end;
   a := 0;
   t := s;
   x := w;
   y := z;
   a := 1;
   {a≥1 & I(a) & I(y) & I(x) & y≥0 & (a≥2 → s=x**(a−2)) &
   I(y+2−a) & y+2−a≥0}
   while a≤y+1 do
      begin
      if a=1 then
        s := 1
      else
        s := x*s;
      a := a+1
      end;
   a := 0;
   if t<s then
      begin
      b := s;
      s := t
        end
      else
        b := t
   {b = max(u**v,w**z) & s = min(u**v,w**z)}
```

Note that the intermediate assertions obtained in the translation are, in general, inadequate for proving the correctness of a target **while** program even if the recursion invariants of the source TR program are adequate for proving it. This situation can occur when there is more than one **while** loop in the target **while** program because the loop invariants do not contain historical (contextual) information. For example, in the second loop invariant, the conjunct

$$t = u{*}{*}v$$

is needed.

6.5. CORRECTNESS OF THE TRANSLATION

In this section, we demonstrate the Semantic Equivalence Lemma and the TR Interpretation Theorem, which are analogs of the Commutativity Lemma and the **While** Interpretation Theorem of Chapter 4. The Semantic Equivalence Lemma states that the translation $\mathfrak{W}$ presented in the preceding section is correct in the sense that execution of a target **while** program ends in the same state as would execution of the source TR program, provided that the TR program's precondition is satisfied. As an immediate consequence of the Semantic Equivalence Lemma, we have the TR Interpretation Theorem, which states that a source TR program P is valid in the free Hoare logic of TR programs iff the target **while** program $\mathfrak{W}_{\mathfrak{P}}[P]$ is valid in the free Hoare logic of **while** programs. Because the semantics of TR programs is denotational, the translation $\mathfrak{W}$ induces a denotational semantics for **while** programs and, conversely, an operational semantics for TR programs. We leave to the reader the useful exercise of working out the details of these semantics.

Proof of the Semantic Equivalence Lemma requires two preliminary results, the **While** Iteration and the TR Activation Lemmas. Intuitively, the operational semantics of **while** programs devoid of **while** statements and the denotational semantics of TR programs free of recursive procedures are the same. The **While** Iteration and the TR Activation Lemmas show the operational semantics of **while** statements and the denotational semantics of tail recursive procedures as converging. We present the **While** Iteration Lemma first because, on a first reading, it is the more intuitive of the two.

WHILE ITERATION LEMMA: Let

$$0\#S \equiv \mathbf{d}$$

$$n\#S \equiv ([n-1]\#S);S \text{ if } n \geqslant 1$$

Then

$\mathfrak{O}[\mathbf{while}\ b\ \mathbf{do}\ S][\mathfrak{N}][\mathfrak{s}] = \mathfrak{s}!$ if there is some $m \geqslant 0$ such that $\mathfrak{s}! = \mathfrak{O}[m\#S][\mathfrak{N}][\mathfrak{s}]$, $\mathfrak{M}_{\mathfrak{E}}[\mathfrak{E}[b]][\mathfrak{N}][\mathfrak{O}[i\#S][\mathfrak{N}][\mathfrak{s}]] \subset \mathfrak{Z}$ for each i from 0 to m, $\mathfrak{M}_{\mathfrak{A}}[b][\mathfrak{N}][\mathfrak{O}[m\#S][\mathfrak{N}][\mathfrak{s}]] = \mathfrak{t}$ for each i from 0 to $m-1$, and $\mathfrak{M}_{\mathfrak{A}}[b][\mathfrak{N}][\mathfrak{O}[m\#S][\mathfrak{N}][\mathfrak{s}]] = \mathfrak{f}$.
$= \perp$ otherwise

Proof: By straightforward (but messy) nested inductions on $m \geqslant 0$ and i such that $0 \leqslant i \leqslant m$, making use of the operational semantics of the dummy and composition statements. □

Let TR **program** $P \equiv$

program pg; Pr_1; . . . ;Pr_k;**begin** $\{p\}A\{q\}$ **end**

with S the statement of A. If $k \geqslant 1$ and **procedure** Pr_k is recursive, we understand its statement body

$$S_{pr_k} \equiv \textbf{if } b \textbf{ then begin } S';\ pr_k \textbf{ end}$$

and take ϕ_j to be as in the TR Fixed Point Theorem as adapted to the semantics of Pr_k. That is,

$$\begin{array}{l}
\phi_0[\mathfrak{N}][\mathfrak{s}] = \bot \\
\phi_{j+1}[\mathfrak{N}][\mathfrak{s}] = \textbf{if } \mathfrak{s} \in \mathfrak{States} \textbf{ then} \\
\qquad\qquad\quad \textbf{if } \mathfrak{s}[a_k] \in \mathfrak{Z} \textbf{ and } \mathfrak{M}_{\mathfrak{E}}[\mathfrak{E}[b]][\mathfrak{N}][\mathfrak{s}] \subset \mathfrak{Z} \textbf{ then} \\
\qquad\qquad\quad\quad \textbf{if } \mathfrak{M}_{\mathfrak{A}}[b][\mathfrak{N}][\mathfrak{s}] = \mathfrak{t} \textbf{ then} \\
\qquad\qquad\quad\quad\quad \phi_j[\mathfrak{N}][(\mathfrak{M}_{\mathfrak{S}}[S'][\mathfrak{p}\mathfrak{s}_{k+1}][\mathfrak{N}][\mathfrak{s}])\{\mathfrak{s}[a_k]+1 \backslash a_k\}] \\
\qquad\qquad\quad\quad \textbf{else} \\
\qquad\qquad\quad\quad\quad \mathfrak{s} \\
\qquad\qquad\quad \textbf{else} \\
\qquad\qquad\quad\quad \bot \\
\qquad\qquad \textbf{else} \\
\qquad\qquad\quad \bot \\
\qquad\qquad\quad\ = \textbf{if } \mathfrak{s} \in \mathfrak{States} \textbf{ then} \\
\qquad\qquad\quad\quad \textbf{if } \mathfrak{s}[a_k] \in \mathfrak{Z} \textbf{ and } \mathfrak{M}_{\mathfrak{E}}[\mathfrak{E}[b]][\mathfrak{N}][\mathfrak{s}] \subset \mathfrak{Z} \textbf{ then} \\
\qquad\qquad\quad\quad\quad \textbf{if } \mathfrak{M}_{\mathfrak{A}}[b][\mathfrak{N}][\mathfrak{s}] = \mathfrak{t} \textbf{ then} \\
\qquad\qquad\quad\quad\quad\quad \phi_j[\mathfrak{N}][\mathfrak{M}_{\mathfrak{S}}[S'; a_k := a_k + 1][\mathfrak{p}\mathfrak{s}_{k+1}][\mathfrak{N}][\mathfrak{s}]] \\
\qquad\qquad\quad\quad\quad \textbf{else} \\
\qquad\qquad\quad\quad\quad\quad \mathfrak{s} \\
\qquad\qquad\quad\quad \textbf{else} \\
\qquad\qquad\quad\quad\quad \bot \\
\qquad\qquad\quad \textbf{else} \\
\qquad\qquad\quad\quad \bot
\end{array}$$

In stating the TR Activation Lemma, which follows, to avoid clutter we drop the subscript k on a_k and the subscript $k+1$ on $\mathfrak{p}\mathfrak{s}_{k+1}$. Note that part (b), converted from a conditional (if) into a biconditional (iff), is equivalent to both (a) and (b).

TR ACTIVATION LEMMA

(a) If $0 \leqslant n \leqslant j-1$, $\mathfrak{s} \in \mathfrak{States}+$, $\mathfrak{s}*$ is a defined state, and
   (1) $\mathfrak{s}* = \mathfrak{M}_{\mathfrak{S}}[n\#(S'; a := a+1)][\mathfrak{p}\mathfrak{s}][\mathfrak{N}][\mathfrak{s}]$
   (2) For each i from 0 to n,
   $\mathfrak{M}_{\mathfrak{E}}[a, \mathfrak{E}[b]][\mathfrak{N}][\mathfrak{M}_{\mathfrak{S}}[i\#(S'; a := a+1)][\mathfrak{p}\mathfrak{s}][\mathfrak{N}][\mathfrak{s}]] \subset \mathfrak{Z}$
   (3) For each i from 0 to $n-1$,
   $\mathfrak{M}_{\mathfrak{A}}[b][\mathfrak{N}][\mathfrak{M}_{\mathfrak{S}}[i\#(S'; a := a+1)][\mathfrak{p}\mathfrak{s}][\mathfrak{N}][\mathfrak{s}]] = \mathfrak{t}$
   (4) $\mathfrak{M}_{\mathfrak{A}}[b][\mathfrak{N}][\mathfrak{M}_{\mathfrak{S}}[n\#(S'; a := a+1)][\mathfrak{p}\mathfrak{s}][\mathfrak{N}][\mathfrak{s}]] = \mathfrak{f}$
   then $\mathfrak{s}* = \phi_j[\mathfrak{N}][\mathfrak{s}]$.

(b) If $j \geqslant 0$, $\mathfrak{s}\in\mathfrak{States}+$, $\mathfrak{s}*$ is a defined state, $\mathfrak{s}* = \phi_j[\mathfrak{N}][\mathfrak{s}]$, then there exists n such that $0 \leqslant n \leqslant j-1$ and

(1) $\mathfrak{s}* = \mathfrak{M}_{\mathfrak{S}}[n\#[S';a{:=}a+1)][\mathfrak{ps}][\mathfrak{N}][\mathfrak{s}]$

(2) For each i from 0 to n,
$\mathfrak{M}_{\mathfrak{E}}[a,\mathfrak{E}[b]][\mathfrak{N}][\mathfrak{M}_{\mathfrak{S}}[i\#(S';a{:=}a+1)][\mathfrak{ps}][\mathfrak{N}][\mathfrak{s}]]\subset\mathfrak{Z}$

(3) For each i from 0 to $n-1$,
$\mathfrak{M}_{\mathfrak{A}}[b][\mathfrak{N}][\mathfrak{M}_{\mathfrak{S}}[i\#(S';a{:=}a+1)][\mathfrak{ps}][\mathfrak{N}][\mathfrak{s}]] = \mathfrak{t}$

(4) $\mathfrak{M}_{\mathfrak{A}}[b][\mathfrak{N}][\mathfrak{M}_{\mathfrak{S}}[n\#(S';a{:=}a+1)][\mathfrak{ps}][\mathfrak{N}][\mathfrak{s}]] = \mathfrak{f}$

Proof: The proofs for both parts (a) and (b) proceed by induction of $j \geqslant 0$. We prove only part (a), leaving part (b) as an exercise. In the basis, when $j = 0$, (a) holds vacuously. So suppose $j \geqslant 1$ and assume the antecedent of (a). We must demonstrate the following:

$\mathfrak{s}* = \phi_j[\mathfrak{N}][\mathfrak{s}]$
  = **if** $\mathfrak{s}\in\mathfrak{States}$
    if $\mathfrak{s}[a]\in\mathfrak{Z}$ **and** $\mathfrak{M}_{\mathfrak{E}}[\mathfrak{E}[b]][\mathfrak{N}][\mathfrak{s}]\subset\mathfrak{Z}$ **then**
      if $\mathfrak{M}_{\mathfrak{A}}[b][\mathfrak{N}][\mathfrak{s}]=\mathfrak{t}$ **then**
        $\phi_{j-1}[\mathfrak{N}][\mathfrak{M}_{\mathfrak{S}}[S';a{:=}a+1][\mathfrak{ps}][\mathfrak{N}][\mathfrak{s}]]$
      else
        $\mathfrak{s}$
    else
      $\perp$
  else
    $\perp$

If $\mathfrak{s}\notin\mathfrak{States}$, $\mathfrak{s}[a]\notin\mathfrak{Z}$, or $\mathfrak{M}_{\mathfrak{E}}[\mathfrak{E}[b]][\mathfrak{N}][\mathfrak{s}]\not\subset\mathfrak{Z}$, then (1) in the antecedent of (a) is false, contradicting the assumption stated above. If $\mathfrak{M}_{\mathfrak{A}}[b][\mathfrak{N}][\mathfrak{s}] = \mathfrak{f}$, we have $n = 0$. Consequently,

$$\begin{aligned}\phi_j[\mathfrak{N}][\mathfrak{s}] &= \mathfrak{s}\\ &= \mathfrak{M}_{\mathfrak{S}}[\mathbf{d}][\mathfrak{ps}][\mathfrak{N}][\mathfrak{s}]\\ &= \mathfrak{M}_{\mathfrak{S}}[0\#(S';a{:=}a+1)][\mathfrak{ps}][\mathfrak{N}][\mathfrak{s}]\\ &= \mathfrak{s}*\end{aligned}$$

So, suppose $\mathfrak{M}_{\mathfrak{A}}[b][\mathfrak{N}][\mathfrak{s}] = \mathfrak{t}$. Let $\mathfrak{s}' = \mathfrak{M}_{\mathfrak{S}}[S';a{:=}a+1][\mathfrak{ps}][\mathfrak{N}][\mathfrak{s}]$. Then, $n \geqslant 1$ from (3), and an application of the *IH* yields the following:

If $0 \leqslant n-1 \leqslant j-2$, $\mathfrak{s}'\in\mathfrak{States}+$, $\mathfrak{s}*$ is a defined state, and

(1′) $\mathfrak{s}* = \mathfrak{M}_{\mathfrak{S}}[[n-1]\#(S';a{:=}a+1)][\mathfrak{ps}][\mathfrak{N}][\mathfrak{s}']$

(2′) For each i from 0 to $n-1$,
$\mathfrak{M}_{\mathfrak{E}}[a,\mathfrak{E}[b]][\mathfrak{N}][\mathfrak{M}_{\mathfrak{S}}[i\#(S';a{:=}a+1)][\mathfrak{ps}][\mathfrak{N}][\mathfrak{s}']]\subset\mathfrak{Z}$

(3′) For each i from 0 to $n-2$,
$\mathfrak{M}_{\mathfrak{A}}[b][\mathfrak{N}][\mathfrak{M}_{\mathfrak{S}}[i\#(S';a{:=}a+1)][\mathfrak{ps}][\mathfrak{N}][\mathfrak{s}']] = \mathfrak{t}$

(4′) $\mathfrak{M}_{\mathfrak{A}}[b][\mathfrak{N}][\mathfrak{M}_{\mathfrak{S}}[[n-1]\#(S';a{:=}a+1)][\mathfrak{ps}][\mathfrak{N}][\mathfrak{s}']] = \mathfrak{f}$

then $\mathfrak{s}* = \phi_{i-1}[\mathfrak{N}][\mathfrak{s}']$.

Because (1)–(4) imply (1′)–(4′), we have $\mathfrak{s}* = \phi_{j-1}[\mathfrak{N}][\mathfrak{s}']$. Since $\mathfrak{M}_{\mathfrak{A}}[b][\mathfrak{N}][\mathfrak{s}] = \mathrm{t}$, we have

$$\begin{aligned}\phi_j[\mathfrak{N}][\mathfrak{s}] &= \phi_{j-1}[\mathfrak{N}][\mathfrak{M}_{\mathfrak{S}}[S';a:=a+1][\mathfrak{ps}][\mathfrak{N}][\mathfrak{s}]] \\ &= \phi_{j-1}[\mathfrak{N}][\mathfrak{s}'] \text{ by the definition of } \mathfrak{s}' \\ &= \mathfrak{s}*\end{aligned}$$

□

SEMANTIC EQUIVALENCE LEMMA: Let P be as before, $\mathfrak{s}$ be any state such that P's precondition p (and all conjuncts of the form $a_{pr_i}=0$ implicit in p) are true, and let $\mathfrak{s}'$ be an a_{pr_1}- . . . -a_{pr_k}-variant of $\mathfrak{s}$. Then

$$\mathfrak{M}_{\mathfrak{P}}[P][\mathfrak{ps}][\mathfrak{N}][\mathfrak{s}] = \mathfrak{D}[\mathfrak{W}_{\mathfrak{P}}[P]][\mathfrak{N}][\mathfrak{s}']$$

Proof: By the definition of $\mathfrak{M}_{\mathfrak{P}}$,

$$\mathfrak{M}_{\mathfrak{P}}[P][\mathfrak{ps}][\mathfrak{N}][\mathfrak{s}] = \mathfrak{M}_{\mathfrak{S}}[S][\mathfrak{ps}_{k+1}][\mathfrak{N}][\mathfrak{s}]$$

Proof that

$$\mathfrak{M}_{\mathfrak{S}}[S][\mathfrak{ps}_{k+1}][\mathfrak{N}][\mathfrak{s}] = \mathfrak{D}[\mathfrak{W}_P[P]][\mathfrak{N}][\mathfrak{s}']$$

proceeds by induction on $k \geqslant 0$, the number of procedures declared in P.

BASIS: $k = 0$.
Because no procedure call can occur in P, $\mathfrak{s}' = \mathfrak{s}$, $\mathfrak{W}_{\mathfrak{P}}[P] = \{p\}S\{q\}$, and so $\mathfrak{D}[\mathfrak{W}_{\mathfrak{P}}[P]][\mathfrak{N}][\mathfrak{s}'] = \mathfrak{D}[S][\mathfrak{N}][\mathfrak{s}]$. Proof that

$$\mathfrak{M}_{\mathfrak{S}}[S][\mathfrak{ps}_1][\mathfrak{N}][\mathfrak{s}] = \mathfrak{D}[S][\mathfrak{N}][\mathfrak{s}]$$

is by a straightforward induction on the complexity of S.

INDUCTION STEP: $k \geqslant 1$.
If no call of **procedure** pr_k occurs in P, the result follows directly from the *IH*. So, suppose one or more calls of **procedure** pr_k occurs in P. The proof now proceeds by a subordinate induction on the complexity of S. We treat only the basis, when $S \equiv pr_k$, as the induction step follows immediately from the *IH*. By the definition of $\mathfrak{W}$, $\mathfrak{W}_{\mathfrak{P}}[P] =$

$\{p\}$

$a_{pr_1} := 0;$

$a_{pr_k} := 0;$

$a_{pr_k} := 1;$

$$\mathfrak{W}_{\mathfrak{A}}[S_{pr_k}, k, Pr_1; \ldots ;Pr_k]$$
$$a_{pr_k} := 0;$$
$$\{q\}$$

Hence, by the definition of $\mathfrak{s}'$ and the operational semantics of **while** programs,

$$\mathfrak{O}[a_{pr_1}:=0; \ldots ;a_{pr_k}:=0][\mathfrak{N}][\mathfrak{s}'] = \mathfrak{s}$$

By the denotational semantics of TR, we have the following:

$$\mathfrak{M}_{\mathfrak{S}}[pr_k][\mathfrak{ps}_{k+1}][\mathfrak{N}][\mathfrak{s}] = (\mathfrak{ps}_{k+1}[pr_k][\mathfrak{N}][\mathfrak{s}\{1\backslash a_{pr_k}\}])\{0\backslash a_{pr_k}\}$$

and, by the operational semantics of **while** programs, we have

$$\mathfrak{O}[a_{pr_k}:=1;\mathfrak{W}_{\mathfrak{A}}[S_{pr_k}];a_{pr_k}:=0][\mathfrak{N}][\mathfrak{s}] = (\mathfrak{O}[\mathfrak{W}_{\mathfrak{A}}[S_{pr_k}]][\mathfrak{N}][\mathfrak{s}\{1\backslash a_{pr_k}\}])\{0\backslash a_{pr_k}\}$$

Let $\mathfrak{s}'' = \mathfrak{s}\{1\backslash a_{pr_k}\}$. If pr_k is not recursive, then

$$\begin{aligned}\mathfrak{ps}_{k+1}[pr_k][\mathfrak{N}][\mathfrak{s}''] &= \mathfrak{M}_{\mathfrak{S}}[S_{pr_k}][\mathfrak{ps}_k][\mathfrak{N}][\mathfrak{s}''] \text{ by the denotational semantics}\\ &= \mathfrak{O}[\mathfrak{W}_{\mathfrak{A}}[S_{pr_k}]][\mathfrak{N}][\mathfrak{s}''] \text{ by the } IH,\end{aligned}$$

and so,

$$\begin{aligned}\mathfrak{M}_{\mathfrak{S}}[pr_k][\mathfrak{ps}_{k+1}][\mathfrak{N}][\mathfrak{s}] &= (\mathfrak{ps}_{k+1}[pr_k][\mathfrak{N}][\mathfrak{s}''])\{0\backslash a_{pr_k}\}\\ &= \mathfrak{O}[\mathfrak{W}_{\mathfrak{A}}[S_{pr_k};a_{pr_k}:=0]][\mathfrak{N}][\mathfrak{s}'']\end{aligned}$$

Hence,

$$\mathfrak{M}_{\mathfrak{S}}[S][\mathfrak{ps}_{k+1}][\mathfrak{N}][\mathfrak{s}] = \mathfrak{O}[\mathfrak{W}_{\mathfrak{P}}[P]][\mathfrak{N}][\mathfrak{s}']$$

On the other hand, suppose pr_k is recursive. Then,

$$\mathfrak{ps}_{k+1}[pr_k][\mathfrak{N}][\mathfrak{s}''] = \mathfrak{lfp}[\Phi]$$

where Φ is as in the semantic equation for recursive procedures in Section 6.2. With $S_{pr_k} \equiv$

if b **then begin** S'; pr_k **end**

we have $\mathfrak{W}_{\mathfrak{A}}[S_{pr_k}] \equiv$

while b **do begin** $\mathfrak{W}_{\mathfrak{A}}[S', k, Pr_1; \ldots ;Pr_k]$; a:=a+1 **end**[2]

[2] Again, we omit the subscript pr_k on pr_k's activation number a_{pr_k} for brevity.

Let $S'' \equiv \mathfrak{W}_{\mathfrak{A}}[S', k, Pr_1; \ldots ;Pr_k]$ and $\mathfrak{O}[S''][\mathfrak{N}][\mathfrak{s}''] = \mathfrak{s}!$. By the **While** Iteration Lemma, either,

(a) $\mathfrak{s}!$ is defined and there exists $m \geqslant 0$ such that
  (1) $\mathfrak{s}! = \mathfrak{O}[m\#(S'';a:=a+1)][\mathfrak{N}][\mathfrak{s}'']$
  (2) For each i from 0 to m,
   $\mathfrak{M}_{\mathfrak{E}}[\mathfrak{E}[b]][\mathfrak{N}][\mathfrak{O}[i\#S][\mathfrak{N}][\mathfrak{s}]] \subset \mathfrak{Z}$
  (3) For each i from 0 to $m-1$,
   $\mathfrak{M}_{\mathfrak{A}}[b][\mathfrak{N}][\mathfrak{O}[m\#S][\mathfrak{N}][\mathfrak{s}]] = \mathfrak{t}$
  (4) $\mathfrak{M}_{\mathfrak{A}}[b][\mathfrak{N}][\mathfrak{O}[m\#S][\mathfrak{N}][\mathfrak{s}]] = \mathfrak{f}$

or

(b) $\mathfrak{s}! = \perp$

Assume (a) that $\mathfrak{s}!$ is a defined state and (1) through (4) hold. We have

$$\mathfrak{O}[S'';a:=a+1][\mathfrak{N}][\mathfrak{s}''] = \mathfrak{M}_{\mathfrak{S}}[S';a:=a+1][\mathfrak{p}\mathfrak{s}_k][\mathfrak{N}][\mathfrak{s}''] \text{ by the } IH.$$

By an inductive argument on i $(0 \leqslant i \leqslant m-1)$, we have

$$\mathfrak{O}[i\#(S'';a:=a+1)][\mathfrak{N}][\mathfrak{s}''] = \mathfrak{M}_{\mathfrak{S}}[i\#(S';a:=a+1)][\mathfrak{p}\mathfrak{s}_k][\mathfrak{N}][\mathfrak{s}'']$$

Hence, by the TR Activation Lemma, part (a), we have $\mathfrak{s}! = \phi_j[\mathfrak{N}][\mathfrak{s}'']$ for every $j \geqslant m+1$, where ϕ_j is as in the TR Activation Lemma. Hence,

$$\begin{aligned}\mathfrak{lfp}[\Phi][\mathfrak{N}][\mathfrak{s}''] &= \mathfrak{lub}[\phi_j][\mathfrak{N}][\mathfrak{s}''] \text{ by the TR Fixed Point Theorem}\\ &= \mathfrak{s}! \text{ because } \mathfrak{States}+ \text{ is a flat cpo}\end{aligned}$$

and again we have

$$\mathfrak{M}_{\mathfrak{S}}[P][\mathfrak{p}\mathfrak{s}_{k+1}][\mathfrak{N}][\mathfrak{s}] = \mathfrak{O}[\mathfrak{W}_{\mathfrak{P}}[P]][\mathfrak{N}][\mathfrak{s}']$$

On the other hand, suppose (b), $\mathfrak{s}! = \perp$. Suppose further that $\mathfrak{lfp}[\Phi][\mathfrak{N}][\mathfrak{s}''] \neq \perp$. Because $\mathfrak{States}+$ is a flat cpo, there is some $j \geqslant 0$ such that $\phi_j[\mathfrak{N}][\mathfrak{s}''] = \mathfrak{lfp}[\Phi][\mathfrak{N}][\mathfrak{s}'']$. Arguing in a manner symmetrical to that employed in case (a), and applying the TR Activation Lemma, part (b), the *IH*, and the **While** Iteration Lemma, we find that $\mathfrak{s}!$ is a defined state, contradicting the assumption stated above. Hence,

$$\mathfrak{lfp}[\Phi][\mathfrak{N}][\mathfrak{s}''] = \perp$$

and, again,

$$\mathfrak{M}_{\mathfrak{S}}[P][\mathfrak{p}\mathfrak{s}_{k+1}][\mathfrak{N}][\mathfrak{s}] = \mathfrak{O}[\mathfrak{W}_{\mathfrak{P}}[P]][\mathfrak{N}][\mathfrak{s}'] \qquad \square$$

Finally, we have the main result of this section, the TR Interpretation Theorem

TR INTERPRETATION THEOREM: $\models P$ in the free Hoare Logic of TR programs iff $\models \mathfrak{W}_{\mathfrak{P}}[P]$ in the free Hoare Logic of **while** programs.

Proof: Immediate from the Semantic Equivalence Lemma. □

6.6. COMPARISON OF THE HOARE AXIOMATIZATION AND THE OPERATIONAL AND DENOTATIONAL SEMANTICS

In this section, we compare the free Hoare Axiomatization for **while** programs—**Hax**—with its semantics, leaving details of the similar comparison of the proof theory and semantics of TR programs to the reader.

Throughout this section, we adopt the following noneffective notion of a proof in free arithmetic: An assertion p is provable ($\vdash p$) if it is valid ($\models p$). The current notion of proof, unlike those we have previously encountered, is not effective because we cannot write a proof-checker in, for example, PROLOG or SNOBOL that can tell us whether an alleged proof is in fact a proof. That is, for any proof-checking algorithm we might devise, there are valid assertions that cannot be determined valid by that algorithm (Gödel).

The advantage of extending the notion of proof in this noneffective manner is that it lets us uncover the source of valid but unprovable asserted statements. The fault lies in (free) arithmetic and not in the Hoare Axiomatization **Hax.** In other words, there is no better axiomatization than **Hax.**

By the argument in Chapter 5, **Hax** is sound (with respect to the operational semantics of **while** programs). We demonstrate in this section that **Hax** is "relatively complete" in the sense that if arithmetic were complete, then so would be **Hax.** Hence, **Hax** matches up with the operational semantics of **while** programs in the sense that an asserted **while** statement AP is valid in the operational semantics iff it is provable. Now, as noted in preceding sections, the translation $\mathfrak{W}$ induces a denotational semantics $\mathfrak{M}'_{\mathfrak{S}}$ for **while** programs that is equivalent to the operational semantics in the sense that $\mathfrak{D}[S][\mathfrak{R}][\mathfrak{s}] = \mathfrak{M}'_{\mathfrak{S}}[S][\mathfrak{R}][\mathfrak{s}]$ for any **while** statement S, any error assignment $\mathfrak{R}$, and any state $\mathfrak{s}$. Hence, **Hax** also matches up with the denotational semantics of **while** programs in the sense that AP is valid in the denotational semantics iff it is provable. That is, **Hax** and the operational and denotational semantics are all equivalent in the sense that they determine the same class of valid asserted statements.

Somewhat similar remarks apply to the free Hoare Axiomatization for TR programs and the denotational and (induced) operational semantics of TR programs.[3]

[3] To obtain a relative completeness result for TR programs, additional constraints are required on variables for local use in procedures. See Exercise 14.

We shall omit details of proofs except for the Relative Completeness Theorem. Proofs of the Weakest Precondition Expressibility Proposition and the Statement Expressibility Proposition, which follow, require technical machinery beyond the scope of this text. The other lemmas and theorems have proofs similar to those found in preceding chapters, and we leave details to the reader.

The notion of the "weakest precondition" of a statement S and a postcondition q has played an important role in recent computer science literature. Roughly, the idea is as follows: The assertion false is usually not a useful precondition in an asserted statement with statement S and postcondition q even though $\{\text{false}\}S\{q\}$ is valid. The assertion false is too "strong" as it implies any assertion. We would like to make the precondition true for all legitimate values of the input variables. That is, if all values are legitimate, we would like to have, if possible, $\{\text{true}\}S\{q\}$ valid. We would like a precondition as "close to" true and as "far from" false as possible. Of course if, for instance, $S \equiv$ **while** true **do** S or $q \equiv$ false, then nothing "weaker" than false will do as a precondition.

The following proposition states that the weakest precondition can be expressed by an assertion. As noted previously, its proof goes beyond the technical devices developed in this text. Suffice it to say that its justification hinges on the fact that each **while** program corresponds to a partial computable function (Böhm-Jacopini), and that each partial computable function can be "represented" by an assertion in arithmetic (Gödel).[4]

WEAKEST PRECONDITION EXPRESSIBILITY PROPOSITION: There is an assertion p such that, for every error assignment $\mathfrak{R}$ and every state $\mathfrak{s}$

(1) $\mathfrak{M}_{\mathfrak{A}}[p][\mathfrak{R}][\mathfrak{s}] = \mathfrak{M}_{\mathfrak{A}}[q][\mathfrak{R}][\mathfrak{D}[S][\mathfrak{R}][\mathfrak{s}]]$

(2) $\mathfrak{ivar}[p] \subset \mathfrak{ivar}[S,q]$

With a slight abuse of notation, we write $\mathfrak{wp}[S,q]$ for an assertion p satisfying (1) and (2) in the Weakest Precondition Expressibility Proposition. An abuse in notation is involved because there are infinitely many syntactically distinct assertions satisfying (1) and (2), as, for example, if p satisfies the conditions, then so do $p\&p$, $p\&p\&p$, ... However, the notation has a semantic justification because, up to equivalence, there is only one $\mathfrak{wp}[S,q]$ —that is, for any assertions p and p' satisfying (1) and (2), we have $\models p \leftrightarrow p'$. As short for the notation $\models \mathfrak{wp}[S,q] \leftrightarrow p$, we will write $\mathfrak{wp}[S,q] = p$.

[4] See Boolos and Jeffrey for a proof that each partial computable function can be represented in arithmetic. (The original proof in Gödel uses somewhat antiquated terminology.) The pathbreaking relative completeness result is due to Cook. See Cook and Loeckx and Sieber for more information on the key role of Gödel's discovery in expressibility propositions such as the one that follows.

In the logic literature, an assertion p is understood to be *weaker* than an assertion q if $\models q \rightarrow p$. Similarly, q is *stronger* than p if p is weaker than q. In light of this established terminology, the following theorem justifies labeling $\mathfrak{wp}[S,q]$ the "weakest precondition" of statement S and assertion q. The proof of this fundamental theorem follows directly from the Weakest Precondition Expressibility Proposition and the definitions of validity and $\mathfrak{wp}[S,q]$.

FUNDAMENTAL THEOREM ABOUT THE WEAKEST PRECONDITION

(1) $\models \{\mathfrak{wp}[S,q]\}S\{q\}$
(2) $\models \{p\}S\{q\}$ iff $\models p \rightarrow \mathfrak{wp}[S,q]$

When attention is restricted to straight-line programs, the proof of the following lemma is constructive because it yields an algorithm, similar to the *VCG* algorithm of Chapter 2, for constructing $\mathfrak{wp}[S,q]$ for any assertion q and any **while**-free statement S. The proof is similar to proofs in preceding chapters.

STRAIGHT-LINE WEAKEST PRECONDITION CHARACTERIZATION THEOREM

(1) $\mathfrak{wp}[d, q] = q$
(2) $\mathfrak{wp}[x{:=}e,q] = \mathrm{I}(e) \& q[e \backslash x]$
(3) $\mathfrak{wp}[S;S',q] = \mathfrak{wp}[S,\mathfrak{wp}[S',q]]$
(4) $\mathfrak{wp}[\textbf{if } b \textbf{ then } S \textbf{ else } S',q] = \mathrm{I}(b) \& (b \rightarrow \mathfrak{wp}[S,q]) \& ({\sim}b \rightarrow \mathfrak{wp}[S',q])$

The Straight-Line Weakest Precondition Characterization Theorem can be extended to **while** statements in a constructive manner by making use of Gödel's result on the β-function. However, the algorithm that can be extracted from the proof yields weakest preconditions that are unintuitive and too complicated to be useful in program verification.[5] It is better for the programmer to discover preconditions creatively (nonalgorithmically), when need be, that are intuitive, as they can be readily expressed in free arithmetic. The results that follow can be assembled into a nonconstructive proof of the **While** Weakest Precondition Characterization Theorem.

Intuitively, the Statement Expressibility Proposition states that **while** statements determine computable partial functions that can be captured in free arithmetic by integer expressions. The justification of this proposition is similar to that of the Weakest Precondition Expressibility Proposition. The

[5] In a logic of partial correctness, Loeckx and Sieber, pp. 166–167, use Gödel's β-function in their construction of an assertion expressing the strongest postcondition of a statement and its precondition.

Termination Lemma states that an adequate Floydian expression for a **while** statement can be captured by a single integer expression and is an immediate consequence of the Statement Expressibility Proposition. Simply put, the adequate Floydian expression gives the number of times the boolean condition b will be tested during execution of the statement **while** b **do** S (beginning in a particular state), and is the analog of the maximum value a procedure's activation number will attain when that procedure is called. The Termination Lemma is an immediate consequence of the Statement Expressibility Proposition.

Throughout the remainder of this section, let S be a statement and x_i $(1 \leqslant i \leqslant n)$ be the $n \geqslant 0$ distinct integer variables occurring in S. By assumption, a valid uniqueness condition for each nonprimitive operation symbol is provable, so we have the following:

STATEMENT EXPRESSIBILITY PROPOSITION: For each i from 1 to n, there exists an integer expression $e_i(x_1, \ldots, x_n)$ in an extension of free arithmetic by explicit definitions such that, for every error assignment $\mathfrak{R}$ and every state $\mathfrak{s}$,

$$\mathfrak{M}_{\mathfrak{E}}[e_i(x_1, \ldots, x_n)][\mathfrak{R}][\mathfrak{s}] = (\mathfrak{D}[S][\mathfrak{R}][\mathfrak{s}])[x_i]$$

Throughout the remainder of this section, let $e_i(x_1, \ldots, x_n)$ $(1 \leqslant i \leqslant n)$ be as in the Statement Expressibility Lemma.

TERMINATION LEMMA: Let $S \equiv$ **while** b **do** S', q be an assertion, and a be a new integer variable. Then, there exists an integer expression $e(x_1, \ldots, x_n)$ in an extension of free arithmetic by explicit definitions such that, for every error assignment $\mathfrak{R}$ and every state $\mathfrak{s}$,

(1) $\mathfrak{M}_{\mathfrak{E}}[e(x_1, \ldots, x_n)][\mathfrak{R}][\mathfrak{s}] =$
$(\mathfrak{D}[a{:=}1;\textbf{while } b \textbf{ do begin } S';a{:=}a+1 \textbf{ end}][\mathfrak{R}][\mathfrak{s}])[a]$

(2) $\models \mathfrak{wp}[S,q]$ & $\mathrm{I}(b)$ & $\sim b \rightarrow e(x_1, \ldots, x_n) = 1$

(3) $\models \mathfrak{wp}[S,q]$ & $\mathrm{I}(b)$ & b & $\mathrm{I}(e(x_1, \ldots, x_n)) \rightarrow$
$\mathrm{I}(e(e_1(x_1, \ldots, x_n), \ldots, e_n(x_1, \ldots, x_n)))$ &
$e(x_1, \ldots, x_n) - 1 = e(e_1(x_1, \ldots, x_n), \ldots, e_n(x_1, \ldots, x_n)) \geqslant 1$

Throughout the remainder of this section, let $e(x_1, \ldots, x_n)$ $(1 \leqslant i \leqslant n)$ be as in the Termination Lemma.

WHILE WEAKEST PRECONDITION CHARACTERIZATION THEOREM: Let $S \equiv$ **while** b **do** S'. Then

$\mathfrak{wp}$[**while** b **do** S',q] =
$\mathrm{I}(b)$ & $\mathrm{I}(e(x_1, \ldots, x_n))$ & $e(x_1, \ldots, x_n) \geqslant 1$ &
($b \rightarrow \mathfrak{wp}[S, \mathfrak{wp}$[**while** b **do** S,q]]) & $(\sim b \rightarrow q)$

As noted earlier, we have extended the concept of a proof in a "noneffective" way. Instead of requiring that an assertion occurring on a line in a proof using *Hax* be provable in free arithmetic, we require instead only that it be valid. That is, we now understand a *proof* in *Hax* to be a finite sequence of lines such that each line is

(1) A valid assertion of arithmetic,
(2) A Dummy or Assignment Axiom, or
(3) Derived from one or more preceding lines by the Composition, Conditional, Consequence, or **While** Rules.

The concept of a proof in *Hax* is no longer effective because of (1).

In the proof of relative completeness, it is convenient to use the following lemma:

INCREMENTAL PROOF VALIDITY PRESERVATION LEMMA: If $\models\{p\}S\{q\}$ and $\models\{p\}S\{q'\}$, then $\models\{p\}S\{q\&q'\}$.

RELATIVE COMPLETENESS OF THE FREE HOARE AXIOMATIZATION FOR WHILE PROGRAMS THEOREM: If $\models\{p\}S\{q\}$, then $\vdash\{p\}S\{q\}$.

Proof: Suppose $\models\{p\}S\{q\}$. The proof proceeds by induction on the complexity of S, and the IH states that, for any asserted statement $AP\equiv\{p'\}S'\{q'\}$ such that $\models AP$ and S' is less complex than S, we have $\vdash AP$. Note that the straight-line program part of the proof (i.e., the proof minus lines that are valid assertions of arithmetic or that were derived by applications of the **While** Rule) is effective.

BASIS: $S\equiv \mathbf{d}$ or $S\equiv x{:=}e$.

Case: $S\equiv \mathbf{d}$.
Because $\mathfrak{wp}[\mathbf{d},q]=q$ by the Straight Line Weakest Precondition Characterization Theorem, part (1), and $\models\{p\}\mathbf{d}\{q\}$ by assumption, we have $\models p\rightarrow q$ by the Fundamental Theorem about the Weakest Precondition. Hence, $\vdash p\rightarrow q$ by the definition of a proof. Further, $\vdash\{q\}\mathbf{d}\{q\}$ by the Dummy Axiom. Applying the Consequence Rule, we have $\vdash\{p\}\mathbf{d}\{q\}$.

Case: $S\equiv x{:=}e$.
Arguing in an entirely similar manner to the previous case, because $\mathfrak{wp}[x{:=}e,q]=\mathrm{I}(x)\&q[e\backslash x]$, $\models\{p\}x{:=}e\{q\}$, $\models p\rightarrow\mathrm{I}(x)\&q[e\backslash x]$, $\vdash p\rightarrow\mathrm{I}(x)\&q[e\backslash x]$, and $\vdash\{\mathrm{I}(e)\&p[e\backslash x]\}x{:=}e\{q\}$, we have $\vdash\{p\}x{:=}e\{q\}$ by the Consequence Rule.

INDUCTION STEP: S is complex.

Case: $S \equiv S';S''$.
We have $\models\{\mathfrak{wp}[S'',q]\}S''\{q\}$ and $\models\{\mathfrak{wp}[S',\mathfrak{wp}[S'',q]]\}S'\{\mathfrak{wp}[S'',q]\}$ by the Fundamental Theorem about the Weakest Precondition, part (1). Hence, $\vdash\{\mathfrak{wp}[S'',q]\}S''\{q\}$ and $\vdash\{\mathfrak{wp}[S',\mathfrak{wp}[S'',q]]\}S'\{\mathfrak{wp}[S'',q]\}$ by the *IH*. Applying the Composition Rule, we have $\vdash\{\mathfrak{wp}[S',\mathfrak{wp}[S'',q]]\}S';S''\{q\}$. Because $\models\{p\}S';S''\{q\}$ by assumption and $\mathfrak{wp}[S';S'',q] = \mathfrak{wp}[S',\mathfrak{wp}[S'',q]]$ by the Straight-Line Weakest Precondition Characterization Lemma, part (3), we have $\models p\rightarrow\mathfrak{wp}[S',\mathfrak{wp}[S'',q]]$ by the Fundamental Theorem about the Weakest Precondition, part (2). Hence, $\vdash p\rightarrow\mathfrak{wp}[S',\mathfrak{wp}[S'',q]]$ by the definition of a proof. Applying the Rule of Consequence, we obtain $\vdash\{p\}S';S''\{q\}$.

Case: $S \equiv$ **if** b **then** S' **else** S''.
Because $\models\{p\}$**if** b **then** S' **else** $S''\{q\}$ by assumption, and $\mathfrak{wp}$[**if** b **then** S' **else** $S'',q] = \mathrm{I}(b)\&(b\rightarrow\mathfrak{wp}[S',q])\&(\sim b\rightarrow\mathfrak{wp}[S'',q])$ by the Straight-Line Weakest Precondition Characterization Theorem, part (4), we have $\models p\rightarrow\mathrm{I}(b)\&(b\rightarrow\mathfrak{wp}[S',q])\&(\sim b\rightarrow\mathfrak{wp}[S'',q])$ by the Fundamental Theorem about the Weakest Precondition, part (2). Hence, $\vdash p\rightarrow\mathrm{I}(b)\&(b\rightarrow\mathfrak{wp}[S',q])\&(\sim b\rightarrow\mathfrak{wp}[S'',q])$ by the definition of a proof. Hence, $\vdash\mathrm{I}(b)\&p\&b\rightarrow\mathfrak{wp}[S',q]$ and $\vdash\mathrm{I}(b)\&p\&\sim b\rightarrow\mathfrak{wp}[S'',q]$. Due to the fact that $\models\{\mathfrak{wp}[S',q]\}S'\{q\}$ and $\models\{\mathfrak{wp}[S'',q]\}S''\{q\}$ by the Fundamental Theorem about the Weakest Precondition, part (1), we have $\vdash\{\mathfrak{wp}[S',q]\}S'\{q\}$ and $\vdash\{\mathfrak{wp}[S'',q]\}S''\{q\}$ by the *IH*. Applying the Consequence Rule, we obtain $\vdash\{\mathrm{I}(b)\&p\&b\}S'\{q\}$ and $\vdash\mathrm{I}(b)\&p\&\sim b\}S''\{q\}$. Hence, $\vdash\{\mathrm{I}(b)\&p\}$**if** b **then** S' **else** $S''\{q\}$ by the Conditional Rule. Because $\vdash p\rightarrow p\&\mathrm{I}(b)$, we have $\vdash\{p\}$**if** b **then** S' **else** $S''\{q\}$ by the Consequence Rule.

Case: $S \equiv$ **while** b **do** S'.
Let y be an integer variable foreign to $\{p\}$**while** b **do** $S'\{q\}$ and $AP \equiv$

$\{\mathrm{I}(b)\&\mathfrak{wp}$[**while** b **do** $S',q]\&\mathrm{I}(e(x_1, \ldots, x_n))\&e(x_1, \ldots, x_n)\geq 0\}$
  while b **do** S'
$\{\mathrm{I}(b)\&\mathfrak{wp}$[**while** b **do** $S',q]\&\mathrm{I}(e(x_1, \ldots, x_n))\&e(x_1, \ldots, x_n)\geq 0$
$\&\sim b\}$

and let $AP' \equiv$

$\{\mathrm{I}(b)\&\mathfrak{wp}$[**while** b **do** $S',q]\&\mathrm{I}(e(x_1, \ldots, x_n))\&e(x_1, \ldots, x_n)\geq 0$
$\&b\&y=e(x_1, \ldots, x_n)\}$
  S'
$\{\mathrm{I}(b)\&\mathfrak{wp}$[**while** b **do** $S',q]\&\mathrm{I}(e(x_1, \ldots, x_n))\&e(x_1, \ldots, x_n)\geq 0\&$
$y>e(x_1, \ldots, x_n)\}$

Shortly, we will show

$(*) \models AP'$

By the *IH*, we have $\vdash AP'$ because S' is less complex than S. Applying the **While** Rule to AP', we have

(1) $\vdash AP$

Because $\mathfrak{wp}[\textbf{while } b \textbf{ do } S', q] =$

$$\mathrm{I}(b) \mathbin{\&} \mathrm{I}(e(x_1, \ldots, x_n)) \mathbin{\&} e(x_1, \ldots, x_n) \geqslant 1 \mathbin{\&} (b \rightarrow \mathfrak{wp}[S', \mathfrak{wp}[\textbf{while } b \textbf{ do } S', q]]) \mathbin{\&} ({\sim}b \rightarrow q)$$

by the **While** Weakest Precondition Characterization Theorem, we have

$$\models \mathfrak{wp}[\textbf{while } b \textbf{ do } S', q] \rightarrow \mathrm{I}(b) \mathbin{\&} \mathfrak{wp}[\textbf{while } b \textbf{ do } S', q] \mathbin{\&} \mathrm{I}(e(x_1, \ldots, x_n)) \mathbin{\&} e(x_1, \ldots, x_n) \geqslant 0$$

Furthermore,

$$\models p \rightarrow \mathfrak{wp}[\textbf{while } b \textbf{ do } S', q]$$

by the Fundamental Theorem about the Weakest Precondition. Hence,

(2) $\vdash p \rightarrow \mathrm{I}(b) \mathbin{\&} \mathfrak{wp}[\textbf{while } b \textbf{ do } S', q] \mathbin{\&} \mathrm{I}(e(x_1, \ldots, x_n)) \mathbin{\&} e(x_1, \ldots, x_n) \geqslant 0$

by the transitivity of implication and the definition of a proof. Again applying the **While** Weakest Precondition Characterization Theorem and the definition of a proof, we have

(3) $\vdash \mathrm{I}(b) \mathbin{\&} \mathfrak{wp}\ [\textbf{while } b \textbf{ do } S', q] \mathbin{\&} \mathrm{I}(e(x_1, \ldots, x_n)) \mathbin{\&} e(x_1, \ldots, x_n) \geqslant 0 \mathbin{\&} {\sim}b \rightarrow q$

Hence, applying the Rule of Consequence to (1)–(3), we have $\vdash \{p\}S\{q\}$.

We now turn to proof of (*) $\models AP'$. By the **While** Weakest Precondition Characterization Theorem, it suffices to show

(4) $\models AP''$

where $AP'' \equiv$

$$\{\mathfrak{wp}[\textbf{while } b \textbf{ do } S', q] \mathbin{\&} b \mathbin{\&} y = e(x_1, \ldots, x_n)\}$$
$$S'$$
$$\{\mathfrak{wp}[\textbf{while } b \textbf{ do } S', q] \mathbin{\&} y > e(x_1, \ldots, x_n)\}$$

Because

$$\models \mathfrak{wp}[\textbf{while } b \textbf{ do } S', q] \mathbin{\&} b \rightarrow \mathfrak{wp}[S', \mathfrak{wp}[\textbf{while } b \textbf{ do } S', q]]$$

by the **While** Weakest Precondition Characterization Theorem, again, and

$$\models\{\mathfrak{wp}[S',\mathfrak{wp}[\mathbf{while}\ b\ \mathbf{do}\ S',q]]\}S'\{\mathfrak{wp}[\mathbf{while}\ b\ \mathbf{do}\ S',q]\}$$

by the Fundamental Theorem about the Weakest Precondition, we have:

$$(5)\ \models\{\mathfrak{wp}[\mathbf{while}\ b\ \mathbf{do}\ S',q]\&b\}\ S'\ \{\mathfrak{wp}[\mathbf{while}\ b\ \mathbf{do}\ S',q]\}$$

by the Consequence Validity Preservation Lemma. Let $\mathfrak{R}$ be any error assignment, and $\mathfrak{s}$ and $\mathfrak{s}'$ be any states such that

$$\mathfrak{M}_{\mathfrak{A}}[\mathfrak{wp}[\mathbf{while}\ b\ \mathbf{do}\ S',q]\ \&\ b\ \&\ y=e(x_1,\ .\ .\ .\ ,x_n)][\mathfrak{R}][\mathfrak{s}]=\mathrm{t}$$

and $\mathfrak{s}'=\mathfrak{D}[\mathbf{while}\ b\ \mathbf{do}\ S'][\mathfrak{R}][\mathfrak{s}]$. Due to the fact that

$$\models\mathfrak{wp}[\mathbf{while}\ b\ \mathbf{do}\ S',q]\rightarrow \mathrm{I}(e(x_1,\ .\ .\ .\ ,x_n))\ \&\ e(x_1,\ .\ .\ .\ ,x_n)\geqslant 0,$$

$\mathfrak{s}'\in\mathfrak{States}$. So, we have

$$\begin{aligned}\mathfrak{s}[y]&=\mathfrak{s}[e[x_1,\ .\ .\ .\ ,x_n)]\\&=\mathfrak{s}'[e(x_1,\ .\ .\ .\ ,x_n)]+1\ \text{by the Termination Lemma.}\end{aligned}$$

Because $\mathfrak{s}'[y]=\mathfrak{s}[y]$ by the Setting Lemma, we have $\mathfrak{s}'[y]>\mathfrak{s}'[e[x_1,\ .\ .\ .\ ,x_n)]$. Hence,

$$(6)\ \models\{\mathfrak{wp}[\mathbf{while}\ b\ \mathbf{do}\ S',q]\ \&\ b\ \&\ y=e[x_1,\ .\ .\ .\ ,x_n)\}\ S'\ \{y>e(x_1,\ .\ .\ .\ ,x_n)\}$$

by the definition of validity. Applying the Incremental Proof Validity Preservation Lemma to (5) and (6), we obtain (4). □

EXERCISES

Proving Programs Correct

In each of the exercises in this section, your first task is to write a TR program consisting of a main program and the procedure described in the exercise. Second, prove your procedure correct in the free Hoare Axiomatization for TR programs **Htr.** Third, prove the program correct in an appropriate extended free Hoare Axiomatization for TR programs. For illustration, see Exercise 1, where we exhibit the (main) program to be used.

1. Write a tail recursive **procedure** *pradd* to compute $x + y$ using only the unary operation symbols 'abs', 'pred', and 'succ'. **Procedure** *pradd* has the two input variable x and y. **Procedure** *pradd* should be constructed efficiently by using the smaller of abs(x) and abs(y) in its boolean guard. The precondition of **procedure** *pradd* is I(x)&I(y), and the postcondition is $z = x + y$, where z is *pr*'s only output variable. The program calling **procedure** *pradd* is

```
program exercise1pr;
procedure pradd;
      begin
      {I(x) & I(y)}
         :
      {z = x+y}
      end;
var x,y,z;
begin
{I(x)&I(y)}
pradd
{z=x+y}
end
```

2. Write a **procedure** *prdiv* to compute x/y using only the operation symbols 'abs', 'pred', and 'succ'. The precondition of *prdiv* is I(x) & I(y) & $y \geqslant 1$, and its postcondition is $z = x/y$.
3. Write a **procedure** *prprime* to determine if an integer x is prime. The precondition of *prprime* is I(x), and its postcondition is z=chprime(x), where chprime is the characteristic operation for the predicate prime. (Do not use either the predicate prime or its characteristic operation chprime in *prprime*'s statement body.)
4. Write a **procedure** *prgcd* to compute the greatest common divisor of x and y using only the operation symbol '−' and the predicate symbols '>' and '='. The precondition of *prgcd* is I(x) & I(y) & $x \geqslant 1$ & $y \geqslant 1$, and its postcondition is $z = \text{gcd}(x,y)$.
5. Write a **procedure** *prsqrt* to compute the integer square root of x using only the operation symbol '+' and the predicate symbol '$\leqslant$'. The precondition is I(x) & $x \geqslant 0$, and the postcondition is $z = \text{sqrt}(x)$.

Semantics

Except when stated otherwise, the following exercises are understood to deal with **while** programs.

6. Let $(C,\sqsubseteq)$ be a cpo and $f \in C \rightarrow C$. Function f is said to be *monotonic* if $f(x) \sqsubseteq f(y)$ for every $x,y \in C$ such that $x \sqsubseteq y$. A monotonic function f is

continuous if, for every chain $\langle x_i \rangle$ in C, $f(\mathfrak{lub}[x_i]) \sqsubseteq \mathfrak{lub}[f(x_i)]$. Prove

(a) A monotonic function f is continuous iff, for every chain $\langle x_i \rangle$ in C, $f(\mathfrak{lub}[x_i]) = \mathfrak{lub}[f(x_i)]$.

(b) The function ϕ giving the denotational semantics of tail recursive procedures (Section 6.2) is continuous.

(c) (The Fixed Point Theorem) Let f be continuous,

$$f_0 = \lambda x.x \quad \text{and} \quad f_{i+1} = \lambda x.f(f_i(x)).$$

Then, f has a least fixed point $\mathfrak{lfp}[f] = \mathfrak{lub}[f_i]$.

7. Prove that the Converse Conditional Rule,

$$\frac{\{\mathrm{I}(b) \& p\}\textbf{if } b \textbf{ then } S \textbf{ else } S'\{q\}}{\{\mathrm{I}(b) \& p \& b\}S\{q\}, \quad \{\mathrm{I}(b) \& p \& {\sim} b\}S'\{q\}}$$

is validity preserving.

8. (a) Can the conjunct $\mathrm{I}(e)$ in the precondition of the Assignment Axiom $\{\mathrm{I}(e) \& p[e \backslash x]\}x := e\{p\}$ be dropped and relative completeness be retained? Soundness?

(b) Answer the same question as (a) for the occurrences of the conjunct $\mathrm{I}(b)$ in the Conditional Rule

$$\frac{\{\mathrm{I}(b) \& p \& b\}S\{q\}, \quad \{\mathrm{I}(b) \& p \& {\sim} b\}S'\{q\}}{\{\mathrm{I}(b) \& p\}\textbf{if } b \textbf{ then } S \textbf{ else } S'\{q\}}$$

(c) Answer the same question as (a) for the occurrences of the conjunct $\mathrm{I}(b)$ in the Converse Conditional Rule of Exercise 7.

(d) Answer the same question as (a) for the occurrences of the conjuncts $\mathrm{I}(b)$ and $\mathrm{I}(e_1) \& \ldots \& \mathrm{I}(e_k)$ in the **While** Rule:

$$\frac{\begin{array}{l}\{\mathrm{I}(b) \& r \& \mathrm{I}(e_1) \& \ldots \& \mathrm{I}(e_k) \& \langle e_1, \ldots, e_k \rangle \not> \langle 0 \rangle \& b \& \\ \langle y_1, \ldots, y_k \rangle = \langle e_1, \ldots, e_k \rangle\} \\ \quad S \\ \{\mathrm{I}(b) \& r \& \mathrm{I}(e_1) \& \ldots \& \mathrm{I}(e_k) \& \langle e_1, \ldots, e_k \rangle \not> \langle 0 \rangle \& \\ \langle y_1, \ldots, y_k \rangle \succ \langle e_1, \ldots, e_k \rangle\}\end{array}}{\begin{array}{l}\{\mathrm{I}(b) \& r \& \mathrm{I}(e_1) \& \ldots \& \mathrm{I}(e_k) \& \langle e_1, \ldots, e_k \rangle \not> \langle 0 \rangle\} \\ \quad \textbf{while } b \textbf{ do } S \\ \{\mathrm{I}(b) \& r \& \mathrm{I}(e_1) \& \ldots \& \mathrm{I}(e_k) \& \langle e_1, \ldots, e_k \rangle \not> \langle 0 \rangle \& {\sim} b\}\end{array}}$$

9. Prove that, for any error assignments $\mathfrak{R}$ and $\mathfrak{R}'$,

$$\mathfrak{O}[S][\mathfrak{R}][\mathfrak{s}] = \mathfrak{O}[S][\mathfrak{R}'][\mathfrak{s}]^{6}$$

[6] Given the present repertoire of statement forms and their semantics, this result justifies replacing the current definition of $\mathfrak{O}$ in the operational semantics with $\mathfrak{O}'$, which is such that, for

10. (a) Prove $\models \{p\}S;S'\{q\}$ iff $\models \{p\}S\{\mathfrak{wp}[S',q]\}$

(b) Consider a proof system consisting of the valid assertions of arithmetic and the one rule of inference.

$$\frac{p \rightarrow \mathfrak{wp}[S,q]}{\{p\}S\{q\}}$$

Prove that the system is relatively complete. Discuss the relative merits of this proof system versus the free Hoare Axiomatization for **while** programs *Hax*.

11. Supplement the integer expressions with the error constant 'error' and the domain $\mathfrak{Z}+$ with the object $error_{\mathfrak{Z}}$, which is to be the denotation of 'error' and other integer expressions that can be detected readily at run-time to be in error. $\bot_{\mathfrak{Z}}$ is still to be understood as the denotation of an integer expression e in the undefined state $\bot_{\mathfrak{States}}$. We understand that $\bot_{\mathfrak{Z}} \sqsubseteq error_{\mathfrak{Z}}$, $error_{\mathfrak{Z}} \notin \mathfrak{Z}$, and, for every integer m, neither $error_{\mathfrak{Z}} \sqsubseteq m$ nor $m \sqsubseteq error_{\mathfrak{Z}}$. Develop the following:

(a) An appropriate semantics and deductive systems for free arithmetic.

(b) An appropriate denotational semantics and Hoare Axiomatization for TR programs.

12. (a) For the Hoare logic of partial correctness, as presented in Chapter 1, the concepts of the *weakest liberal precondition* $\mathfrak{wlp}[S,q]$ of a statement S and a postcondition q and the *strongest postcondition* $\mathfrak{sp}[q,S]$ of precondition q and a statement S are developed in the literature. Semantically, using the notation of the present chapter, $\mathfrak{wlp}[S,q]$ is an assertion such that

$$\begin{aligned}\mathfrak{M}_{\mathfrak{A}}[\mathfrak{wlp}[S,q]][\mathfrak{N}][\mathfrak{s}] &= \mathfrak{t} \text{ if } \mathfrak{M}_{\mathfrak{A}}[q][\mathfrak{N}][\mathfrak{s}][\mathfrak{D}[S][\mathfrak{N}][\mathfrak{s}]] = \mathfrak{t} \\ &\qquad \text{or } \mathfrak{D}[S][\mathfrak{N}][\mathfrak{s}] = \bot \\ &= \mathfrak{f} \text{ otherwise}\end{aligned}$$

and $\mathfrak{sp}[q,S]$ is an assertion such that

$$\begin{aligned}\mathfrak{M}_{\mathfrak{A}}[\mathfrak{sp}[q,S]][\mathfrak{N}][\mathfrak{s}] &= \mathfrak{t} \text{ if there is a state } \mathfrak{s}' \text{ such that } \mathfrak{s}=\mathfrak{D}[S][\mathfrak{N}][\mathfrak{s}'] \text{ and} \\ &\qquad \mathfrak{M}_{\mathfrak{A}}[q][\mathfrak{N}][\mathfrak{s}']=\mathfrak{t} \\ &= \mathfrak{f} \text{ otherwise}\end{aligned}$$

In the free Hoare logic of partial correctness, we understand the seman-

---

any error assignment $\mathfrak{N}$,

$$\mathfrak{D}'[S][\mathfrak{s}] = \mathfrak{D}[S][\mathfrak{N}][\mathfrak{s}]$$

A similar remark applies to $\mathfrak{M}_{\mathfrak{S}}$ in the denotational semantics of TR programs.

tics of asserted programs to be given by the following semantic equation:

$$\mathfrak{M}'_{\mathfrak{AP}}[\{p\}S\{q\}][N][s] = \mathfrak{t} \text{ if } \mathfrak{M}_{\mathfrak{A}}[q][\mathfrak{N}][\mathfrak{O}[S][\mathfrak{N}][\mathfrak{s}]] = \mathfrak{t} \text{ or } \mathfrak{M}_{\mathfrak{A}}[p][\mathfrak{N}][\mathfrak{s}] = \mathfrak{f} \text{ or } \mathfrak{O}[S][\mathfrak{N}][\mathfrak{s}] = \perp$$
$$= \mathfrak{f} \text{ otherwise}$$

and validity to be defined in the usual manner. State and prove characterization theorems for $\mathfrak{wlp}[S,q]$ and $\mathfrak{sp}[q,S]$ in the free Hoare logic of partial correctness. Why is there no counterpart of the strongest postcondition in the Hoare logic of total correctness?

(b) Develop an axiomatization for the free Hoare logic of partial correctness, and prove the soundness and relative completeness of your axiomatization.

13. Develop the operational semantics of TR programs induced by the translation $\mathfrak{W}$ (Section 6.4). Prove the equivalence of the operational and denotational semantics.

14. Because the variables for local use in a **procedure** *pr* may not be initialized when *pr* is called, variables for local use have much the same problematic status as ALGOL60 OWN variables.

(a) Prove that the Hoare Axiomatizations, the $\mathbf{Htr}_{PCA}$'s, are not relatively complete by exhibiting a valid program with valid procedures, each having the precondition true, that cannot be proven correct.

(b) Modify the semantics of TR programs so that variables for local use in a **procedure** *pr* are initialized to 0, and modify the translation $\mathfrak{W}$ and the proof of the TR Interpretation Theorem appropriately.

15. Develop the denotational semantics of **while** programs induced by the translation $\mathfrak{W}$. Prove the equivalence of the operational and denotational semantics.

16. (a) Develop a free semantics for the FC programs of Chapter 2. Redefine the VCG algorithm and the concepts of verification, well-foundedness, and termination conditions in an appropriate manner. Prove the VCG Correctness Theorem.

(b) Extend the results of part (a) to the FC+ programs of Chapter 3.

17. (a) Show that any asserted **while** statement $AP \equiv \{p\}S\{q\}$ that is a full program can be translated into another full program $AP' \equiv \{p\}S'\{q\}$ such that

(1) For any state $\mathfrak{s}$ and any integer variable x occurring in AP, $(\mathfrak{O}[S][\mathfrak{N}][\mathfrak{s}])[x] = (\mathfrak{O}[S'][\mathfrak{N}][\mathfrak{s}])[x]$, and

(2) AP' is the target program of some source TR program under the translation $\mathfrak{W}$ (i.e., there is some TR program P such that $\mathfrak{W}[P] = AP'$.)

(b) It is known that a **while** program containing at most one **while** statement as a constituent can compute any computable partial function (Böhm-Jacopini). Using this result and part (a), show that a TR program containing at most one procedure can compute any computable partial function.

18. Presume that variables for local use in a procedure are initialized to 0 (see Exercise 14).

(a) State a Weakest Precondition Expressibility Proposition for the class of TR statements analogous to that in Section 6.6 for **while** statements.

(b) State and prove a Weakest Precondition Characterization Theorem for the class of TR statements.

19. Presume that variables for local use in a procedure are initialized to 0 (see Exercise 14). Also, build from the results of Exercise 18.

We seek to establish the relative completeness of the free Hoare Axiomatization for TR programs containing at most one procedure. (See Exercise 17.) Let the input variables of **procedure** *pr* be $x_i(1 \leq i \leq m)$ and the output variables be $z_i(1 \leq i \leq n)$, and let $e_i(x_1, \ldots, x_m)$ $(1 \leq i \leq m)$ be as in the following TR Statement Expressibility Proposition:

For each i from 1 to n, there exists an integer expression $e_i(x_1, \ldots, x_m)$ in an extension of free arithmetic by explicit definitions such that, for every error assignment $\mathfrak{N}$ and every state $\mathfrak{s}$,

$$\mathfrak{M}_{\mathfrak{E}}[e_i(x_1, \ldots, x_m)][\mathfrak{N}][\mathfrak{s}] = (\mathfrak{M}_{\mathfrak{S}}[S][\mathfrak{N}][\mathfrak{s}])[x_i]$$

Let the precondition of procedure *pr* be $\mathfrak{wp}[S_{pr}, \text{true}]$, and its postcondition be

$$z_1 = e_1(x_1, \ldots, x_m) \;\&\; \ldots \;\&\; z_n = e_n(x_1, \ldots, x_m)$$

Prove $\vdash P$ if $\models P$.

20. This exercise presupposes Exercise 13. Modify the syntax, operational semantics, and concept of an extended free Hoare Axiomatization for TR programs so that parameters can be passed to procedures by value and by reference. You will need to develop a dynamic storage allocation scheme (presumably, a run-time stack). As in the preceding chapter, prohibit references to global variables in procedure bodies.

21. This exercise presupposes Exercise 13. Modify the syntax, operational semantics, and concept of an extended free Hoare Axiomatization for TR programs so that parameters can be passed to procedures by *name* (as in ALGOL60 and SIMULA67).

22. This exercise is similar to Exercise 20 except, in this case, permit a procedure to refer to global variables but not change their values. Impose appropriate syntactic restrictions on procedures and, if need be, redefine the concept of validity.

23. This exercise is similar to Exercise 20, except that instead of procedures with value and reference parameters, you are to allow functions with value parameters.

Programming Projects

24. Implement the translation $\mathfrak{W}$ of TR programs into **while** programs in your favorite programming language.
25. (a) Define a direct translation of TR programs into FC programs. (That is, write out the equations in full and do not give as an answer simply, "The composition of the translation in Chapter 4 with the translation in the present chapter.")

    (b) Implement your solution to part (a).
26. Implement an interpreter for the class of **while** programs described in this chapter.
27. This exercise presupposes Exercise 13. Write an interpreter for the class of TR programs.
28. Implement the algorithm that can be extracted from the Straight-Line Weakest Precondition Characterization Theorem. In other words, your program is to output $\mathfrak{wp}[S,q]$ for any straight-line **while** program S and any postcondition q.
29. Write a proof-checker for the free Hoare Axiomatization for **while** programs **Hax.** Skip validity tests for assertions. That is, if a line in a proof is an assertion, assume that it is valid.
30. Write a proof-checker for extended free Hoare Axiomatizations for TR programs. Skip validity tests for assertions.

SUGGESTIONS FOR FURTHER READING

Histories of the development of programming logic and denotational semantics can be found in the papers by Apt and Scott (1977), respectively.

The natural deduction system for first-order logic (Chapter 0) is taken from Leblanc and Wisdom, supplemented with rules for identity as in Copi, and adapted to free logic following hints in Lambert and van Fraassen. The axiomatization of arithmetic (Chapter 0) appears to be new although, presumably, it is derivable from the axiomatization in Feferman. The axiomatization of free arithmetic (Chapter 5) is new. The Hoare Axiomatization (Chapter 1) is common in the literature, but the axiomatizations developed in Chapters 4 to 6 to handle more sophisticated data types and programming constructs have novel features. The operational semantics are based on those of Cook as simplified by de Bakker. The denotational semantics of tail recursive procedures (Chapter 6) is derived from the usual denotational semantics of **while** programs. Our translational semantics is based on material frequently covered in freshman- or sophomore-level computer science courses.

We have annotated the following bibliography in the hope of guiding the interested reader to topics touched on but not fully addressed in this text. The annotations are not intended to summarize the contents of these works. The reader who has completed this text should be able to find more accessible texts that are noted as advanced.

Alagic, S., and M. A. Arbib, *The Design of Well-Structured and Correct Programs,* Springer, New York, 1978.

Emphasizes program construction and proving as complementary activities.

Anderson, R. B., *Proving Programs Correct,* Wiley, New York, 1979.

Well-written. Very introductory and informal.

Apt, K. R., "Ten Years of Hoare's Logic, a Survey," *ACM Trans. on Prog. Lang. and Sys.,* **3,** 431–483 (1981).

Ashcroft, E. A. and W. W. Wadge, "℞ for Semantics," *ACM Trans. on Prog. Lang. and Sys.,* **4,** 283–294 (1982).

Argues that both axiomatic and denotational semantic descriptions are clean when attention is restricted to reasonable programming language constructs.

de Bakker, J. W., *Mathematical Theory of Program Correctness,* Prentice-Hall, Englewood Cliffs, N.J., 1980.

Excellent advanced, relatively comprehensive text on programming logics.

Berg, H. K., et al., *Formal Methods of Program Verification and Specification,* Prentice-Hall, Englewood Cliffs, N.J., 1982.

Survey of verification and specification techniques.

Berztiss, A. T., *Data Structures: Theory and Practice,* Academic Press, New York, 1975.

Contains a discussion of the Roy-Warshall algorithm.

Böhm, C. and G. Jacopini, "Flow Diagrams, Turing Machines, and Languages with only Two Formation Rules," *Comm. of the ACM,* **9,** 366–371 (1966).

All the computable functions are computable by **while** programs.

Boolos, G. S., "A Curious Inference," *Journal of Philosophical Logic,* **16,** 1–12 (1987).

Suggests that first-order logic is "practically incomplete" by demonstrating that a proof about an Ackermann-like function is "beyond the bounds of physical possibility" in first-order arithmetic but is of manageable length in second-order arithmetic. Might be read in conjunction with Shapiro's paper.

Boolos, G. S., and R. C. Jeffrey, *Computability and Logic,* 2nd ed., Cambridge, London/New York, 1980.

Text for second course in logic covering Kleene's normal form theorem, arithmetic (including Gödel's results) and first and second-order logic.

de Bouvere, K. L., *A Method in Proofs of Undefinability; with Applications to Functions in the Arithmetic of Natural Numbers,* North-Holland, Amsterdam, 1959.

An advanced text. Contains a demonstration that exponentiation is explicitly but not equationally definable.

Clarke, E. M., "The Characterization Problem for Hoare Logics." In Hoare, C. A. R., and J. C. Shepherdson (eds.), *Mathematical Logic and Programming Languages,* 89–104, Prentice-Hall, Englewood Cliffs, N.J., 1985.

Suggests the existence of a sound and relatively complete Hoare logic as a possible design criterion for programming languages. Might be read in conjunction with the paper by Ashcroft and Wadge.

Constable, R. L., and M. J. O'Donnell, *A Programming Logic,* Winthrop, Cambridge, Mass. 1978.

Programming logic for a dialect of PL/I. Treats many basic types (integers, booleans, strings) in an underlying many-sorted logic.

Cook, S. A., "Soundness and Completeness of an Axiom System for Program Verification," *SIAM J. on Computing,* **7,** 70–90 (1978).

The pioneering work on relative completeness.

Copi, I. M., *Symbolic Logic,* 2nd ed., Macmillan, New York, 1965.

Introduction to natural deduction for first-order logic with identity.

Department of Defense Trusted Computer System Evaluation Criteria, CSC-STD-001-83, DoD Computer Security Center, Fort Meade, Md., 1983.

Verification required for the highest evaluation.

Dijkstra, E. W., *A Discipline of Programming,* Prentice-Hall, Englewood Cliffs, N.J., 1976.

Advanced text on program proving and construction. Introduced the concept of the weakest precondition.

Donahue, J. E., *Complementary Definitions of Programming Language Semantics, Lecture Notes in Computer Science,* **42,** Springer, New York, 1976.

The first comprehensive text on programming logics.

Feferman, S., *The Number Systems: Foundations of Algebra and Analysis*, Addison-Wesley, Reading, Mass., 1964.

Advanced, classic text developing the theory of integers in terms of the natural numbers.

Floyd, R. W., "Assigning Meaning to Programs." In Schwartz, J. T., (ed.), *Mathematical Aspects of Computer Science, Proc. Symp. on Appl. Math.*, American Mathematical Society, **19,** 19-32 (1967).

Introduced the Floyd method.

Friedman, F. L., and E. B. Koffman, *Problem Solving and Structured Programming in BASIC,* Addison-Wesley, Reading, Mass., 1979.

Gallier, J. H., *Logic for Computer Science: Foundations of Automatic Theorem Proving,* Harper & Row, New York, 1986.

Somewhat more advanced than Kleene (1967). Covers resolution, semantics of PROLOG, and many-sorted logics.

Gödel, K., "Über Formal Unentscheidbare Sätze der Principia Mathematica und Verwandte Systeme, I," *Monatsh. Math. Phys.*, **38,** 173-198 (1931).

Gödel proves that the computable functions are representable in arithmetic on his way to proving the incompleteness of arithmetic.

Goguen, J. A., "Abstract Errors for Abstract Data Types." In Neuhold, E. J. (ed.), *Formal Description of Programming Concepts,* 491-522. North Holland, Amsterdam.

Should every domain have only one error object?

Gordon, M. J. C., *The Denotational Description of Programming Languages,* Springer, New York, 1979.

Introduction to writing denotational descriptions.

Greibach, S. A., *Theory of Program Structures: Schemes, Semantics, Verification, Lecture Notes in Computer Science,* **36,** Springer, New York, 1975.

*Contains material on **for** and **while** programs that might be read after reading Harel's and Ledgard and Marcotty's discussion of the Böhm-Jacopin theorem.*

Gries, D., *The Science of Programming,* Springer, New York, 1981.

Emphasizes program construction and proving as complementary activities.

Gumb, R. D., "An Extended Joint Consistency Theorem for Free Logic with Equality," *Notre Dame Journal of Formal Logic,* **20,** 321-335 (1979).

Free logic has a reasonable model theory.

Gumb, R. D., "On the Underlying Logics of Specification Languages," *ACM Software Engineering Notes,* **4,** 21-23 (1982).

Possible criteria for evaluating specification languages. Might be read in conjunction with the papers by Gurevitch and Shapiro.

Gurevitch, Y., "Toward Logic Tailored for Computational Complexity," *CRL-TR-3-84,* Computing Research Laboratory, University of Michigan, Ann Arbor, 1984.

Considers logics between first-order and second-order for use in computer science. Contains a proof that the transitive closure property is not first-order.

Harel, D., "On Folk Theorems," *Comm. of the ACM,* **23,** 379–389 (1980).

Traces the history of the Böhm-Jacopini Theorem from its roots in Kleene's normal form theorem in recursive function theory.

Hoare, C. A. R., "An Axiomatic Basis of Computer Programming," *Comm. of the ACM,* **12,** 576–583 (1969).

Introduced the Hoare axiomatizations. Treatment of existential quantifications suggests the underlying first-order logic is naturally free.

Hoare, C. A. R., and P. E. Lauer, "Consistent and Complementary Formal Theories of the Semantics of Programming Languages," *Acta Informatica,* **3,** 135–153 (1974).

Pioneering paper showing the equivalence of several semantics, adumbrating work on the soundness and completeness of Hoare logics.

Hoare, C. A. R., and N. Wirth, "An Axiomatic Definition of the Programming Language PASCAL," *Acta Informatica,* **2,** 335–355 (1973).

Kirkerud, B., "Completeness of Hoare-Calculi Revisited," *BIT,* **22,** 402–418 (1982).

Uses free logic to handle undefined expressions.

Kleene, S. C., *Introduction to Metamathematics,* North-Holland, Amsterdam, 1952.

This advanced text treats the second recursion theorem, fundamental to the development of denotational semantics.

Kleene, S. C., *Mathematical Logic,* Wiley, New York, 1967.

Introductory logic text, more advanced and comprehensive than Copi or Leblanc and Wisdom, less advanced than Kleene (1952), Boolos and Jeffrey, or Shoenfeld.

Lambert, K., "On the Philosophical Foundations of Free Logic, *Inquiry,*" **24,** 147–203 (1981).

A history of free logic.

Lambert, K. and B. van Fraassen, *Derivation and Counterexample: An Introduction to Philosophical Logic,* Dickenson, Belmont, Calif., 1972.

Contains an introduction to free logic.

Leblanc, H., *Truth-Value Semantics,* North Holland, Amsterdam, 1976.

Advanced, comprehensive treatment of first- and higher-order logic, free logic, and a variety of other logics.

Leblanc, H., et al., *Essays in Epistemology and Semantics,* Haven, New York, 1983.

Contains some basic papers on free intuitionistic logic.

Leblanc, H., and W. A. Wisdom, *Deductive Logic,* Allyn and Bacon, Rockleigh, N.J., 1972.

Introduction to natural deduction, including a soundness proof.

Lewis, H. R., and C. H. Papadimitriou, *Elements of the Theory of Computation,* Prentice-Hall, Englewood Cliffs, N.J., 1981.

Some relevant topics covered by this introductory text are formal languages, computability, uncomputability, and logic.

Loeckx, J., and K. Sieber, *The Foundations of Program Verification,* Wiley, New York, 1984.

Presupposes more mathematical maturity than our text. Excellent in relating pro-

gram verification to logic. Contains a detailed sketch of the β-function representation of the strongest postcondition of a **while** *statement.*

Manna, Z., *Mathematical Theory of Computation,* McGraw–Hill, New York, 1974.

Thorough treatment of the Floyd method applied to flowcharts. Introduction to the mathematics of denotational semantics.

Manna, Z., and A. Pnueli, "Axiomatic Approach to Total Correctness of Programs," *Acta Informatica,* **3,** 242–263 (1974).

The pioneering work on proving total correctness in Hoare logic.

Manna, Z., and R. Waldinger, *The Logical Basis for Computer Programming-Volume 1: Deductive Reasoning,* Addison–Wesley, Reading, Mass., 1985.

Introduction to logic for computer scientists.

Marcotty, M., and H. F. Ledgard, *Programming Language Landscape: Syntax, Semantics, Implementation,* 2nd ed., Science Research Associates, Chicago, 1986.

Introduction to concepts of programming languages with intuitive explanations of the Böhm-Jacopini theorem, fixpoint theory, and the role of consistent and complementary semantic descriptions.

McCarthy, J., "Torwards a Mathematical Science of Computation." In Popplewell, C. M., (ed.), *Proc. IFIP Congress,* **62,** 21–28 (1963).

A pioneering work in the semantics of programming languages.

McCarthy, J., and J. A. Painter, "Correctness of a Compiler for Arithmetic Expressions." In Schwartz, J. T., (ed.), *Proceedings of a Symposium in Applied Mathematics, Mathematical Aspects of Computer Science,* **19,** 33–41, American Mathematical Society, (1967).

A pioneering work in translational semantics.

Melliar–Smith, P. M., and R. L. Schwartz, "Formal Specification and Mechanical Verification of SIFT: A Fault-Tolerant Flight Control System, " *IEEE Transactions on Computers,* **31,** 616–630 (1982).

Attempts to use program verification to insure airplane safety.

Merchant, M. J., *FORTRAN 77: Language and Style,* Wadsworth, Belmont, Calif., 1981.

Structured programming in FORTRAN.

Meyer, A. R., and D. M. Ritchie, "The Complexity of Loop Programs," *Proc. of the ACM 22nd National Conference,* 465–469, 1967.

The **for** *programs compute the primitive recursive functions.*

Mili, A., *An Introduction to Formal Program Verification,* Van Nostrand–Reinhold, Princeton, N.J., 1985.

Examines eight different verification techniques.

De Millo, R., et al., "Social Processes and Proofs of Theorems and Programs," *Conf. Record of 1977 ACM Conf. on Principles of Programming Languages,* 206–214, 1977.

Interesting critique of verification. In my opinion, however, the arguments in this paper do not establish that program verification can never become a practical activity.

Nelson, G., and D. Redell, "The Star Wars Computer System," *CPSR Educational Materials,* Computer Professionals for Social Responsibility, Palo Alto, CA., 1985.

A critical look at an advanced computer system for which some program verification may be attempted.

Nilsson, N. J., *Principles of Artificial Intelligence,* Morgan Kaufmann, Los Altos, CA, 1980.

Includes treatments of resolution theorem-proving and methods of program synthesis.

O'Donnell, M. J., "A Critique of the Foundations of Hoare Style Programming Logics," *Comm. of the ACM,* **25,** 927–935 (1982).

Emphasizes that insufficient attention has been paid to soundness in much of the literature. Suggests that there may be a need to return to the Floyd method to handle cleanly **goto***'s and related constructs.*

Pagan, F. G., *Formal Specification of Programming Languages: A Panoramic View,* Prentice–Hall, Englewood Cliffs, N.J., 1981.

Survey of syntactic and semantic devices.

Parnas, D. L., "Why Software is Unreliable," *CPSR Educational Materials,* Computer Professionals for Social Responsibility, Palo Alto CA, 1985.

A thought-provoking review, with a skeptical view of verification, by a leading software engineer.

Reynolds, J., *The Craft of Programming,* Prentice–Hall, Englewood Cliffs, N.J., 1981.

Advanced treatment of program construction and proving as complementary activities.

Russell, B., "Correctness of the Compiling Process Based on Axiomatic Semantics," *Acta Informatica,* **14,** 1–20 (1980).

Schmidt, D. A., *Denotational Semantics: A Methodology for Language Development,* Allyn and Bacon, Rockleigh, N.J., 1986.

This advanced text contains material on compiler generation from denotational descriptions.

Scott, D. S., "Existence and Description in Formal Logic." In Schoenmann, R., (ed.), *Bertrand Russell, Philosopher of the Century,* 181–200, Allen and Unwin, London, 1967.

Prepared the way for mathematical applications of free logic.

Scott, D. S., "Outline of a Mathematical Theory of Computation," *4th Annual Princeton Conference on Information Science and Systems,* 109–176 (1970).

A pioneering work in denotational semantics.

Scott, D. S., "Logic and Programming Language," *Comm. of the ACM,* **20,** 634–641 (1977).

Scott, D. S., "Identity and Existence in Intuitionistic Logic." In Fourman M. P., (ed.), *Applications of Sheaves, Lecture Notes in Mathematics,* **735,** 660–696, Springer, New York, 1979.

Constructive mathematics using free intuitionistic logic.

Shapiro, S., "Second-Order Languages and Mathematical Practice," *Journal of Symbolic Logic,* **50,** 714–742 (1985).

Philosophical treatment of some of the advantages of second-order logic.

Shoenfield, J. R., *Mathematical Logic,* Addison–Wesley, Reading, Mass. 1967.

A comprehensive, advanced text.

Smith, B. C., "Limits of Correctness in Computers," *CPSR Educational Materials,* Computer Professionals for Social Responsibility, Palo Alto, CA, 1985.

Discusses the limitations of formal specifications.

Smith, S., and J. Harp, *Machine Organization and Assembly Language: Using Data General AOS and AOS/VS Systems,* Ginn Press, Waltham, Mass., 1986.

Structured programming in assembly language.

Stevenson, J. T., "Roundabout the Runabout Inference-Ticket," *Analysis,* **21,** 124–128 (1961).

Emphasizes the importance of soundness in vindicating a rule of inference.

Stoy, J., *Denotational Semantics: The Scott-Strachey Approach to Programming Language Theory,* MIT Press, Cambridge, Mass., 1977.

An advanced text on the mathematics of denotational semantics.

Suppes, P. *Axiomatic Set Theory,* Dover, New York, 1972.

Introductory presentation of the theory of definitions and the natural numbers.

Tenenbaum, A. M., and M. J. Augenstein, *Data Structures Using Pascal,* Prentice–Hall, Englewood Cliffs, N.J., 1981.

Tennant, R. D., "A Note on Undefined Expression Values in Programming Logics," *Information Processing Letters,* **24,** 331–333 (1987).

Uses free logic in a novel treatment of the semantics of boolean expressions.

Tennant, R. D., *Principles of Programming Languages,* Prentice–Hall, Englewood Cliffs, N.J., 1981.

A more advanced text than Ledgard and Marcotty. Emphasizes denotational semantics.

Turner, R., *Logics for Artificial Intelligence,* Ellis Horwood, Chichester, 1984.

Carefully done introductory treatment of dynamic logic and other logics used in program verification and semantics.

Wand, M., *Induction, Recursion, and Programming,* North Holland, Amsterdam, 1980.

An introduction to discrete structures with an emphasis on applications to program verification and semantics.

Index of Notations

CHAPTER 0. MATHEMATICAL PRELIMINARIES

CHAPTER 1. THE PARTIAL CORRECTNESS OF WHILE PROGRAMS

CHAPTER 2. THE TOTAL CORRECTNESS OF FLOWCHART PROGRAMS

CHAPTER 3. THE TOTAL CORRECTNESS OF FLOWCHART PROGRAMS WITH ARRAYS AND INPUT AND OUTPUT

CHAPTER 4. THE TRANSLATION OF WHILE PROGRAMS WITH ARRAYS, INPUT AND OUTPUT, AND A STACK INTO FLOW-CHART PROGRAMS

CHAPTER 5. THE TOTAL CORRECTNESS OF WHILE PROGRAMS WITH PROCEDURES AND FUNCTIONS

CHAPTER 6. THE TRANSLATION OF TAIL RECURSIVE PROCEDURES INTO WHILE PROGRAMS

Index of Definitions of Arithmetic

EXPLICIT AND EQUATIONAL DEFINITIONS

SYMBOLS INTRODUCED WITH NONCREATIVE AXIOMS

Index of Lemmas, Propositions, and Theorems

CHAPTER 0. MATHEMATICAL PRELIMINARIES

CHAPTER 1. THE PARTIAL CORRECTNESS OF WHILE PROGRAMS

CHAPTER 2. THE TOTAL CORRECTNESS OF FLOWCHART PROGRAMS

CHAPTER 3. THE TOTAL CORRECTNESS OF FLOWCHART PROGRAMS WITH ARRAYS AND INPUT AND OUTPUT

CHAPTER 4. THE TRANSLATION OF WHILE PROGRAMS WITH ARRAYS, INPUT AND OUTPUT, AND A STACK INTO FLOWCHART PROGRAMS

CHAPTER 5. THE TOTAL CORRECTNESS OF WHILE PROGRAMS WITH PROCEDURES AND FUNCTIONS

CHAPTER 6. THE TRANSLATION OF TAIL RECURSIVE PROCEDURES INTO WHILE PROGRAMS

Subject Index